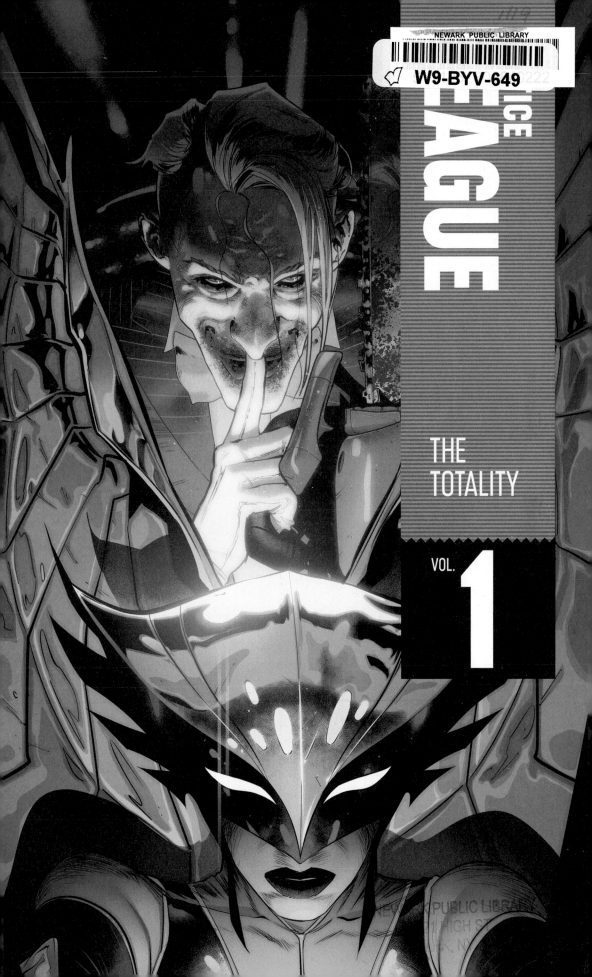

JUSTICE LEAGUE

THE TOTALITY

VOL. **1**

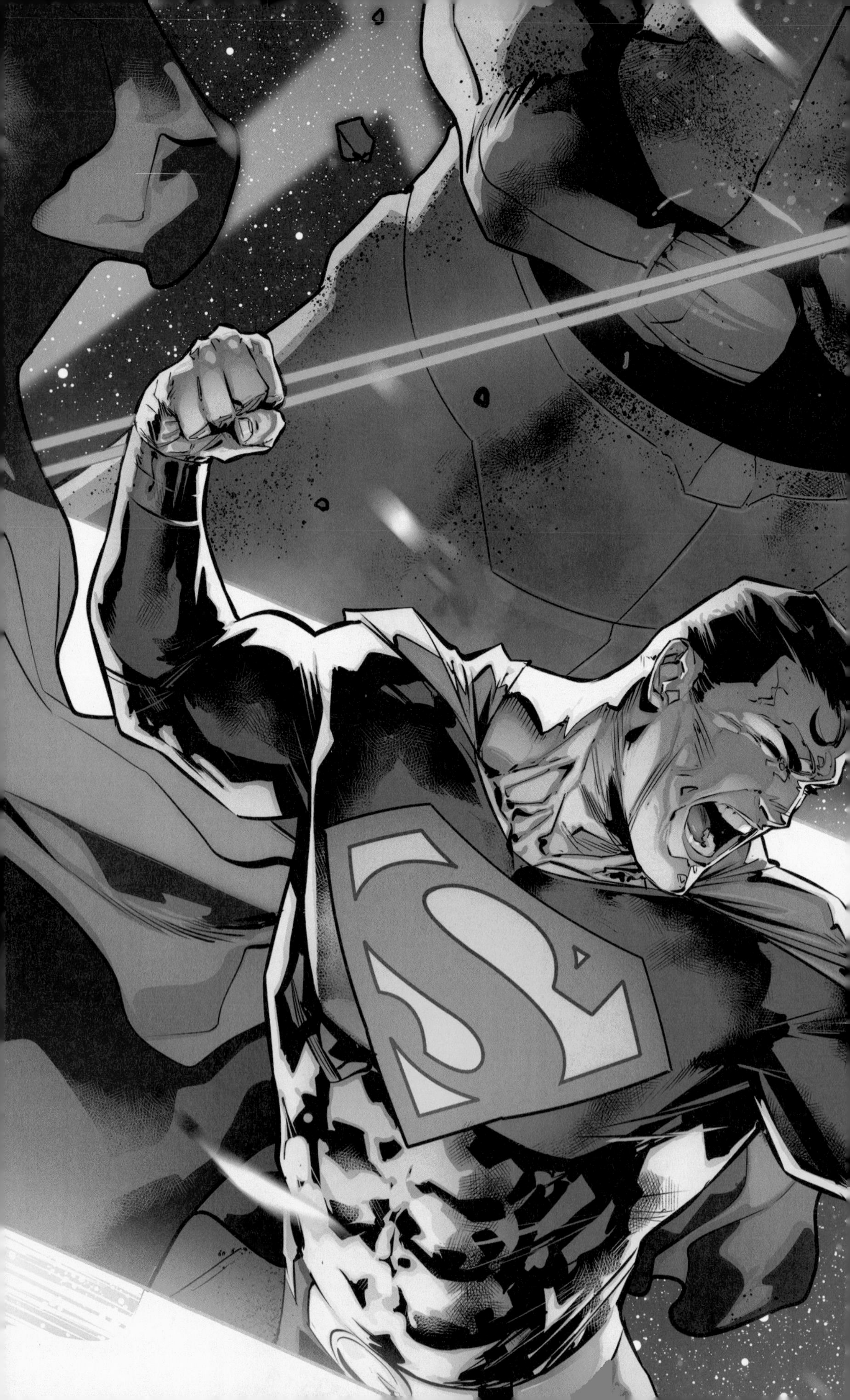

JUSTICE
LEAGUE
THE TOTALITY

writers
SCOTT SNYDER
JAMES TYNION IV

pencillers
JORGE JIMENEZ
JIM CHEUNG
DOUG MAHNKE

inkers
JORGE JIMENEZ
MARK MORALES
JAIME MENDOZA
WALDEN WONG
JIM CHEUNG

colorists
ALEJANDRO SANCHEZ
TOMEU MOREY
WIL QUINTANA

letterer
TOM NAPOLITANO

collection cover artists
JIM CHEUNG and LAURA MARTIN

SUPERMAN created by
JERRY SIEGEL and JOE SHUSTER
By special arrangement with
the Jerry Siegel family

VOL.
1

REBECCA TAYLOR PAUL KAMINSKI Editors – Original Series
ROB LEVIN Associate Editor – Original Series
ANDREW MARINO Assistant Editor – Original Series
JEB WOODARD Group Editor – Collected Editions
ROBIN WILDMAN Editor – Collected Edition
STEVE COOK Design Director – Books
DAMIAN RYLAND Publication Design

BOB HARRAS Senior VP – Editor-in-Chief, DC Comics
PAT McCALLUM Executive Editor, DC Comics

DAN DiDIO Publisher
JIM LEE Publisher & Chief Creative Officer
AMIT DESAI Executive VP – Business & Marketing Strategy, Direct to
              Consumer & Global Franchise Management
BOBBIE CHASE VP & Executive Editor, Young Reader & Talent Development
MARK CHIARELLO Senior VP – Art, Design & Collected Editions
JOHN CUNNINGHAM Senior VP – Sales & Trade Marketing
BRIAR DARDEN VP – Business Affairs
ANNE DePIES Senior VP – Business Strategy, Finance & Administration
DON FALLETTI VP – Manufacturing Operations
LAWRENCE GANEM VP – Editorial Administration & Talent Relations
ALISON GILL Senior VP – Manufacturing & Operations
JASON GREENBERG VP – Business Strategy & Finance
HANK KANALZ Senior VP – Editorial Strategy & Administration
JAY KOGAN Senior VP – Legal Affairs
NICK J. NAPOLITANO VP – Manufacturing Administration
LISETTE OSTERLOH VP – Digital Marketing & Events
EDDIE SCANNELL VP – Consumer Marketing
COURTNEY SIMMONS Senior VP – Publicity & Communications
JIM (SKI) SOKOLOWSKI VP – Comic Book Specialty Sales & Trade Marketing
NANCY SPEARS VP – Mass, Book, Digital Sales & Trade Marketing
MICHELE R. WELLS VP – Content Strategy

JUSTICE LEAGUE VOL. 1: THE TOTALITY

DC Comics, 2900 West Alameda Ave., Burbank, CA 91505
Printed by LSC Communications, Kendallville, IN, USA. 10/19/18. First Printing.
ISBN: 978-1-4012-8499-2

Library of Congress Cataloging-in-Publication Data is available.

MIX
Paper from
responsible sources
FSC® C132124

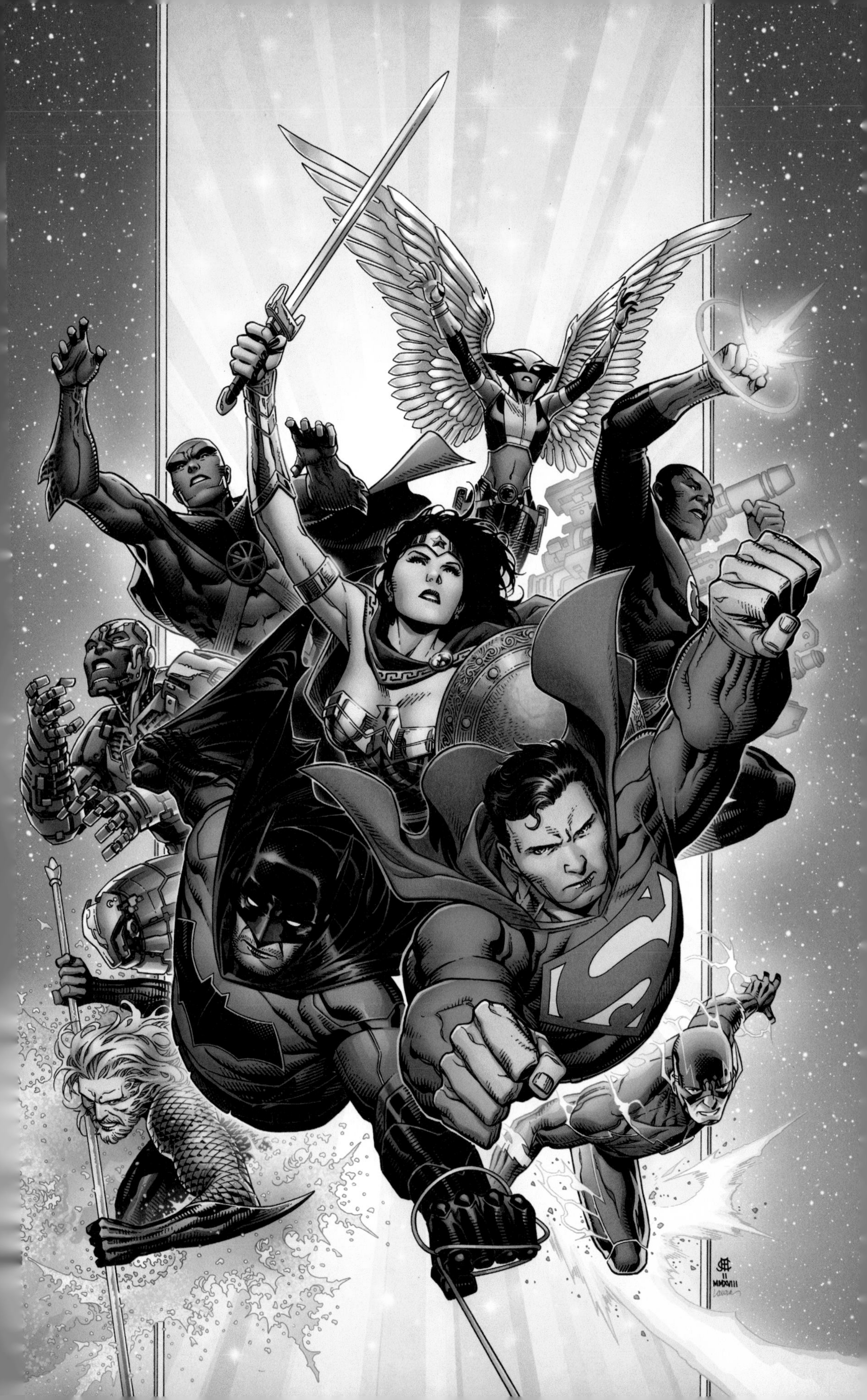

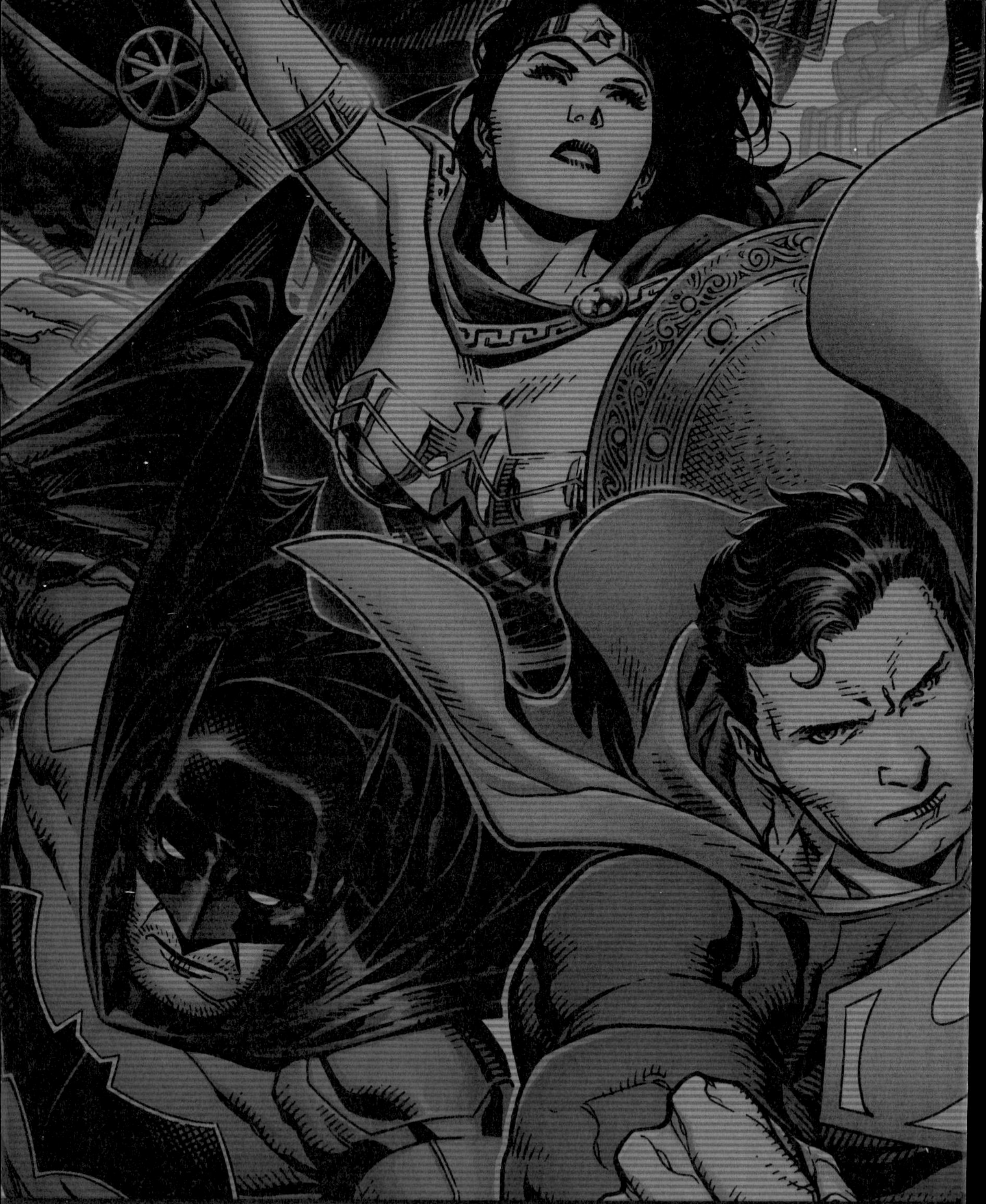

JUSTICE
LEAGUE
#1

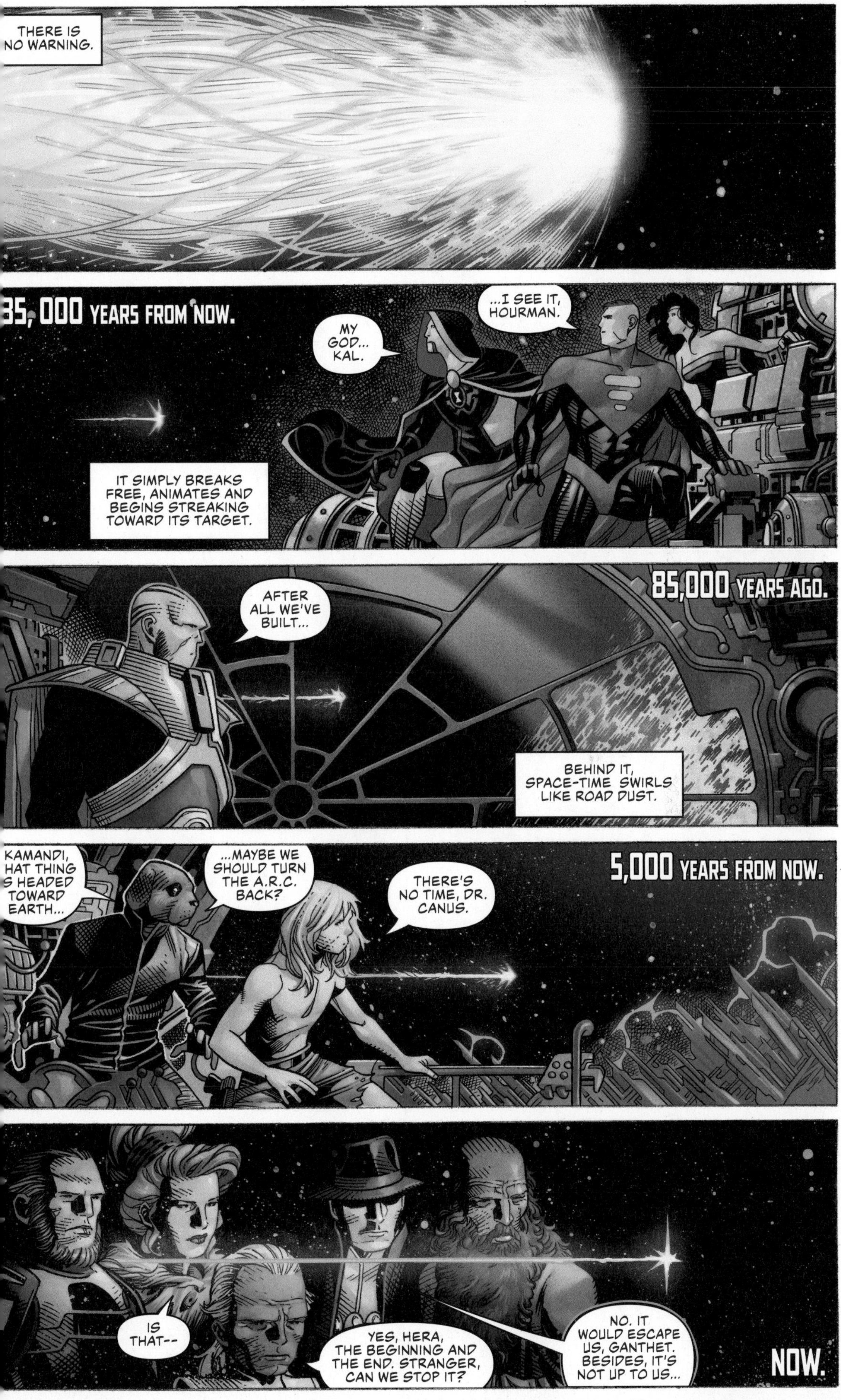
THERE IS NO WARNING.
35,000 YEARS FROM NOW.
MY GOD... KAL.
...I SEE IT, HOURMAN.
IT SIMPLY BREAKS FREE, ANIMATES AND BEGINS STREAKING TOWARD ITS TARGET.
85,000 YEARS AGO.
AFTER ALL WE'VE BUILT...
BEHIND IT, SPACE-TIME SWIRLS LIKE ROAD DUST.
5,000 YEARS FROM NOW.
KAMANDI, HAT THING S HEADED TOWARD EARTH...
...MAYBE WE SHOULD TURN THE A.R.C. BACK?
THERE'S NO TIME, DR. CANUS.
IS THAT--
YES, HERA, THE BEGINNING AND THE END. STRANGER, CAN WE STOP IT?
NO. IT WOULD ESCAPE US, GANTHET. BESIDES, IT'S NOT UP TO US...
NOW.

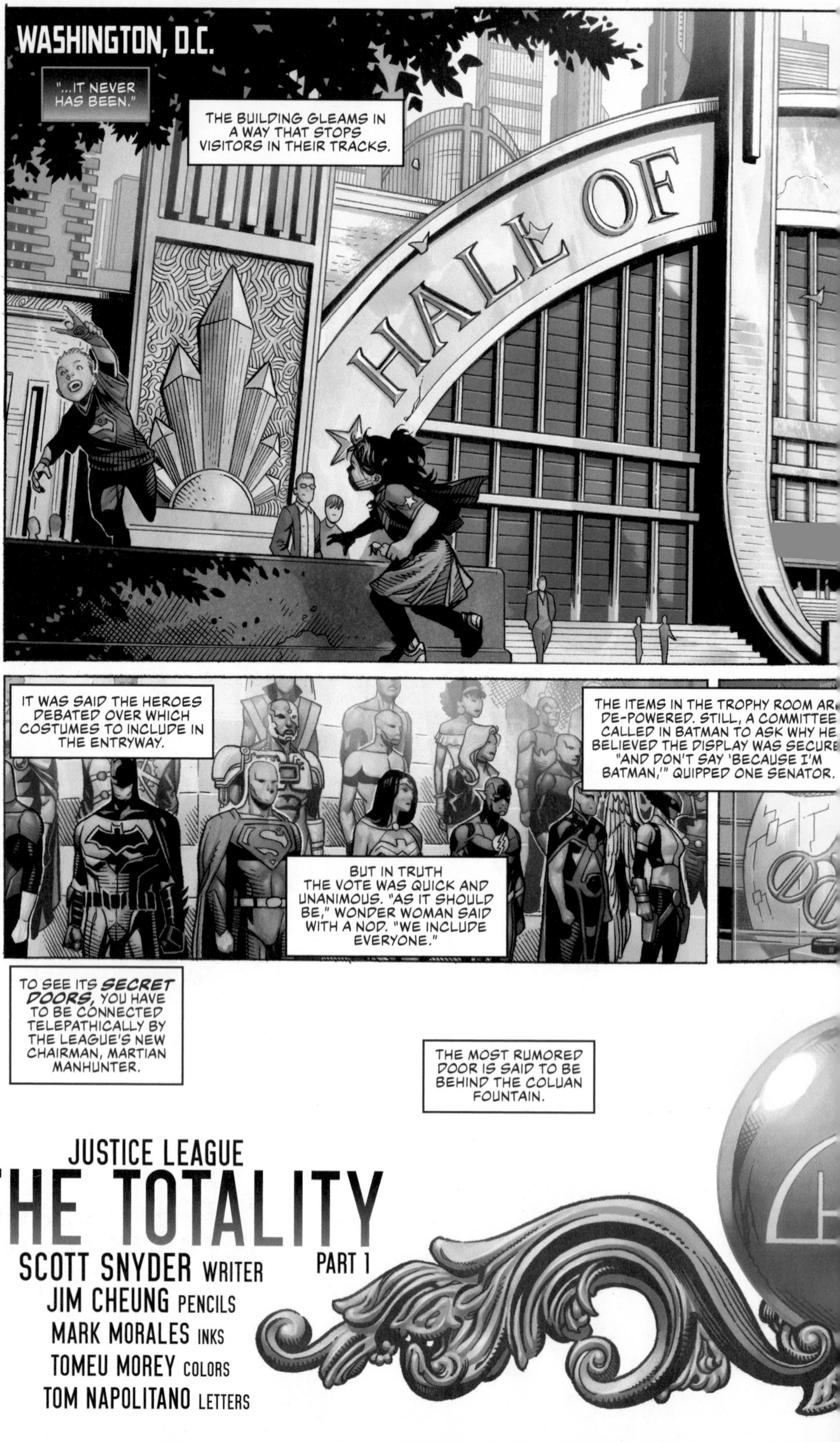

WASHINGTON, D.C.
"...IT NEVER HAS BEEN."
THE BUILDING GLEAMS IN A WAY THAT STOPS VISITORS IN THEIR TRACKS.
HALL OF
IT WAS SAID THE HEROES DEBATED OVER WHICH COSTUMES TO INCLUDE IN THE ENTRYWAY.
BUT IN TRUTH THE VOTE WAS QUICK AND UNANIMOUS. "AS IT SHOULD BE," WONDER WOMAN SAID WITH A NOD. "WE INCLUDE EVERYONE."
THE ITEMS IN THE TROPHY ROOM AR DE-POWERED. STILL, A COMMITTEE CALLED IN BATMAN TO ASK WHY HE BELIEVED THE DISPLAY WAS SECURE "AND DON'T SAY 'BECAUSE I'M BATMAN,'" QUIPPED ONE SENATOR.
TO SEE ITS *SECRET DOORS,* YOU HAVE TO BE CONNECTED TELEPATHICALLY BY THE LEAGUE'S NEW CHAIRMAN, MARTIAN MANHUNTER.
THE MOST RUMORED DOOR IS SAID TO BE BEHIND THE COLUAN FOUNTAIN.
JUSTICE LEAGUE
THE TOTALITY
PART 1
SCOTT SNYDER WRITER
JIM CHEUNG PENCILS
MARK MORALES INKS
TOMEU MOREY COLORS
TOM NAPOLITANO LETTERS

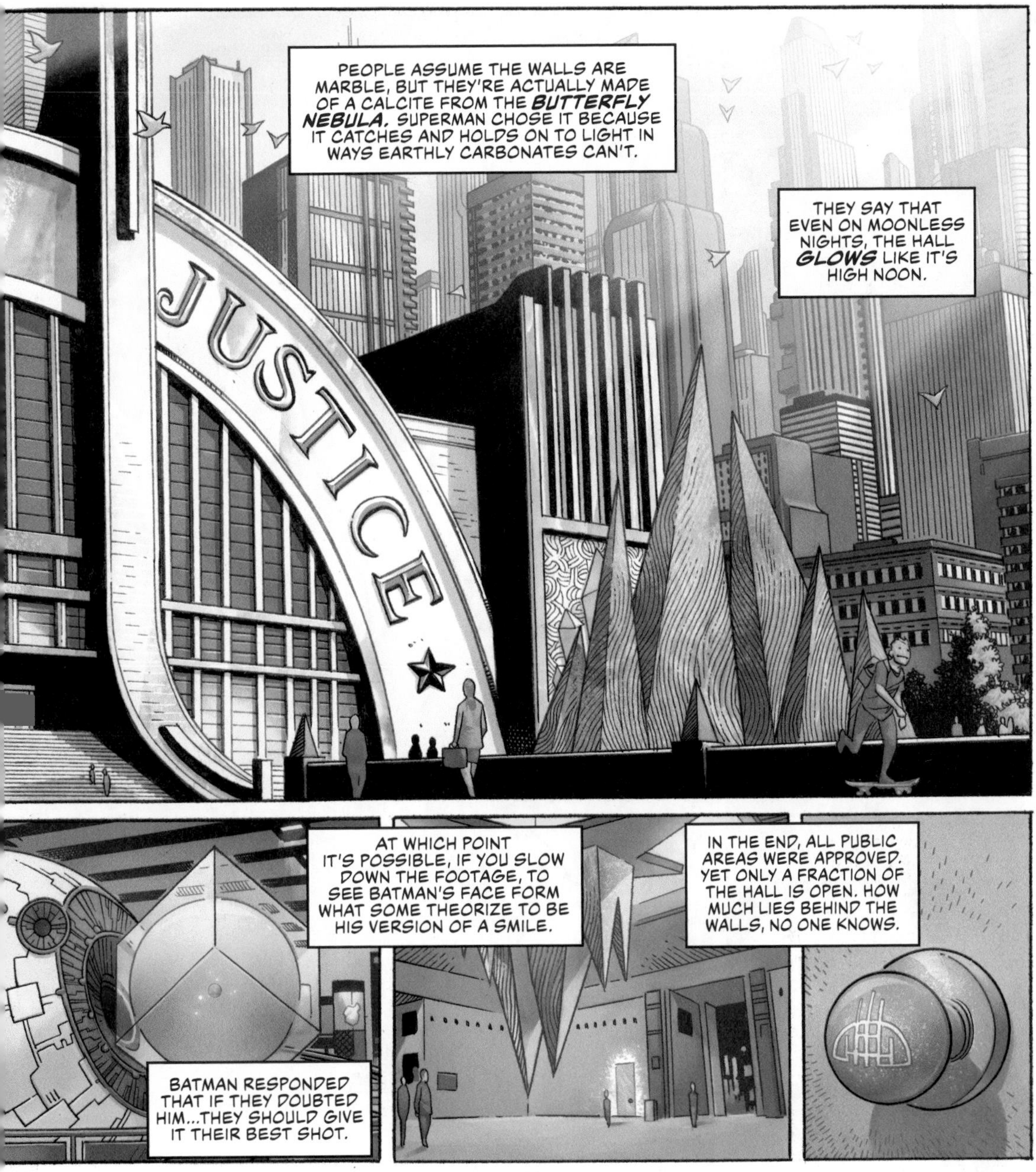
PEOPLE ASSUME THE WALLS ARE MARBLE, BUT THEY'RE ACTUALLY MADE OF A CALCITE FROM THE BUTTERFLY NEBULA. SUPERMAN CHOSE IT BECAUSE IT CATCHES AND HOLDS ON TO LIGHT IN WAYS EARTHLY CARBONATES CAN'T.
THEY SAY THAT EVEN ON MOONLESS NIGHTS, THE HALL GLOWS LIKE IT'S HIGH NOON.
JUSTICE
BATMAN RESPONDED THAT IF THEY DOUBTED HIM...THEY SHOULD GIVE IT THEIR BEST SHOT.
AT WHICH POINT IT'S POSSIBLE, IF YOU SLOW DOWN THE FOOTAGE, TO SEE BATMAN'S FACE FORM WHAT SOME THEORIZE TO BE HIS VERSION OF A SMILE.
IN THE END, ALL PUBLIC AREAS WERE APPROVED. YET ONLY A FRACTION OF THE HALL IS OPEN. HOW MUCH LIES BEHIND THE WALLS, NO ONE KNOWS.

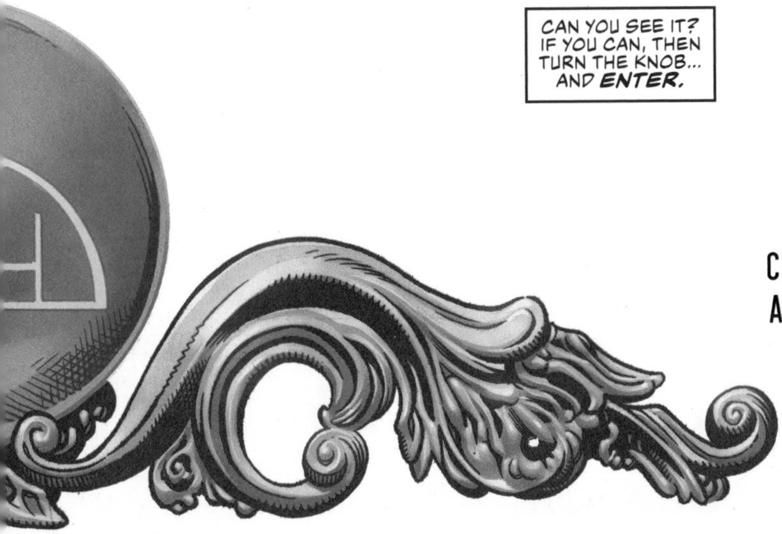
CAN YOU SEE IT? IF YOU CAN, THEN TURN THE KNOB... AND ENTER.

CHEUNG & LAURA MARTIN COVER
ANDREW MARINO ASSISTANT EDITOR
REBECCA TAYLOR EDITOR
MARIE JAVINS GROUP EDITOR

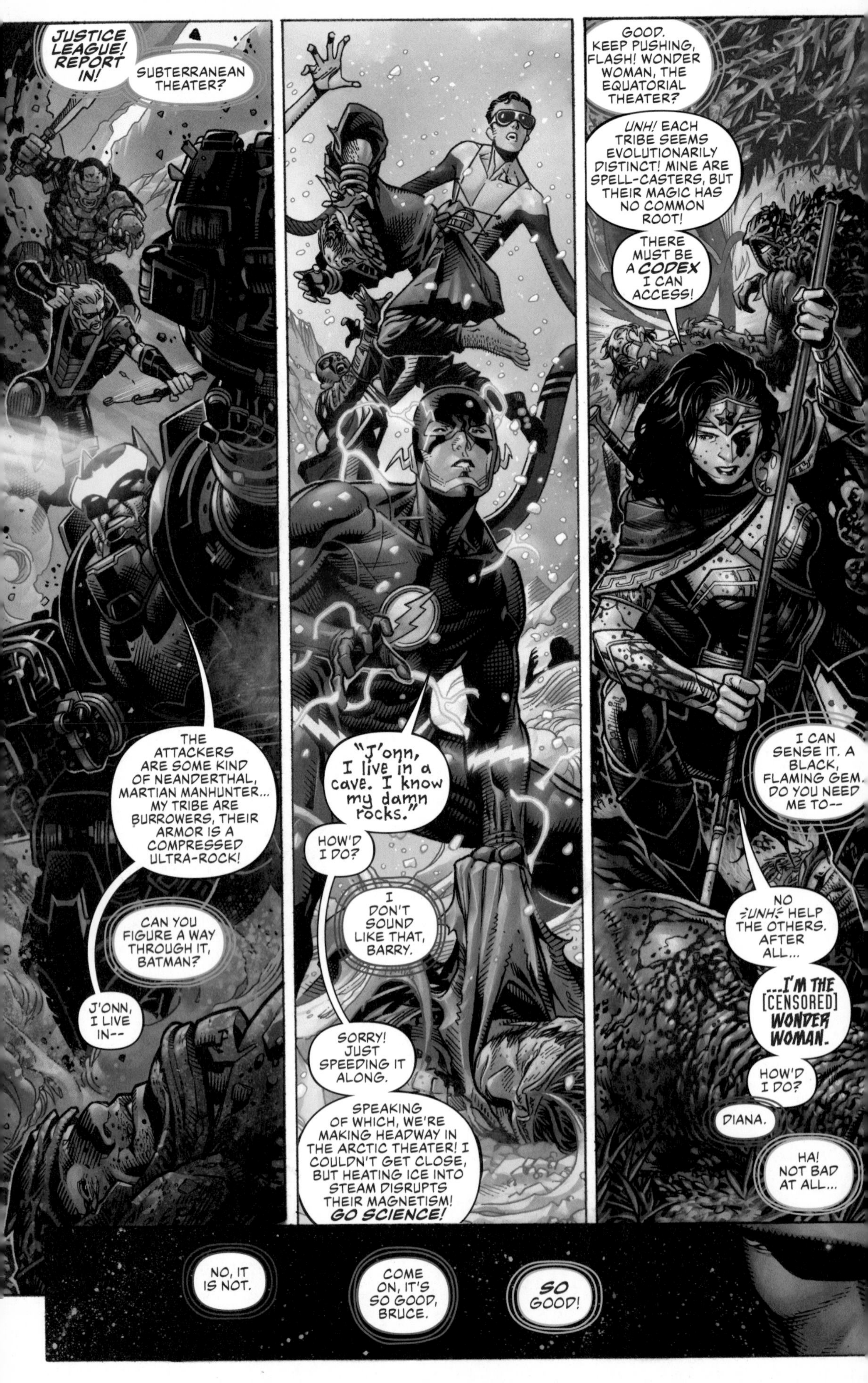
JUSTICE LEAGUE! REPORT IN!
SUBTERRANEAN THEATER?
THE ATTACKERS ARE SOME KIND OF NEANDERTHAL, MARTIAN MANHUNTER... MY TRIBE ARE BURROWERS, THEIR ARMOR IS A COMPRESSED ULTRA-ROCK!
CAN YOU FIGURE A WAY THROUGH IT, BATMAN?
J'ONN, I LIVE IN--
"J'onn, I live in a cave. I know my damn rocks."
HOW'D I DO?
I DON'T SOUND LIKE THAT, BARRY.
SORRY! JUST SPEEDING IT ALONG.
SPEAKING OF WHICH, WE'RE MAKING HEADWAY IN THE ARCTIC THEATER! I COULDN'T GET CLOSE, BUT HEATING ICE INTO STEAM DISRUPTS THEIR MAGNETISM! GO SCIENCE!
GOOD. KEEP PUSHING, FLASH! WONDER WOMAN, THE EQUATORIAL THEATER?
UNH! EACH TRIBE SEEMS EVOLUTIONARILY DISTINCT! MINE ARE SPELL-CASTERS, BUT THEIR MAGIC HAS NO COMMON ROOT!
THERE MUST BE A CODEX I CAN ACCESS!
I CAN SENSE IT. A BLACK, FLAMING GEM. DO YOU NEED ME TO--
NO =UNH= HELP THE OTHERS. AFTER ALL...
...I'M THE [CENSORED] WONDER WOMAN.
HOW'D I DO?
DIANA.
HA! NOT BAD AT ALL...
NO, IT IS NOT.
COME ON, IT'S SO GOOD, BRUCE.
SO GOOD!

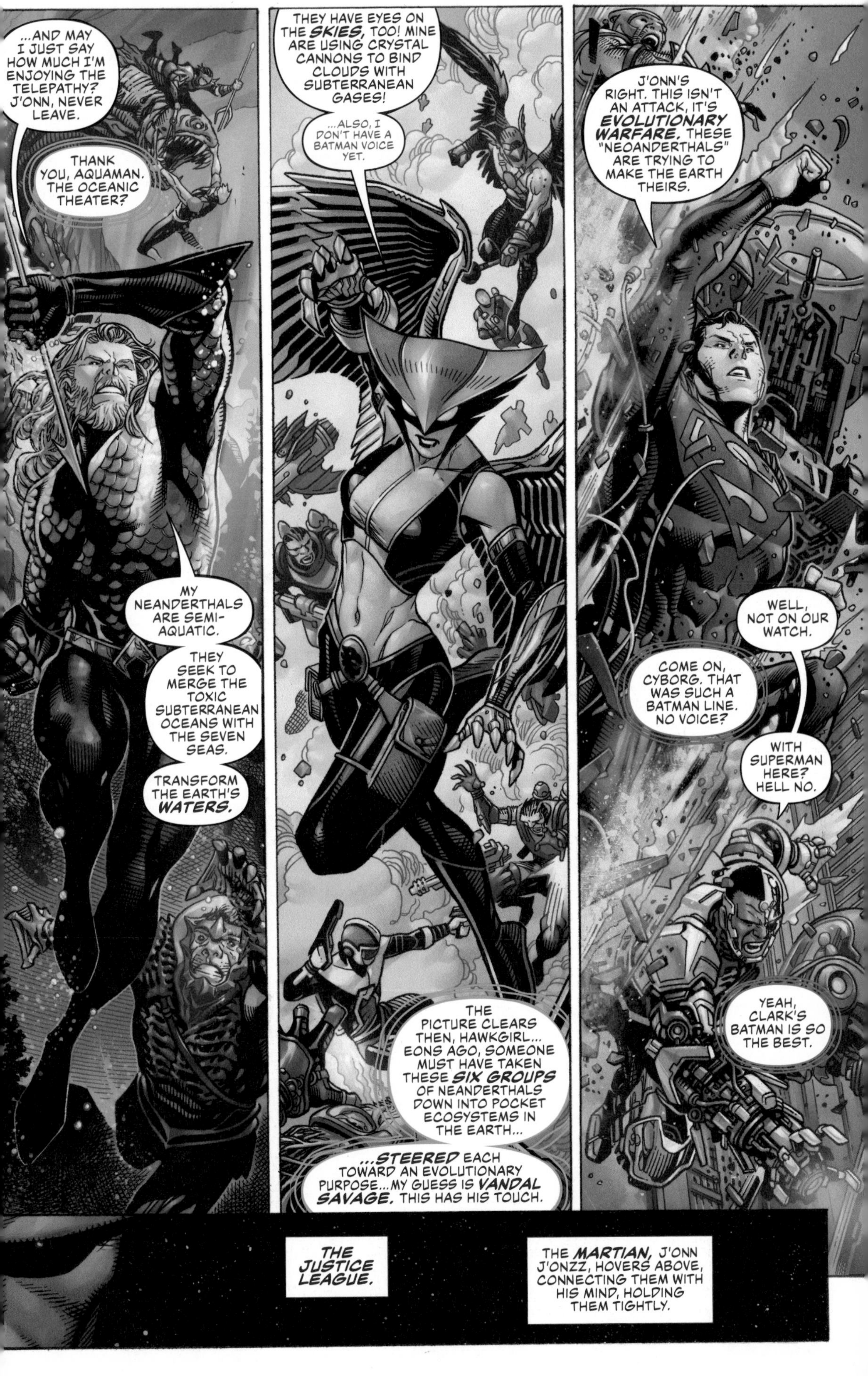
...AND MAY I JUST SAY HOW MUCH I'M ENJOYING THE TELEPATHY? J'ONN, NEVER LEAVE.
THANK YOU, AQUAMAN. THE OCEANIC THEATER?
MY NEANDERTHALS ARE SEMI-AQUATIC.
THEY SEEK TO MERGE THE TOXIC SUBTERRANEAN OCEANS WITH THE SEVEN SEAS.
TRANSFORM THE EARTH'S WATERS.
THEY HAVE EYES ON THE SKIES, TOO! MINE ARE USING CRYSTAL CANNONS TO BIND CLOUDS WITH SUBTERRANEAN GASES!
...ALSO, I DON'T HAVE A BATMAN VOICE YET.
THE PICTURE CLEARS THEN, HAWKGIRL... EONS AGO, SOMEONE MUST HAVE TAKEN THESE SIX GROUPS OF NEANDERTHALS DOWN INTO POCKET ECOSYSTEMS IN THE EARTH...
...STEERED EACH TOWARD AN EVOLUTIONARY PURPOSE...MY GUESS IS VANDAL SAVAGE. THIS HAS HIS TOUCH.
J'ONN'S RIGHT. THIS ISN'T AN ATTACK, IT'S EVOLUTIONARY WARFARE. THESE "NEOANDERTHALS" ARE TRYING TO MAKE THE EARTH THEIRS.
WELL, NOT ON OUR WATCH.
COME ON, CYBORG. THAT WAS SUCH A BATMAN LINE. NO VOICE?
WITH SUPERMAN HERE? HELL NO.
YEAH, CLARK'S BATMAN IS SO THE BEST.
THE JUSTICE LEAGUE.
THE MARTIAN, J'ONN J'ONZZ, HOVERS ABOVE, CONNECTING THEM WITH HIS MIND, HOLDING THEM TIGHTLY.

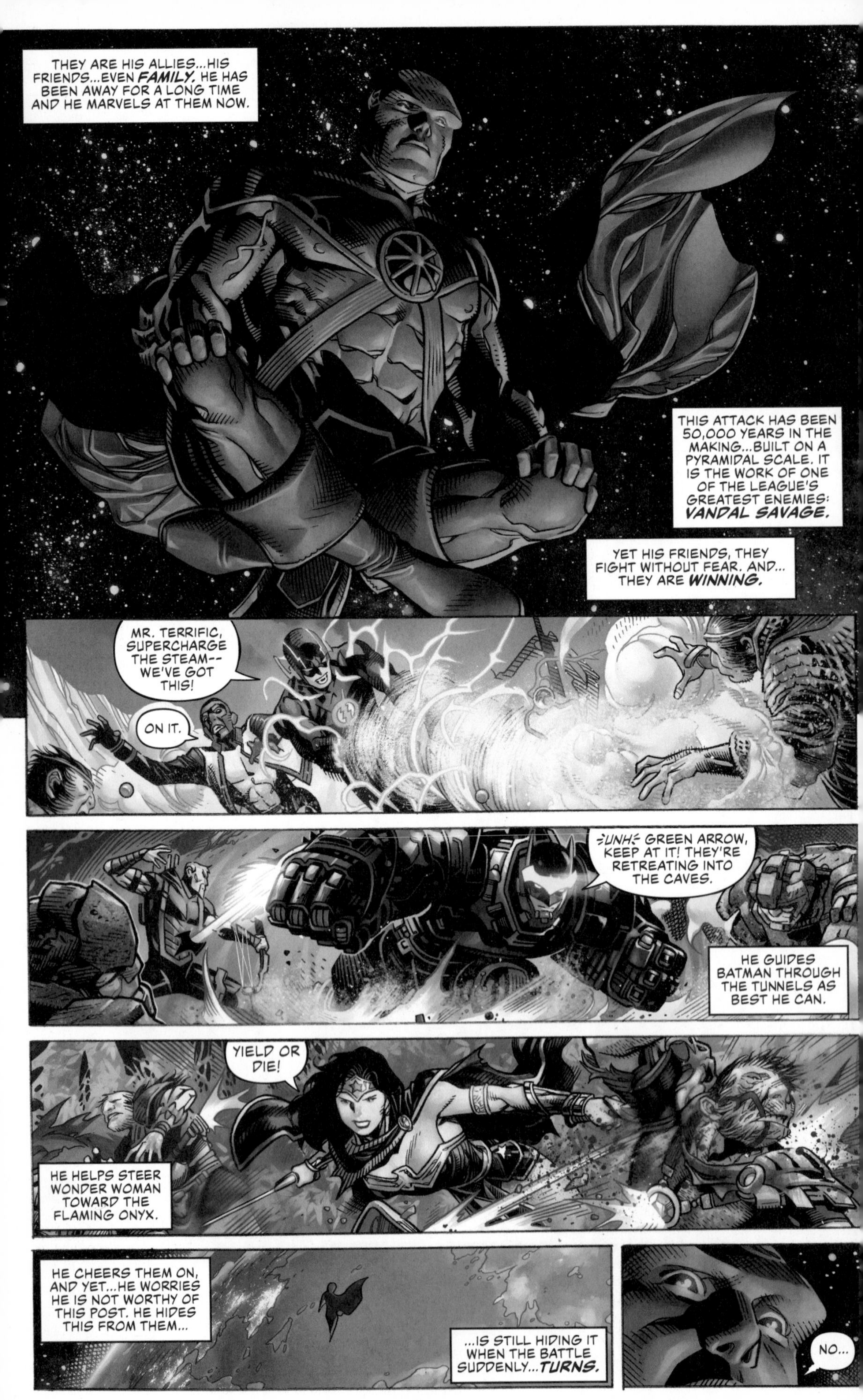
THEY ARE HIS ALLIES...HIS FRIENDS...EVEN FAMILY. HE HAS BEEN AWAY FOR A LONG TIME AND HE MARVELS AT THEM NOW.
THIS ATTACK HAS BEEN 50,000 YEARS IN THE MAKING...BUILT ON A PYRAMIDAL SCALE. IT IS THE WORK OF ONE OF THE LEAGUE'S GREATEST ENEMIES: VANDAL SAVAGE.
YET HIS FRIENDS, THEY FIGHT WITHOUT FEAR. AND... THEY ARE WINNING.
MR. TERRIFIC, SUPERCHARGE THE STEAM-- WE'VE GOT THIS!
ON IT.
UNH GREEN ARROW, KEEP AT IT! THEY'RE RETREATING INTO THE CAVES.
HE GUIDES BATMAN THROUGH THE TUNNELS AS BEST HE CAN.
YIELD OR DIE!
HE HELPS STEER WONDER WOMAN TOWARD THE FLAMING ONYX.
HE CHEERS THEM ON, AND YET...HE WORRIES HE IS NOT WORTHY OF THIS POST. HE HIDES THIS FROM THEM...
...IS STILL HIDING IT WHEN THE BATTLE SUDDENLY...TURNS.
NO...

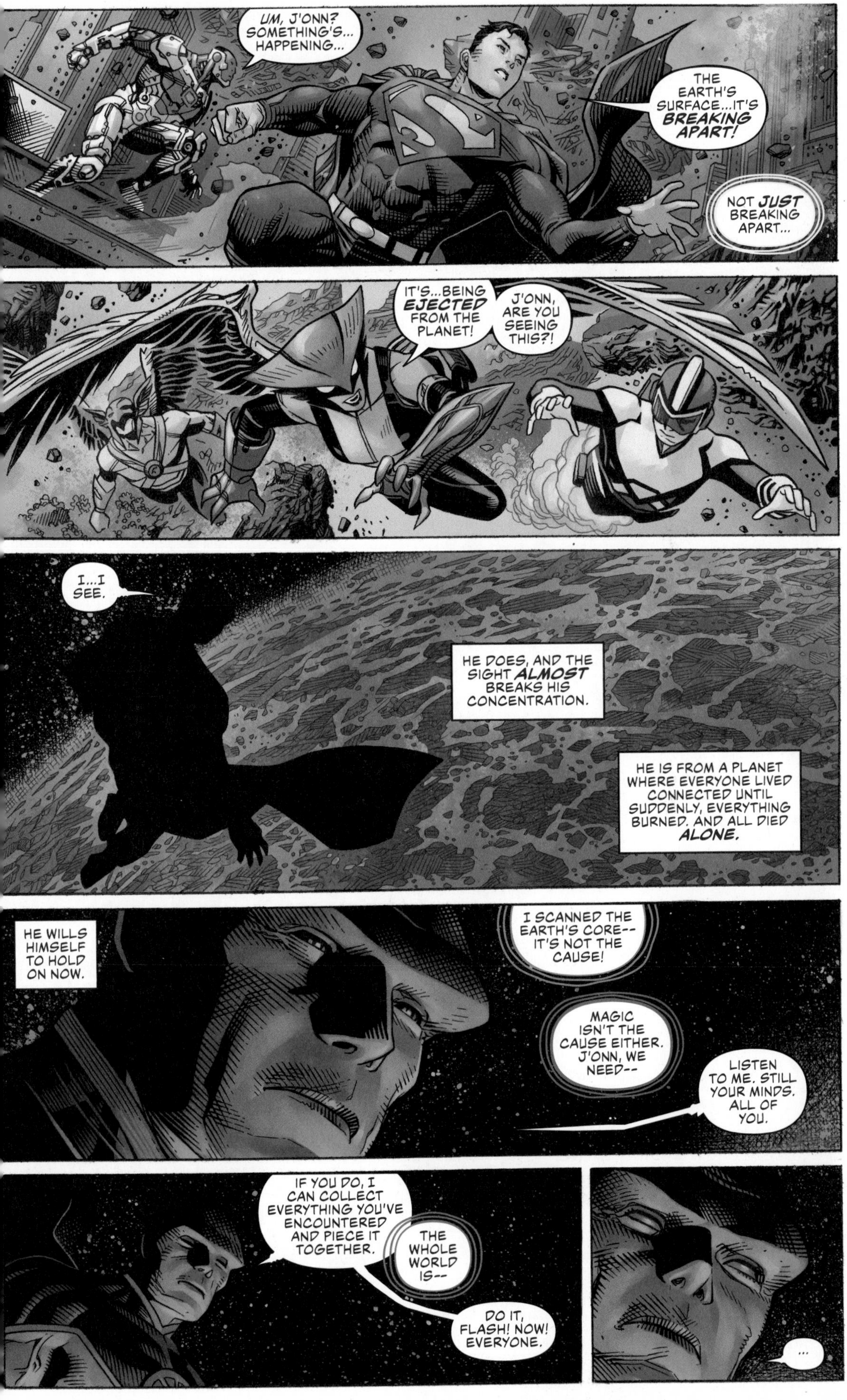

UM, J'ONN? SOMETHING'S... HAPPENING...
THE EARTH'S SURFACE...IT'S BREAKING APART!
NOT JUST BREAKING APART...
IT'S...BEING EJECTED FROM THE PLANET!
J'ONN, ARE YOU SEEING THIS?!
I...I SEE.
HE DOES, AND THE SIGHT ALMOST BREAKS HIS CONCENTRATION.
HE IS FROM A PLANET WHERE EVERYONE LIVED CONNECTED UNTIL SUDDENLY, EVERYTHING BURNED. AND ALL DIED ALONE.
HE WILLS HIMSELF TO HOLD ON NOW.
I SCANNED THE EARTH'S CORE-- IT'S NOT THE CAUSE!
MAGIC ISN'T THE CAUSE EITHER. J'ONN, WE NEED--
LISTEN TO ME. STILL YOUR MINDS. ALL OF YOU.
IF YOU DO, I CAN COLLECT EVERYTHING YOU'VE ENCOUNTERED AND PIECE IT TOGETHER.
THE WHOLE WORLD IS--
DO IT, FLASH! NOW! EVERYONE.
...

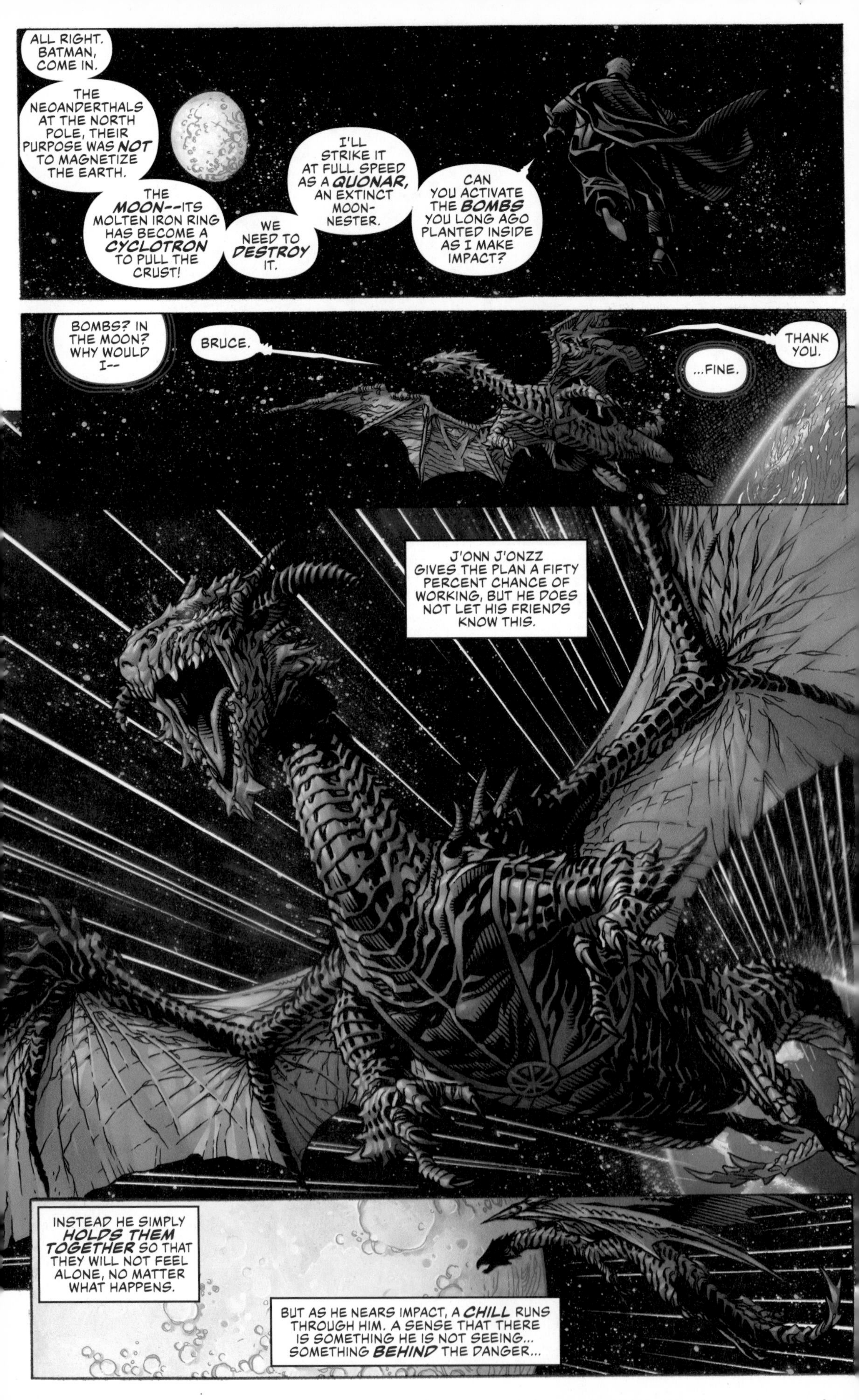
ALL RIGHT. BATMAN, COME IN.
THE NEOANDERTHALS AT THE NORTH POLE, THEIR PURPOSE WAS NOT TO MAGNETIZE THE EARTH.
THE MOON--ITS MOLTEN IRON RING HAS BECOME A CYCLOTRON TO PULL THE CRUST!
WE NEED TO DESTROY IT.
I'LL STRIKE IT AT FULL SPEED AS A QUONAR, AN EXTINCT MOON-NESTER.
CAN YOU ACTIVATE THE BOMBS YOU LONG AGO PLANTED INSIDE AS I MAKE IMPACT?
BOMBS? IN THE MOON? WHY WOULD I--
BRUCE.
...FINE.
THANK YOU.
J'ONN J'ONZZ GIVES THE PLAN A FIFTY PERCENT CHANCE OF WORKING, BUT HE DOES NOT LET HIS FRIENDS KNOW THIS.
INSTEAD HE SIMPLY HOLDS THEM TOGETHER SO THAT THEY WILL NOT FEEL ALONE, NO MATTER WHAT HAPPENS.
BUT AS HE NEARS IMPACT, A CHILL RUNS THROUGH HIM. A SENSE THAT THERE IS SOMETHING HE IS NOT SEEING... SOMETHING BEHIND THE DANGER...

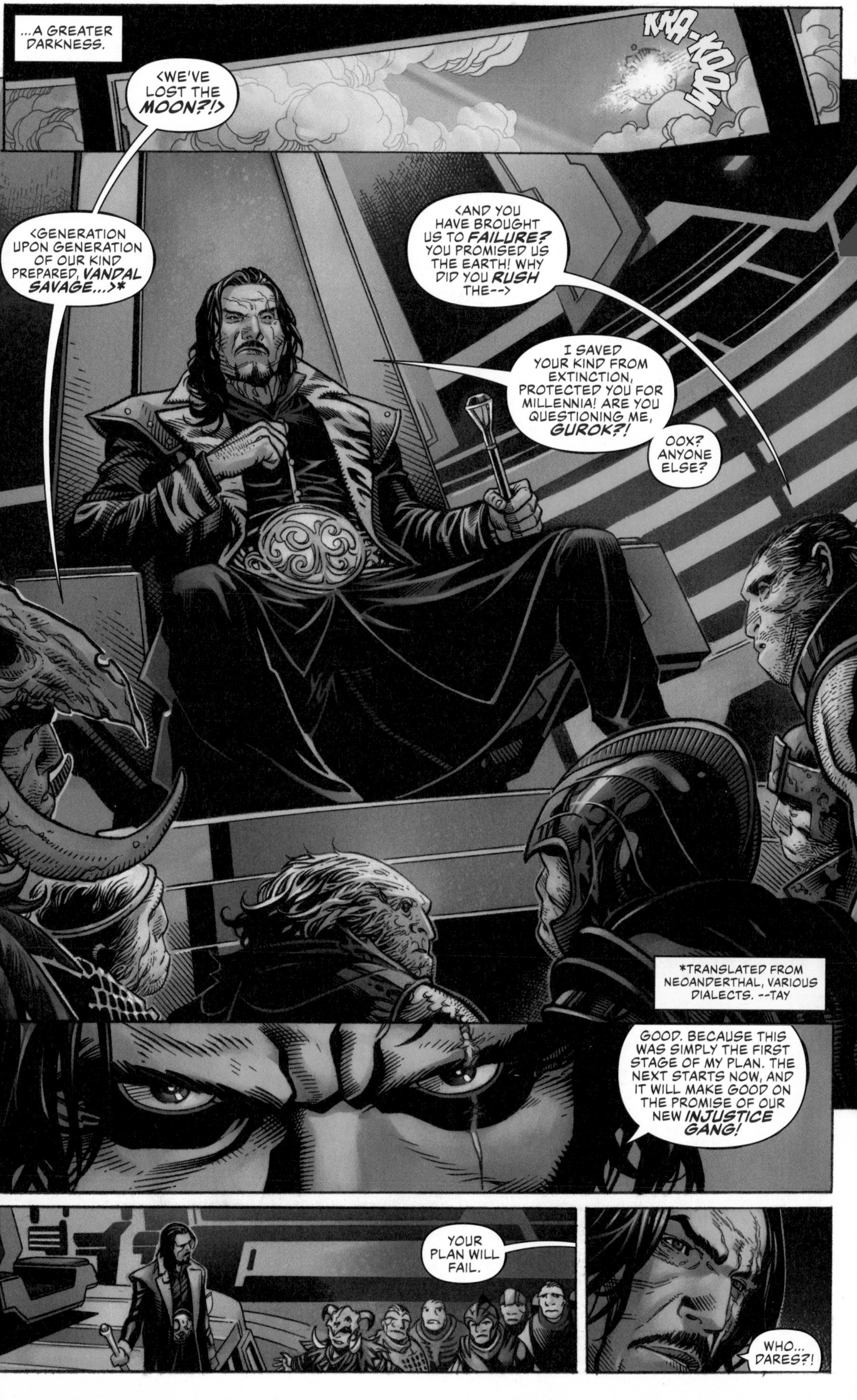

...A GREATER DARKNESS.
KRA-KOOM
<WE'VE LOST THE MOON?!>
<GENERATION UPON GENERATION OF OUR KIND PREPARED, VANDAL SAVAGE...>*
<AND YOU HAVE BROUGHT US TO FAILURE? YOU PROMISED US THE EARTH! WHY DID YOU RUSH THE-->
I SAVED YOUR KIND FROM EXTINCTION, PROTECTED YOU FOR MILLENNIA! ARE YOU QUESTIONING ME, GUROK?!
OOX? ANYONE ELSE?
*TRANSLATED FROM NEOANDERTHAL, VARIOUS DIALECTS. --TAY
GOOD. BECAUSE THIS WAS SIMPLY THE FIRST STAGE OF MY PLAN. THE NEXT STARTS NOW, AND IT WILL MAKE GOOD ON THE PROMISE OF OUR NEW INJUSTICE GANG!
YOUR PLAN WILL FAIL.
WHO... DARES?!

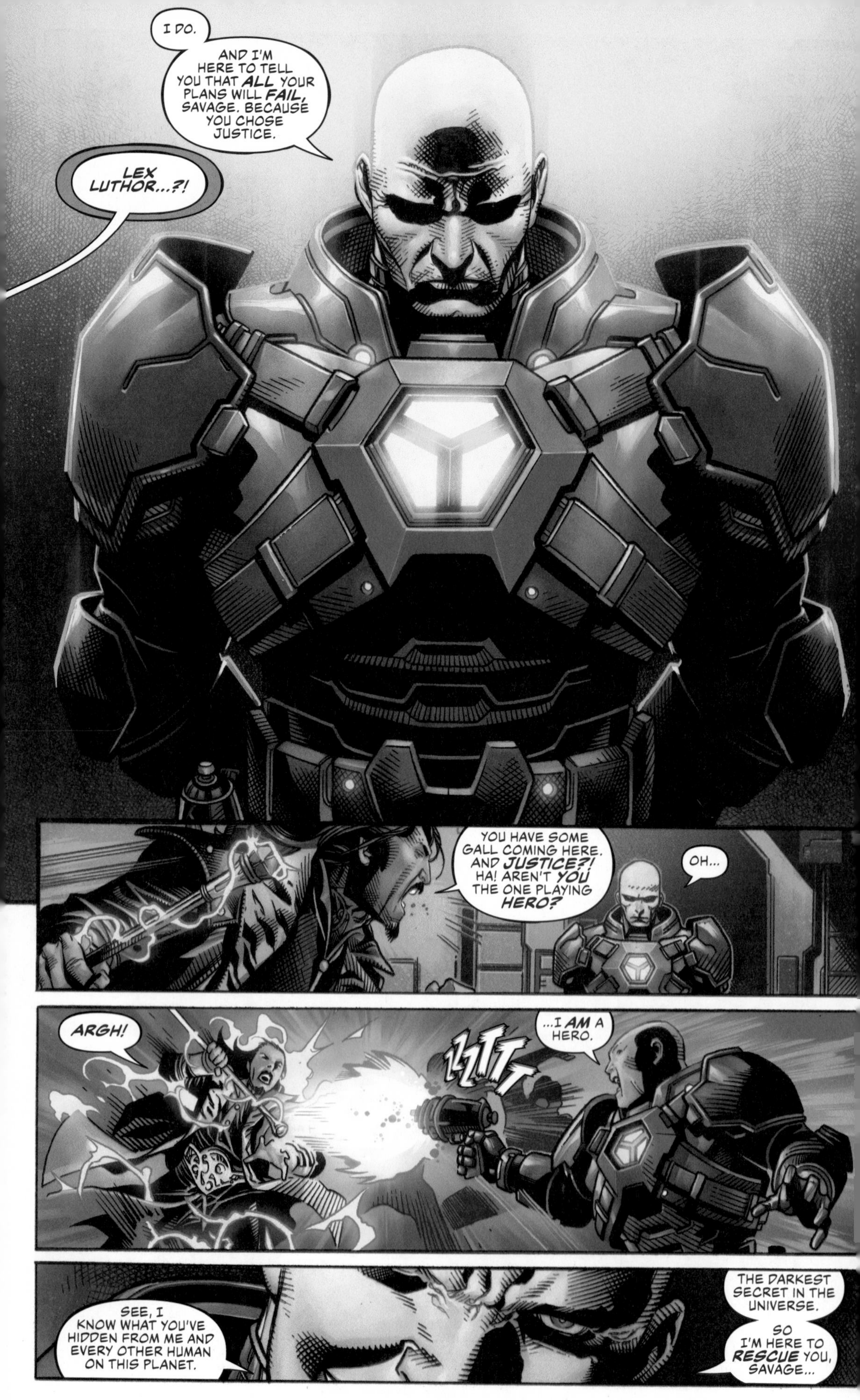
I DO.
AND I'M HERE TO TELL YOU THAT ALL YOUR PLANS WILL FAIL, SAVAGE. BECAUSE YOU CHOSE JUSTICE.
LEX LUTHOR...?!
YOU HAVE SOME GALL COMING HERE. AND JUSTICE?! HA! AREN'T YOU THE ONE PLAYING HERO?
OH...
ARGH!
...I AM A HERO.
ZZZTTT
SEE, I KNOW WHAT YOU'VE HIDDEN FROM ME AND EVERY OTHER HUMAN ON THIS PLANET.
THE DARKEST SECRET IN THE UNIVERSE.
SO I'M HERE TO RESCUE YOU, SAVAGE...

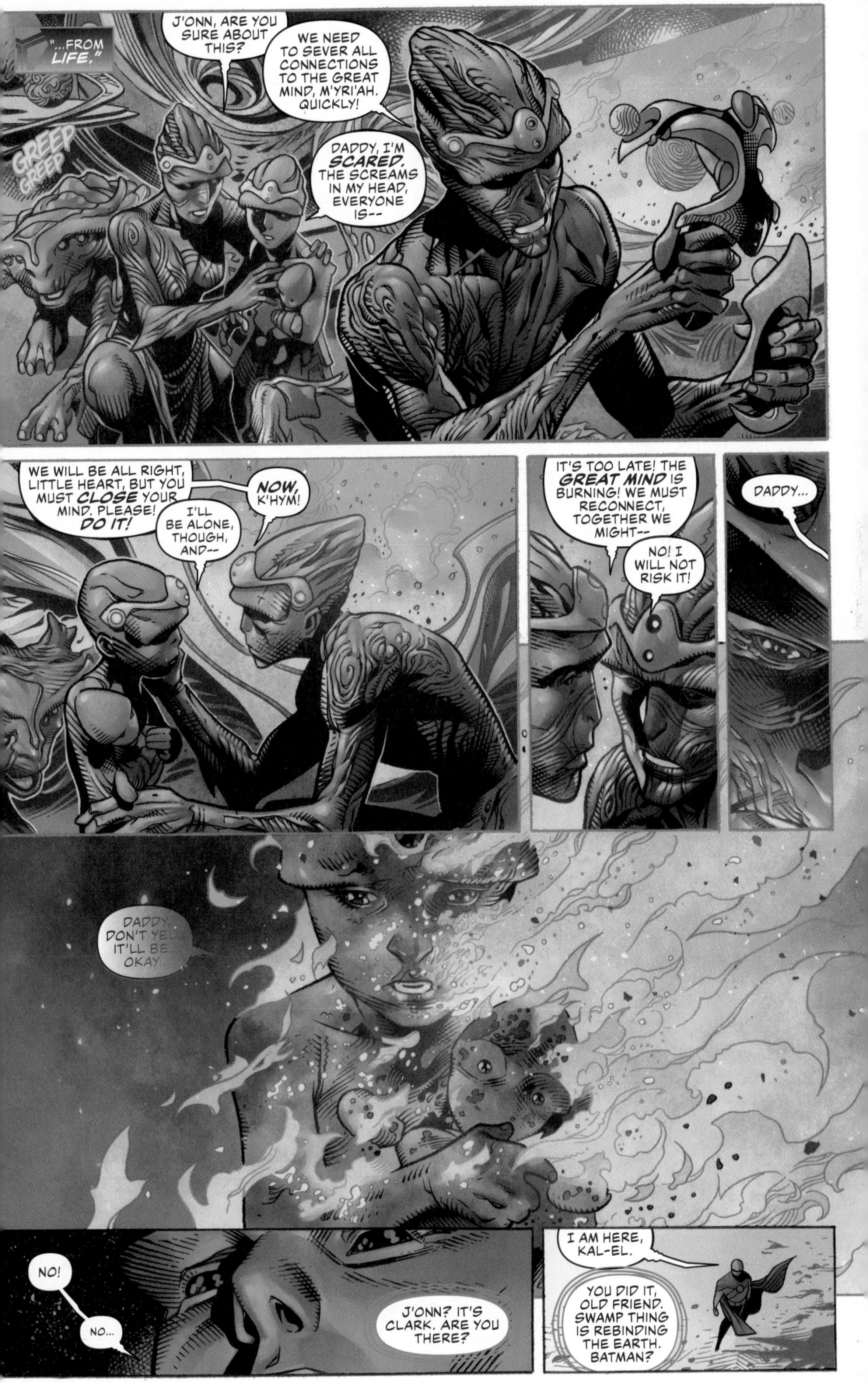
"...FROM LIFE."
J'ONN, ARE YOU SURE ABOUT THIS?
WE NEED TO SEVER ALL CONNECTIONS TO THE GREAT MIND, M'YRI'AH. QUICKLY!
GREEP GREEP
DADDY, I'M SCARED. THE SCREAMS IN MY HEAD, EVERYONE IS--
WE WILL BE ALL RIGHT, LITTLE HEART, BUT YOU MUST CLOSE YOUR MIND. PLEASE! DO IT!
I'LL BE ALONE, THOUGH, AND--
NOW, K'HYM!
IT'S TOO LATE! THE GREAT MIND IS BURNING! WE MUST RECONNECT, TOGETHER WE MIGHT--
NO! I WILL NOT RISK IT!
DADDY...
DADDY, DON'T YELL. IT'LL BE OKAY.
NO!
NO...
J'ONN? IT'S CLARK. ARE YOU THERE?
I AM HERE, KAL-EL.
YOU DID IT, OLD FRIEND. SWAMP THING IS REBINDING THE EARTH. BATMAN?

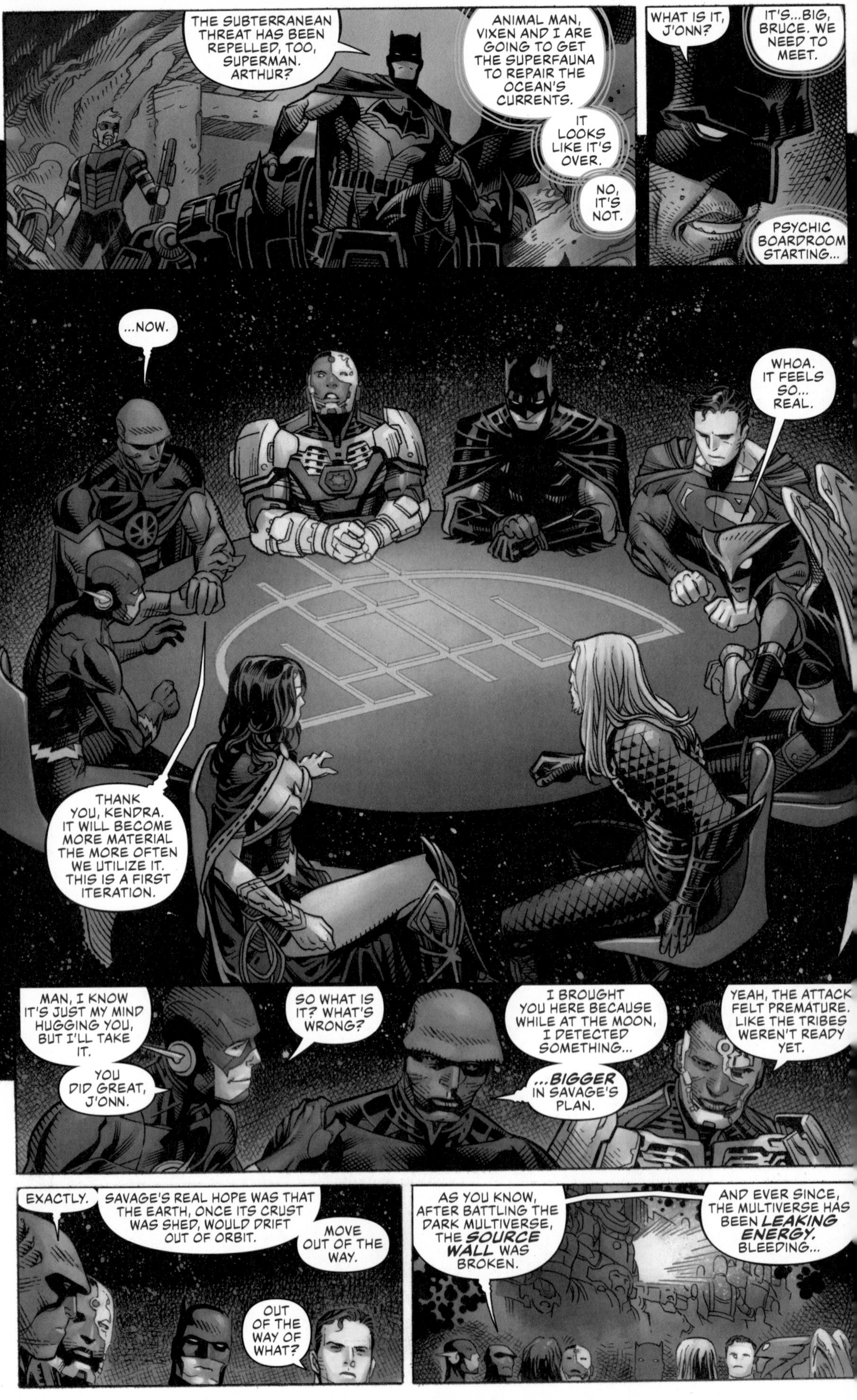

THE SUBTERRANEAN THREAT HAS BEEN REPELLED, TOO, SUPERMAN. ARTHUR?
ANIMAL MAN, VIXEN AND I ARE GOING TO GET THE SUPERFAUNA TO REPAIR THE OCEAN'S CURRENTS.
IT LOOKS LIKE IT'S OVER.
NO, IT'S NOT.
WHAT IS IT, J'ONN?
IT'S...BIG, BRUCE. WE NEED TO MEET.
PSYCHIC BOARDROOM STARTING...
...NOW.
WHOA. IT FEELS SO... REAL.
THANK YOU, KENDRA. IT WILL BECOME MORE MATERIAL THE MORE OFTEN WE UTILIZE IT. THIS IS A FIRST ITERATION.
MAN, I KNOW IT'S JUST MY MIND HUGGING YOU, BUT I'LL TAKE IT.
YOU DID GREAT, J'ONN.
SO WHAT IS IT? WHAT'S WRONG?
I BROUGHT YOU HERE BECAUSE WHILE AT THE MOON, I DETECTED SOMETHING...
...BIGGER IN SAVAGE'S PLAN.
YEAH, THE ATTACK FELT PREMATURE. LIKE THE TRIBES WEREN'T READY YET.
EXACTLY.
SAVAGE'S REAL HOPE WAS THAT THE EARTH, ONCE ITS CRUST WAS SHED, WOULD DRIFT OUT OF ORBIT.
MOVE OUT OF THE WAY.
OUT OF THE WAY OF WHAT?
AS YOU KNOW, AFTER BATTLING THE DARK MULTIVERSE, THE SOURCE WALL WAS BROKEN.
AND EVER SINCE, THE MULTIVERSE HAS BEEN LEAKING ENERGY. BLEEDING...

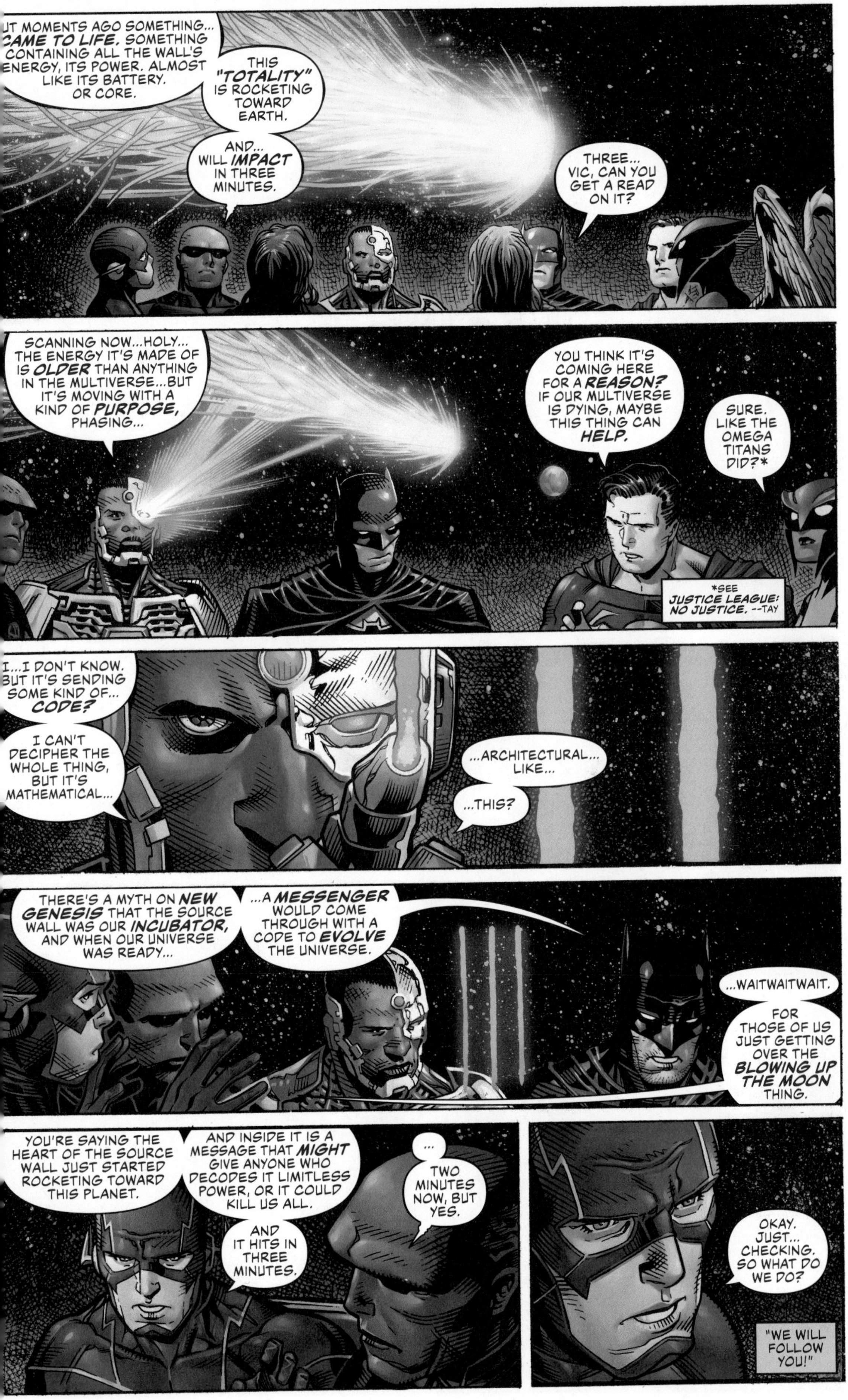
UT MOMENTS AGO SOMETHING... CAME TO LIFE. SOMETHING CONTAINING ALL THE WALL'S ENERGY, ITS POWER. ALMOST LIKE ITS BATTERY. OR CORE.
THIS "TOTALITY" IS ROCKETING TOWARD EARTH.
AND... WILL IMPACT IN THREE MINUTES.
THREE... VIC, CAN YOU GET A READ ON IT?
SCANNING NOW...HOLY... THE ENERGY IT'S MADE OF IS OLDER THAN ANYTHING IN THE MULTIVERSE...BUT IT'S MOVING WITH A KIND OF PURPOSE, PHASING...
YOU THINK IT'S COMING HERE FOR A REASON? IF OUR MULTIVERSE IS DYING, MAYBE THIS THING CAN HELP.
SURE. LIKE THE OMEGA TITANS DID?*
*SEE JUSTICE LEAGUE: NO JUSTICE. --TAY
I...I DON'T KNOW. BUT IT'S SENDING SOME KIND OF... CODE?
I CAN'T DECIPHER THE WHOLE THING, BUT IT'S MATHEMATICAL...
...ARCHITECTURAL... LIKE...
...THIS?
THERE'S A MYTH ON NEW GENESIS THAT THE SOURCE WALL WAS OUR INCUBATOR, AND WHEN OUR UNIVERSE WAS READY...
...A MESSENGER WOULD COME THROUGH WITH A CODE TO EVOLVE THE UNIVERSE.
...WAITWAITWAIT.
FOR THOSE OF US JUST GETTING OVER THE BLOWING UP THE MOON THING.
YOU'RE SAYING THE HEART OF THE SOURCE WALL JUST STARTED ROCKETING TOWARD THIS PLANET.
AND INSIDE IT IS A MESSAGE THAT MIGHT GIVE ANYONE WHO DECODES IT LIMITLESS POWER, OR IT COULD KILL US ALL.
AND IT HITS IN THREE MINUTES.
...
TWO MINUTES NOW, BUT YES.
OKAY. JUST... CHECKING. SO WHAT DO WE DO?
"WE WILL FOLLOW YOU!"

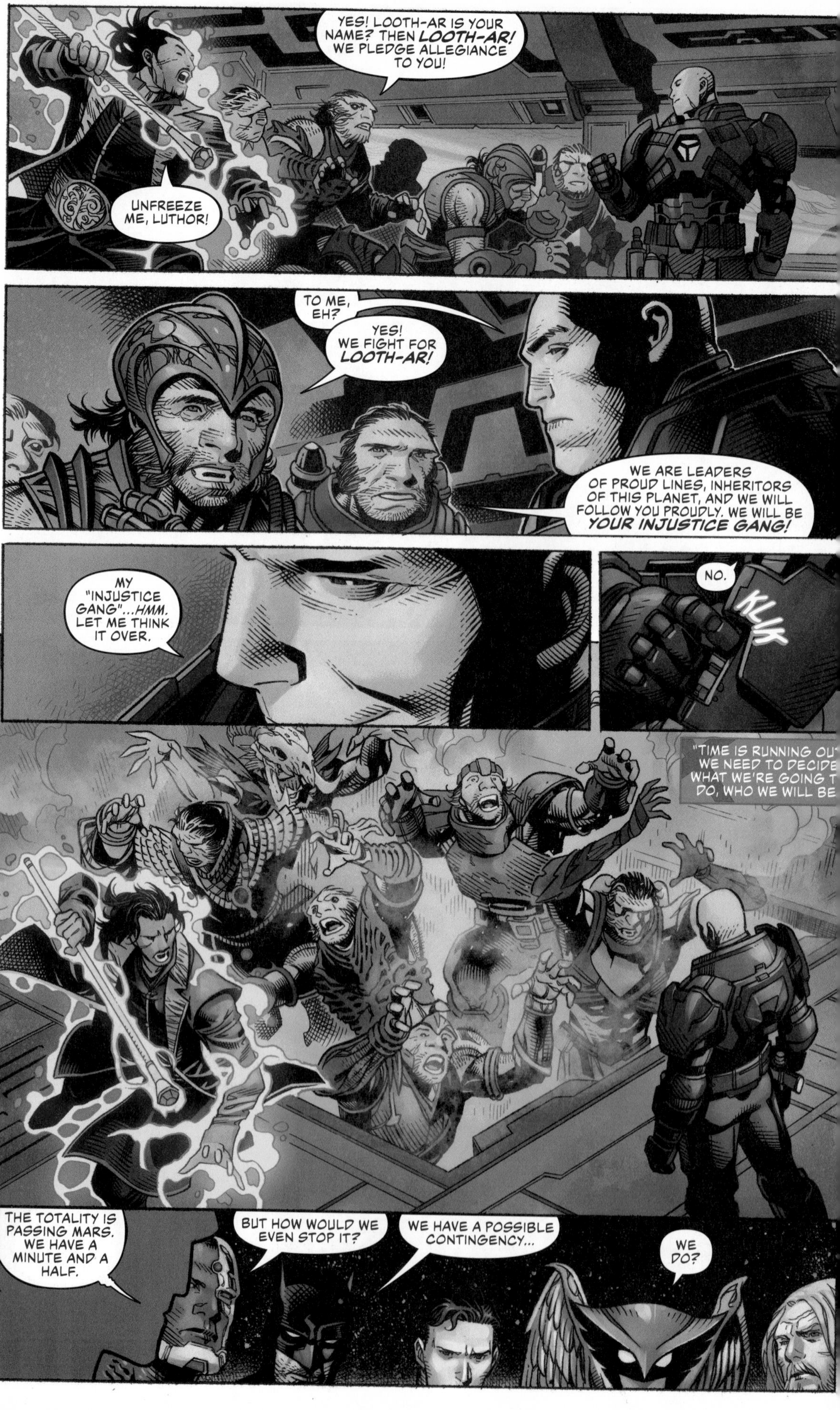

YES! LOOTH-AR IS YOUR NAME? THEN LOOTH-AR! WE PLEDGE ALLEGIANCE TO YOU!
UNFREEZE ME, LUTHOR!
TO ME, EH?
YES! WE FIGHT FOR LOOTH-AR!
WE ARE LEADERS OF PROUD LINES, INHERITORS OF THIS PLANET, AND WE WILL FOLLOW YOU PROUDLY. WE WILL BE YOUR INJUSTICE GANG!
MY "INJUSTICE GANG"...HMM. LET ME THINK IT OVER.
NO.
KLIK
"TIME IS RUNNING OU WE NEED TO DECIDE WHAT WE'RE GOING T DO, WHO WE WILL BE
THE TOTALITY IS PASSING MARS. WE HAVE A MINUTE AND A HALF.
BUT HOW WOULD WE EVEN STOP IT?
WE HAVE A POSSIBLE CONTINGENCY...
WE DO?

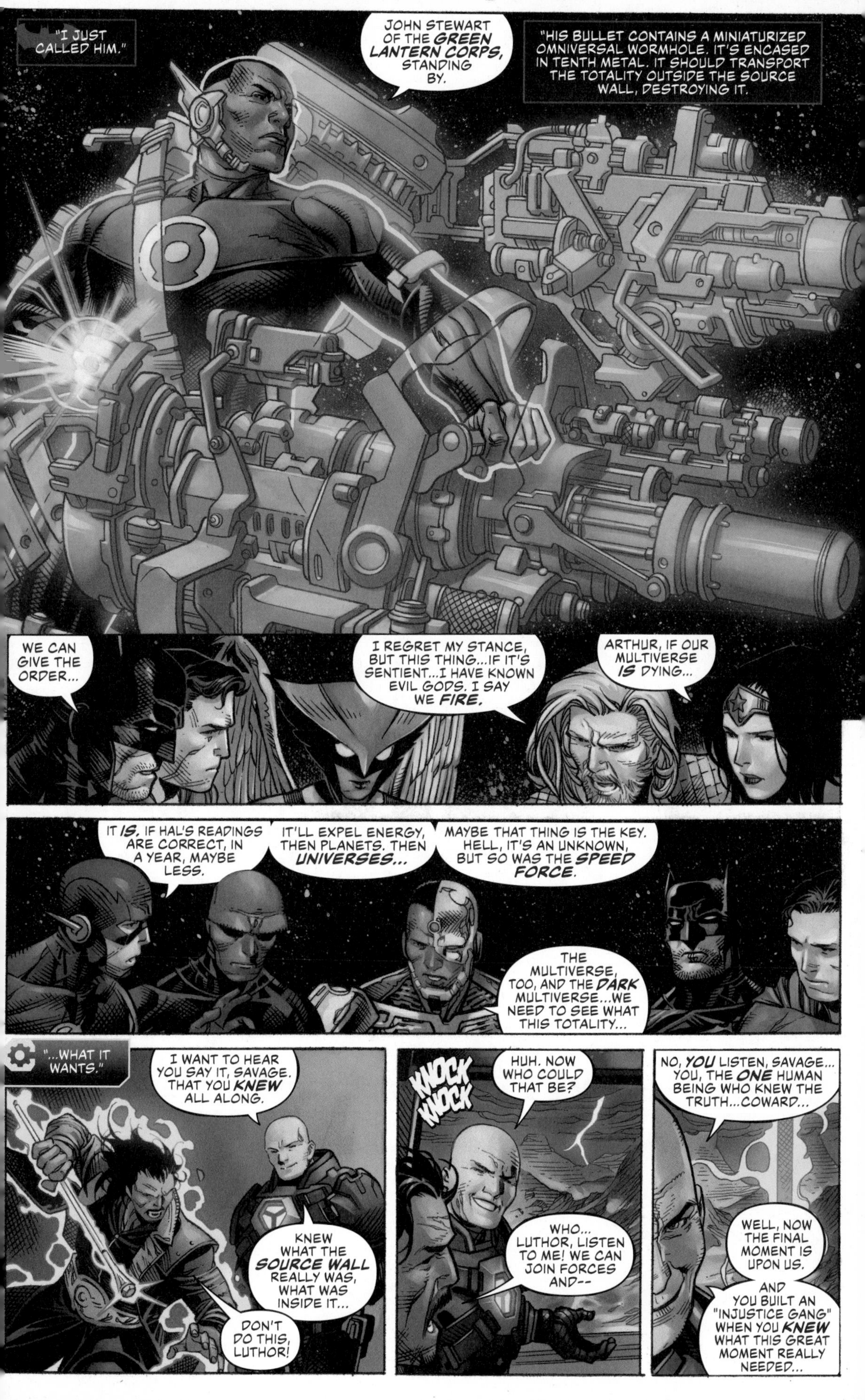
"I JUST CALLED HIM."
JOHN STEWART OF THE GREEN LANTERN CORPS, STANDING BY.
"HIS BULLET CONTAINS A MINIATURIZED OMNIVERSAL WORMHOLE. IT'S ENCASED IN TENTH METAL. IT SHOULD TRANSPORT THE TOTALITY OUTSIDE THE SOURCE WALL, DESTROYING IT.
WE CAN GIVE THE ORDER...
I REGRET MY STANCE, BUT THIS THING...IF IT'S SENTIENT...I HAVE KNOWN EVIL GODS. I SAY WE FIRE.
ARTHUR, IF OUR MULTIVERSE IS DYING...
IT IS. IF HAL'S READINGS ARE CORRECT, IN A YEAR, MAYBE LESS.
IT'LL EXPEL ENERGY, THEN PLANETS. THEN UNIVERSES...
MAYBE THAT THING IS THE KEY. HELL, IT'S AN UNKNOWN, BUT SO WAS THE SPEED FORCE.
THE MULTIVERSE, TOO, AND THE DARK MULTIVERSE...WE NEED TO SEE WHAT THIS TOTALITY...
"...WHAT IT WANTS."
I WANT TO HEAR YOU SAY IT, SAVAGE. THAT YOU KNEW ALL ALONG.
KNEW WHAT THE SOURCE WALL REALLY WAS, WHAT WAS INSIDE IT...
DON'T DO THIS, LUTHOR!
KNOCK KNOCK
HUH. NOW WHO COULD THAT BE?
WHO... LUTHOR, LISTEN TO ME! WE CAN JOIN FORCES AND--
NO, YOU LISTEN, SAVAGE... YOU, THE ONE HUMAN BEING WHO KNEW THE TRUTH...COWARD...
WELL, NOW THE FINAL MOMENT IS UPON US.
AND YOU BUILT AN "INJUSTICE GANG" WHEN YOU KNEW WHAT THIS GREAT MOMENT REALLY NEEDED...

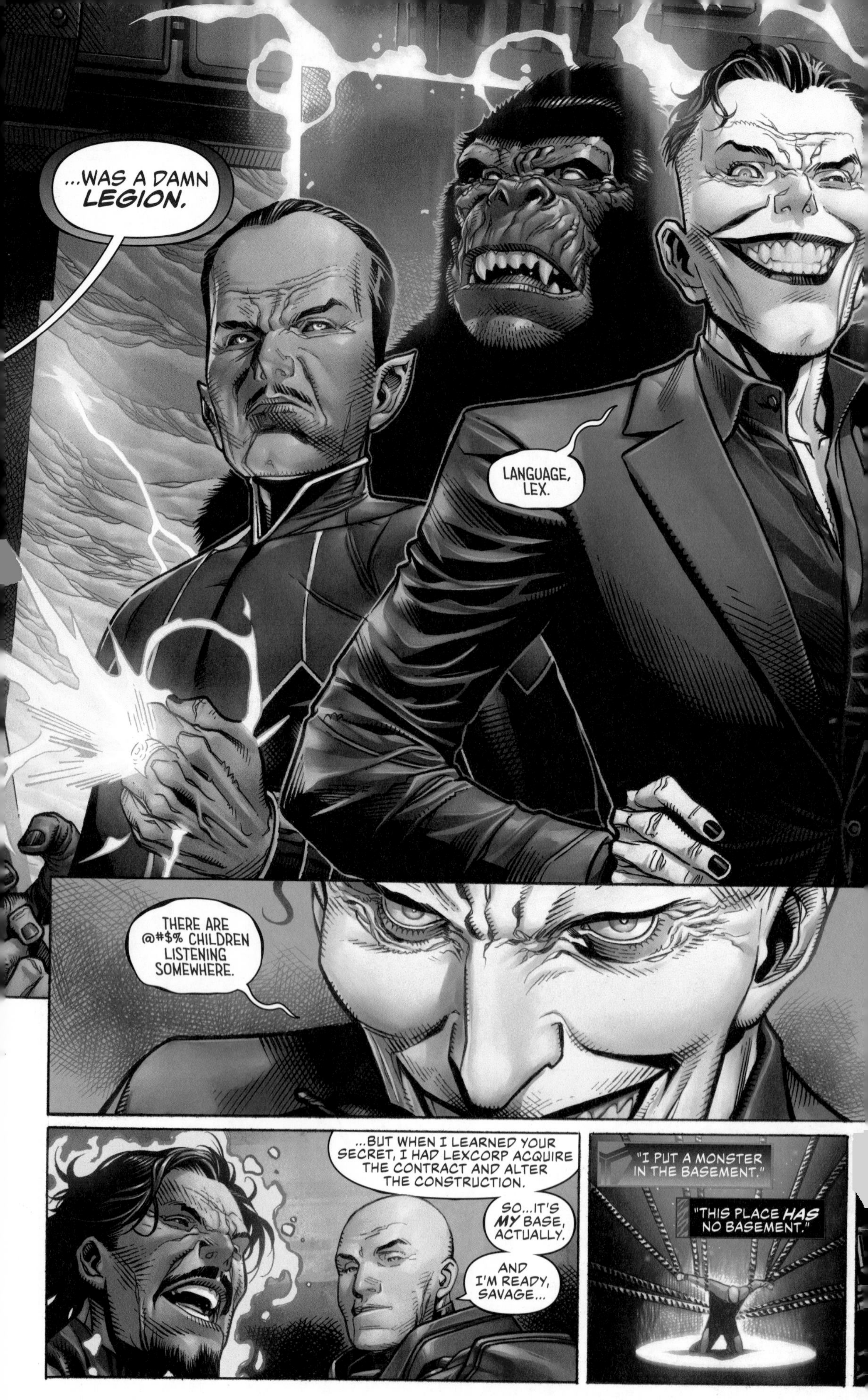
...WAS A DAMN LEGION.
LANGUAGE, LEX.
THERE ARE @#$% CHILDREN LISTENING SOMEWHERE.
...BUT WHEN I LEARNED YOUR SECRET, I HAD LEXCORP ACQUIRE THE CONTRACT AND ALTER THE CONSTRUCTION.
SO...IT'S MY BASE, ACTUALLY.
AND I'M READY, SAVAGE...
"I PUT A MONSTER IN THE BASEMENT."
"THIS PLACE HAS NO BASEMENT."

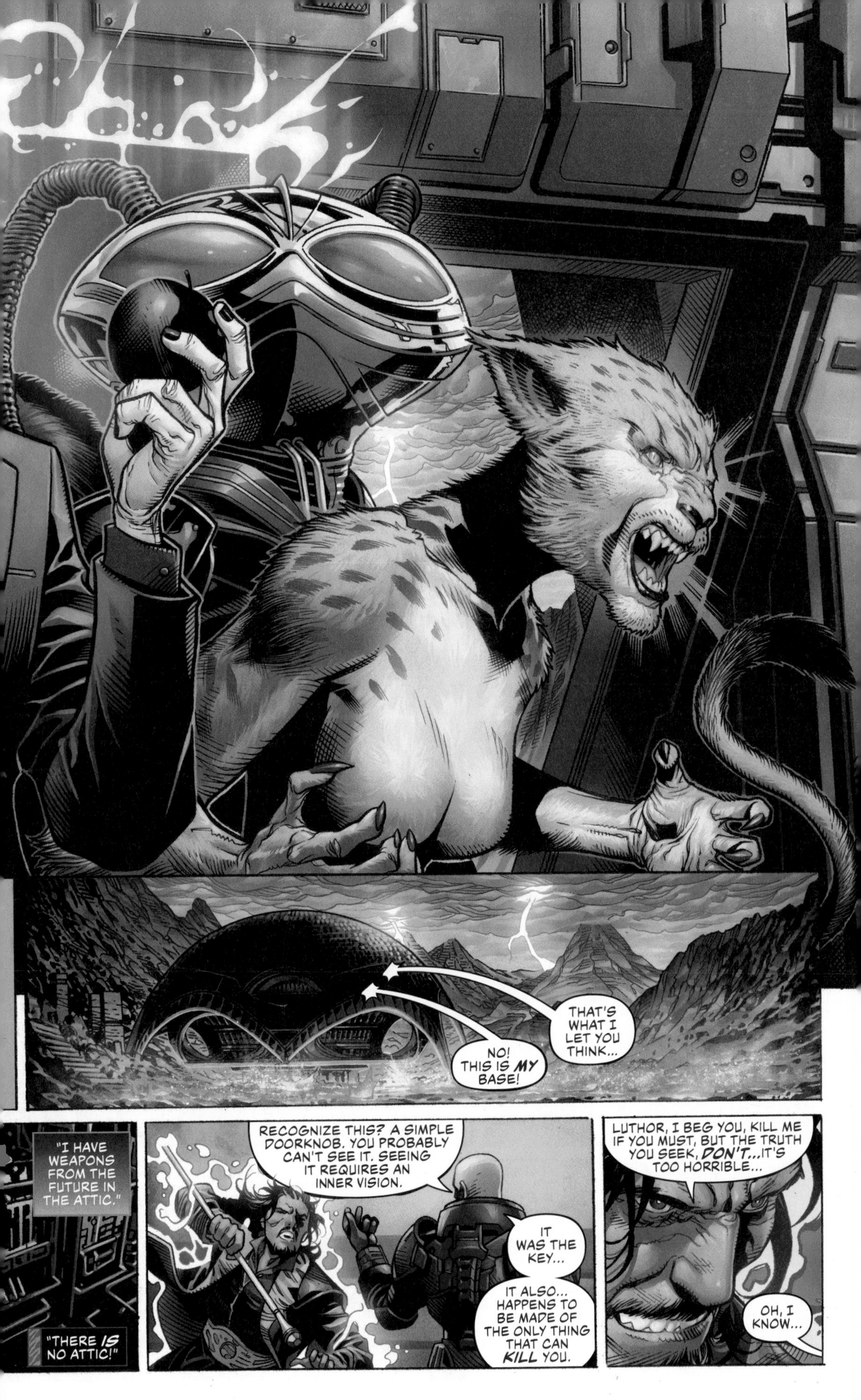
NO! THIS IS MY BASE!
THAT'S WHAT I LET YOU THINK...
"I HAVE WEAPONS FROM THE FUTURE IN THE ATTIC."
"THERE IS NO ATTIC!"
RECOGNIZE THIS? A SIMPLE DOORKNOB. YOU PROBABLY CAN'T SEE IT. SEEING IT REQUIRES AN INNER VISION.
IT WAS THE KEY...
IT ALSO... HAPPENS TO BE MADE OF THE ONLY THING THAT CAN KILL YOU.
LUTHOR, I BEG YOU, KILL ME IF YOU MUST, BUT THE TRUTH YOU SEEK, DON'T... IT'S TOO HORRIBLE...
OH, I KNOW...

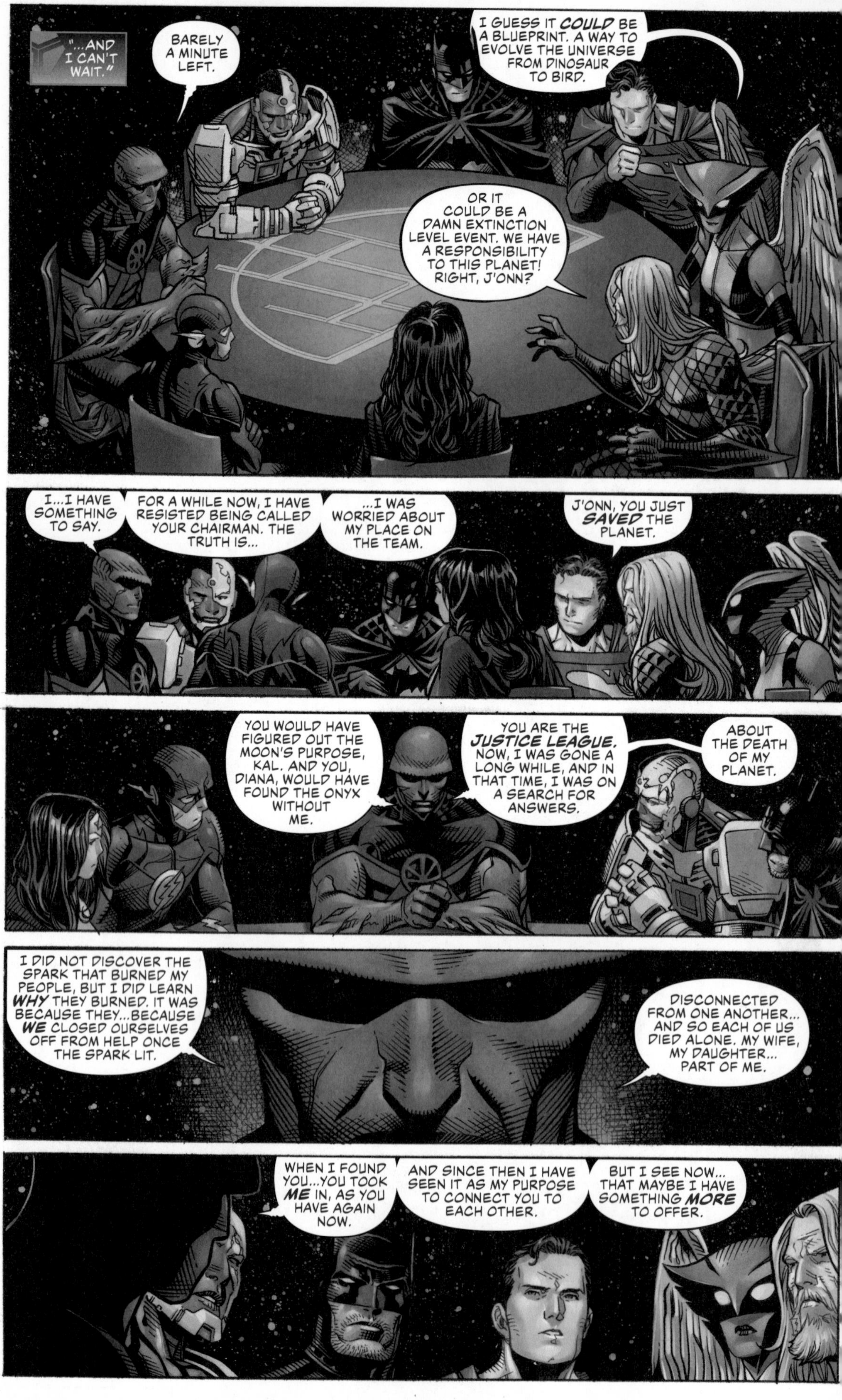
"...AND I CAN'T WAIT."
BARELY A MINUTE LEFT.
I GUESS IT COULD BE A BLUEPRINT. A WAY TO EVOLVE THE UNIVERSE FROM DINOSAUR TO BIRD.
OR IT COULD BE A DAMN EXTINCTION LEVEL EVENT. WE HAVE A RESPONSIBILITY TO THIS PLANET! RIGHT, J'ONN?
I...I HAVE SOMETHING TO SAY.
FOR A WHILE NOW, I HAVE RESISTED BEING CALLED YOUR CHAIRMAN. THE TRUTH IS...
...I WAS WORRIED ABOUT MY PLACE ON THE TEAM.
J'ONN, YOU JUST SAVED THE PLANET.
YOU WOULD HAVE FIGURED OUT THE MOON'S PURPOSE, KAL. AND YOU, DIANA, WOULD HAVE FOUND THE ONYX WITHOUT ME.
YOU ARE THE JUSTICE LEAGUE. NOW, I WAS GONE A LONG WHILE, AND IN THAT TIME, I WAS ON A SEARCH FOR ANSWERS.
ABOUT THE DEATH OF MY PLANET.
I DID NOT DISCOVER THE SPARK THAT BURNED MY PEOPLE, BUT I DID LEARN WHY THEY BURNED. IT WAS BECAUSE THEY...BECAUSE WE CLOSED OURSELVES OFF FROM HELP ONCE THE SPARK LIT.
DISCONNECTED FROM ONE ANOTHER... AND SO EACH OF US DIED ALONE. MY WIFE, MY DAUGHTER... PART OF ME.
WHEN I FOUND YOU...YOU TOOK ME IN, AS YOU HAVE AGAIN NOW.
AND SINCE THEN I HAVE SEEN IT AS MY PURPOSE TO CONNECT YOU TO EACH OTHER.
BUT I SEE NOW... THAT MAYBE I HAVE SOMETHING MORE TO OFFER.

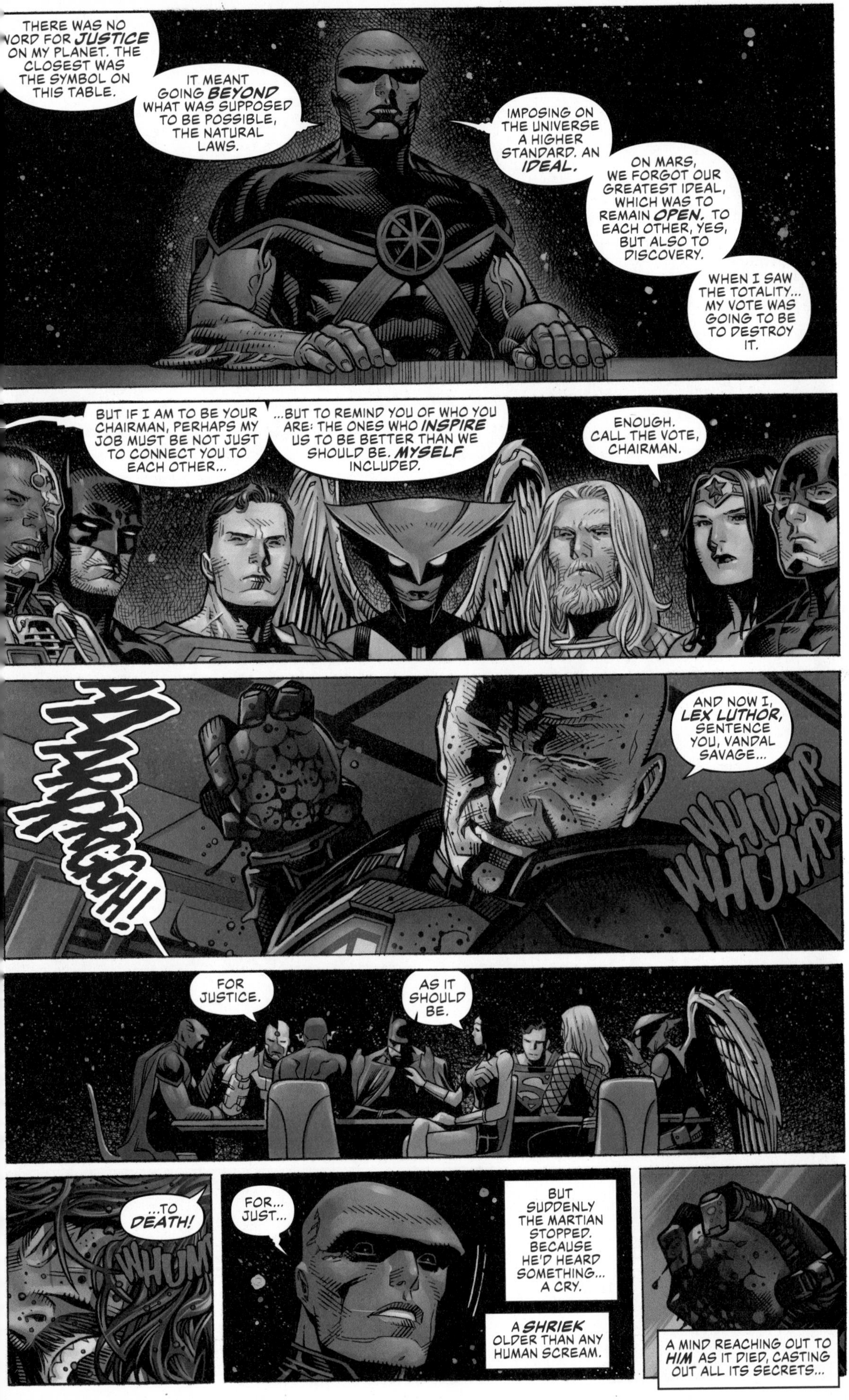

THERE WAS NO WORD FOR JUSTICE ON MY PLANET. THE CLOSEST WAS THE SYMBOL ON THIS TABLE.
IT MEANT GOING BEYOND WHAT WAS SUPPOSED TO BE POSSIBLE, THE NATURAL LAWS.
IMPOSING ON THE UNIVERSE A HIGHER STANDARD. AN IDEAL.
ON MARS, WE FORGOT OUR GREATEST IDEAL, WHICH WAS TO REMAIN OPEN. TO EACH OTHER, YES, BUT ALSO TO DISCOVERY.
WHEN I SAW THE TOTALITY... MY VOTE WAS GOING TO BE TO DESTROY IT.
BUT IF I AM TO BE YOUR CHAIRMAN, PERHAPS MY JOB MUST BE NOT JUST TO CONNECT YOU TO EACH OTHER...
...BUT TO REMIND YOU OF WHO YOU ARE: THE ONES WHO INSPIRE US TO BE BETTER THAN WE SHOULD BE. MYSELF INCLUDED.
ENOUGH. CALL THE VOTE, CHAIRMAN.
AND NOW I, LEX LUTHOR, SENTENCE YOU, VANDAL SAVAGE...
WHUMP WHUMP
FOR JUSTICE.
AS IT SHOULD BE.
...TO DEATH!
WHUM
FOR... JUST...
BUT SUDDENLY THE MARTIAN STOPPED. BECAUSE HE'D HEARD SOMETHING... A CRY.
A SHRIEK OLDER THAN ANY HUMAN SCREAM.
A MIND REACHING OUT TO HIM AS IT DIED, CASTING OUT ALL ITS SECRETS...

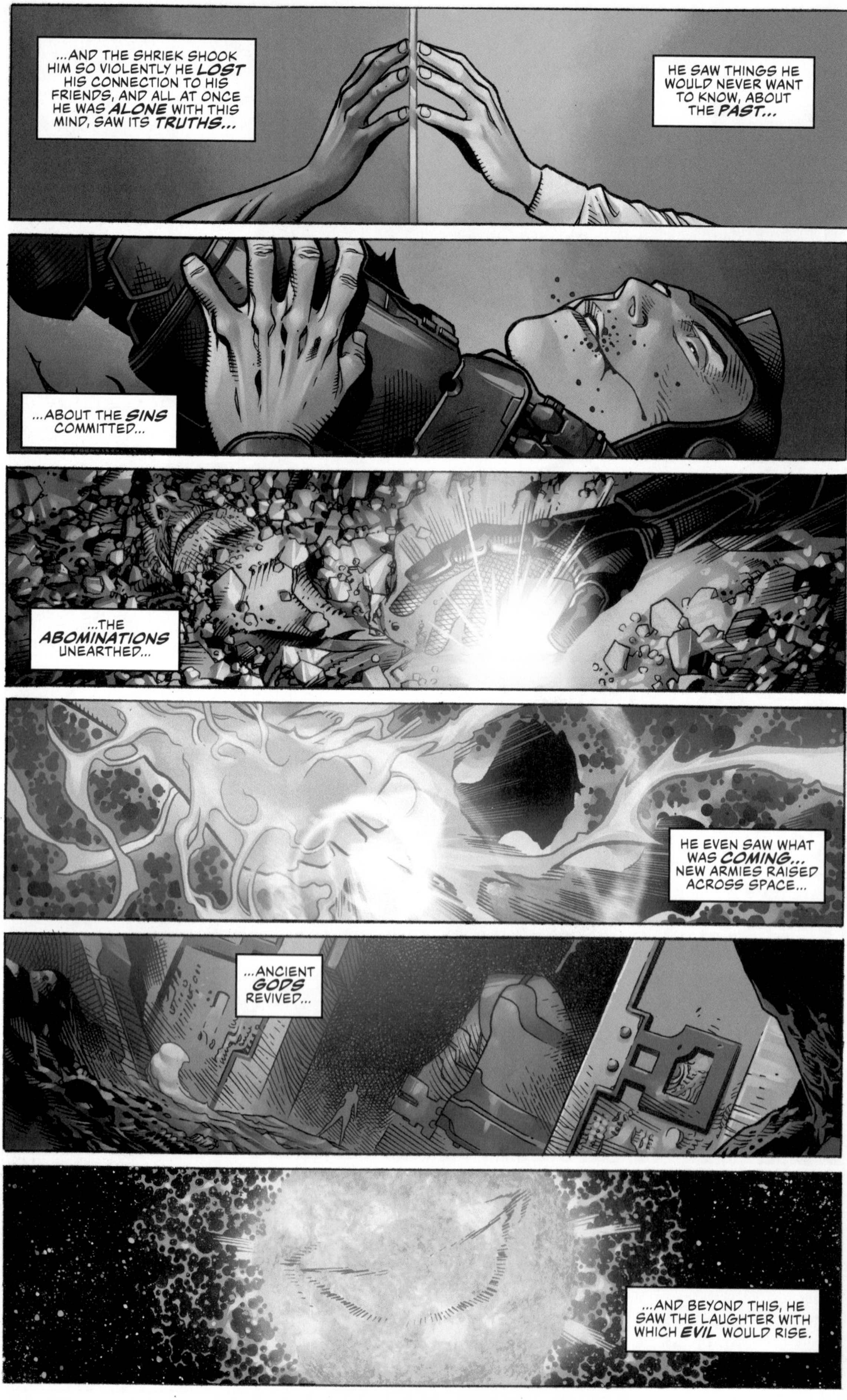
...AND THE SHRIEK SHOOK HIM SO VIOLENTLY HE LOST HIS CONNECTION TO HIS FRIENDS, AND ALL AT ONCE HE WAS ALONE WITH THIS MIND, SAW ITS TRUTHS...
HE SAW THINGS HE WOULD NEVER WANT TO KNOW, ABOUT THE PAST...
...ABOUT THE SINS COMMITTED...
...THE ABOMINATIONS UNEARTHED...
HE EVEN SAW WHAT WAS COMING... NEW ARMIES RAISED ACROSS SPACE...
...ANCIENT GODS REVIVED...
...AND BEYOND THIS, HE SAW THE LAUGHTER WITH WHICH EVIL WOULD RISE.

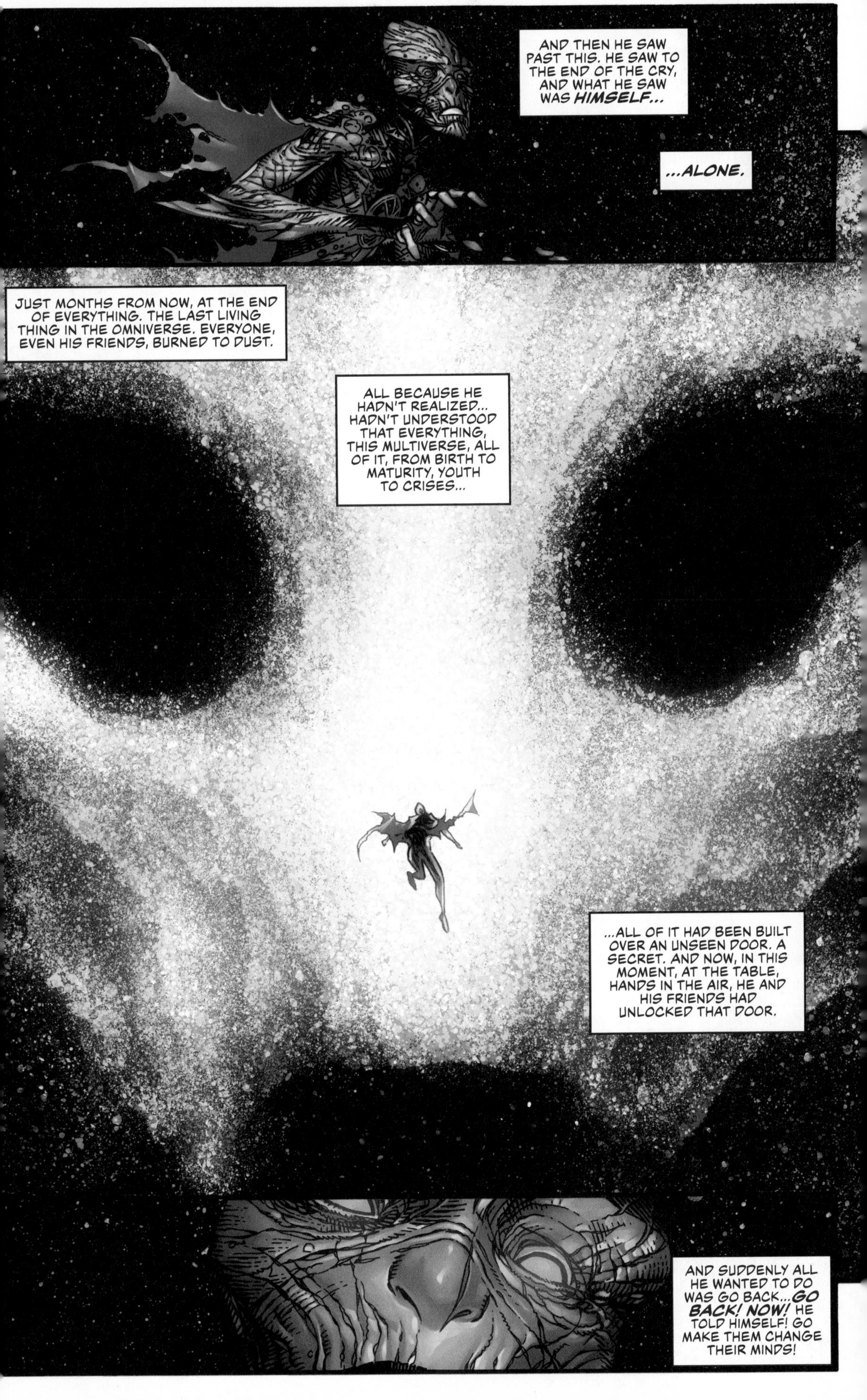
AND THEN HE SAW PAST THIS. HE SAW TO THE END OF THE CRY, AND WHAT HE SAW WAS HIMSELF...
...ALONE.
JUST MONTHS FROM NOW, AT THE END OF EVERYTHING. THE LAST LIVING THING IN THE OMNIVERSE. EVERYONE, EVEN HIS FRIENDS, BURNED TO DUST.
ALL BECAUSE HE HADN'T REALIZED... HADN'T UNDERSTOOD THAT EVERYTHING, THIS MULTIVERSE, ALL OF IT, FROM BIRTH TO MATURITY, YOUTH TO CRISES...
...ALL OF IT HAD BEEN BUILT OVER AN UNSEEN DOOR. A SECRET. AND NOW, IN THIS MOMENT, AT THE TABLE, HANDS IN THE AIR, HE AND HIS FRIENDS HAD UNLOCKED THAT DOOR.
AND SUDDENLY ALL HE WANTED TO DO WAS GO BACK...GO BACK! NOW! HE TOLD HIMSELF! GO MAKE THEM CHANGE THEIR MINDS!

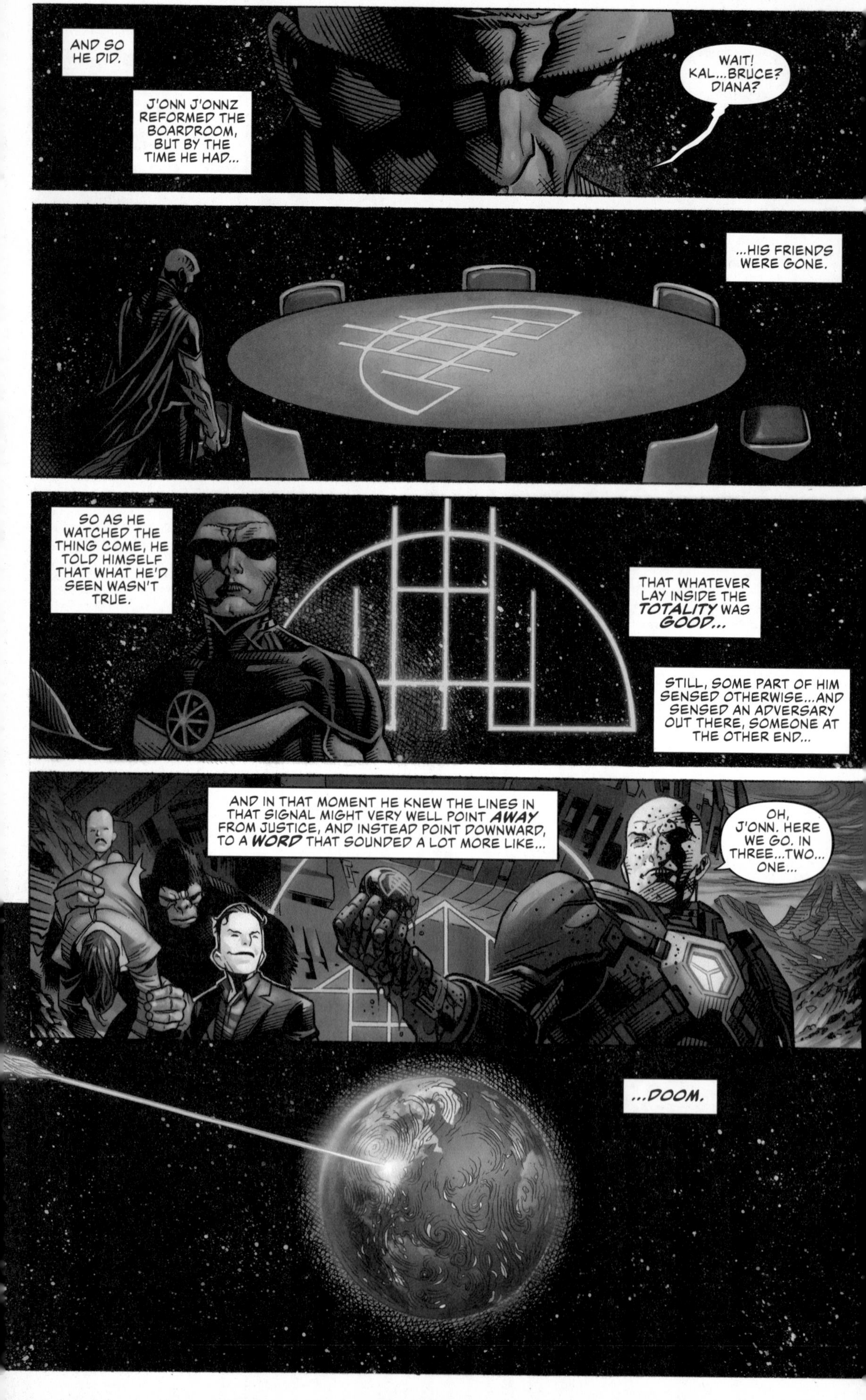
AND SO HE DID.
J'ONN J'ONNZ REFORMED THE BOARDROOM, BUT BY THE TIME HE HAD...
WAIT! KAL...BRUCE? DIANA?
...HIS FRIENDS WERE GONE.
SO AS HE WATCHED THE THING COME, HE TOLD HIMSELF THAT WHAT HE'D SEEN WASN'T TRUE.
THAT WHATEVER LAY INSIDE THE TOTALITY WAS GOOD...
STILL, SOME PART OF HIM SENSED OTHERWISE...AND SENSED AN ADVERSARY OUT THERE, SOMEONE AT THE OTHER END...
AND IN THAT MOMENT HE KNEW THE LINES IN THAT SIGNAL MIGHT VERY WELL POINT AWAY FROM JUSTICE, AND INSTEAD POINT DOWNWARD, TO A WORD THAT SOUNDED A LOT MORE LIKE...
OH, J'ONN. HERE WE GO. IN THREE...TWO... ONE...
...DOOM.

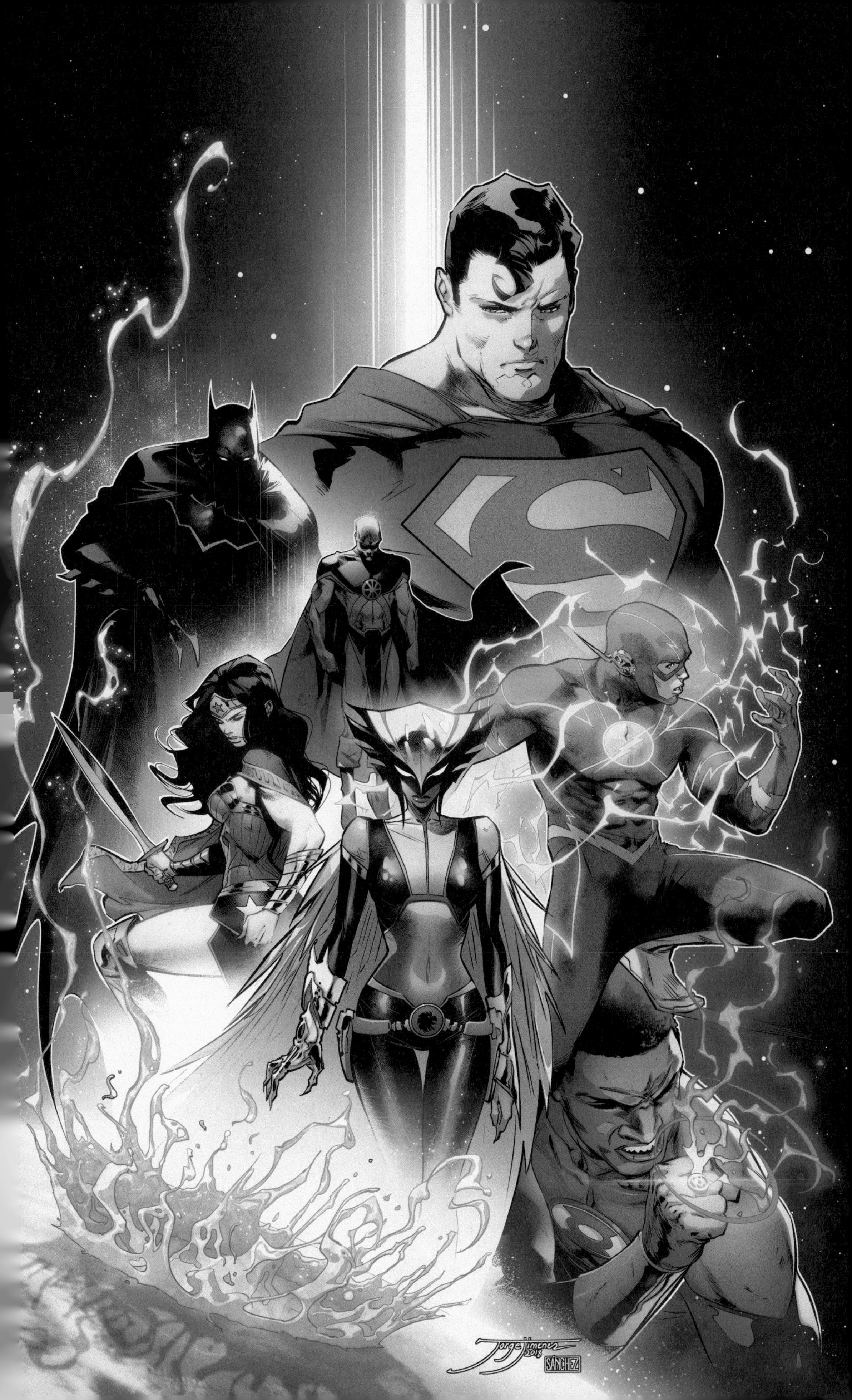
Jorge Jimenez 2018
SÁNCHEZ

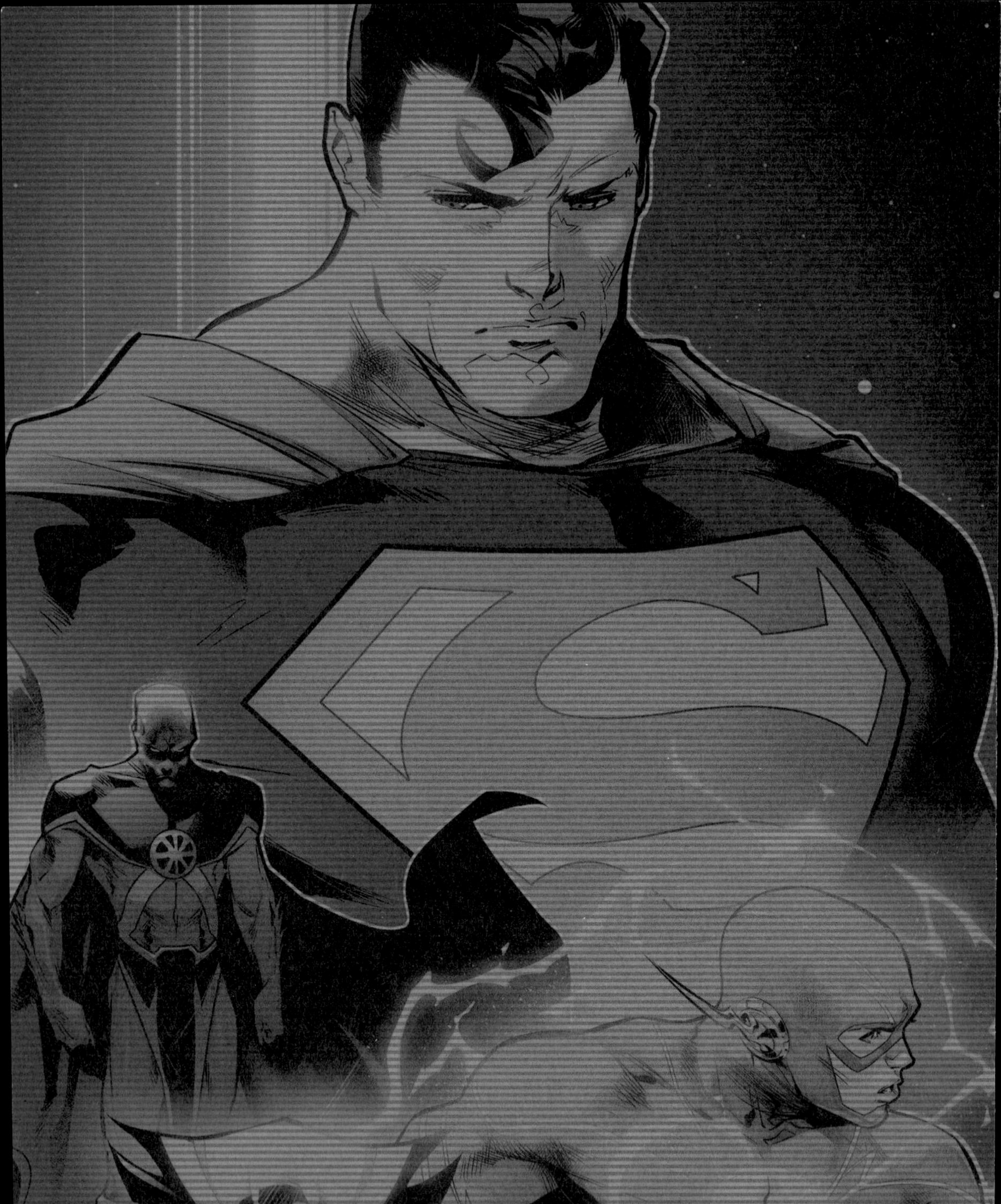

JUSTICE
LEAGUE
#2

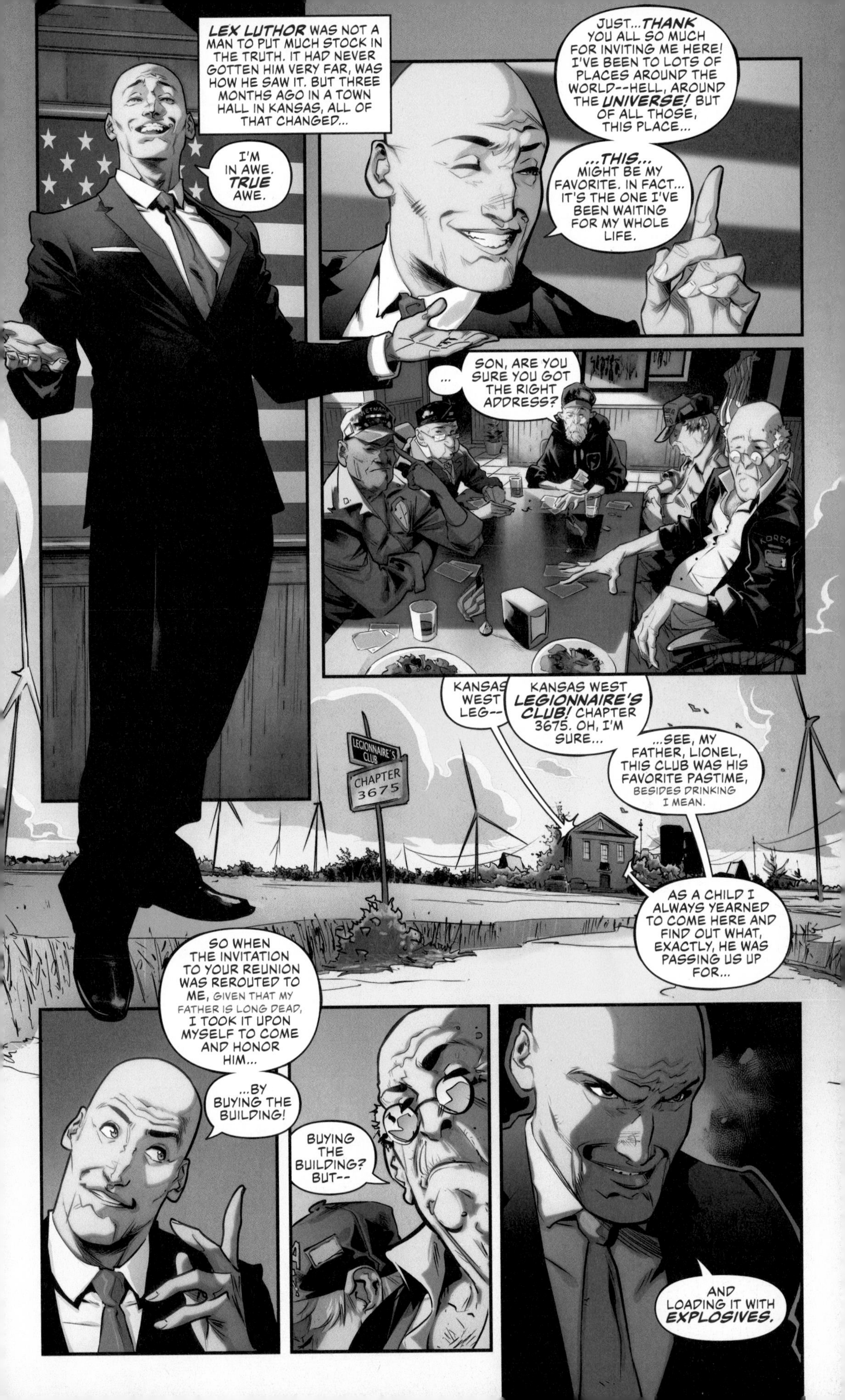
LEX LUTHOR WAS NOT A MAN TO PUT MUCH STOCK IN THE TRUTH. IT HAD NEVER GOTTEN HIM VERY FAR, WAS HOW HE SAW IT. BUT THREE MONTHS AGO IN A TOWN HALL IN KANSAS, ALL OF THAT CHANGED...
I'M IN AWE. TRUE AWE.
JUST...THANK YOU ALL SO MUCH FOR INVITING ME HERE! I'VE BEEN TO LOTS OF PLACES AROUND THE WORLD--HELL, AROUND THE UNIVERSE! BUT OF ALL THOSE, THIS PLACE...
...THIS... MIGHT BE MY FAVORITE. IN FACT... IT'S THE ONE I'VE BEEN WAITING FOR MY WHOLE LIFE.
...
SON, ARE YOU SURE YOU GOT THE RIGHT ADDRESS?
KANSAS WEST LEG--
KANSAS WEST LEGIONNAIRE'S CLUB! CHAPTER 3675. OH, I'M SURE...
LEGIONNAIRE'S CLUB
CHAPTER 3675
...SEE, MY FATHER, LIONEL, THIS CLUB WAS HIS FAVORITE PASTIME, BESIDES DRINKING I MEAN.
AS A CHILD I ALWAYS YEARNED TO COME HERE AND FIND OUT WHAT, EXACTLY, HE WAS PASSING US UP FOR...
SO WHEN THE INVITATION TO YOUR REUNION WAS REROUTED TO ME, GIVEN THAT MY FATHER IS LONG DEAD, I TOOK IT UPON MYSELF TO COME AND HONOR HIM...
...BY BUYING THE BUILDING!
BUYING THE BUILDING? BUT--
AND LOADING IT WITH EXPLOSIVES.

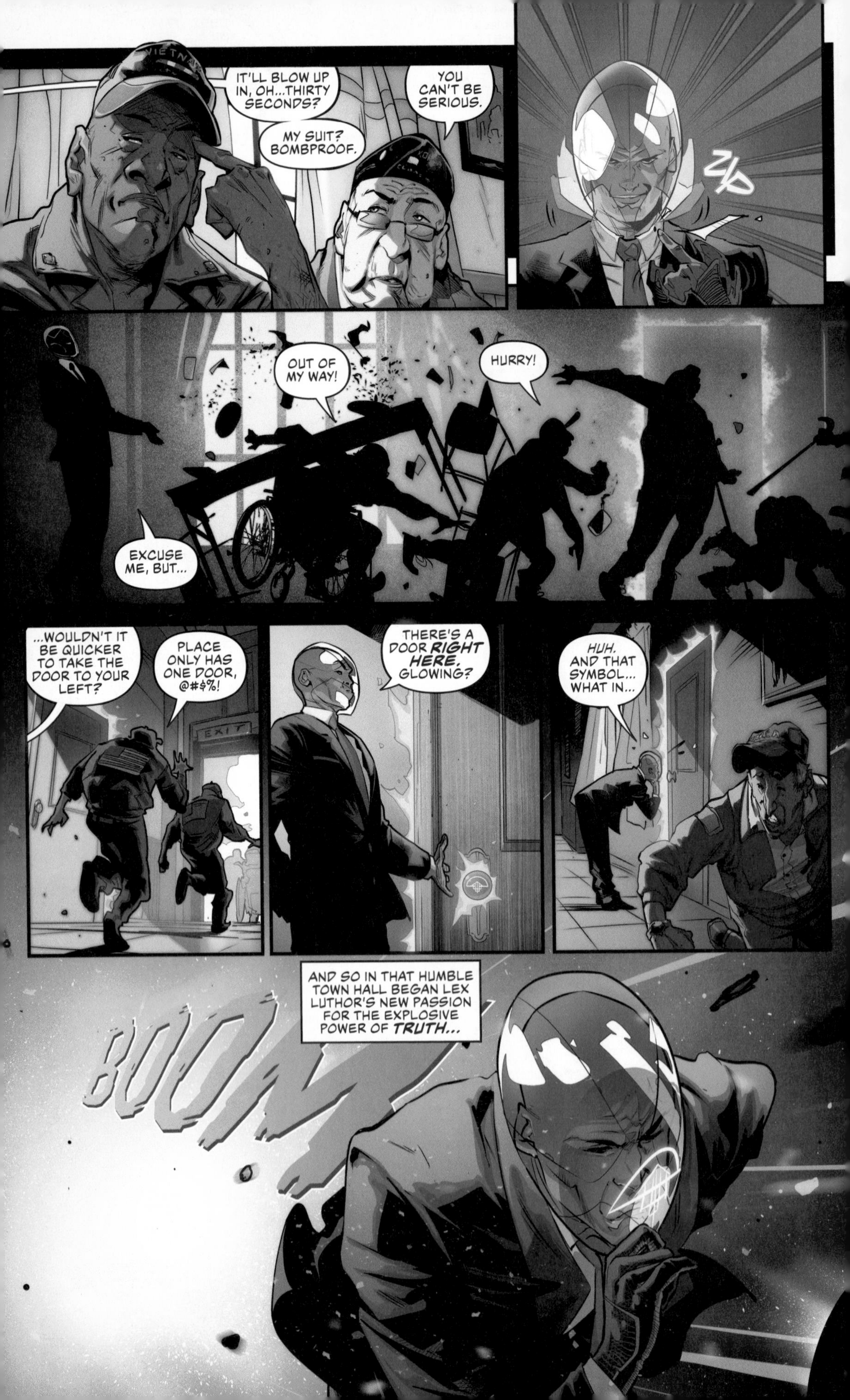
IT'LL BLOW UP IN, OH...THIRTY SECONDS?
YOU CAN'T BE SERIOUS.
MY SUIT? BOMBPROOF.
ZIP
OUT OF MY WAY!
HURRY!
EXCUSE ME, BUT...
...WOULDN'T IT BE QUICKER TO TAKE THE DOOR TO YOUR LEFT?
PLACE ONLY HAS ONE DOOR, @#$%!
EXIT
THERE'S A DOOR RIGHT HERE. GLOWING?
HUH. AND THAT SYMBOL... WHAT IN...
AND SO IN THAT HUMBLE TOWN HALL BEGAN LEX LUTHOR'S NEW PASSION FOR THE EXPLOSIVE POWER OF TRUTH...
BOOM

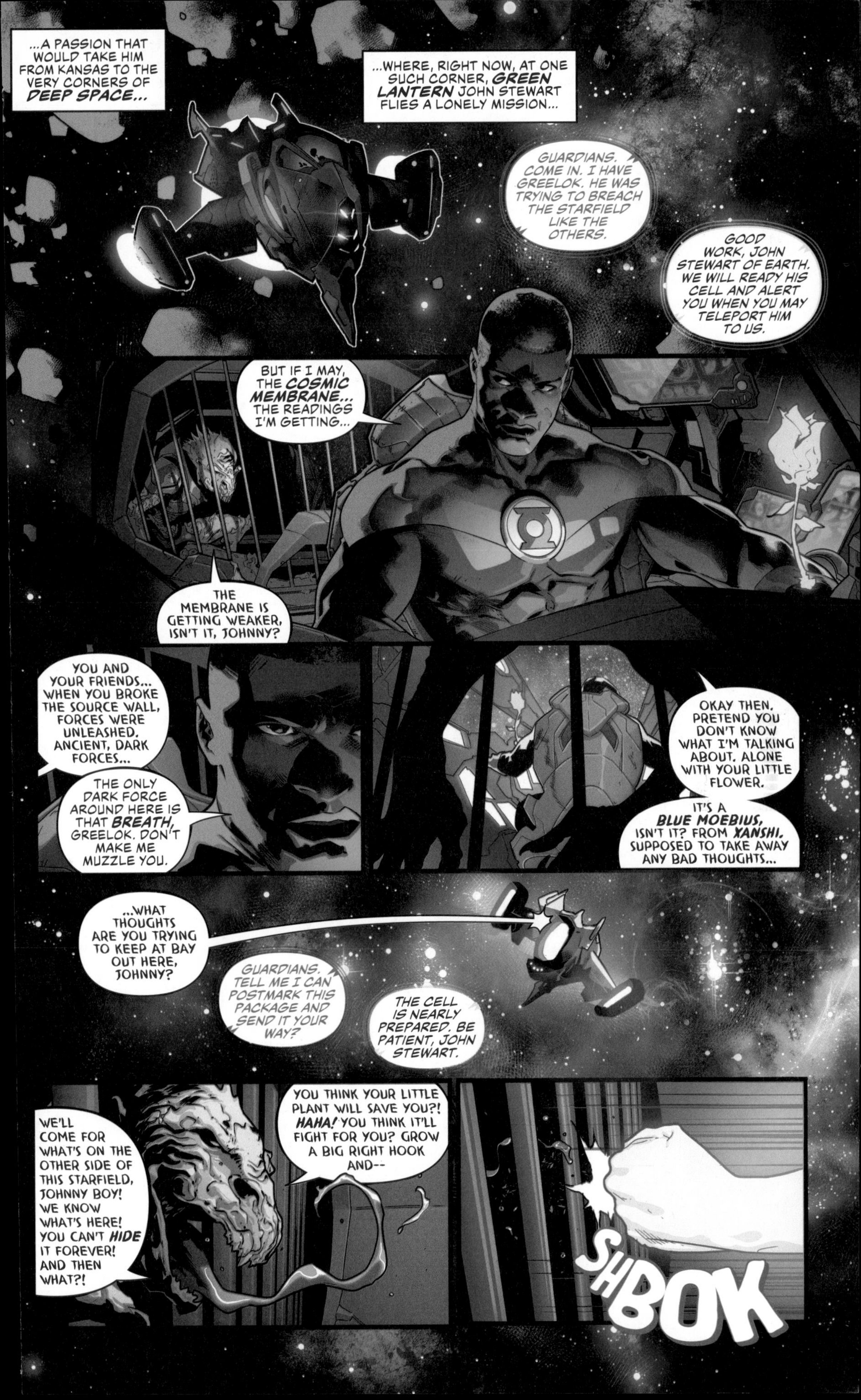
...A PASSION THAT WOULD TAKE HIM FROM KANSAS TO THE VERY CORNERS OF DEEP SPACE...
...WHERE, RIGHT NOW, AT ONE SUCH CORNER, GREEN LANTERN JOHN STEWART FLIES A LONELY MISSION...
GUARDIANS. COME IN. I HAVE GREELOK. HE WAS TRYING TO BREACH THE STARFIELD LIKE THE OTHERS.
GOOD WORK, JOHN STEWART OF EARTH. WE WILL READY HIS CELL AND ALERT YOU WHEN YOU MAY TELEPORT HIM TO US.
BUT IF I MAY, THE COSMIC MEMBRANE... THE READINGS I'M GETTING...
THE MEMBRANE IS GETTING WEAKER, ISN'T IT, JOHNNY?
YOU AND YOUR FRIENDS... WHEN YOU BROKE THE SOURCE WALL, FORCES WERE UNLEASHED. ANCIENT, DARK FORCES...
THE ONLY DARK FORCE AROUND HERE IS THAT BREATH, GREELOK. DON'T MAKE ME MUZZLE YOU.
OKAY THEN. PRETEND YOU DON'T KNOW WHAT I'M TALKING ABOUT. ALONE WITH YOUR LITTLE FLOWER.
IT'S A BLUE MOEBIUS, ISN'T IT? FROM XANSHI. SUPPOSED TO TAKE AWAY ANY BAD THOUGHTS...
...WHAT THOUGHTS ARE YOU TRYING TO KEEP AT BAY OUT HERE, JOHNNY?
GUARDIANS. TELL ME I CAN POSTMARK THIS PACKAGE AND SEND IT YOUR WAY?
THE CELL IS NEARLY PREPARED. BE PATIENT, JOHN STEWART.
WE'LL COME FOR WHAT'S ON THE OTHER SIDE OF THIS STARFIELD, JOHNNY BOY! WE KNOW WHAT'S HERE! YOU CAN'T HIDE IT FOREVER! AND THEN WHAT?!
YOU THINK YOUR LITTLE PLANT WILL SAVE YOU?! HAHA! YOU THINK IT'LL FIGHT FOR YOU? GROW A BIG RIGHT HOOK AND--
SHBOK

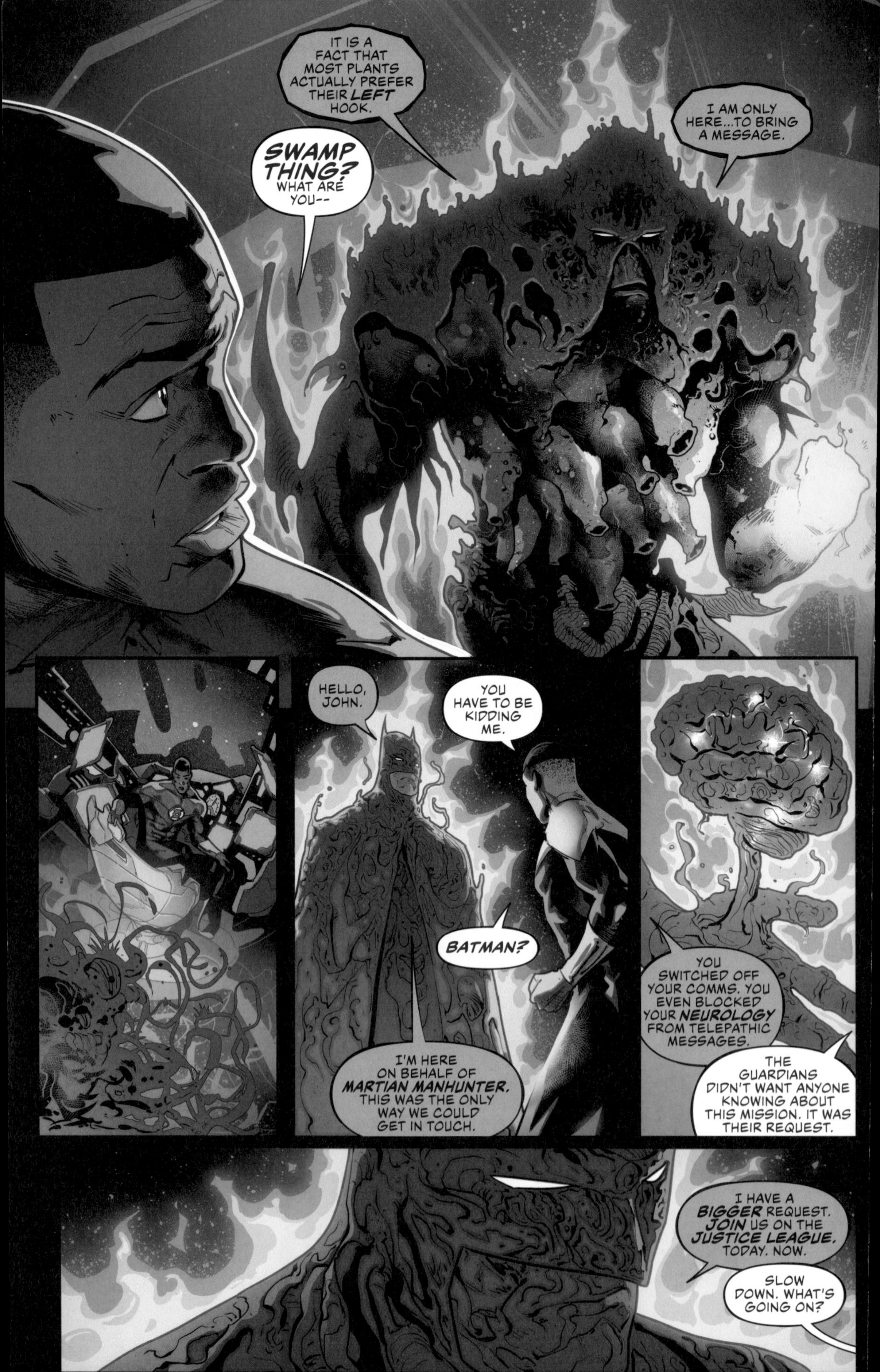
IT IS A FACT THAT MOST PLANTS ACTUALLY PREFER THEIR LEFT HOOK.
SWAMP THING? WHAT ARE YOU--
I AM ONLY HERE...TO BRING A MESSAGE.
HELLO, JOHN.
YOU HAVE TO BE KIDDING ME.
BATMAN?
I'M HERE ON BEHALF OF MARTIAN MANHUNTER. THIS WAS THE ONLY WAY WE COULD GET IN TOUCH.
YOU SWITCHED OFF YOUR COMMS. YOU EVEN BLOCKED YOUR NEUROLOGY FROM TELEPATHIC MESSAGES.
THE GUARDIANS DIDN'T WANT ANYONE KNOWING ABOUT THIS MISSION. IT WAS THEIR REQUEST.
I HAVE A BIGGER REQUEST. JOIN US ON THE JUSTICE LEAGUE. TODAY. NOW.
SLOW DOWN. WHAT'S GOING ON?

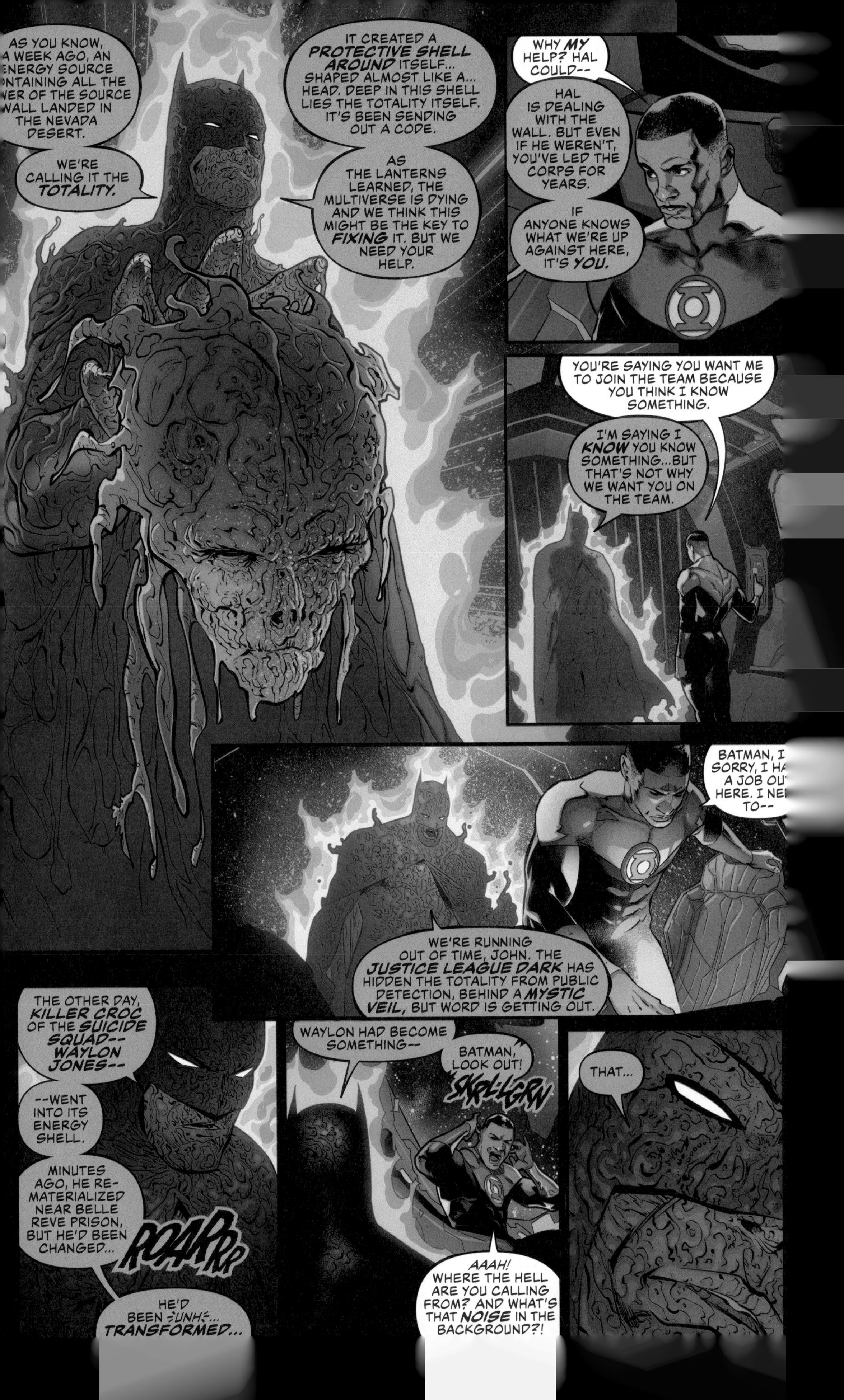

AS YOU KNOW, A WEEK AGO, AN ENERGY SOURCE ONTAINING ALL THE WER OF THE SOURCE WALL LANDED IN THE NEVADA DESERT.
WE'RE CALLING IT THE TOTALITY.
IT CREATED A PROTECTIVE SHELL AROUND ITSELF... SHAPED ALMOST LIKE A... HEAD. DEEP IN THIS SHELL LIES THE TOTALITY ITSELF. IT'S BEEN SENDING OUT A CODE.
AS THE LANTERNS LEARNED, THE MULTIVERSE IS DYING AND WE THINK THIS MIGHT BE THE KEY TO FIXING IT. BUT WE NEED YOUR HELP.
WHY MY HELP? HAL COULD--
HAL IS DEALING WITH THE WALL. BUT EVEN IF HE WEREN'T, YOU'VE LED THE CORPS FOR YEARS.
IF ANYONE KNOWS WHAT WE'RE UP AGAINST HERE, IT'S YOU.
YOU'RE SAYING YOU WANT ME TO JOIN THE TEAM BECAUSE YOU THINK I KNOW SOMETHING.
I'M SAYING I KNOW YOU KNOW SOMETHING...BUT THAT'S NOT WHY WE WANT YOU ON THE TEAM.
BATMAN, I SORRY, I HA A JOB OU HERE. I NE TO--
WE'RE RUNNING OUT OF TIME, JOHN. THE JUSTICE LEAGUE DARK HAS HIDDEN THE TOTALITY FROM PUBLIC DETECTION, BEHIND A MYSTIC VEIL, BUT WORD IS GETTING OUT.
THE OTHER DAY, KILLER CROC OF THE SUICIDE SQUAD-- WAYLON JONES--
--WENT INTO ITS ENERGY SHELL.
MINUTES AGO, HE RE-MATERIALIZED NEAR BELLE REVE PRISON, BUT HE'D BEEN CHANGED...
ROARRRR
HE'D BEEN -UNH-... TRANSFORMED...
WAYLON HAD BECOME SOMETHING--
BATMAN, LOOK OUT!
SKRL-LGRN
AAAH! WHERE THE HELL ARE YOU CALLING FROM? AND WHAT'S THAT NOISE IN THE BACKGROUND?!
THAT...

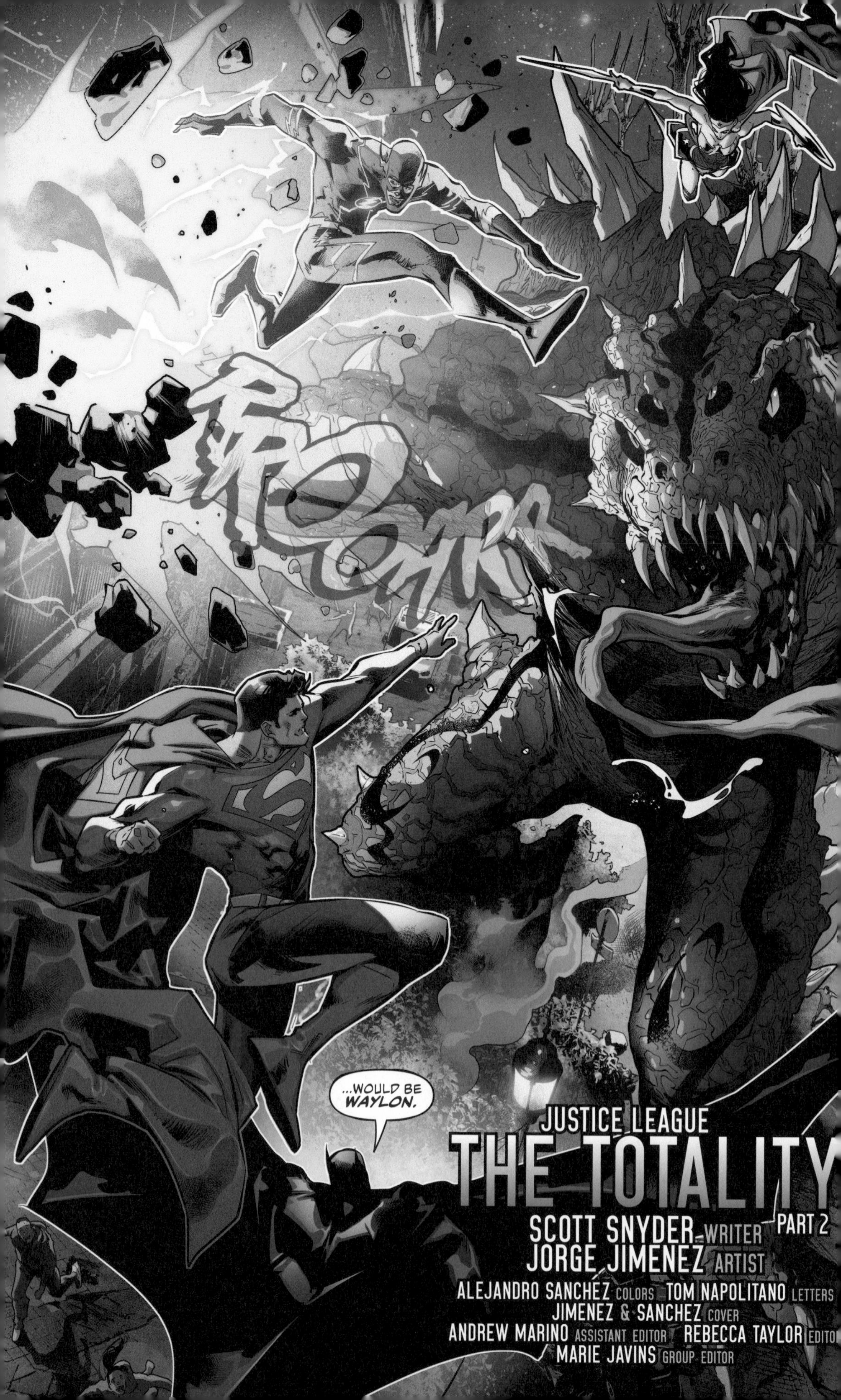
...WOULD BE WAYLON.
JUSTICE LEAGUE
THE TOTALITY
PART 2
SCOTT SNYDER WRITER
JORGE JIMENEZ ARTIST
ALEJANDRO SANCHEZ COLORS TOM NAPOLITANO LETTERS
JIMENEZ & SANCHEZ COVER
ANDREW MARINO ASSISTANT EDITOR REBECCA TAYLOR EDITO
MARIE JAVINS GROUP EDITOR

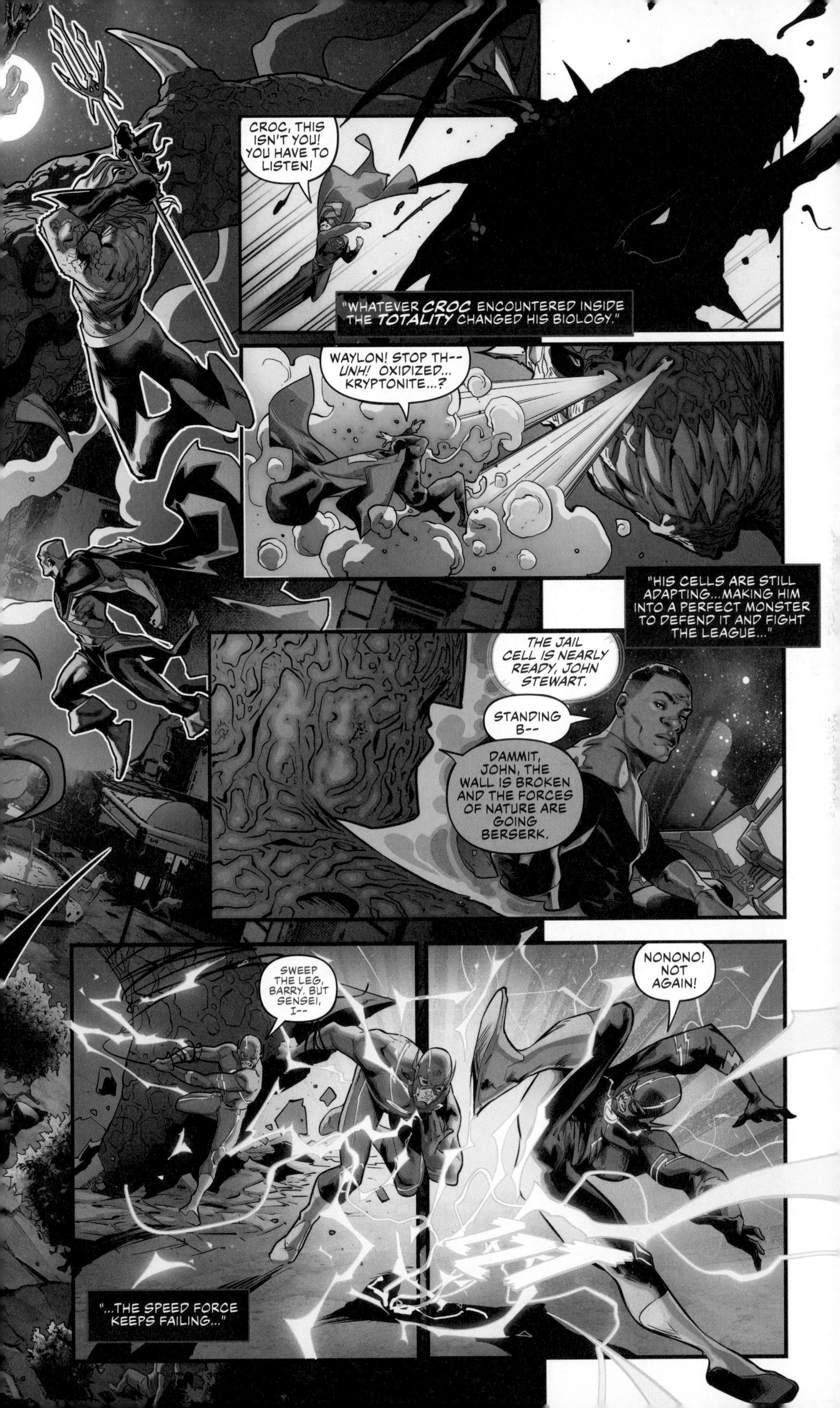
CROC, THIS ISN'T YOU! YOU HAVE TO LISTEN!
"WHATEVER CROC ENCOUNTERED INSIDE THE TOTALITY CHANGED HIS BIOLOGY."
WAYLON! STOP TH-- UNH! OXIDIZED... KRYPTONITE...?
"HIS CELLS ARE STILL ADAPTING...MAKING HIM INTO A PERFECT MONSTER TO DEFEND IT AND FIGHT THE LEAGUE..."
THE JAIL CELL IS NEARLY READY, JOHN STEWART.
STANDING B--
DAMMIT, JOHN, THE WALL IS BROKEN AND THE FORCES OF NATURE ARE GOING BERSERK.
SWEEP THE LEG, BARRY. BUT SENSEI, I--
NONONO! NOT AGAIN!
"...THE SPEED FORCE KEEPS FAILING..."

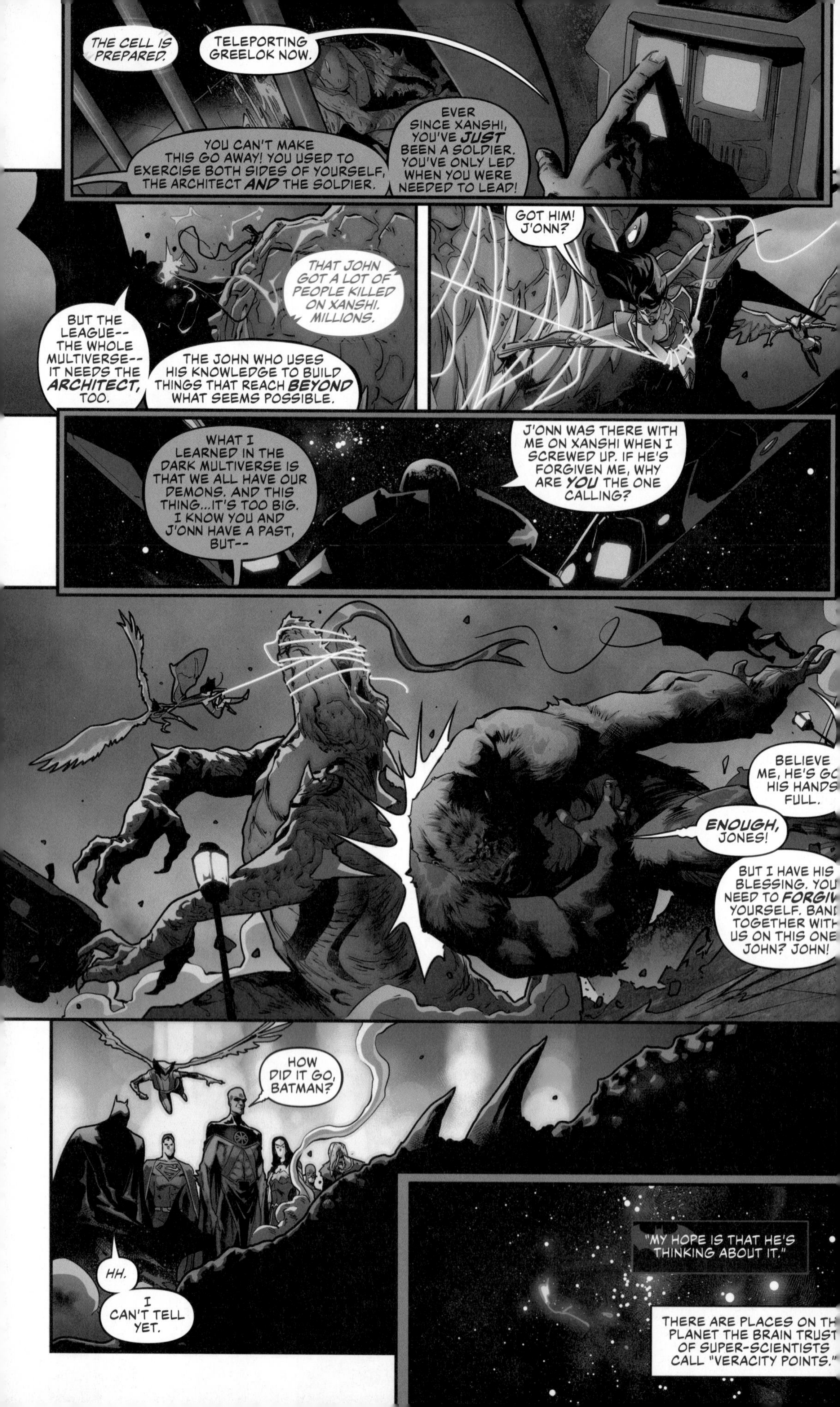

THE CELL IS PREPARED.
TELEPORTING GREELOK NOW.
YOU CAN'T MAKE THIS GO AWAY! YOU USED TO EXERCISE BOTH SIDES OF YOURSELF, THE ARCHITECT AND THE SOLDIER.
EVER SINCE XANSHI, YOU'VE JUST BEEN A SOLDIER. YOU'VE ONLY LED WHEN YOU WERE NEEDED TO LEAD!
THAT JOHN GOT A LOT OF PEOPLE KILLED ON XANSHI. MILLIONS.
BUT THE LEAGUE-- THE WHOLE MULTIVERSE-- IT NEEDS THE ARCHITECT, TOO.
THE JOHN WHO USES HIS KNOWLEDGE TO BUILD THINGS THAT REACH BEYOND WHAT SEEMS POSSIBLE.
GOT HIM! J'ONN?
WHAT I LEARNED IN THE DARK MULTIVERSE IS THAT WE ALL HAVE OUR DEMONS. AND THIS THING...IT'S TOO BIG. I KNOW YOU AND J'ONN HAVE A PAST, BUT--
J'ONN WAS THERE WITH ME ON XANSHI WHEN I SCREWED UP. IF HE'S FORGIVEN ME, WHY ARE YOU THE ONE CALLING?
BELIEVE ME, HE'S GO HIS HANDS FULL.
ENOUGH, JONES!
BUT I HAVE HIS BLESSING. YOU NEED TO FORGIV YOURSELF. BAN TOGETHER WITH US ON THIS ONE JOHN? JOHN!
HOW DID IT GO, BATMAN?
HH.
I CAN'T TELL YET.
"MY HOPE IS THAT HE'S THINKING ABOUT IT."
THERE ARE PLACES ON TH PLANET THE BRAIN TRUST OF SUPER-SCIENTISTS CALL "VERACITY POINTS."

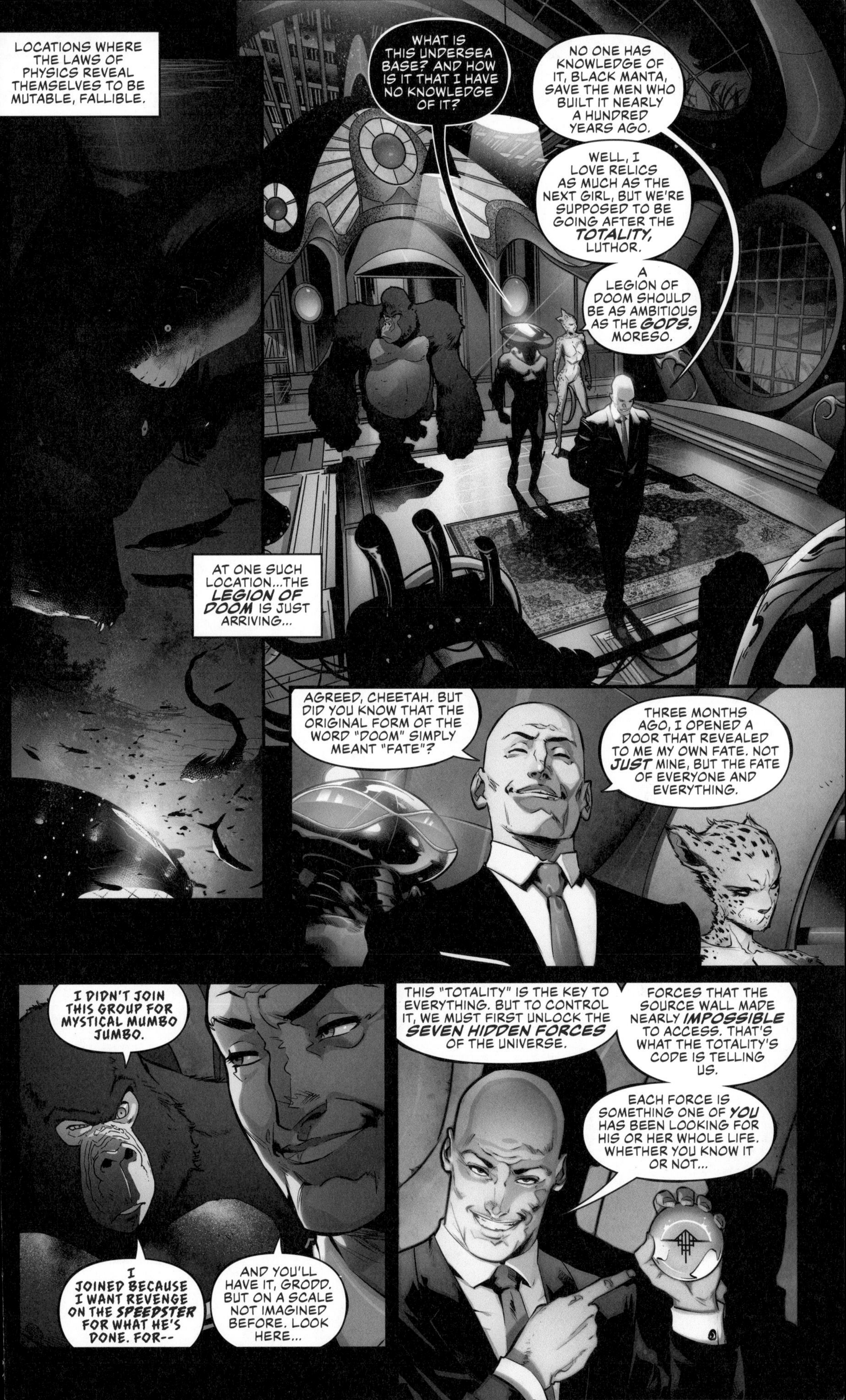
LOCATIONS WHERE THE LAWS OF PHYSICS REVEAL THEMSELVES TO BE MUTABLE, FALLIBLE.
WHAT IS THIS UNDERSEA BASE? AND HOW IS IT THAT I HAVE NO KNOWLEDGE OF IT?
NO ONE HAS KNOWLEDGE OF IT, BLACK MANTA, SAVE THE MEN WHO BUILT IT NEARLY A HUNDRED YEARS AGO.
WELL, I LOVE RELICS AS MUCH AS THE NEXT GIRL, BUT WE'RE SUPPOSED TO BE GOING AFTER THE TOTALITY, LUTHOR.
A LEGION OF DOOM SHOULD BE AS AMBITIOUS AS THE GODS. MORESO.
AT ONE SUCH LOCATION...THE LEGION OF DOOM IS JUST ARRIVING...
AGREED, CHEETAH. BUT DID YOU KNOW THAT THE ORIGINAL FORM OF THE WORD "DOOM" SIMPLY MEANT "FATE"?
THREE MONTHS AGO, I OPENED A DOOR THAT REVEALED TO ME MY OWN FATE. NOT JUST MINE, BUT THE FATE OF EVERYONE AND EVERYTHING.
I DIDN'T JOIN THIS GROUP FOR MYSTICAL MUMBO JUMBO.
I JOINED BECAUSE I WANT REVENGE ON THE SPEEDSTER FOR WHAT HE'S DONE. FOR--
AND YOU'LL HAVE IT, GRODD. BUT ON A SCALE NOT IMAGINED BEFORE. LOOK HERE...
THIS "TOTALITY" IS THE KEY TO EVERYTHING. BUT TO CONTROL IT, WE MUST FIRST UNLOCK THE SEVEN HIDDEN FORCES OF THE UNIVERSE.
FORCES THAT THE SOURCE WALL MADE NEARLY IMPOSSIBLE TO ACCESS. THAT'S WHAT THE TOTALITY'S CODE IS TELLING US.
EACH FORCE IS SOMETHING ONE OF YOU HAS BEEN LOOKING FOR HIS OR HER WHOLE LIFE. WHETHER YOU KNOW IT OR NOT...

WILL DESTROY *YOUR* ENEMY, GRODD.

COULDN'T HAVE DONE IT WITHOUT THE HELP OF A *TRUE EVIL GENIUS*... WHO'S RIGHT OVER HERE.

COME SAY HELLO TO YOUR NEW PARTNER, GRODD. AND DON'T BE AFRAID...

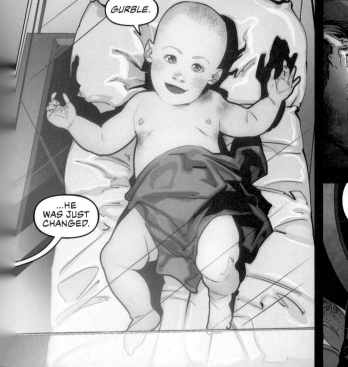

GURBLE.

...HE WAS JUST CHANGED.

WHAT THE HELL IS THIS?

IT'S A BABY, GRODD. PICK IT UP.

WAIT... IS THIS WHO I THINK IT IS?

CONNECT TO HIM AND FIND OUT.

AS FOR THE *SECOND* HIDDEN FORCE, SINESTRO IS ALREADY ON HIS WAY TO CLAIM IT. A SECTION OF THE EMOTIONAL SPECTRUM OFF LIMITS... UNTIL NOW.

BEYOND THAT WALL, THEY THINK WE'RE TINY, INSIGNIFICANT. "FIREFLIES FLICKERING AROUND A GRAVEYARD" WAITING TO BE JARRED...

MY GOD...THE POWER...

BUT THAT'S NOT WHAT WE ARE. OR RATHER, NOT WHAT WE *WERE* MEANT TO BE...

THE TRUTH IS, THE STARS ARE THE FIREFLIES. US...WE'RE THE ONES BUILDING THE DAMN JAR. SO THAT WALL? IT WAS THERE TO PROTECT *THEM* FROM *US*.

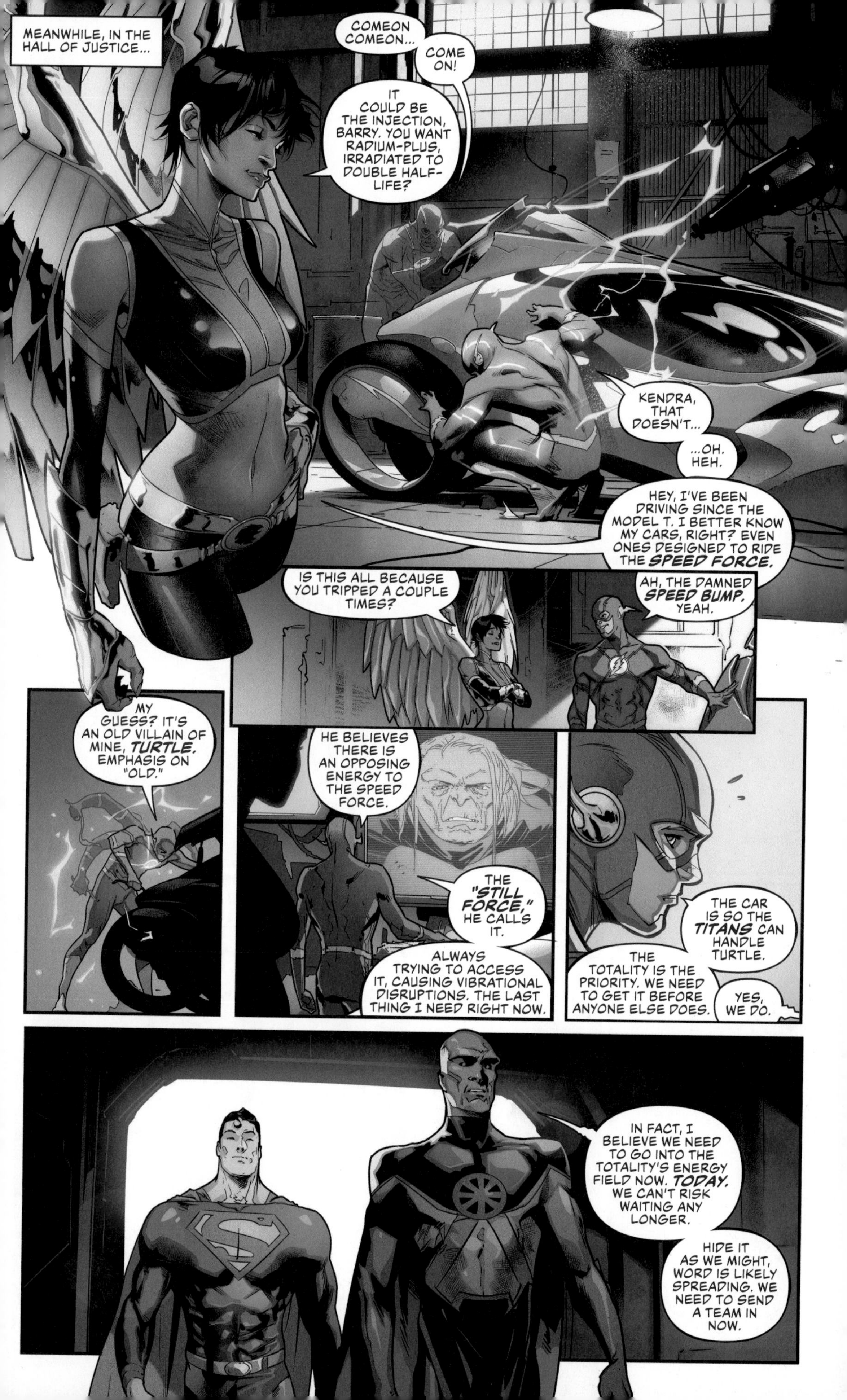

MEANWHILE, IN THE HALL OF JUSTICE...
COMEON COMEON...
COME ON!
IT COULD BE THE INJECTION, BARRY. YOU WANT RADIUM-PLUS, IRRADIATED TO DOUBLE HALF-LIFE?
KENDRA, THAT DOESN'T...
...OH. HEH.
HEY, I'VE BEEN DRIVING SINCE THE MODEL T. I BETTER KNOW MY CARS, RIGHT? EVEN ONES DESIGNED TO RIDE THE SPEED FORCE.
IS THIS ALL BECAUSE YOU TRIPPED A COUPLE TIMES?
AH, THE DAMNED SPEED BUMP. YEAH.
MY GUESS? IT'S AN OLD VILLAIN OF MINE, TURTLE. EMPHASIS ON "OLD."
HE BELIEVES THERE IS AN OPPOSING ENERGY TO THE SPEED FORCE.
THE "STILL FORCE," HE CALLS IT.
ALWAYS TRYING TO ACCESS IT, CAUSING VIBRATIONAL DISRUPTIONS. THE LAST THING I NEED RIGHT NOW.
THE CAR IS SO THE TITANS CAN HANDLE TURTLE.
THE TOTALITY IS THE PRIORITY. WE NEED TO GET IT BEFORE ANYONE ELSE DOES.
YES, WE DO.
IN FACT, I BELIEVE WE NEED TO GO INTO THE TOTALITY'S ENERGY FIELD NOW. TODAY. WE CAN'T RISK WAITING ANY LONGER.
HIDE IT AS WE MIGHT, WORD IS LIKELY SPREADING. WE NEED TO SEND A TEAM IN NOW.

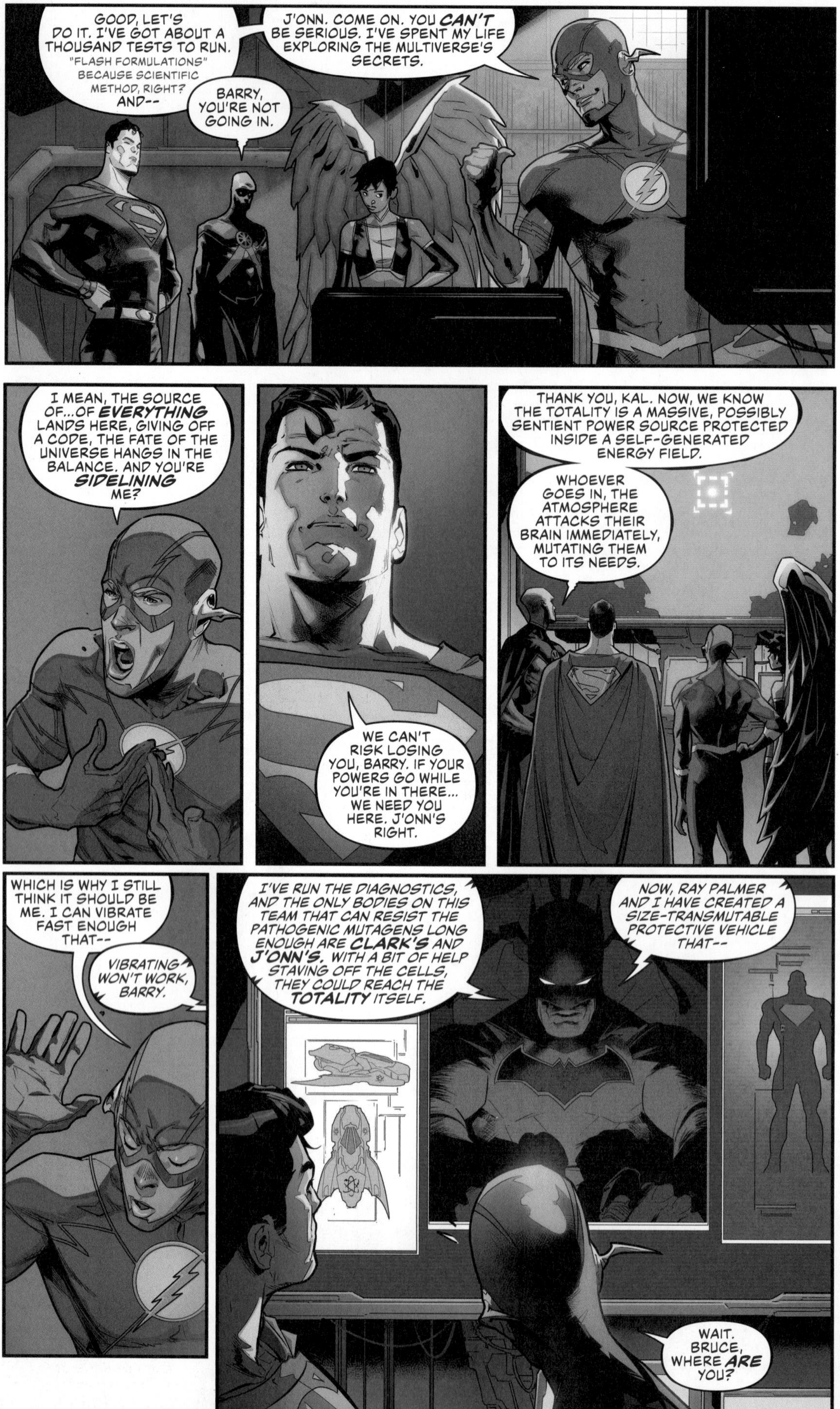
GOOD, LET'S DO IT. I'VE GOT ABOUT A THOUSAND TESTS TO RUN. "FLASH FORMULATIONS" BECAUSE SCIENTIFIC METHOD, RIGHT? AND--
BARRY, YOU'RE NOT GOING IN.
J'ONN. COME ON. YOU CAN'T BE SERIOUS. I'VE SPENT MY LIFE EXPLORING THE MULTIVERSE'S SECRETS.
I MEAN, THE SOURCE OF...OF EVERYTHING LANDS HERE, GIVING OFF A CODE, THE FATE OF THE UNIVERSE HANGS IN THE BALANCE. AND YOU'RE SIDELINING ME?
WE CAN'T RISK LOSING YOU, BARRY. IF YOUR POWERS GO WHILE YOU'RE IN THERE... WE NEED YOU HERE. J'ONN'S RIGHT.
THANK YOU, KAL. NOW, WE KNOW THE TOTALITY IS A MASSIVE, POSSIBLY SENTIENT POWER SOURCE PROTECTED INSIDE A SELF-GENERATED ENERGY FIELD.
WHOEVER GOES IN, THE ATMOSPHERE ATTACKS THEIR BRAIN IMMEDIATELY, MUTATING THEM TO ITS NEEDS.
WHICH IS WHY I STILL THINK IT SHOULD BE ME. I CAN VIBRATE FAST ENOUGH THAT--
VIBRATING WON'T WORK, BARRY.
I'VE RUN THE DIAGNOSTICS, AND THE ONLY BODIES ON THIS TEAM THAT CAN RESIST THE PATHOGENIC MUTAGENS LONG ENOUGH ARE CLARK'S AND J'ONN'S. WITH A BIT OF HELP STAVING OFF THE CELLS, THEY COULD REACH THE TOTALITY ITSELF.
NOW, RAY PALMER AND I HAVE CREATED A SIZE-TRANSMUTABLE PROTECTIVE VEHICLE THAT--
WAIT. BRUCE, WHERE ARE YOU?

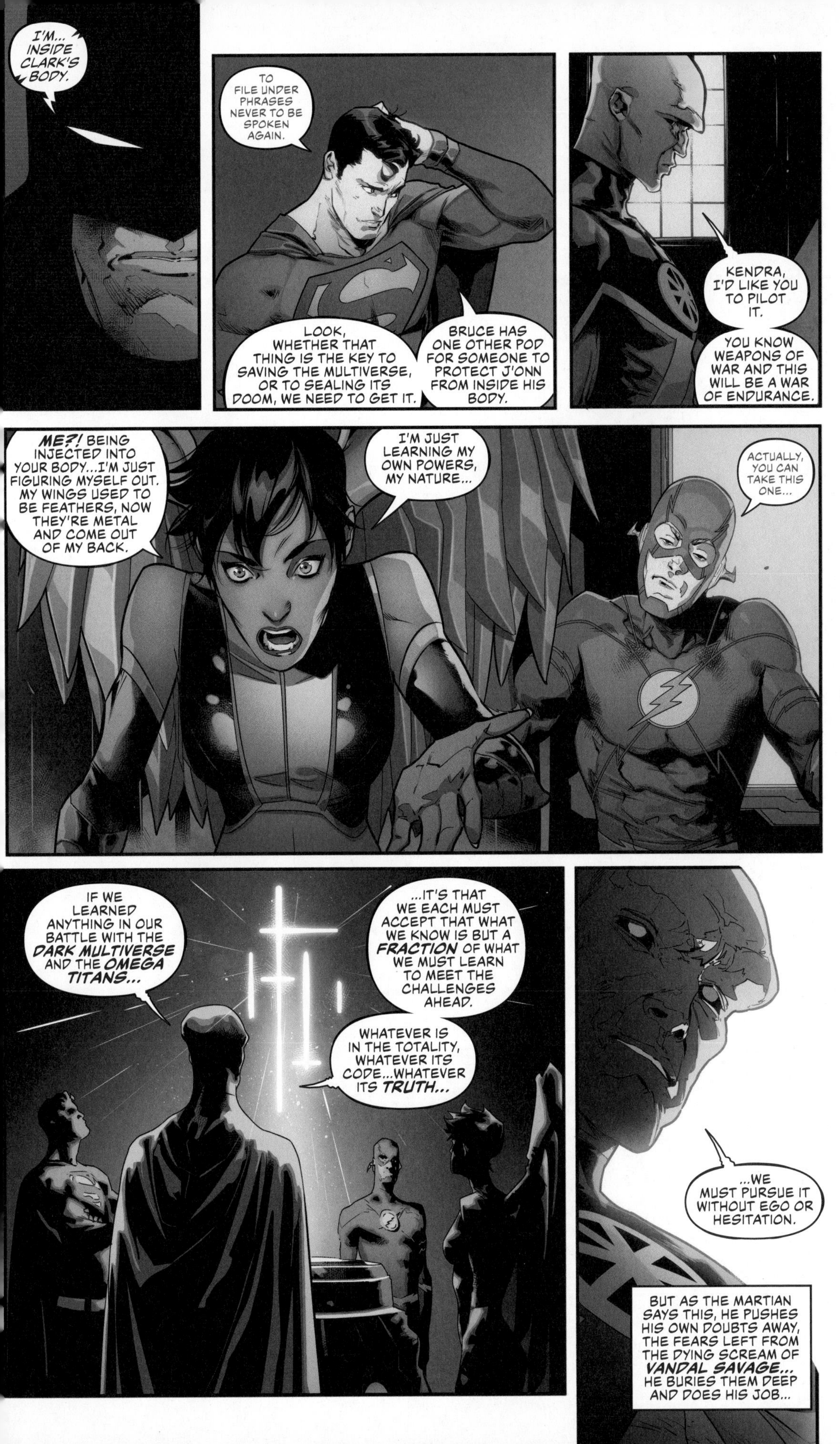
I'M... INSIDE CLARK'S BODY.
TO FILE UNDER PHRASES NEVER TO BE SPOKEN AGAIN.
LOOK, WHETHER THAT THING IS THE KEY TO SAVING THE MULTIVERSE, OR TO SEALING ITS DOOM, WE NEED TO GET IT.
BRUCE HAS ONE OTHER POD FOR SOMEONE TO PROTECT J'ONN FROM INSIDE HIS BODY.
KENDRA, I'D LIKE YOU TO PILOT IT.
YOU KNOW WEAPONS OF WAR AND THIS WILL BE A WAR OF ENDURANCE.
ME?! BEING INJECTED INTO YOUR BODY...I'M JUST FIGURING MYSELF OUT. MY WINGS USED TO BE FEATHERS, NOW THEY'RE METAL AND COME OUT OF MY BACK.
I'M JUST LEARNING MY OWN POWERS, MY NATURE...
ACTUALLY, YOU CAN TAKE THIS ONE...
IF WE LEARNED ANYTHING IN OUR BATTLE WITH THE DARK MULTIVERSE AND THE OMEGA TITANS...
...IT'S THAT WE EACH MUST ACCEPT THAT WHAT WE KNOW IS BUT A FRACTION OF WHAT WE MUST LEARN TO MEET THE CHALLENGES AHEAD.
WHATEVER IS IN THE TOTALITY, WHATEVER ITS CODE...WHATEVER ITS TRUTH...
...WE MUST PURSUE IT WITHOUT EGO OR HESITATION.
BUT AS THE MARTIAN SAYS THIS, HE PUSHES HIS OWN DOUBTS AWAY, THE FEARS LEFT FROM THE DYING SCREAM OF VANDAL SAVAGE... HE BURIES THEM DEEP AND DOES HIS JOB...

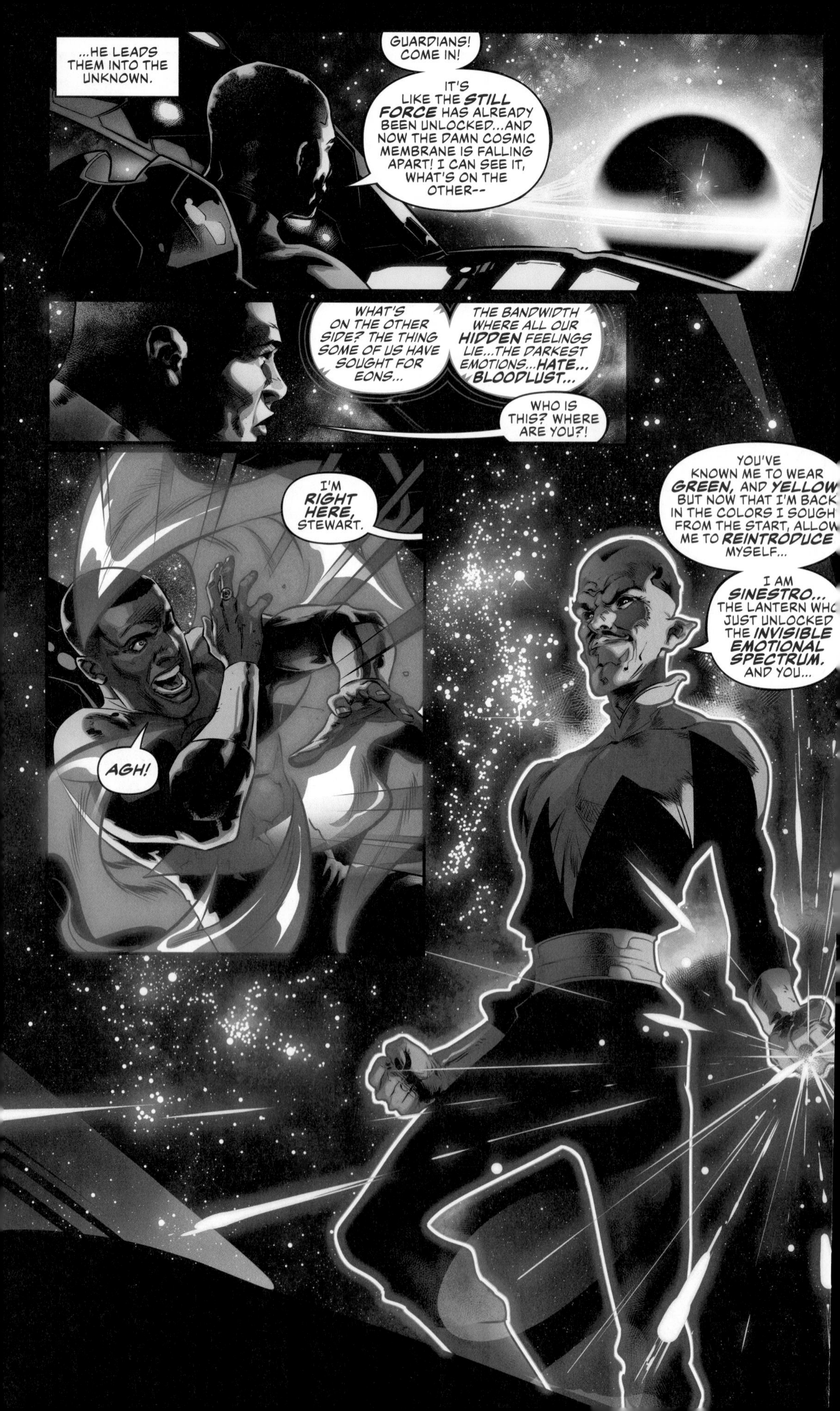

...HE LEADS THEM INTO THE UNKNOWN.
GUARDIANS! COME IN!
IT'S LIKE THE STILL FORCE HAS ALREADY BEEN UNLOCKED...AND NOW THE DAMN COSMIC MEMBRANE IS FALLING APART! I CAN SEE IT, WHAT'S ON THE OTHER--
WHAT'S ON THE OTHER SIDE? THE THING SOME OF US HAVE SOUGHT FOR EONS...
THE BANDWIDTH WHERE ALL OUR HIDDEN FEELINGS LIE...THE DARKEST EMOTIONS...HATE... BLOODLUST...
WHO IS THIS? WHERE ARE YOU?!
I'M RIGHT HERE, STEWART.
AGH!
YOU'VE KNOWN ME TO WEAR GREEN, AND YELLOW BUT NOW THAT I'M BACK IN THE COLORS I SOUGH FROM THE START, ALLOW ME TO REINTRODUCE MYSELF...
I AM SINESTRO... THE LANTERN WHO JUST UNLOCKED THE INVISIBLE EMOTIONAL SPECTRUM. AND YOU...

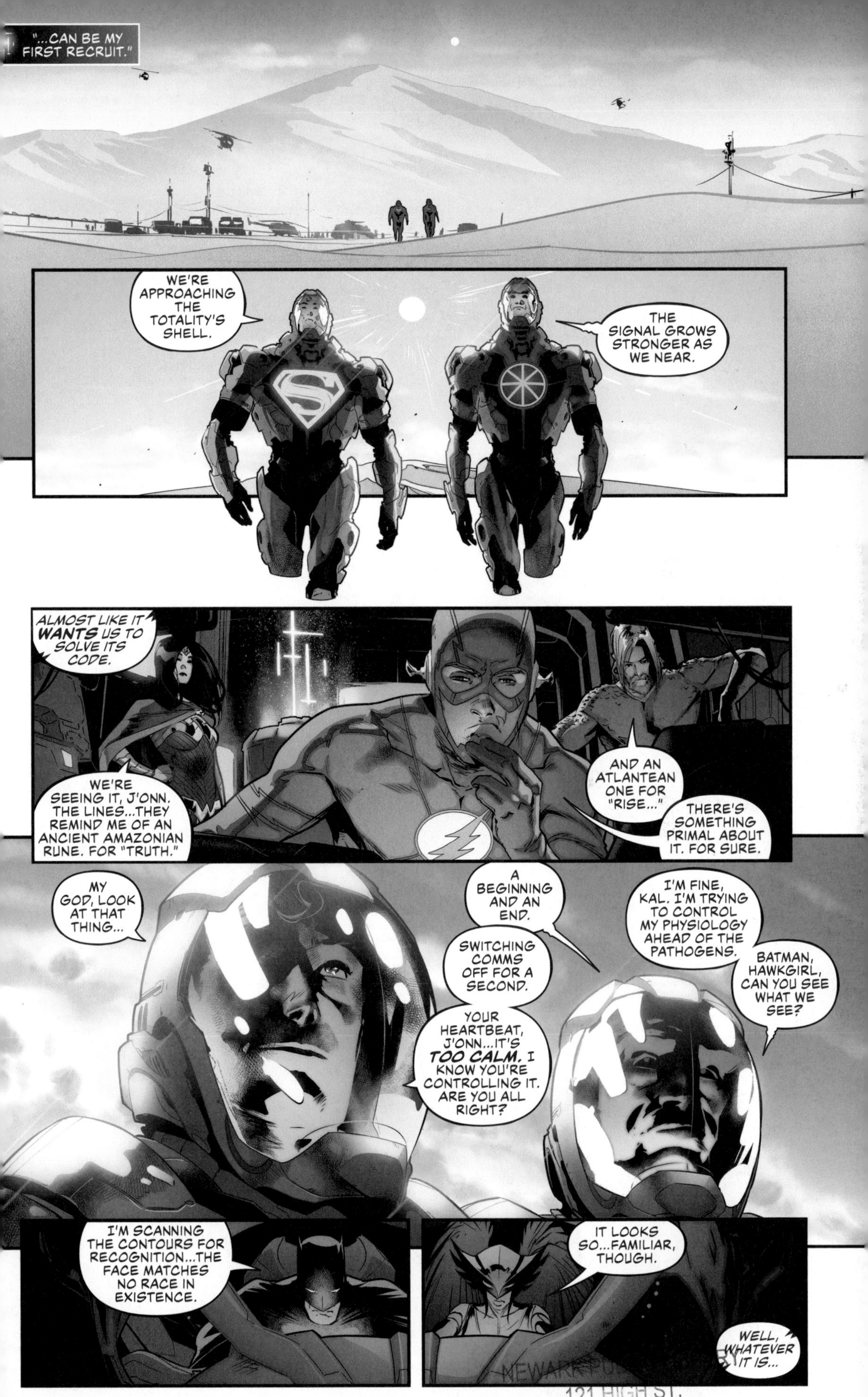
"...CAN BE MY FIRST RECRUIT."
WE'RE APPROACHING THE TOTALITY'S SHELL.
THE SIGNAL GROWS STRONGER AS WE NEAR.
ALMOST LIKE IT WANTS US TO SOLVE ITS CODE.
WE'RE SEEING IT, J'ONN. THE LINES...THEY REMIND ME OF AN ANCIENT AMAZONIAN RUNE. FOR "TRUTH."
AND AN ATLANTEAN ONE FOR "RISE..."
THERE'S SOMETHING PRIMAL ABOUT IT. FOR SURE.
MY GOD, LOOK AT THAT THING...
A BEGINNING AND AN END.
SWITCHING COMMS OFF FOR A SECOND.
YOUR HEARTBEAT, J'ONN...IT'S TOO CALM. I KNOW YOU'RE CONTROLLING IT. ARE YOU ALL RIGHT?
I'M FINE, KAL. I'M TRYING TO CONTROL MY PHYSIOLOGY AHEAD OF THE PATHOGENS.
BATMAN, HAWKGIRL, CAN YOU SEE WHAT WE SEE?
I'M SCANNING THE CONTOURS FOR RECOGNITION...THE FACE MATCHES NO RACE IN EXISTENCE.
IT LOOKS SO...FAMILIAR, THOUGH.
WELL, WHATEVER IT IS...

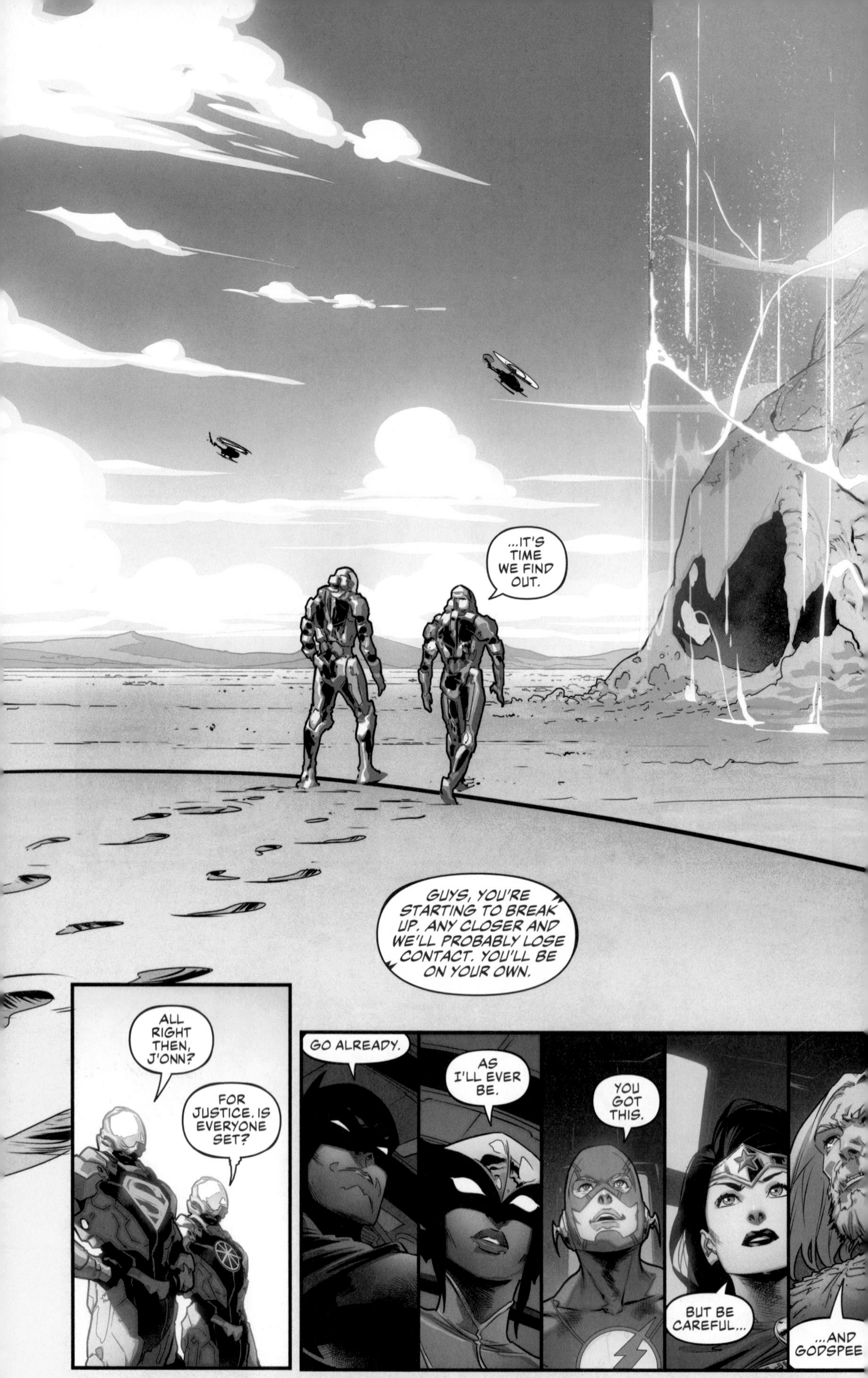
...IT'S TIME WE FIND OUT.
GUYS, YOU'RE STARTING TO BREAK UP. ANY CLOSER AND WE'LL PROBABLY LOSE CONTACT. YOU'LL BE ON YOUR OWN.
ALL RIGHT THEN, J'ONN?
FOR JUSTICE. IS EVERYONE SET?
GO ALREADY.
AS I'LL EVER BE.
YOU GOT THIS.
BUT BE CAREFUL...
...AND GODSPEE

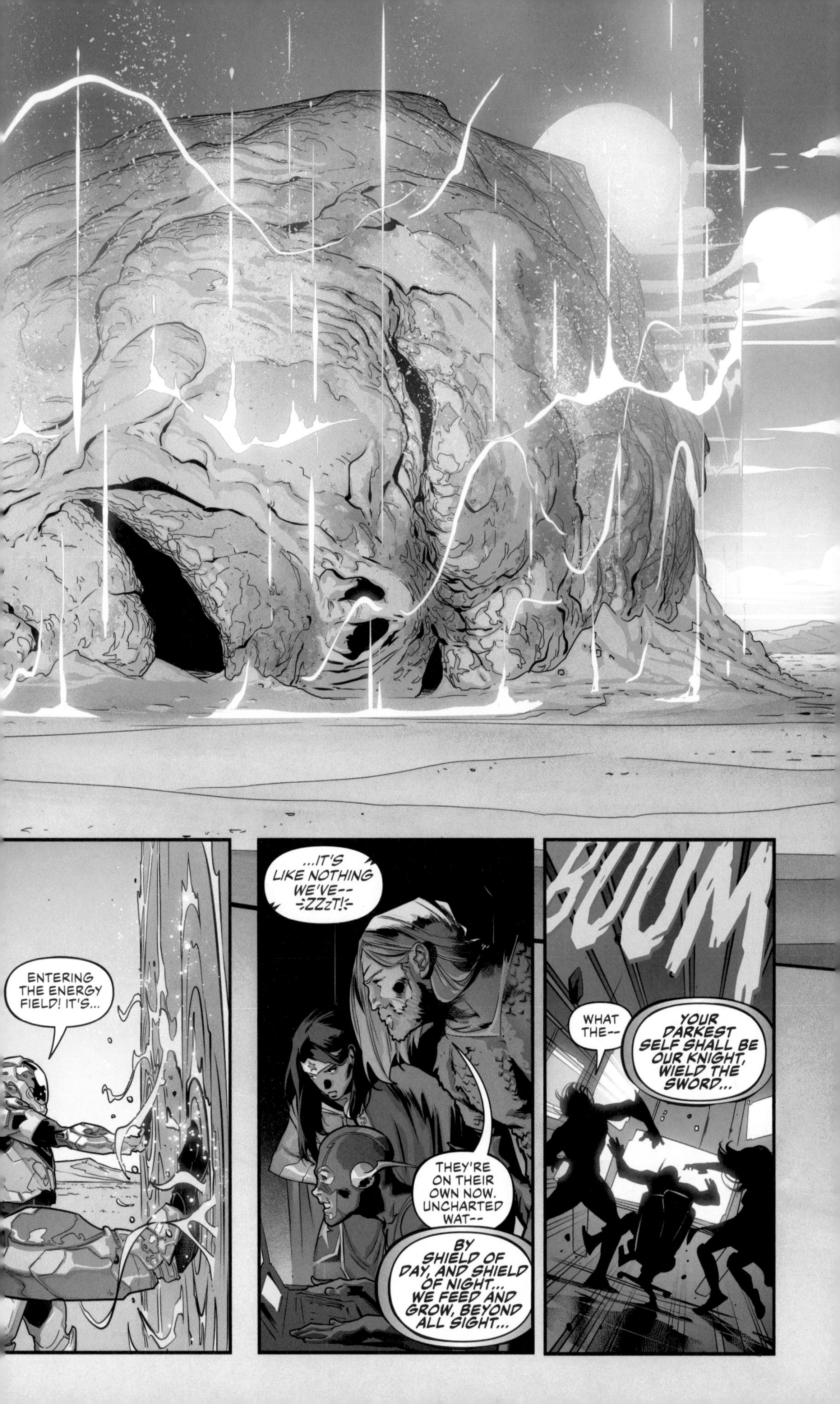
ENTERING THE ENERGY FIELD! IT'S...
...IT'S LIKE NOTHING WE'VE-- -ZZzT!-
THEY'RE ON THEIR OWN NOW. UNCHARTED WAT--
BY SHIELD OF DAY, AND SHIELD OF NIGHT... WE FEED AND GROW, BEYOND ALL SIGHT...
BOOM
WHAT THE--
YOUR DARKEST SELF SHALL BE OUR KNIGHT, WIELD THE SWORD...

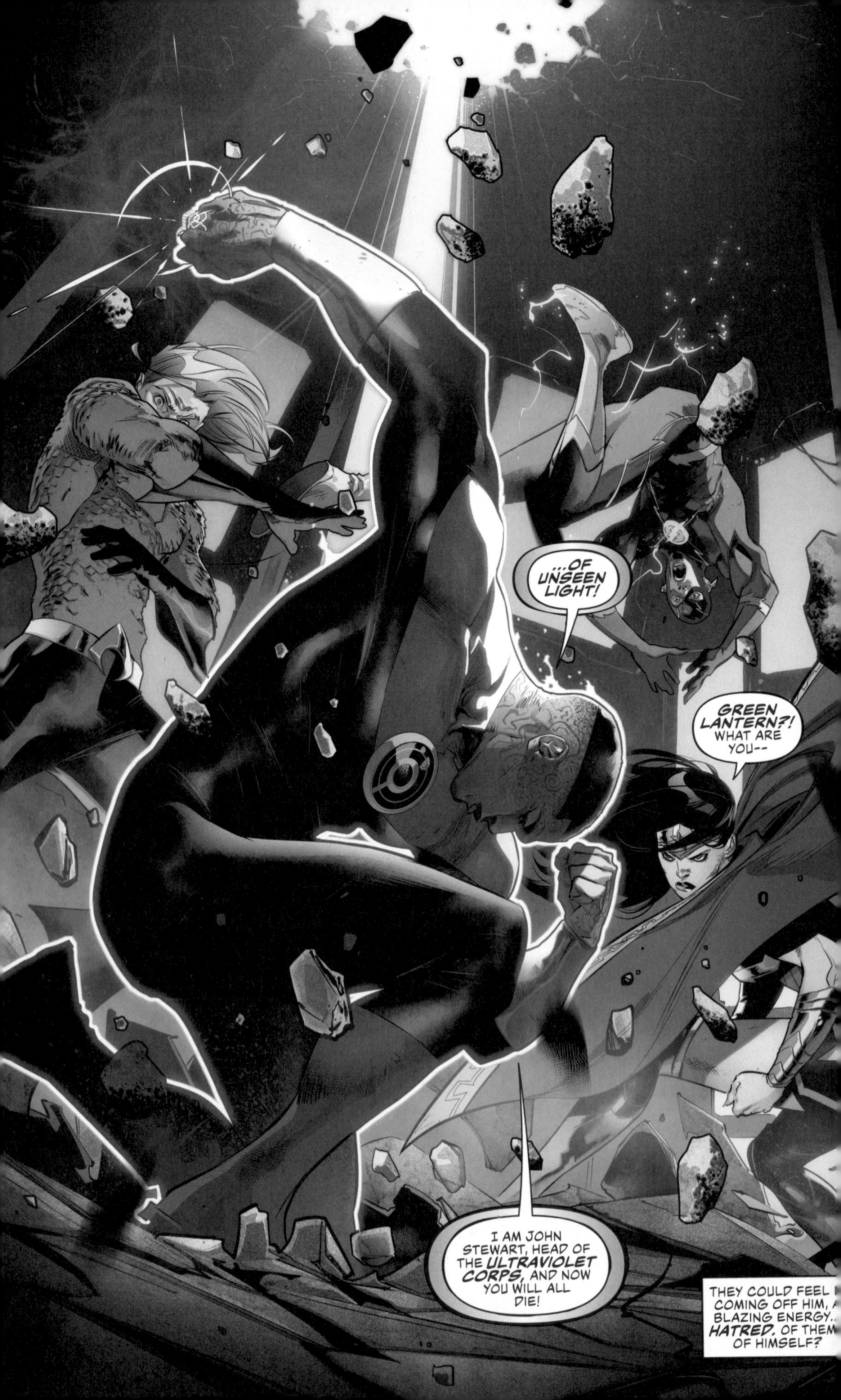
...OF UNSEEN LIGHT!
GREEN LANTERN?! WHAT ARE YOU--
I AM JOHN STEWART, HEAD OF THE ULTRAVIOLET CORPS, AND NOW YOU WILL ALL DIE!
THEY COULD FEEL
COMING OFF HIM,
BLAZING ENERGY.
HATRED. OF THEM
OF HIMSELF?

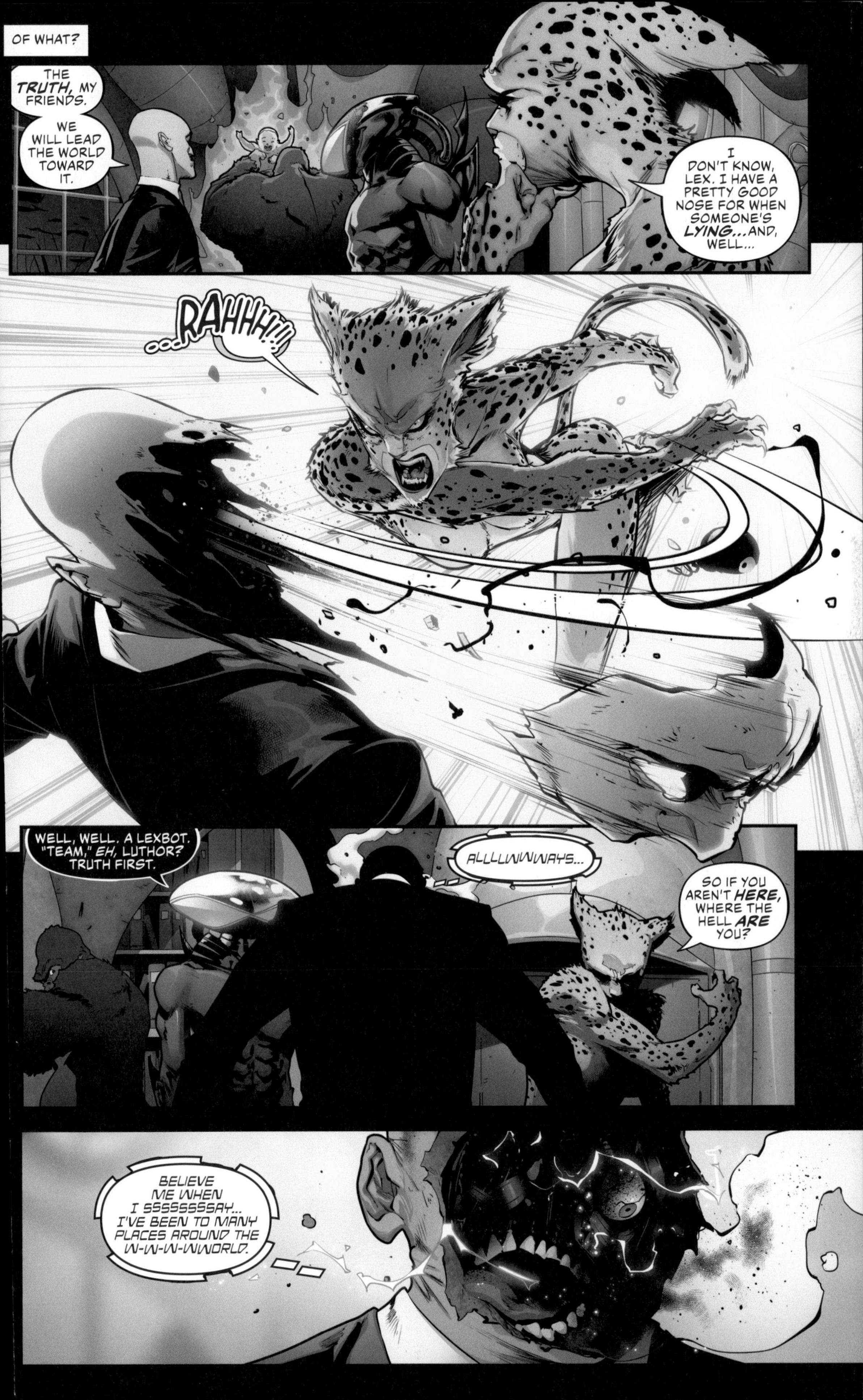
OF WHAT?
THE TRUTH, MY FRIENDS.
WE WILL LEAD THE WORLD TOWARD IT.
I DON'T KNOW, LEX. I HAVE A PRETTY GOOD NOSE FOR WHEN SOMEONE'S LYING...AND, WELL...
...RAHHH!!!!
WELL, WELL. A LEXBOT. "TEAM," EH, LUTHOR? TRUTH FIRST.
ALLLLWWWAYS...
SO IF YOU AREN'T HERE, WHERE THE HELL ARE YOU?
BELIEVE ME WHEN I SSSSSSSSAY... I'VE BEEN TO MANY PLACES AROUND THE W-W-W-WWORLD.

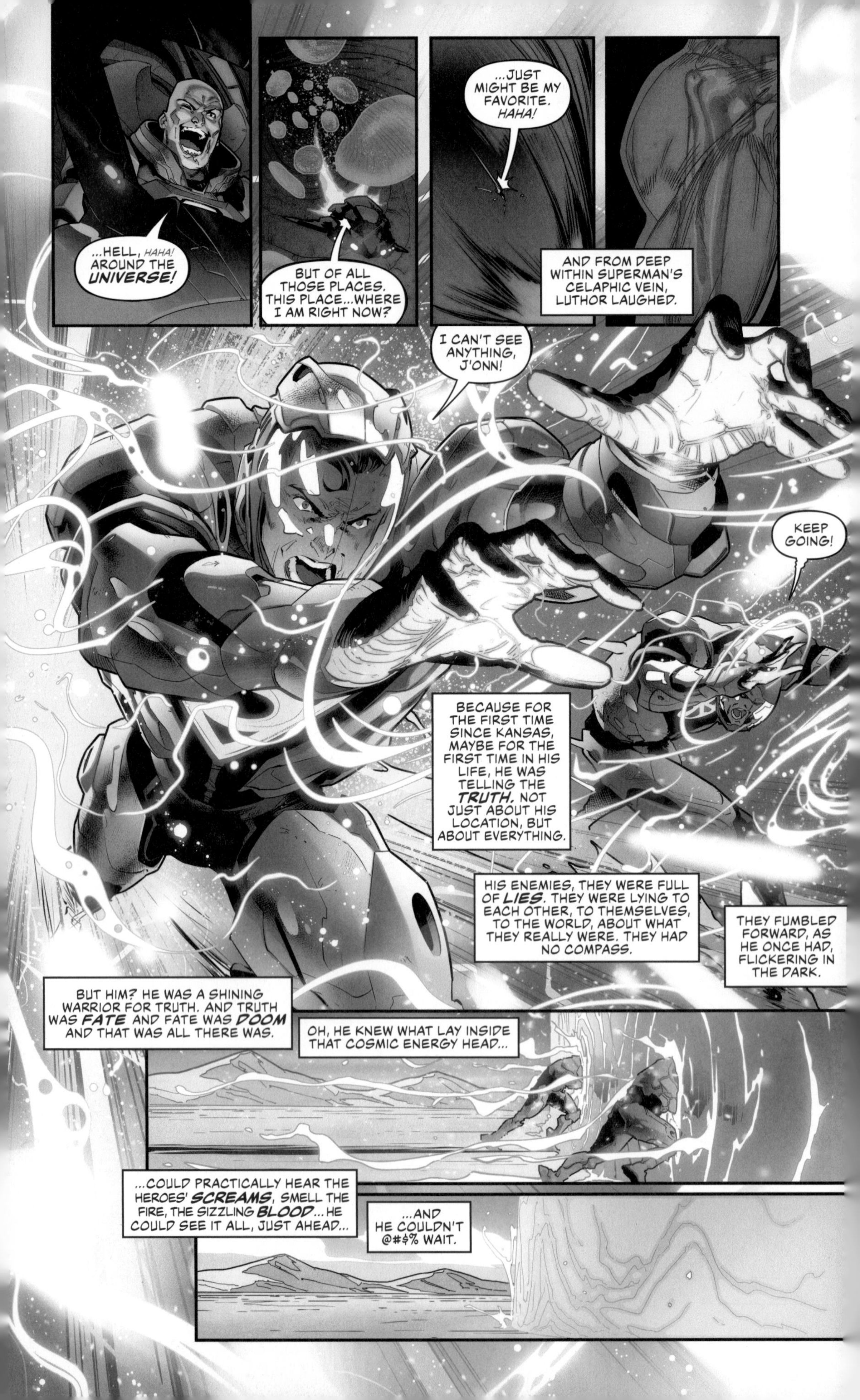
...HELL, HAHA! AROUND THE UNIVERSE!
BUT OF ALL THOSE PLACES. THIS PLACE...WHERE I AM RIGHT NOW?
...JUST MIGHT BE MY FAVORITE. HAHA!
AND FROM DEEP WITHIN SUPERMAN'S CELAPHIC VEIN, LUTHOR LAUGHED.
I CAN'T SEE ANYTHING, J'ONN!
KEEP GOING!
BECAUSE FOR THE FIRST TIME SINCE KANSAS, MAYBE FOR THE FIRST TIME IN HIS LIFE, HE WAS TELLING THE TRUTH. NOT JUST ABOUT HIS LOCATION, BUT ABOUT EVERYTHING.
HIS ENEMIES, THEY WERE FULL OF LIES. THEY WERE LYING TO EACH OTHER, TO THEMSELVES, TO THE WORLD, ABOUT WHAT THEY REALLY WERE. THEY HAD NO COMPASS.
THEY FUMBLED FORWARD, AS HE ONCE HAD, FLICKERING IN THE DARK.
BUT HIM? HE WAS A SHINING WARRIOR FOR TRUTH. AND TRUTH WAS FATE AND FATE WAS DOOM AND THAT WAS ALL THERE WAS.
OH, HE KNEW WHAT LAY INSIDE THAT COSMIC ENERGY HEAD...
...COULD PRACTICALLY HEAR THE HEROES' SCREAMS, SMELL THE FIRE, THE SIZZLING BLOOD... HE COULD SEE IT ALL, JUST AHEAD...
...AND HE COULDN'T @#$% WAIT.

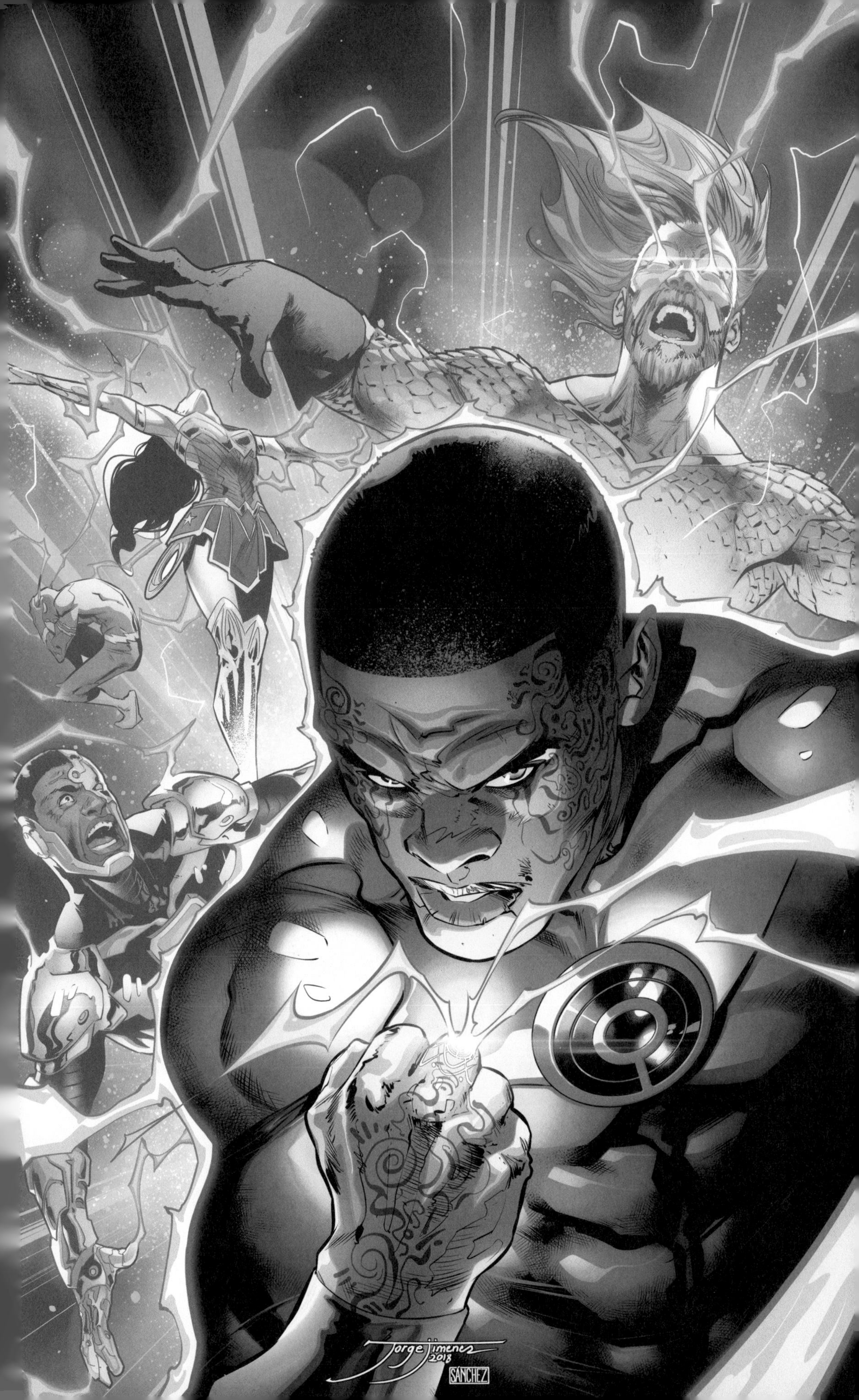
Jorge Jimenez
2018
SANCHEZ

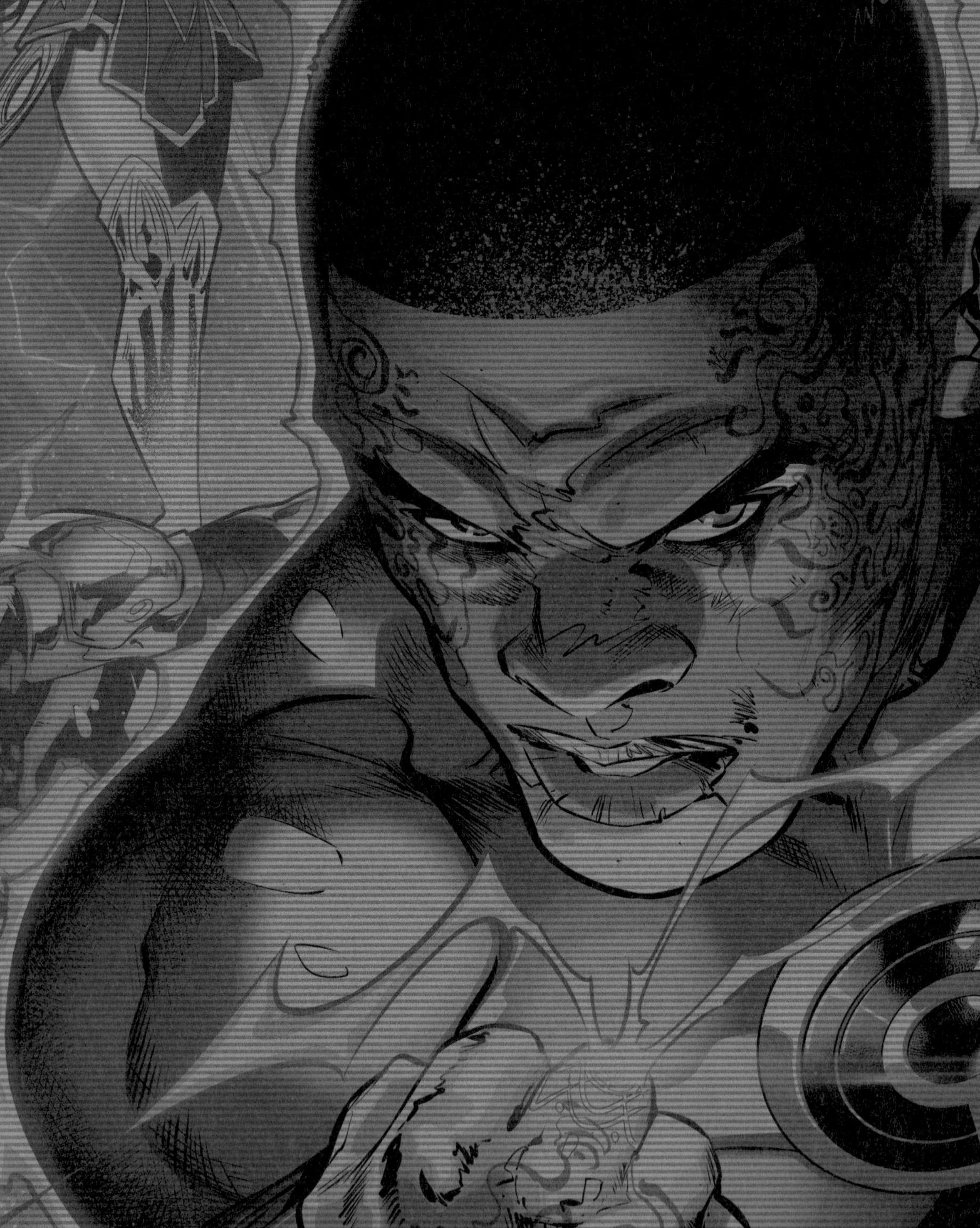

JUSTICE
LEAGUE
#3

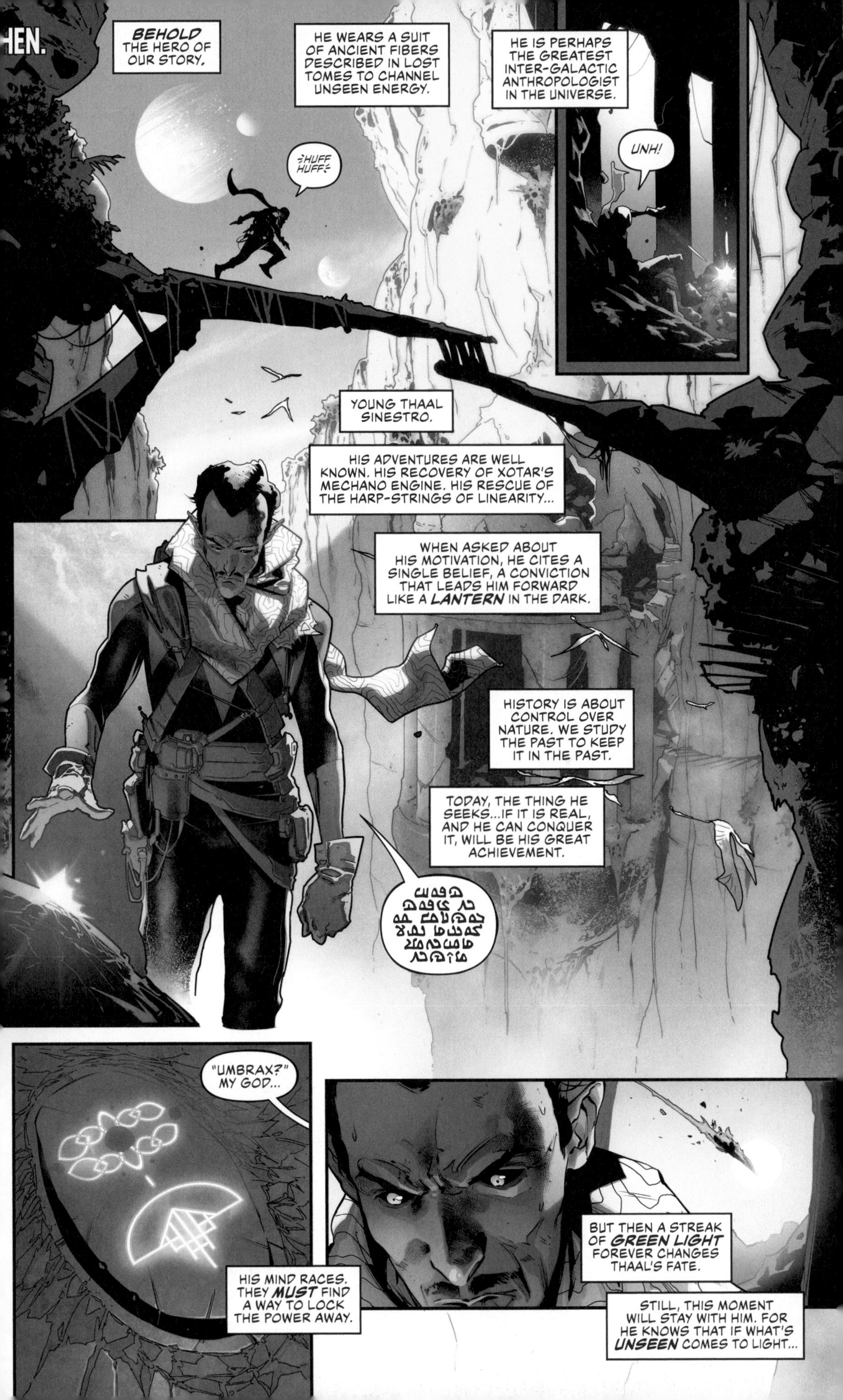
HEN.
BEHOLD THE HERO OF OUR STORY.
HE WEARS A SUIT OF ANCIENT FIBERS DESCRIBED IN LOST TOMES TO CHANNEL UNSEEN ENERGY.
HE IS PERHAPS THE GREATEST INTER-GALACTIC ANTHROPOLOGIST IN THE UNIVERSE.
HUFF HUFF
UNH!
YOUNG THAAL SINESTRO.
HIS ADVENTURES ARE WELL KNOWN. HIS RECOVERY OF XOTAR'S MECHANO ENGINE. HIS RESCUE OF THE HARP-STRINGS OF LINEARITY...
WHEN ASKED ABOUT HIS MOTIVATION, HE CITES A SINGLE BELIEF, A CONVICTION THAT LEADS HIM FORWARD LIKE A LANTERN IN THE DARK.
HISTORY IS ABOUT CONTROL OVER NATURE. WE STUDY THE PAST TO KEEP IT IN THE PAST.
TODAY, THE THING HE SEEKS...IF IT IS REAL, AND HE CAN CONQUER IT, WILL BE HIS GREAT ACHIEVEMENT.
"UMBRAX?" MY GOD...
HIS MIND RACES. THEY MUST FIND A WAY TO LOCK THE POWER AWAY.
BUT THEN A STREAK OF GREEN LIGHT FOREVER CHANGES THAAL'S FATE.
STILL, THIS MOMENT WILL STAY WITH HIM. FOR HE KNOWS THAT IF WHAT'S UNSEEN COMES TO LIGHT...

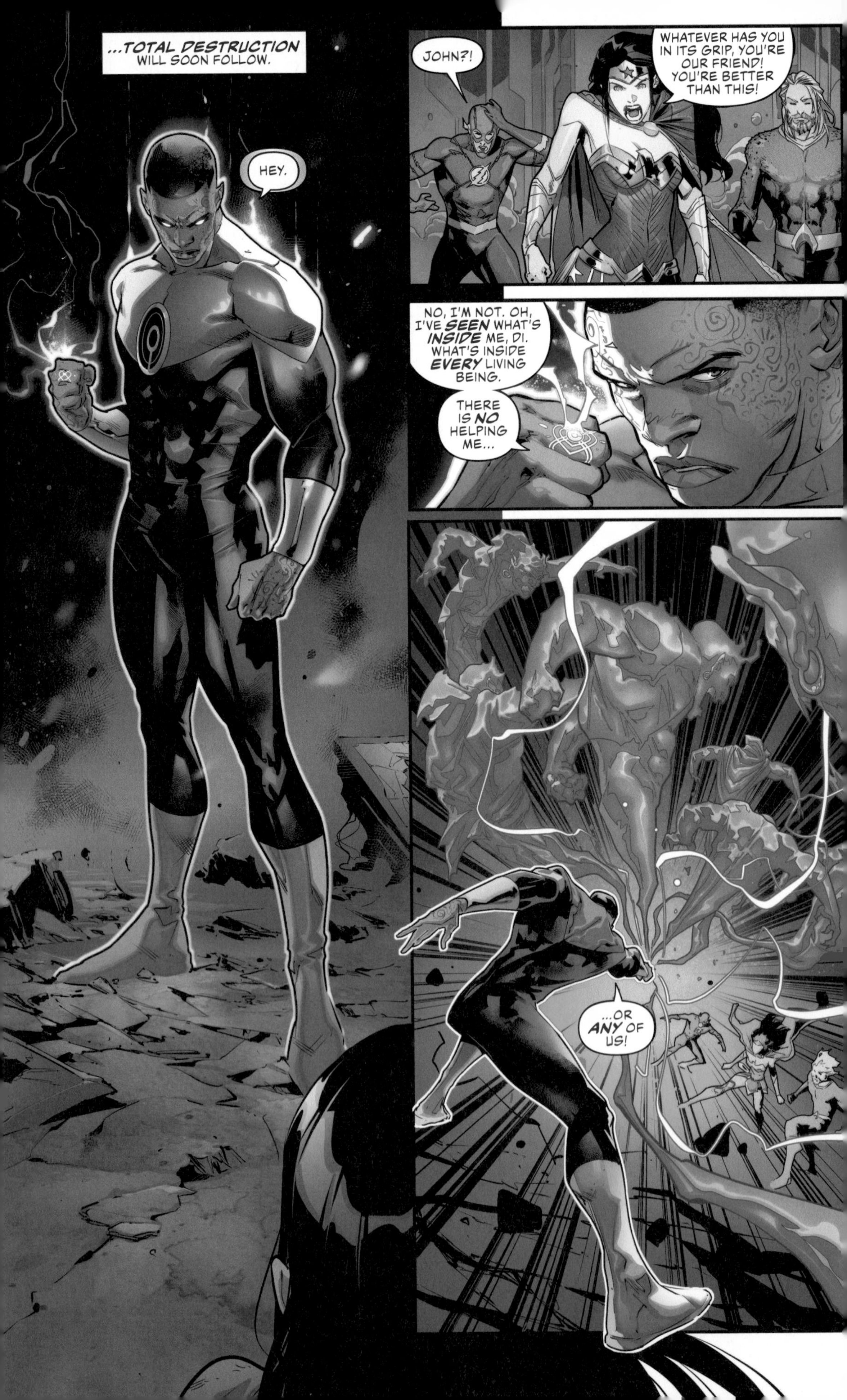
...TOTAL DESTRUCTION WILL SOON FOLLOW.
HEY.
JOHN?!
WHATEVER HAS YOU IN ITS GRIP, YOU'RE OUR FRIEND! YOU'RE BETTER THAN THIS!
NO, I'M NOT. OH, I'VE SEEN WHAT'S INSIDE ME, DI. WHAT'S INSIDE EVERY LIVING BEING.
THERE IS NO HELPING ME...
...OR ANY OF US!

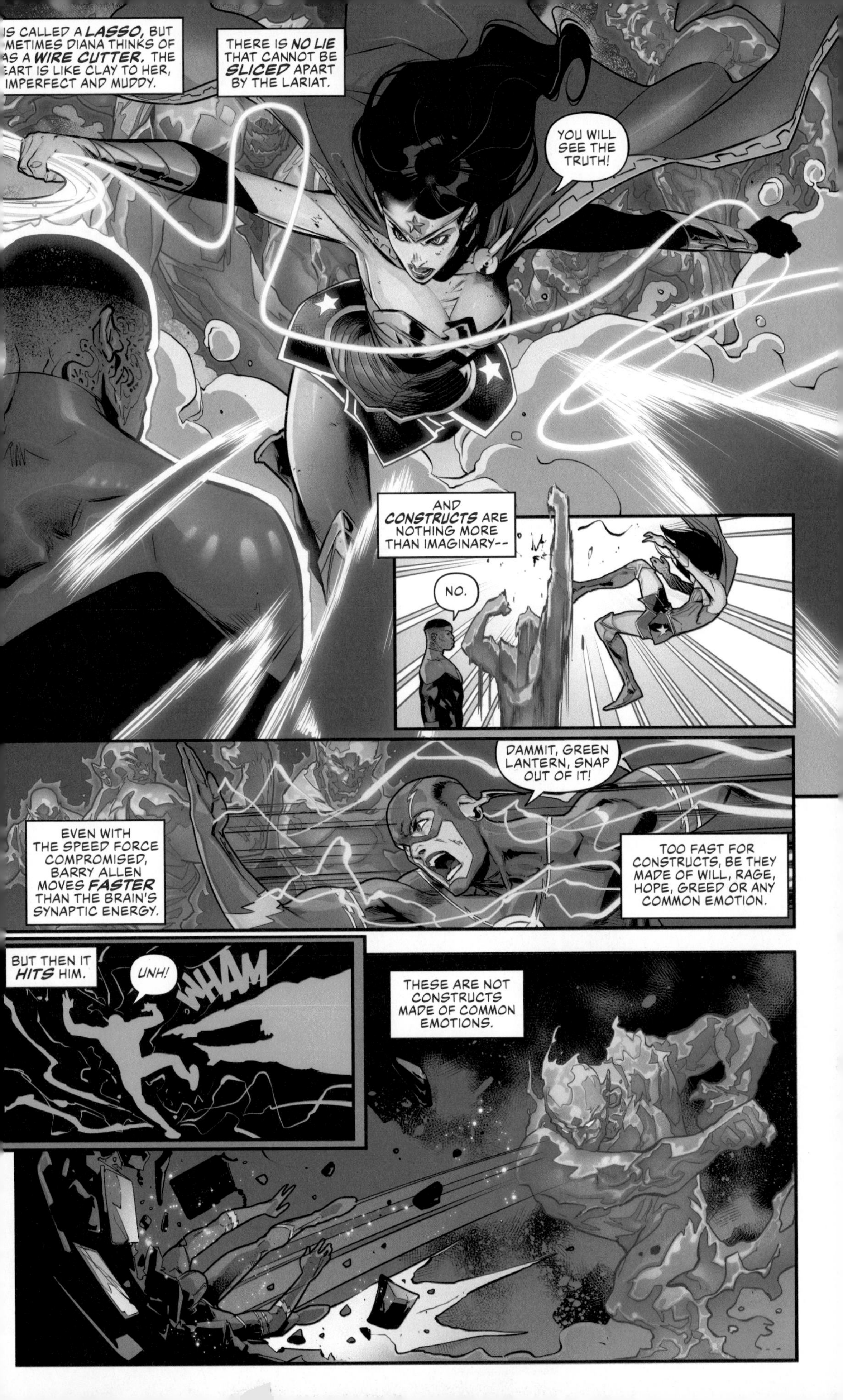

IS CALLED A LASSO, BUT METIMES DIANA THINKS OF AS A WIRE CUTTER. THE EART IS LIKE CLAY TO HER, IMPERFECT AND MUDDY.
THERE IS NO LIE THAT CANNOT BE SLICED APART BY THE LARIAT.
YOU WILL SEE THE TRUTH!
AND CONSTRUCTS ARE NOTHING MORE THAN IMAGINARY--
NO.
DAMMIT, GREEN LANTERN, SNAP OUT OF IT!
EVEN WITH THE SPEED FORCE COMPROMISED, BARRY ALLEN MOVES FASTER THAN THE BRAIN'S SYNAPTIC ENERGY.
TOO FAST FOR CONSTRUCTS, BE THEY MADE OF WILL, RAGE, HOPE, GREED OR ANY COMMON EMOTION.
BUT THEN IT HITS HIM.
UNH!
WHAM
THESE ARE NOT CONSTRUCTS MADE OF COMMON EMOTIONS.

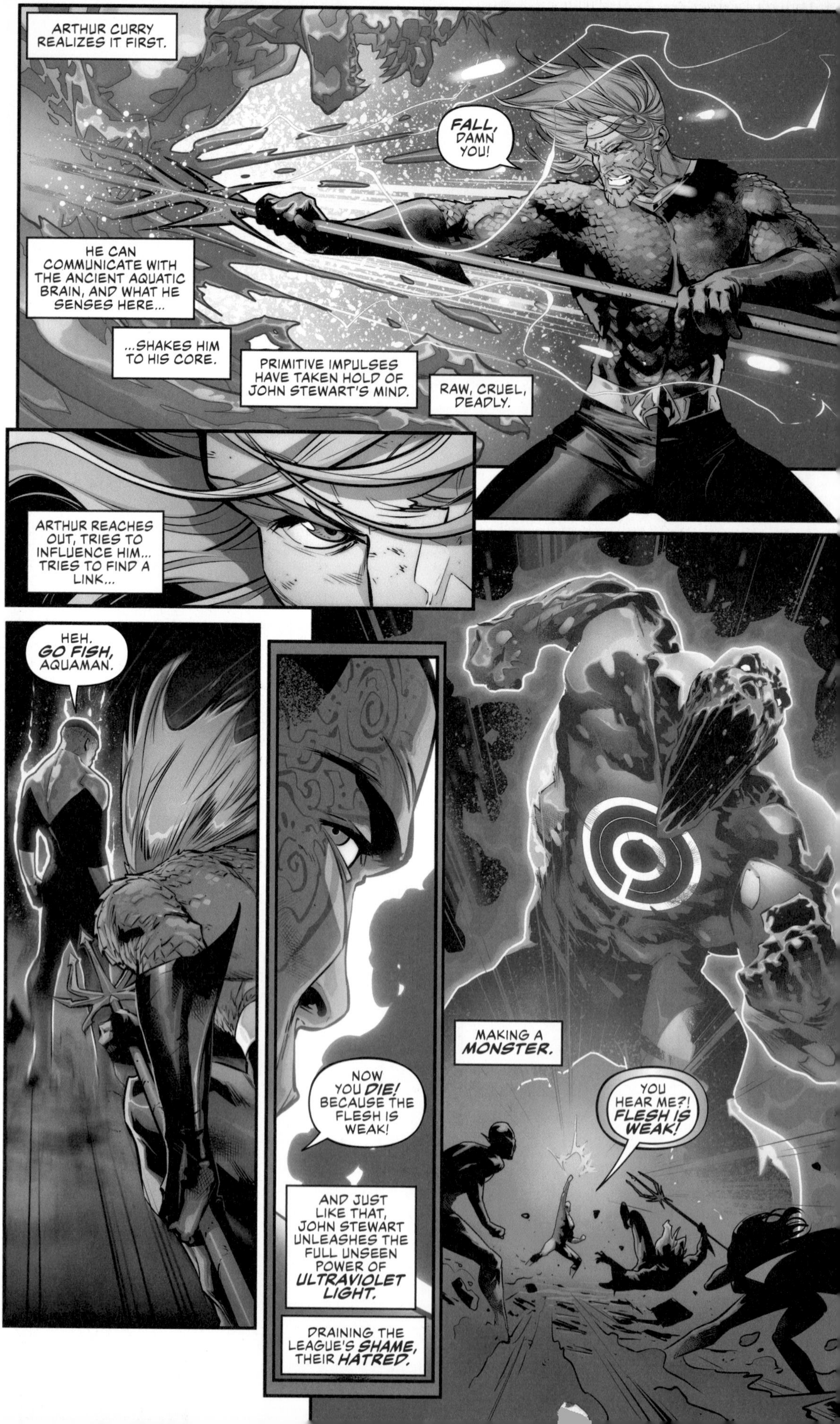
ARTHUR CURRY REALIZES IT FIRST.
FALL, DAMN YOU!
HE CAN COMMUNICATE WITH THE ANCIENT AQUATIC BRAIN, AND WHAT HE SENSES HERE...
...SHAKES HIM TO HIS CORE.
PRIMITIVE IMPULSES HAVE TAKEN HOLD OF JOHN STEWART'S MIND.
RAW, CRUEL, DEADLY.
ARTHUR REACHES OUT, TRIES TO INFLUENCE HIM... TRIES TO FIND A LINK...
HEH. GO FISH, AQUAMAN.
MAKING A MONSTER.
NOW YOU DIE! BECAUSE THE FLESH IS WEAK!
YOU HEAR ME?! FLESH IS WEAK!
AND JUST LIKE THAT, JOHN STEWART UNLEASHES THE FULL UNSEEN POWER OF ULTRAVIOLET LIGHT.
DRAINING THE LEAGUE'S SHAME, THEIR HATRED.

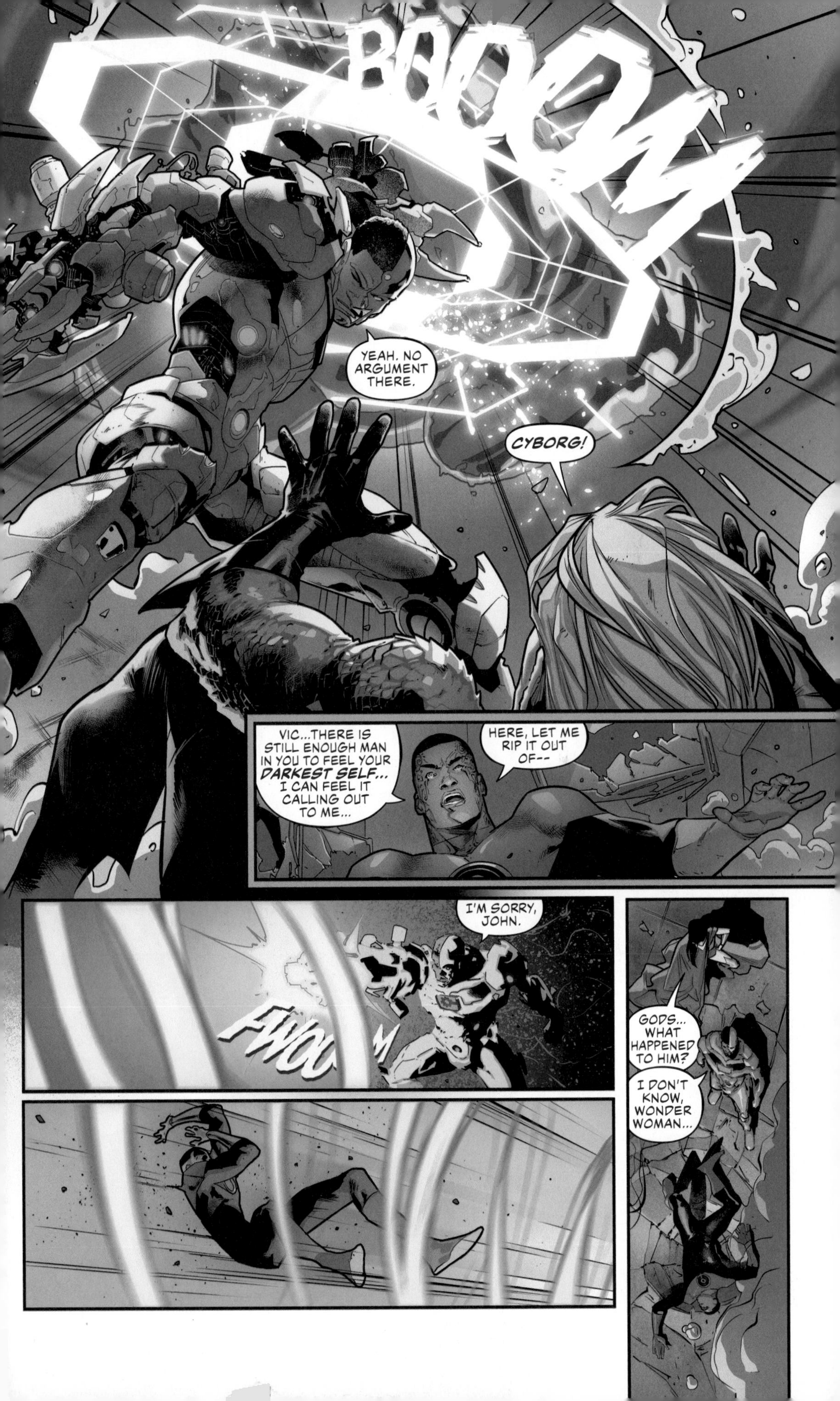
BOOOOM
YEAH. NO ARGUMENT THERE.
CYBORG!
VIC...THERE IS STILL ENOUGH MAN IN YOU TO FEEL YOUR DARKEST SELF... I CAN FEEL IT CALLING OUT TO ME...
HERE, LET ME RIP IT OUT OF--
I'M SORRY, JOHN.
FWOOM
GODS... WHAT HAPPENED TO HIM?
I DON'T KNOW, WONDER WOMAN...

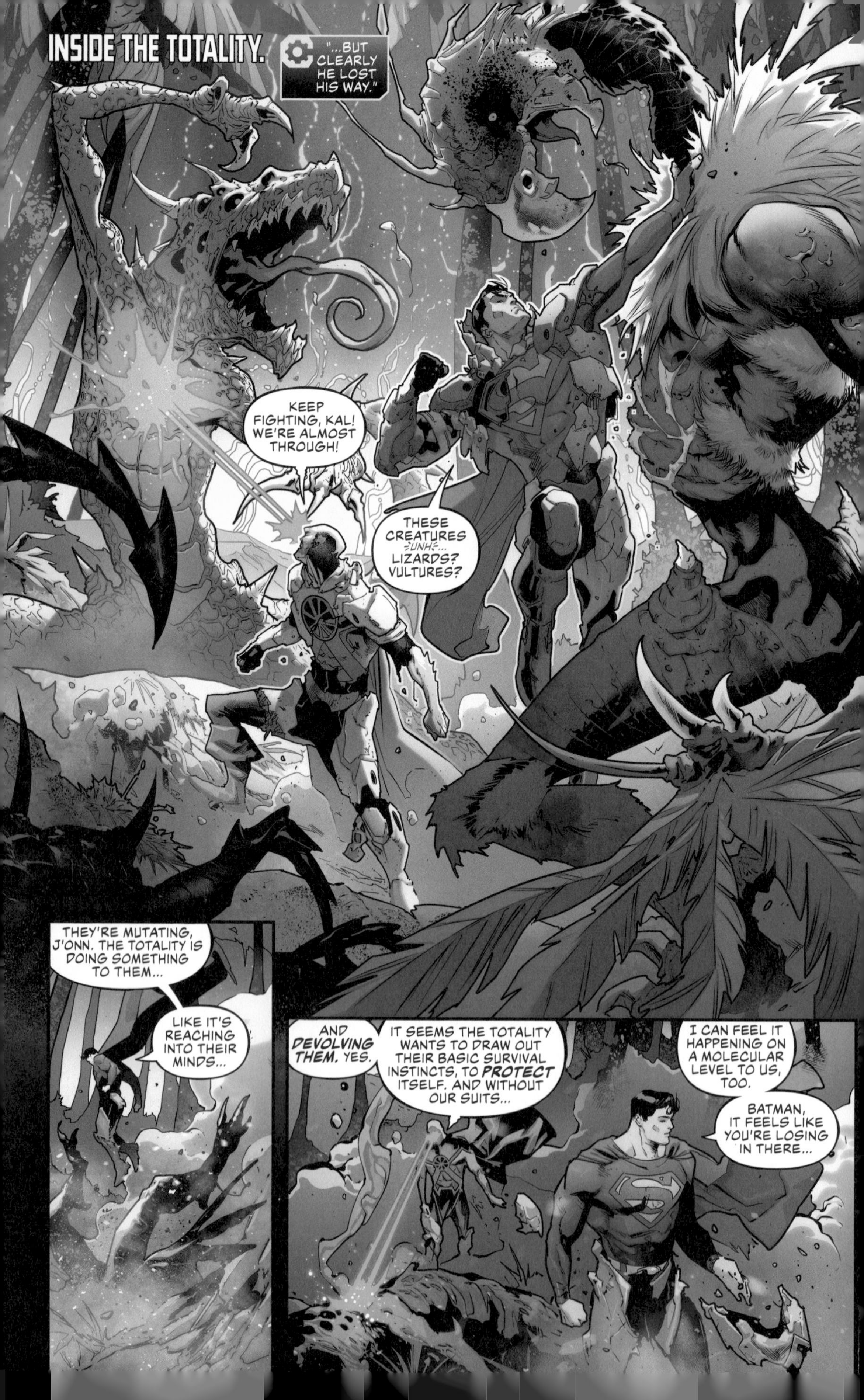
INSIDE THE TOTALITY.
"...BUT CLEARLY HE LOST HIS WAY."
KEEP FIGHTING, KAL! WE'RE ALMOST THROUGH!
THESE CREATURES --UNH-- ... LIZARDS? VULTURES?
THEY'RE MUTATING, J'ONN. THE TOTALITY IS DOING SOMETHING TO THEM...
LIKE IT'S REACHING INTO THEIR MINDS...
AND DEVOLVING THEM. YES.
IT SEEMS THE TOTALITY WANTS TO DRAW OUT THEIR BASIC SURVIVAL INSTINCTS, TO PROTECT ITSELF. AND WITHOUT OUR SUITS...
I CAN FEEL IT HAPPENING ON A MOLECULAR LEVEL TO US, TOO.
BATMAN, IT FEELS LIKE YOU'RE LOSING IN THERE...

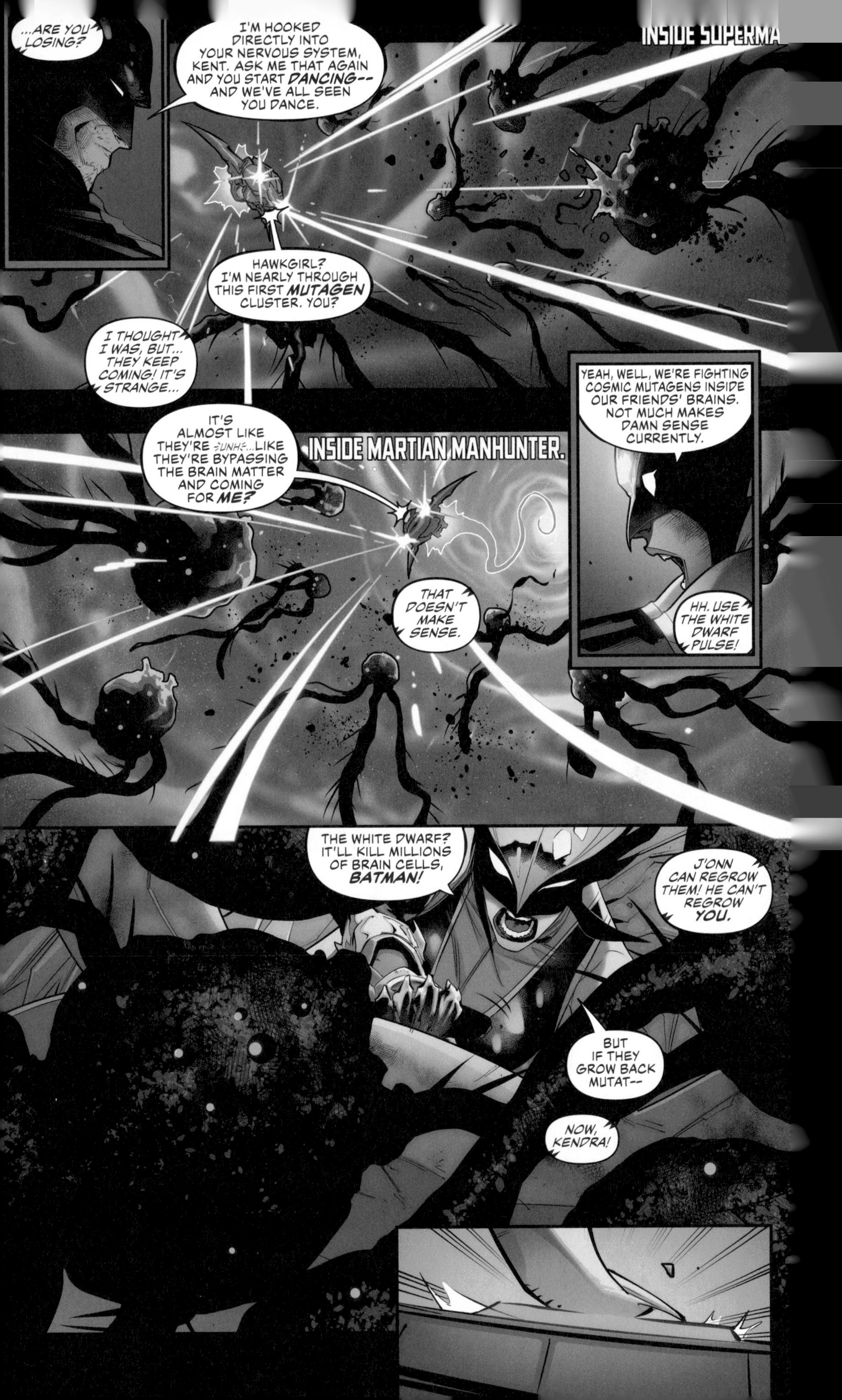

...ARE YOU LOSING?
INSIDE SUPERMA
I'M HOOKED DIRECTLY INTO YOUR NERVOUS SYSTEM, KENT. ASK ME THAT AGAIN AND YOU START DANCING-- AND WE'VE ALL SEEN YOU DANCE.
HAWKGIRL? I'M NEARLY THROUGH THIS FIRST MUTAGEN CLUSTER. YOU?
I THOUGHT I WAS, BUT... THEY KEEP COMING! IT'S STRANGE...
YEAH, WELL, WE'RE FIGHTING COSMIC MUTAGENS INSIDE OUR FRIENDS' BRAINS. NOT MUCH MAKES DAMN SENSE CURRENTLY.
IT'S ALMOST LIKE THEY'RE UNH...LIKE THEY'RE BYPASSING THE BRAIN MATTER AND COMING FOR ME?
INSIDE MARTIAN MANHUNTER.
THAT DOESN'T MAKE SENSE.
HH. USE THE WHITE DWARF PULSE!
THE WHITE DWARF? IT'LL KILL MILLIONS OF BRAIN CELLS, BATMAN!
J'ONN CAN REGROW THEM! HE CAN'T REGROW YOU.
BUT IF THEY GROW BACK MUTAT--
NOW, KENDRA!

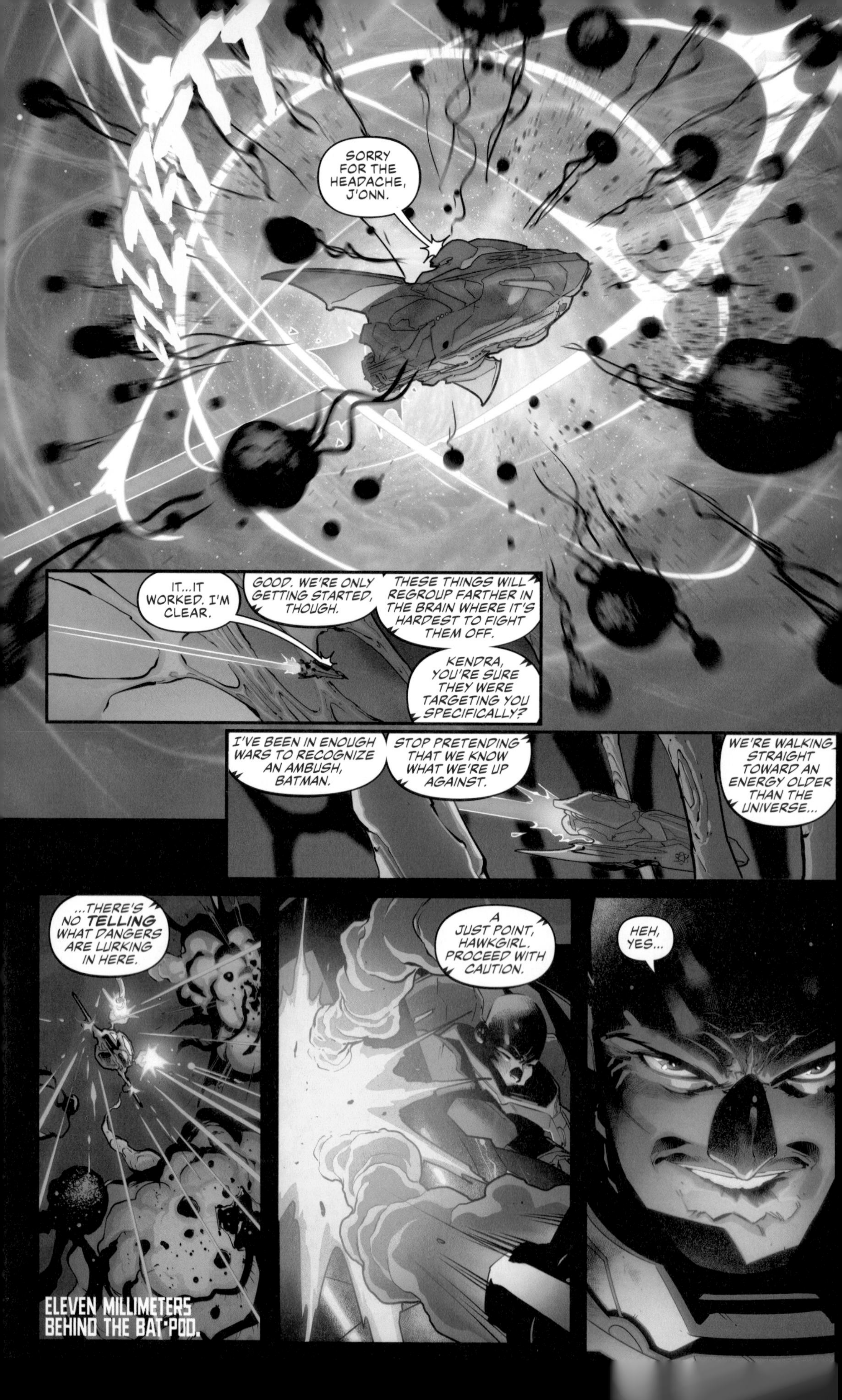
SORRY FOR THE HEADACHE, J'ONN.
IT...IT WORKED. I'M CLEAR.
GOOD. WE'RE ONLY GETTING STARTED, THOUGH.
THESE THINGS WILL REGROUP FARTHER IN THE BRAIN WHERE IT'S HARDEST TO FIGHT THEM OFF.
KENDRA, YOU'RE SURE THEY WERE TARGETING YOU SPECIFICALLY?
I'VE BEEN IN ENOUGH WARS TO RECOGNIZE AN AMBUSH, BATMAN.
STOP PRETENDING THAT WE KNOW WHAT WE'RE UP AGAINST.
WE'RE WALKING STRAIGHT TOWARD AN ENERGY OLDER THAN THE UNIVERSE...
...THERE'S NO TELLING WHAT DANGERS ARE LURKING IN HERE.
ELEVEN MILLIMETERS BEHIND THE BAT-POD.
A JUST POINT, HAWKGIRL. PROCEED WITH CAUTION.
HEH, YES...

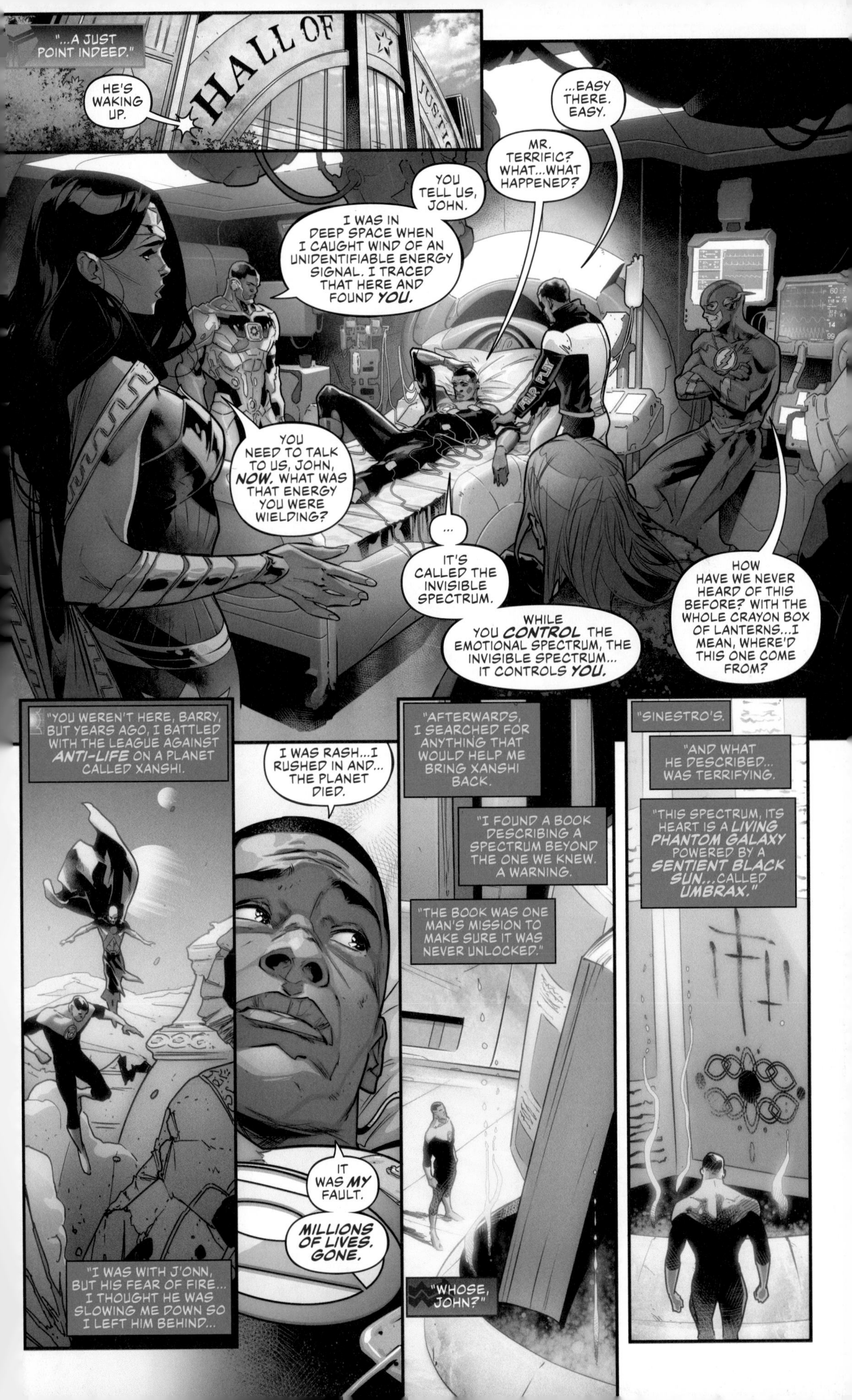
"...A JUST POINT INDEED."
HALL OF
JUSTIC
HE'S WAKING UP.
...EASY THERE. EASY.
MR. TERRIFIC? WHAT...WHAT HAPPENED?
YOU TELL US, JOHN.
I WAS IN DEEP SPACE WHEN I CAUGHT WIND OF AN UNIDENTIFIABLE ENERGY SIGNAL. I TRACED THAT HERE AND FOUND YOU.
YOU NEED TO TALK TO US, JOHN, NOW. WHAT WAS THAT ENERGY YOU WERE WIELDING?
...
IT'S CALLED THE INVISIBLE SPECTRUM.
WHILE YOU CONTROL THE EMOTIONAL SPECTRUM, THE INVISIBLE SPECTRUM... IT CONTROLS YOU.
HOW HAVE WE NEVER HEARD OF THIS BEFORE? WITH THE WHOLE CRAYON BOX OF LANTERNS...I MEAN, WHERE'D THIS ONE COME FROM?
"YOU WEREN'T HERE, BARRY, BUT YEARS AGO, I BATTLED WITH THE LEAGUE AGAINST ANTI-LIFE ON A PLANET CALLED XANSHI.
"I WAS WITH J'ONN, BUT HIS FEAR OF FIRE... I THOUGHT HE WAS SLOWING ME DOWN SO I LEFT HIM BEHIND...
I WAS RASH...I RUSHED IN AND... THE PLANET DIED.
IT WAS MY FAULT.
MILLIONS OF LIVES. GONE.
"AFTERWARDS, I SEARCHED FOR ANYTHING THAT WOULD HELP ME BRING XANSHI BACK.
"I FOUND A BOOK DESCRIBING A SPECTRUM BEYOND THE ONE WE KNEW. A WARNING.
"THE BOOK WAS ONE MAN'S MISSION TO MAKE SURE IT WAS NEVER UNLOCKED."
"WHOSE, JOHN?"
"SINESTRO'S.
"AND WHAT HE DESCRIBED... WAS TERRIFYING.
"THIS SPECTRUM, ITS HEART IS A LIVING PHANTOM GALAXY POWERED BY A SENTIENT BLACK SUN... CALLED UMBRAX."

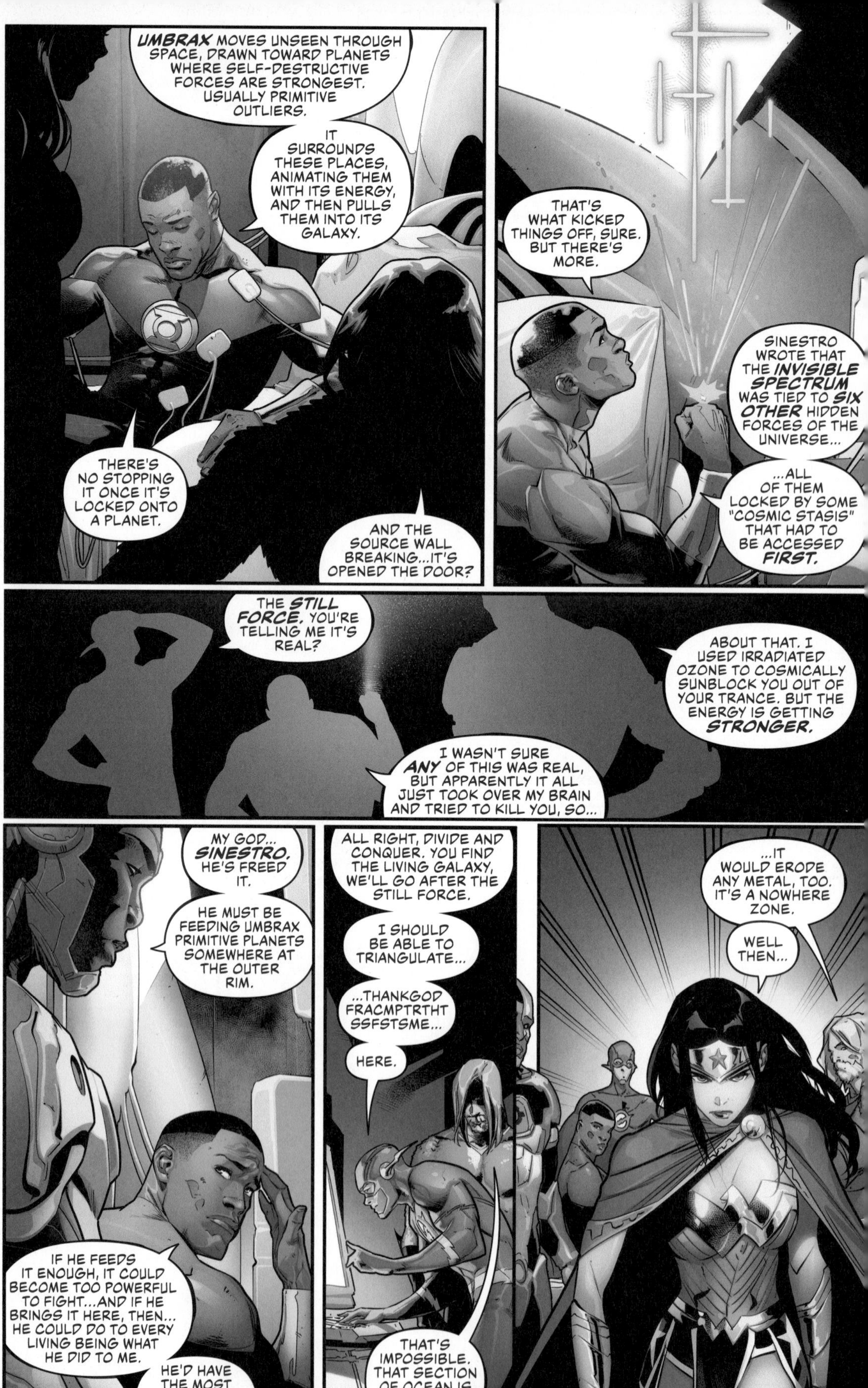
UMBRAX MOVES UNSEEN THROUGH SPACE, DRAWN TOWARD PLANETS WHERE SELF-DESTRUCTIVE FORCES ARE STRONGEST. USUALLY PRIMITIVE OUTLIERS.
IT SURROUNDS THESE PLACES, ANIMATING THEM WITH ITS ENERGY, AND THEN PULLS THEM INTO ITS GALAXY.
THERE'S NO STOPPING IT ONCE IT'S LOCKED ONTO A PLANET.
AND THE SOURCE WALL BREAKING...IT'S OPENED THE DOOR?
THAT'S WHAT KICKED THINGS OFF, SURE. BUT THERE'S MORE.
SINESTRO WROTE THAT THE INVISIBLE SPECTRUM WAS TIED TO SIX OTHER HIDDEN FORCES OF THE UNIVERSE...
...ALL OF THEM LOCKED BY SOME "COSMIC STASIS" THAT HAD TO BE ACCESSED FIRST.
THE STILL FORCE. YOU'RE TELLING ME IT'S REAL?
ABOUT THAT. I USED IRRADIATED OZONE TO COSMICALLY SUNBLOCK YOU OUT OF YOUR TRANCE. BUT THE ENERGY IS GETTING STRONGER.
I WASN'T SURE ANY OF THIS WAS REAL, BUT APPARENTLY IT ALL JUST TOOK OVER MY BRAIN AND TRIED TO KILL YOU, SO...
MY GOD... SINESTRO. HE'S FREED IT.
HE MUST BE FEEDING UMBRAX PRIMITIVE PLANETS SOMEWHERE AT THE OUTER RIM.
IF HE FEEDS IT ENOUGH, IT COULD BECOME TOO POWERFUL TO FIGHT...AND IF HE BRINGS IT HERE, THEN... HE COULD DO TO EVERY LIVING BEING WHAT HE DID TO ME.
HE'D HAVE THE MOST POWERFUL CORPS IN THE UNIVERSE...
ALL RIGHT, DIVIDE AND CONQUER. YOU FIND THE LIVING GALAXY, WE'LL GO AFTER THE STILL FORCE.
I SHOULD BE ABLE TO TRIANGULATE...
...THANKGOD FRACMPTRTHT SSFSTSME...
HERE.
THAT'S IMPOSSIBLE. THAT SECTION OF OCEAN IS TOXIC TO ALL LIFE...
...IT WOULD ERODE ANY METAL, TOO. IT'S A NOWHERE ZONE.
WELL THEN...

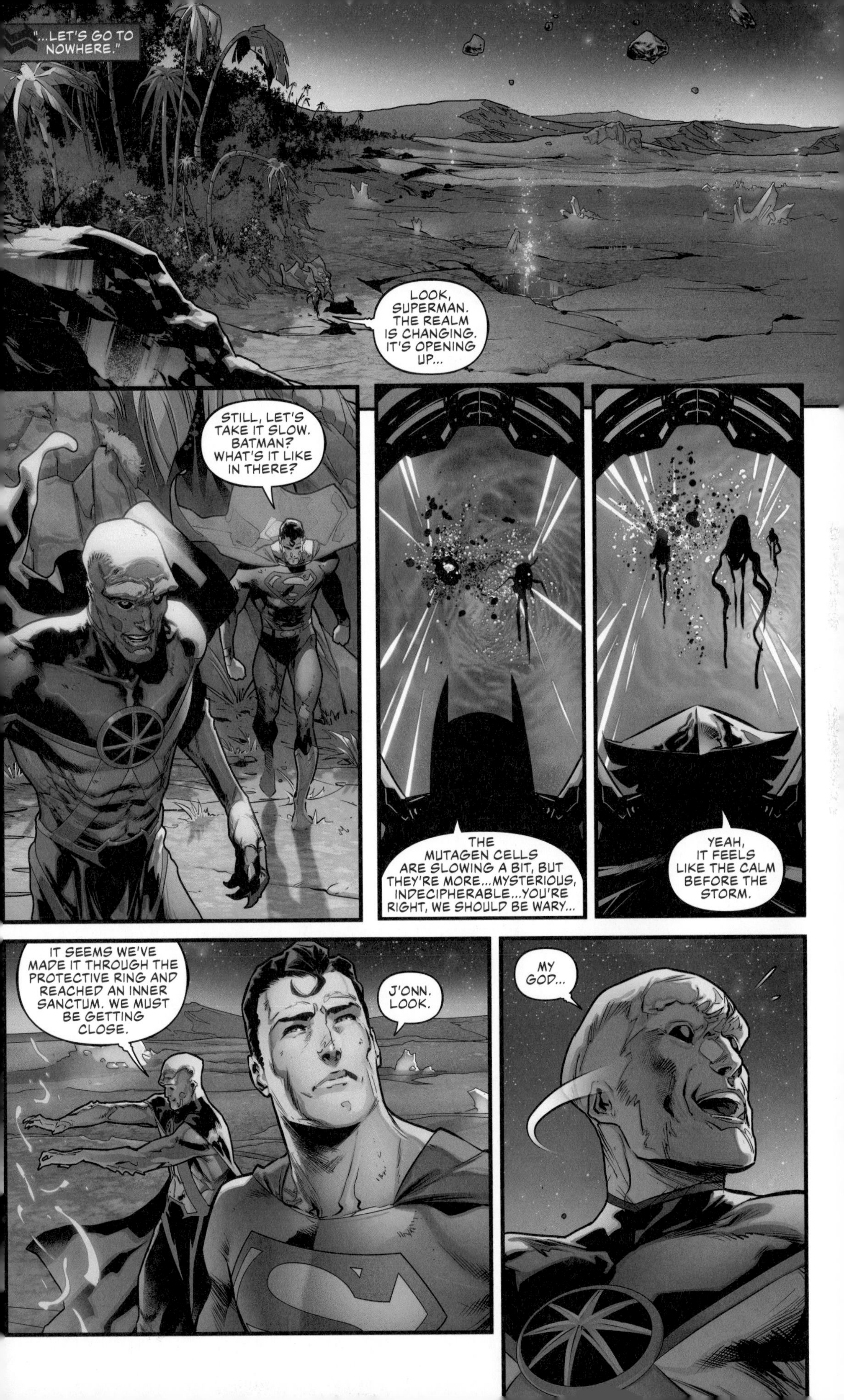
"...LET'S GO TO NOWHERE."
LOOK, SUPERMAN. THE REALM IS CHANGING. IT'S OPENING UP...
STILL, LET'S TAKE IT SLOW. BATMAN? WHAT'S IT LIKE IN THERE?
THE MUTAGEN CELLS ARE SLOWING A BIT, BUT THEY'RE MORE...MYSTERIOUS, INDECIPHERABLE...YOU'RE RIGHT, WE SHOULD BE WARY...
YEAH, IT FEELS LIKE THE CALM BEFORE THE STORM.
IT SEEMS WE'VE MADE IT THROUGH THE PROTECTIVE RING AND REACHED AN INNER SANCTUM. WE MUST BE GETTING CLOSE.
J'ONN. LOOK.
MY GOD...

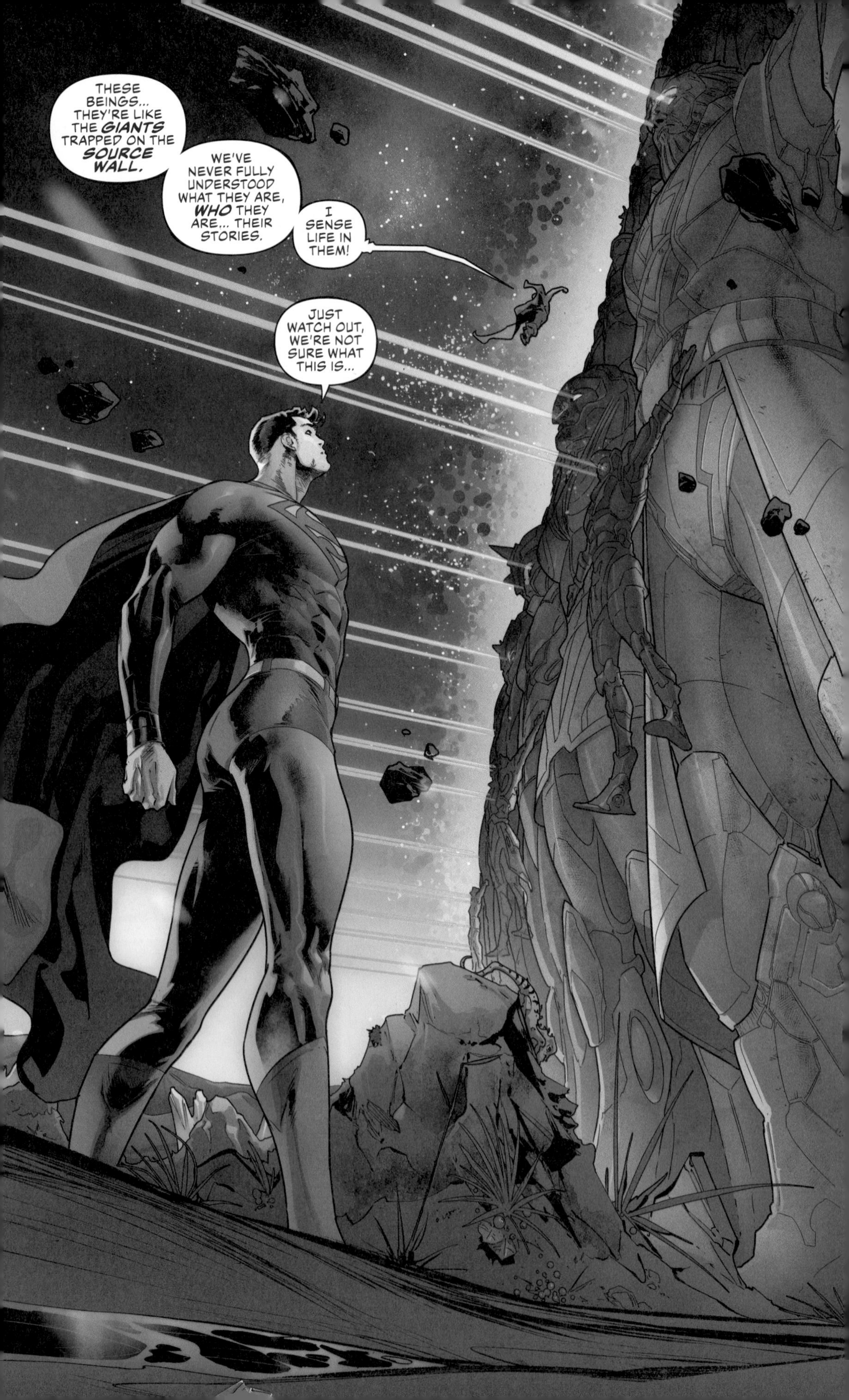
THESE BEINGS... THEY'RE LIKE THE GIANTS TRAPPED ON THE SOURCE WALL.
WE'VE NEVER FULLY UNDERSTOOD WHAT THEY ARE, WHO THEY ARE... THEIR STORIES.
I SENSE LIFE IN THEM!
JUST WATCH OUT, WE'RE NOT SURE WHAT THIS IS...

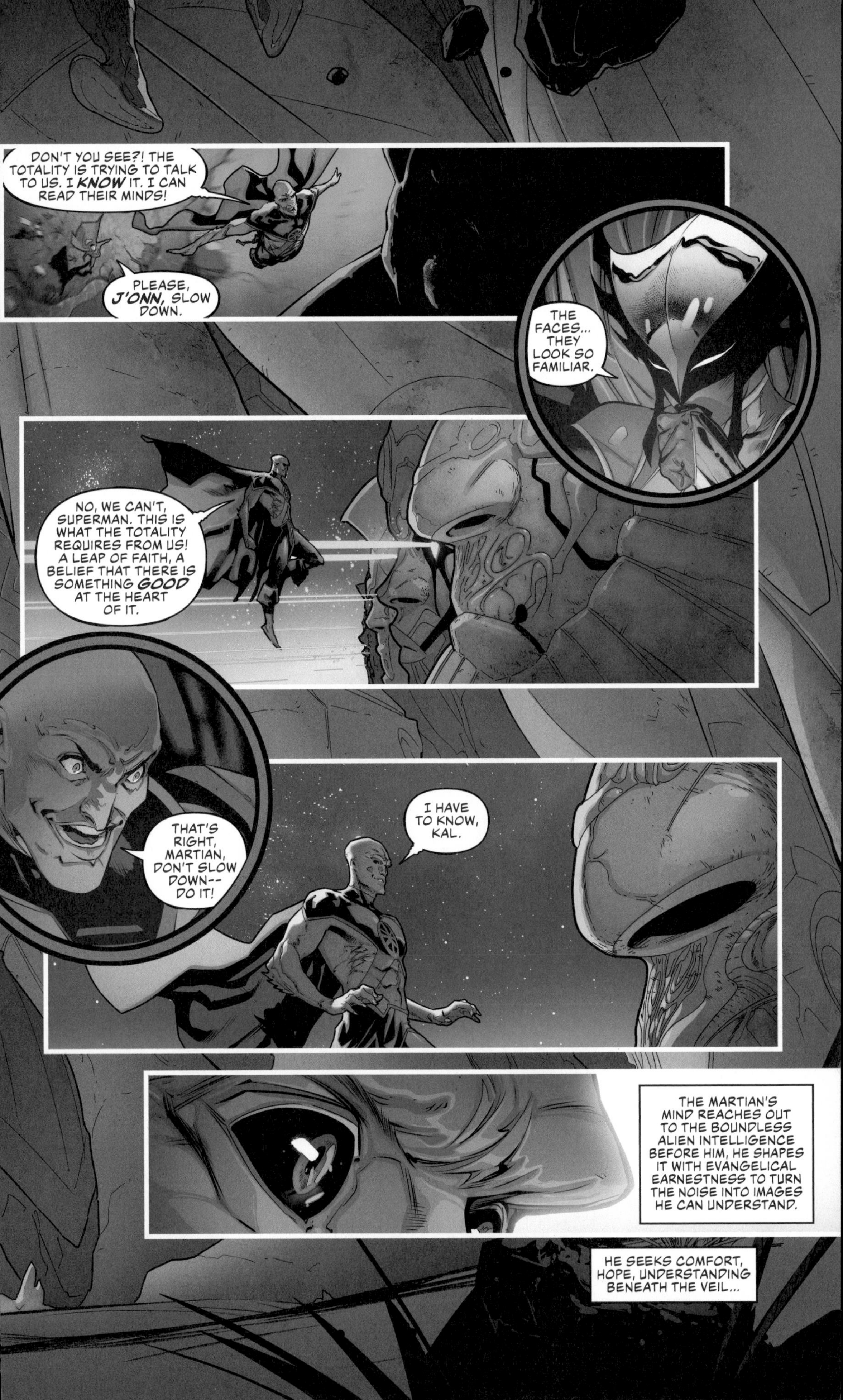

DON'T YOU SEE?! THE TOTALITY IS TRYING TO TALK TO US. I KNOW IT. I CAN READ THEIR MINDS!
PLEASE, J'ONN, SLOW DOWN.
THE FACES... THEY LOOK SO FAMILIAR.
NO, WE CAN'T, SUPERMAN. THIS IS WHAT THE TOTALITY REQUIRES FROM US! A LEAP OF FAITH, A BELIEF THAT THERE IS SOMETHING GOOD AT THE HEART OF IT.
THAT'S RIGHT, MARTIAN, DON'T SLOW DOWN-- DO IT!
I HAVE TO KNOW, KAL.
THE MARTIAN'S MIND REACHES OUT TO THE BOUNDLESS ALIEN INTELLIGENCE BEFORE HIM, HE SHAPES IT WITH EVANGELICAL EARNESTNESS TO TURN THE NOISE INTO IMAGES HE CAN UNDERSTAND.
HE SEEKS COMFORT, HOPE, UNDERSTANDING BENEATH THE VEIL...

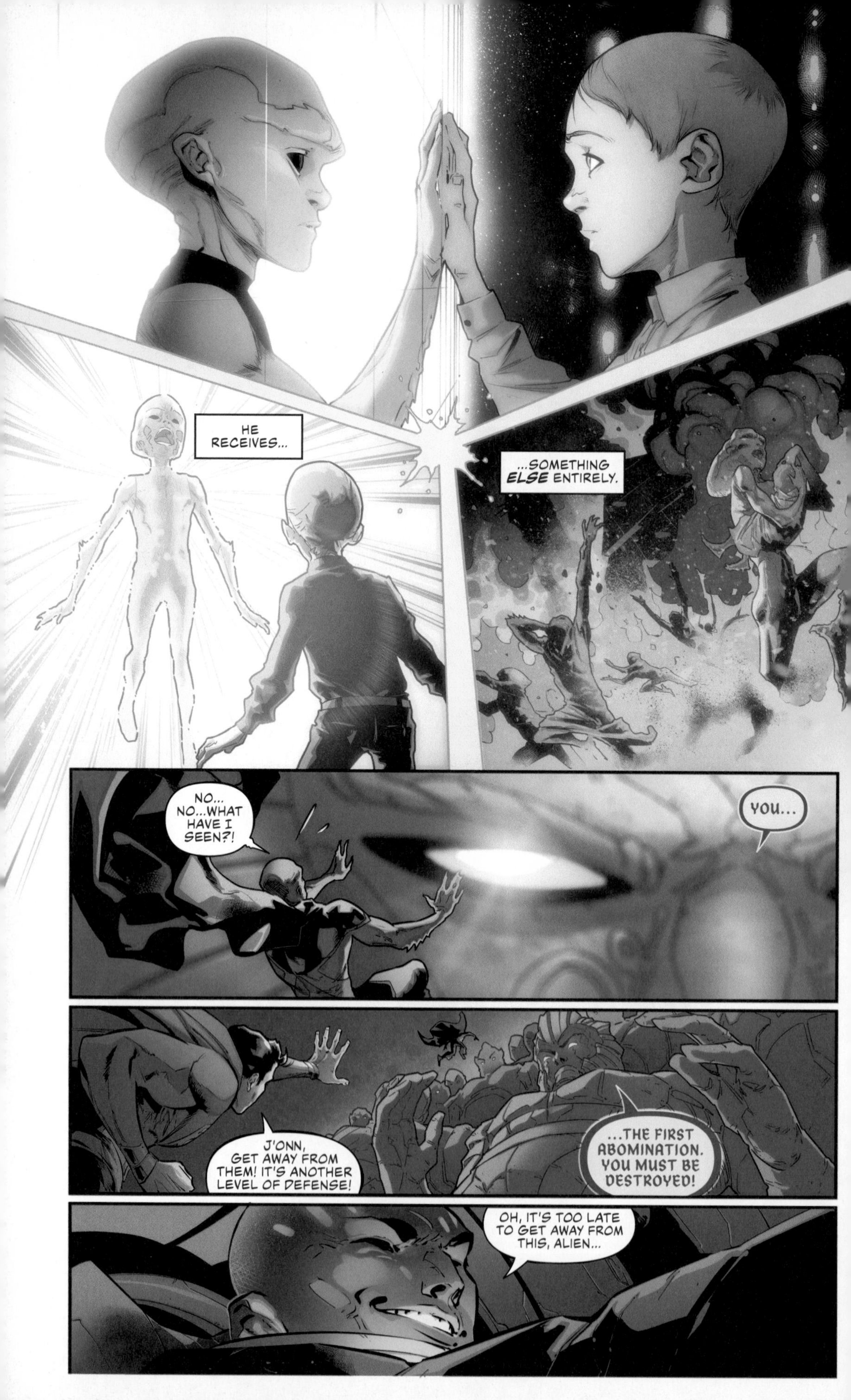

HE RECEIVES...
...SOMETHING ELSE ENTIRELY.
NO... NO...WHAT HAVE I SEEN?!
YOU...
J'ONN, GET AWAY FROM THEM! IT'S ANOTHER LEVEL OF DEFENSE!
...THE FIRST ABOMINATION. YOU MUST BE DESTROYED!
OH, IT'S TOO LATE TO GET AWAY FROM THIS, ALIEN...

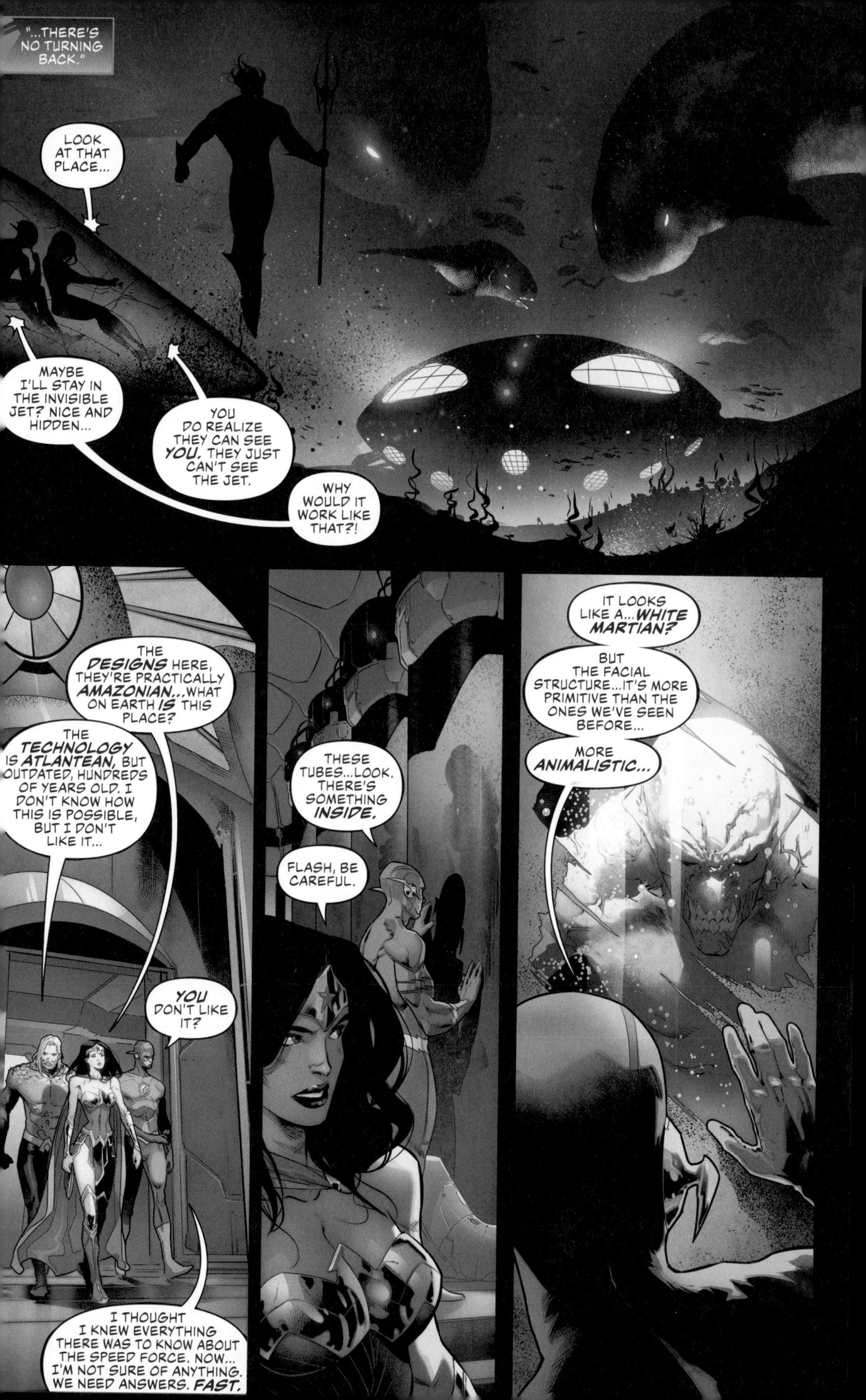
"...THERE'S NO TURNING BACK."
LOOK AT THAT PLACE...
MAYBE I'LL STAY IN THE INVISIBLE JET? NICE AND HIDDEN...
YOU DO REALIZE THEY CAN SEE YOU. THEY JUST CAN'T SEE THE JET.
WHY WOULD IT WORK LIKE THAT?!
THE DESIGNS HERE, THEY'RE PRACTICALLY AMAZONIAN...WHAT ON EARTH IS THIS PLACE?
THE TECHNOLOGY IS ATLANTEAN, BUT OUTDATED, HUNDREDS OF YEARS OLD. I DON'T KNOW HOW THIS IS POSSIBLE, BUT I DON'T LIKE IT...
YOU DON'T LIKE IT?
I THOUGHT I KNEW EVERYTHING THERE WAS TO KNOW ABOUT THE SPEED FORCE. NOW... I'M NOT SURE OF ANYTHING. WE NEED ANSWERS. FAST.
THESE TUBES...LOOK. THERE'S SOMETHING INSIDE.
FLASH, BE CAREFUL.
IT LOOKS LIKE A...WHITE MARTIAN?
BUT THE FACIAL STRUCTURE...IT'S MORE PRIMITIVE THAN THE ONES WE'VE SEEN BEFORE...
MORE ANIMALISTIC...

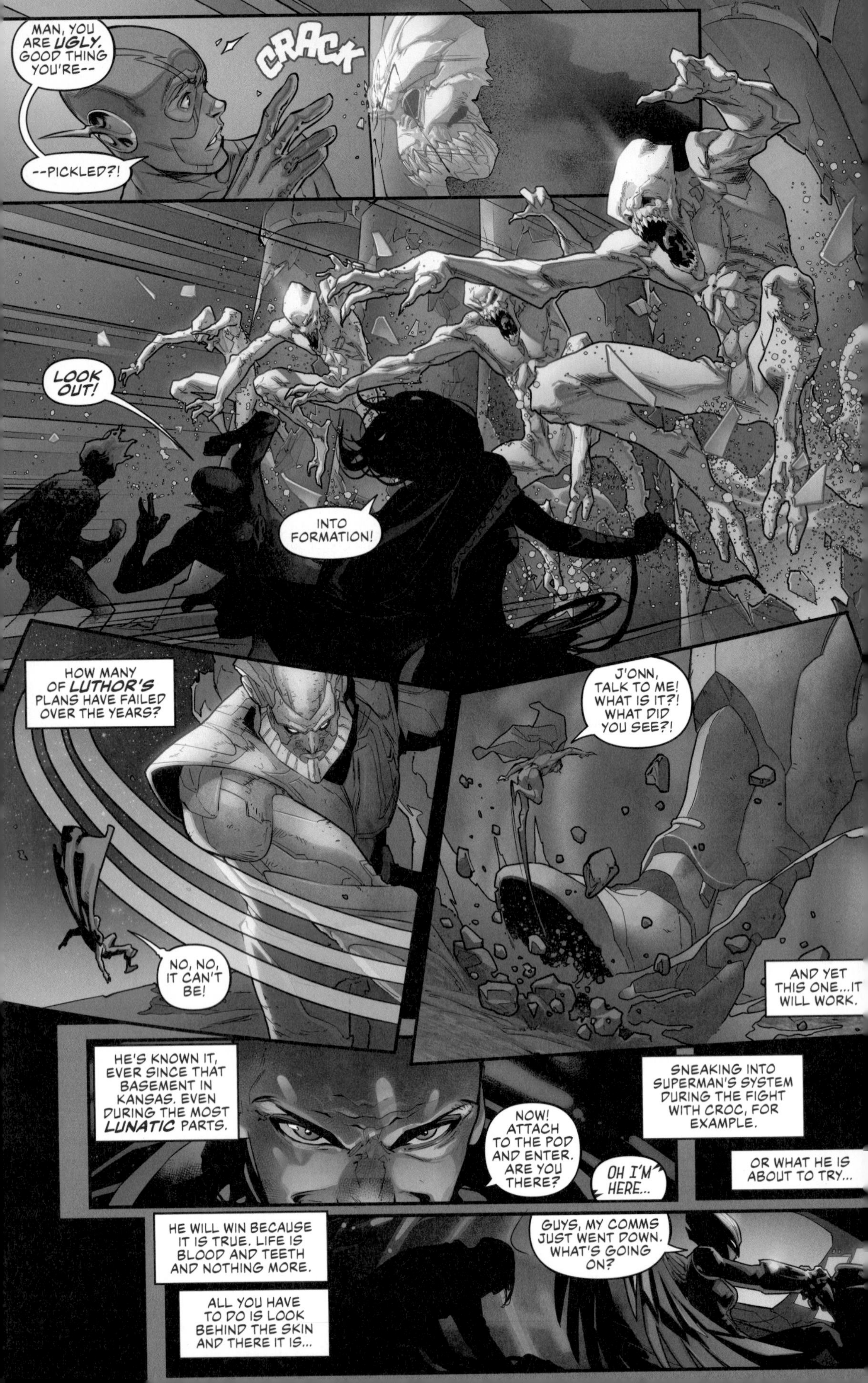
MAN, YOU ARE UGLY. GOOD THING YOU'RE--
--PICKLED?!
CRACK
LOOK OUT!
INTO FORMATION!
HOW MANY OF LUTHOR'S PLANS HAVE FAILED OVER THE YEARS?
NO, NO, IT CAN'T BE!
J'ONN, TALK TO ME! WHAT IS IT?! WHAT DID YOU SEE?!
AND YET THIS ONE...IT WILL WORK.
HE'S KNOWN IT, EVER SINCE THAT BASEMENT IN KANSAS. EVEN DURING THE MOST LUNATIC PARTS.
NOW! ATTACH TO THE POD AND ENTER. ARE YOU THERE?
OH I'M HERE...
SNEAKING INTO SUPERMAN'S SYSTEM DURING THE FIGHT WITH CROC, FOR EXAMPLE.
OR WHAT HE IS ABOUT TO TRY...
HE WILL WIN BECAUSE IT IS TRUE. LIFE IS BLOOD AND TEETH AND NOTHING MORE.
ALL YOU HAVE TO DO IS LOOK BEHIND THE SKIN AND THERE IT IS...
GUYS, MY COMMS JUST WENT DOWN. WHAT'S GOING ON?

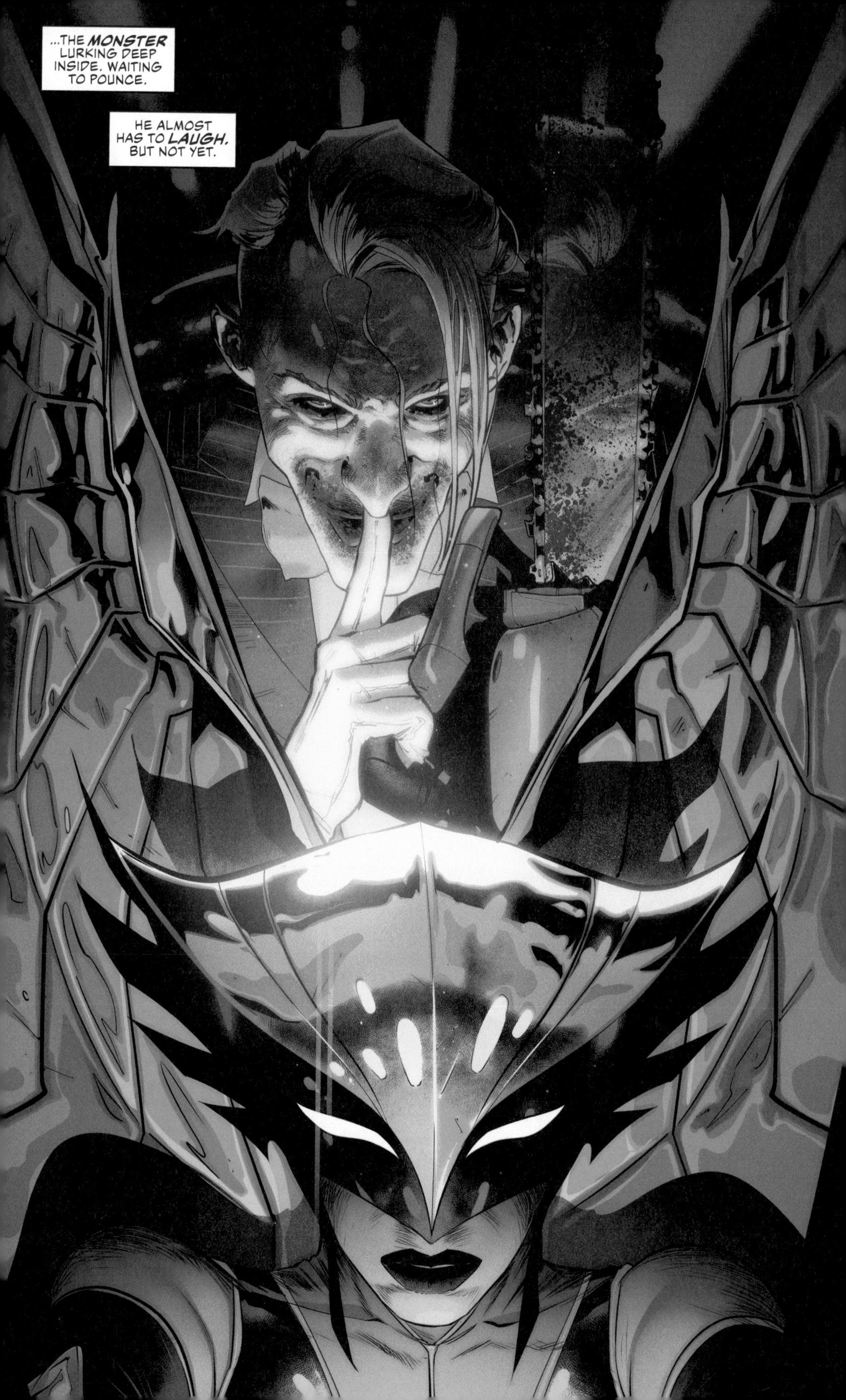
...THE MONSTER LURKING DEEP INSIDE. WAITING TO POUNCE.
HE ALMOST HAS TO LAUGH. BUT NOT YET.

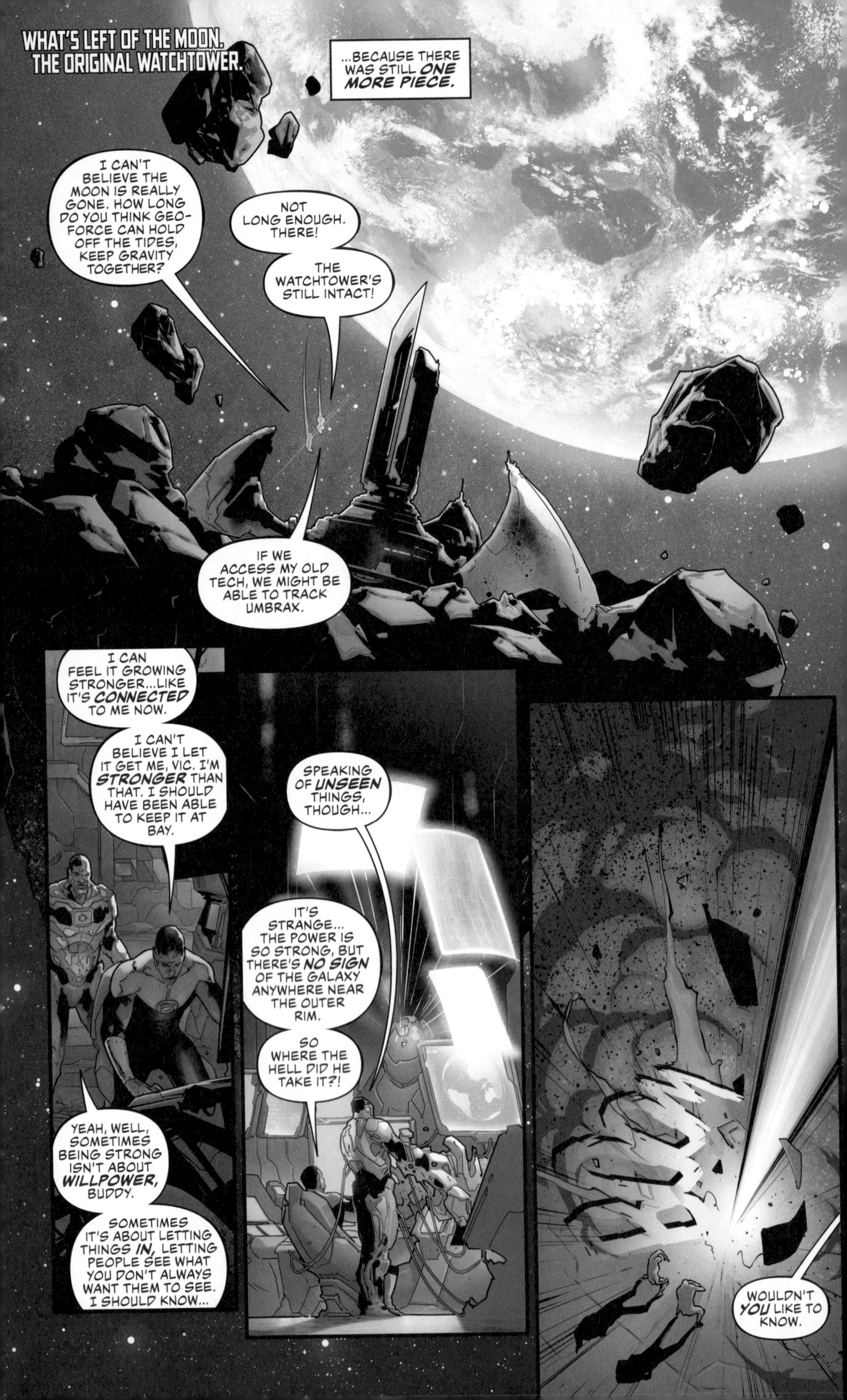
WHAT'S LEFT OF THE MOON. THE ORIGINAL WATCHTOWER.
...BECAUSE THERE WAS STILL ONE MORE PIECE.
I CAN'T BELIEVE THE MOON IS REALLY GONE. HOW LONG DO YOU THINK GEO-FORCE CAN HOLD OFF THE TIDES, KEEP GRAVITY TOGETHER?
NOT LONG ENOUGH. THERE!
THE WATCHTOWER'S STILL INTACT!
IF WE ACCESS MY OLD TECH, WE MIGHT BE ABLE TO TRACK UMBRAX.
I CAN FEEL IT GROWING STRONGER...LIKE IT'S CONNECTED TO ME NOW.
I CAN'T BELIEVE I LET IT GET ME, VIC. I'M STRONGER THAN THAT. I SHOULD HAVE BEEN ABLE TO KEEP IT AT BAY.
YEAH, WELL, SOMETIMES BEING STRONG ISN'T ABOUT WILLPOWER, BUDDY.
SOMETIMES IT'S ABOUT LETTING THINGS IN, LETTING PEOPLE SEE WHAT YOU DON'T ALWAYS WANT THEM TO SEE. I SHOULD KNOW...
SPEAKING OF UNSEEN THINGS, THOUGH...
IT'S STRANGE... THE POWER IS SO STRONG, BUT THERE'S NO SIGN OF THE GALAXY ANYWHERE NEAR THE OUTER RIM.
SO WHERE THE HELL DID HE TAKE IT?!
WOULDN'T YOU LIKE TO KNOW.

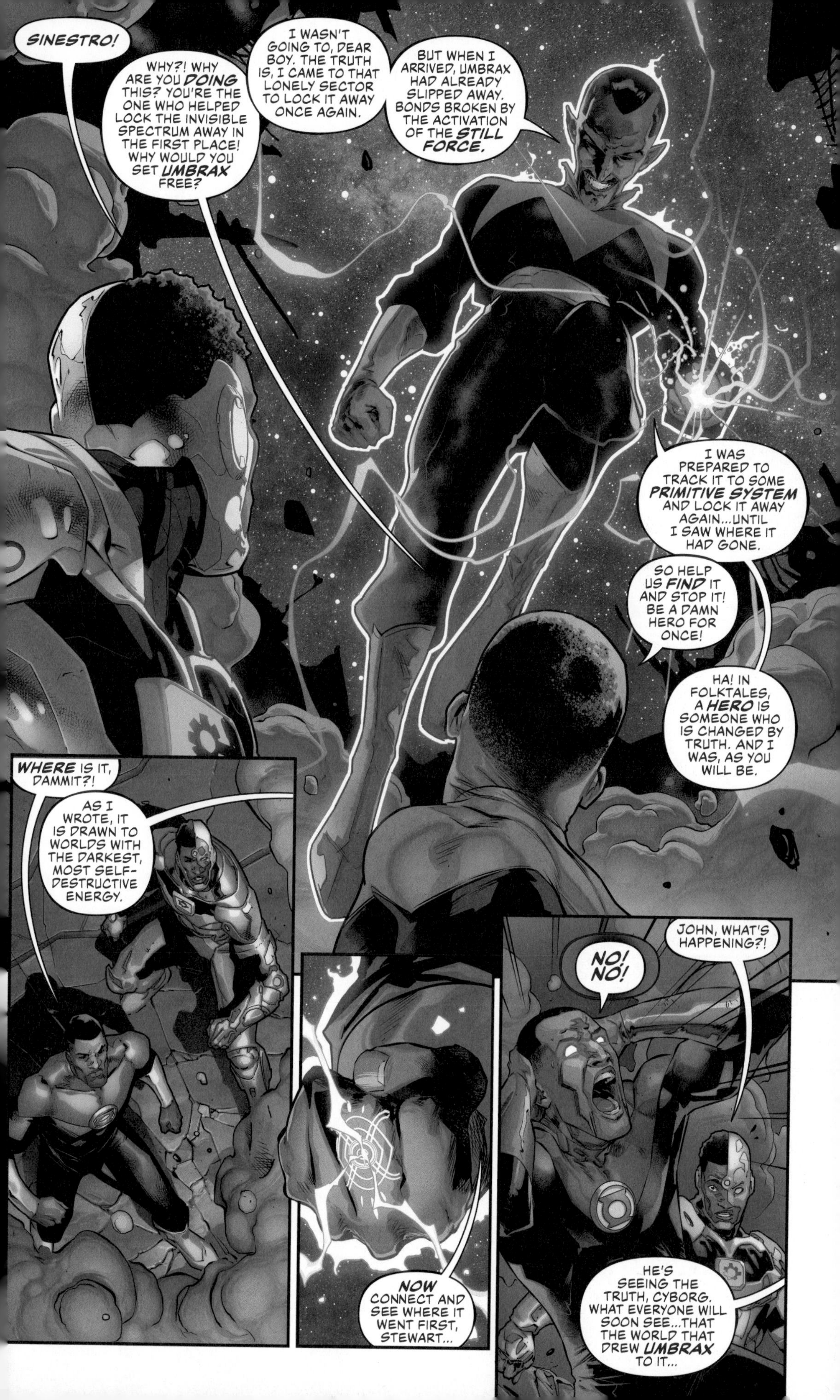
SINESTRO!
WHY?! WHY ARE YOU DOING THIS? YOU'RE THE ONE WHO HELPED LOCK THE INVISIBLE SPECTRUM AWAY IN THE FIRST PLACE! WHY WOULD YOU SET UMBRAX FREE?
I WASN'T GOING TO, DEAR BOY. THE TRUTH IS, I CAME TO THAT LONELY SECTOR TO LOCK IT AWAY ONCE AGAIN.
BUT WHEN I ARRIVED, UMBRAX HAD ALREADY SLIPPED AWAY. BONDS BROKEN BY THE ACTIVATION OF THE STILL FORCE.
I WAS PREPARED TO TRACK IT TO SOME PRIMITIVE SYSTEM AND LOCK IT AWAY AGAIN...UNTIL I SAW WHERE IT HAD GONE.
SO HELP US FIND IT AND STOP IT! BE A DAMN HERO FOR ONCE!
HA! IN FOLKTALES, A HERO IS SOMEONE WHO IS CHANGED BY TRUTH. AND I WAS, AS YOU WILL BE.
WHERE IS IT, DAMMIT?!
AS I WROTE, IT IS DRAWN TO WORLDS WITH THE DARKEST, MOST SELF-DESTRUCTIVE ENERGY.
NOW CONNECT AND SEE WHERE IT WENT FIRST, STEWART...
NO! NO!
JOHN, WHAT'S HAPPENING?!
HE'S SEEING THE TRUTH, CYBORG. WHAT EVERYONE WILL SOON SEE...THAT THE WORLD THAT DREW UMBRAX TO IT...

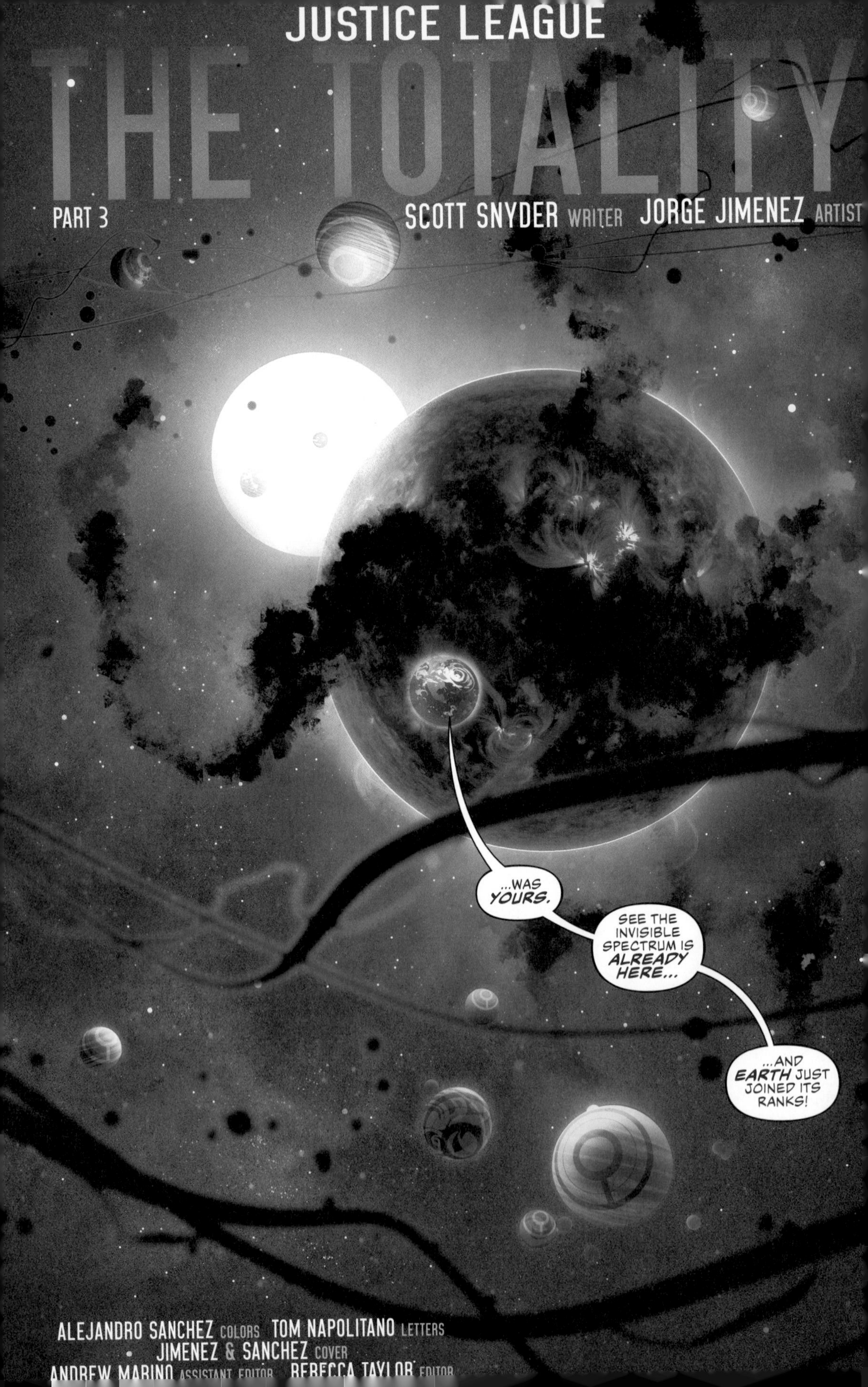
JUSTICE LEAGUE
THE TOTALITY
PART 3
SCOTT SNYDER WRITER JORGE JIMENEZ ARTIST
...WAS YOURS.
SEE THE INVISIBLE SPECTRUM IS ALREADY HERE...
...AND EARTH JUST JOINED ITS RANKS!
ALEJANDRO SANCHEZ COLORS TOM NAPOLITANO LETTERS
JIMENEZ & SANCHEZ COVER
ANDREW MARINO ASSISTANT EDITOR REBECCA TAYLOR EDITOR

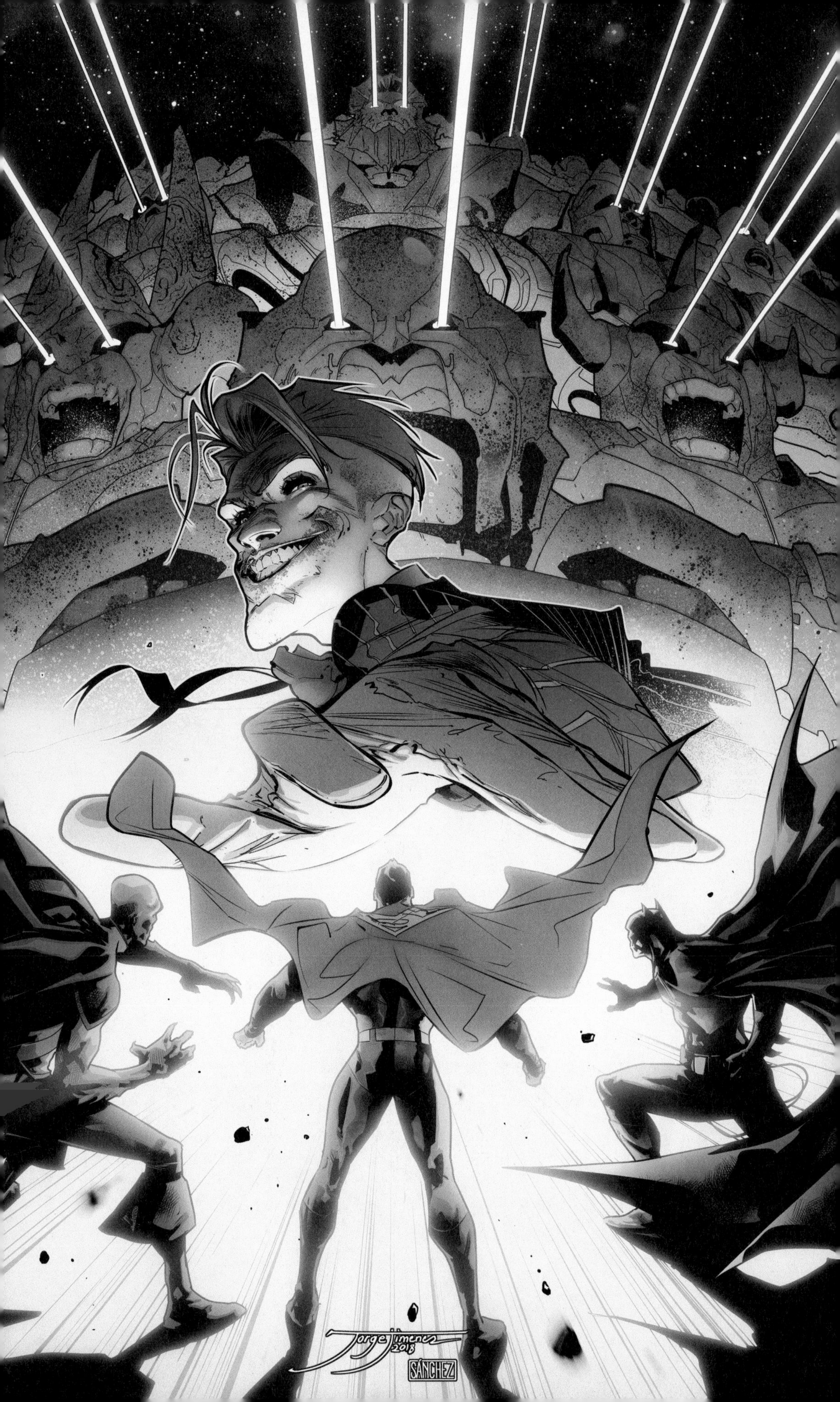
Jorge Jimenez 2018
SÁNCHEZ

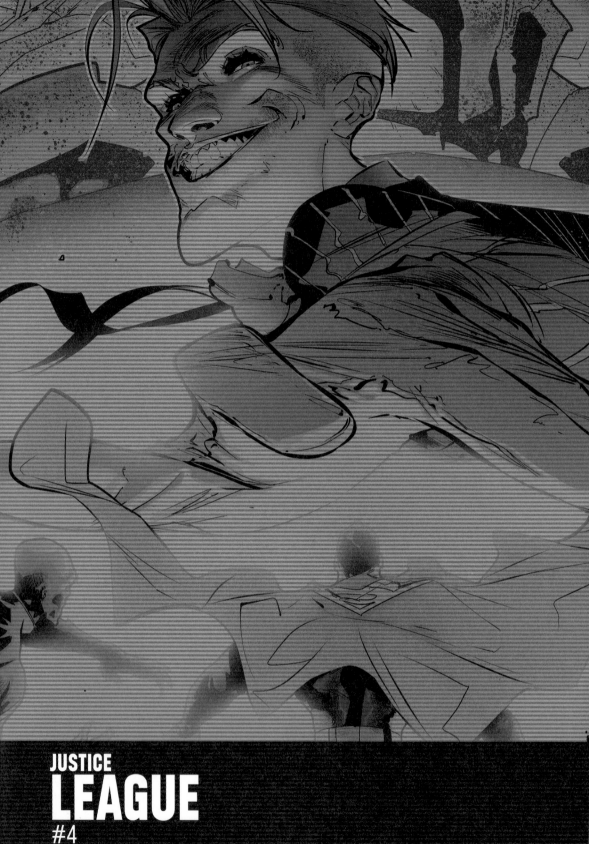

JUSTICE
LEAGUE
#4

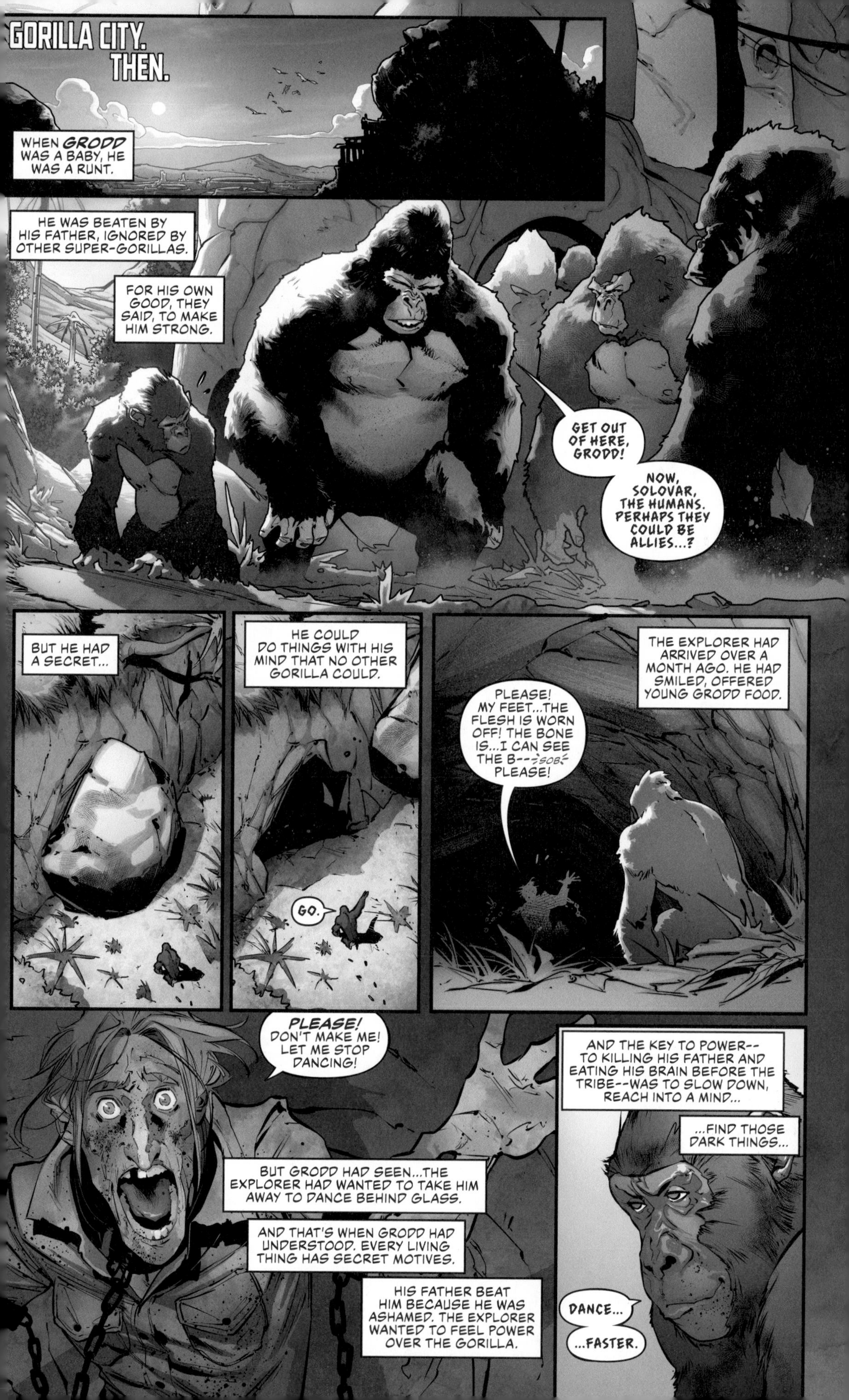
GORILLA CITY.
THEN.
WHEN GRODD WAS A BABY, HE WAS A RUNT.
HE WAS BEATEN BY HIS FATHER, IGNORED BY OTHER SUPER-GORILLAS.
FOR HIS OWN GOOD, THEY SAID, TO MAKE HIM STRONG.
GET OUT OF HERE, GRODD!
NOW, SOLOVAR, THE HUMANS. PERHAPS THEY COULD BE ALLIES...?
BUT HE HAD A SECRET...
HE COULD DO THINGS WITH HIS MIND THAT NO OTHER GORILLA COULD.
GO.
THE EXPLORER HAD ARRIVED OVER A MONTH AGO. HE HAD SMILED, OFFERED YOUNG GRODD FOOD.
PLEASE! MY FEET...THE FLESH IS WORN OFF! THE BONE IS...I CAN SEE THE B-- SOB PLEASE!
PLEASE! DON'T MAKE ME! LET ME STOP DANCING!
BUT GRODD HAD SEEN...THE EXPLORER HAD WANTED TO TAKE HIM AWAY TO DANCE BEHIND GLASS.
AND THAT'S WHEN GRODD HAD UNDERSTOOD. EVERY LIVING THING HAS SECRET MOTIVES.
HIS FATHER BEAT HIM BECAUSE HE WAS ASHAMED. THE EXPLORER WANTED TO FEEL POWER OVER THE GORILLA.
AND THE KEY TO POWER--TO KILLING HIS FATHER AND EATING HIS BRAIN BEFORE THE TRIBE--WAS TO SLOW DOWN, REACH INTO A MIND...
...FIND THOSE DARK THINGS...
DANCE...
...FASTER.

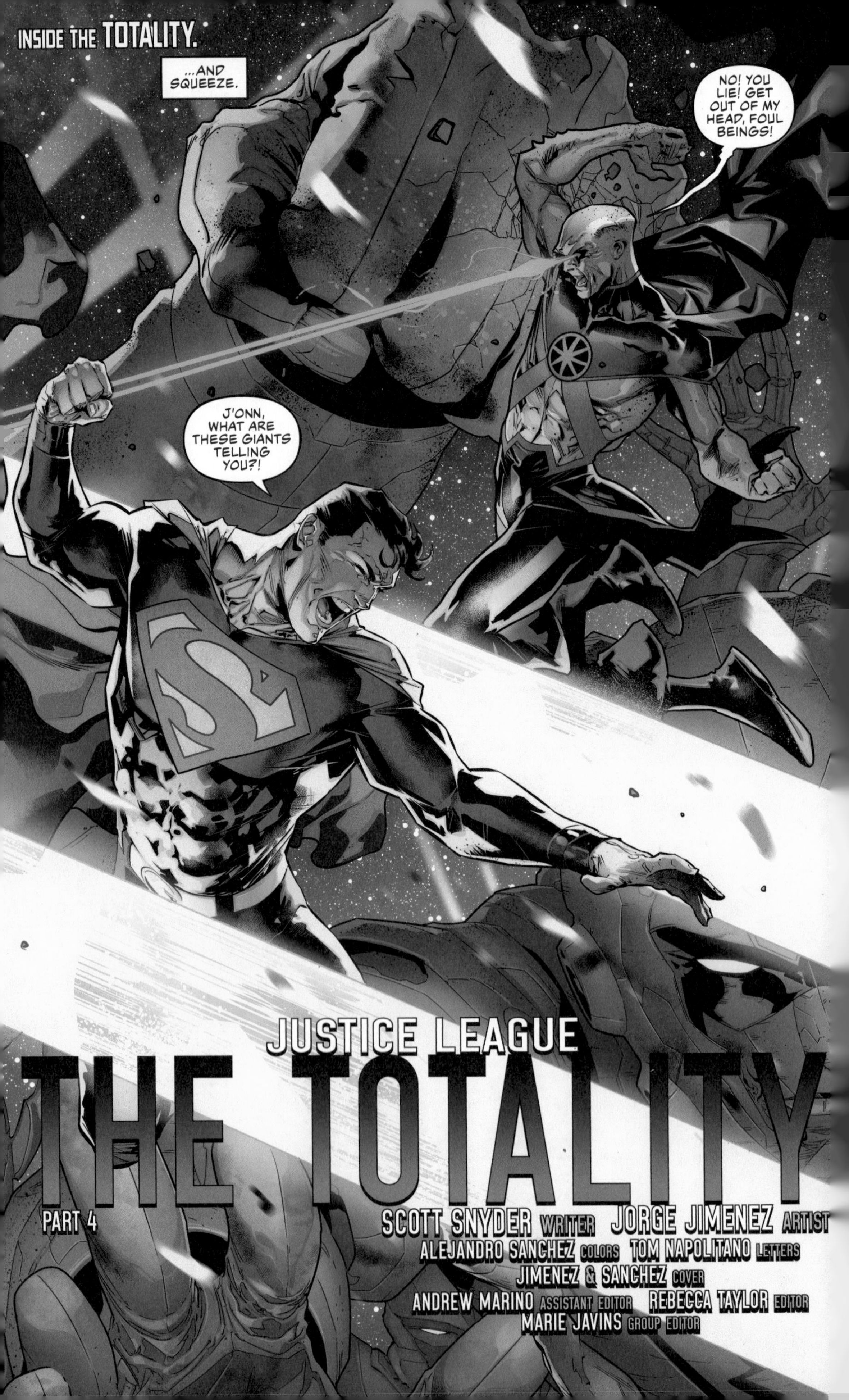
INSIDE THE TOTALITY.
...AND SQUEEZE.
NO! YOU LIE! GET OUT OF MY HEAD, FOUL BEINGS!
J'ONN, WHAT ARE THESE GIANTS TELLING YOU?!
JUSTICE LEAGUE
THE TOTALITY
PART 4
SCOTT SNYDER WRITER JORGE JIMENEZ ARTIST
ALEJANDRO SANCHEZ COLORS TOM NAPOLITANO LETTERS
JIMENEZ & SANCHEZ COVER
ANDREW MARINO ASSISTANT EDITOR REBECCA TAYLOR EDITOR
MARIE JAVINS GROUP EDITOR

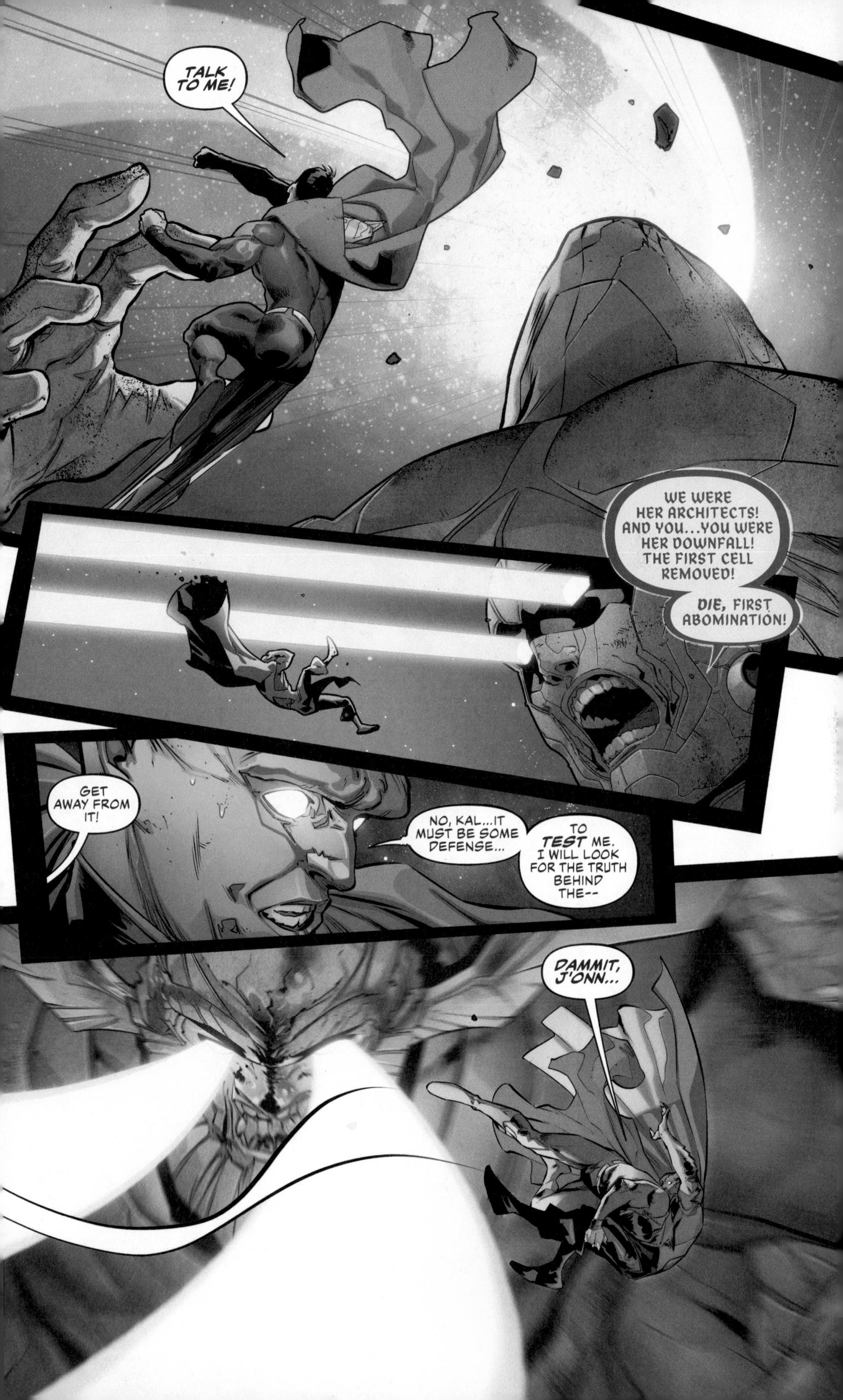
TALK TO ME!
WE WERE HER ARCHITECTS! AND YOU...YOU WERE HER DOWNFALL! THE FIRST CELL REMOVED!
DIE, FIRST ABOMINATION!
GET AWAY FROM IT!
NO, KAL...IT MUST BE SOME DEFENSE...
TO TEST ME. I WILL LOOK FOR THE TRUTH BEHIND THE--
DAMMIT, J'ONN...

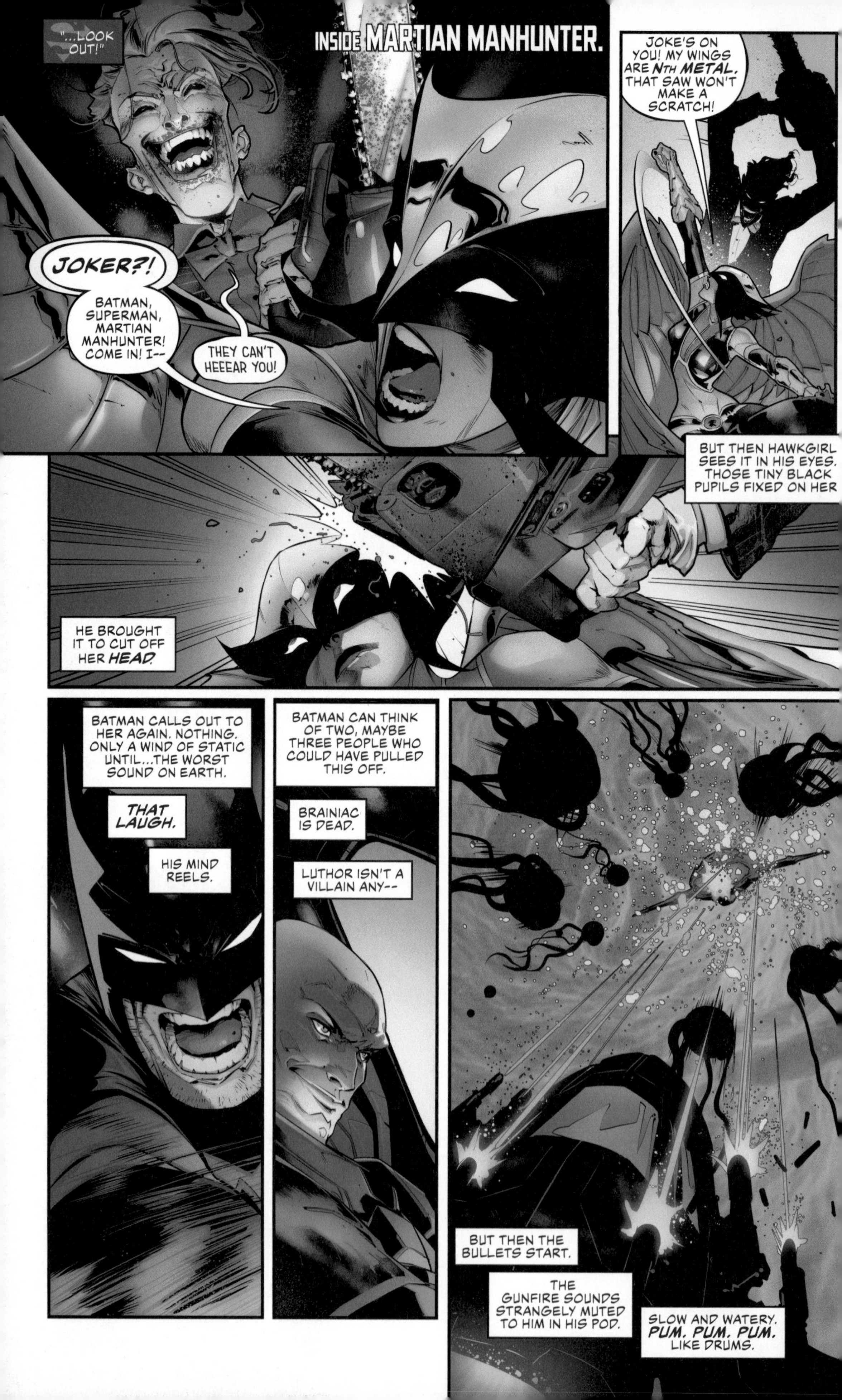

"...LOOK OUT!"
INSIDE MARTIAN MANHUNTER.
JOKER?!
BATMAN, SUPERMAN, MARTIAN MANHUNTER! COME IN! I--
THEY CAN'T HEEEAR YOU!
JOKE'S ON YOU! MY WINGS ARE NTH METAL. THAT SAW WON'T MAKE A SCRATCH!
BUT THEN HAWKGIRL SEES IT IN HIS EYES. THOSE TINY BLACK PUPILS FIXED ON HER
HE BROUGHT IT TO CUT OFF HER HEAD.
BATMAN CALLS OUT TO HER AGAIN. NOTHING. ONLY A WIND OF STATIC UNTIL...THE WORST SOUND ON EARTH.
THAT LAUGH.
HIS MIND REELS.
BATMAN CAN THINK OF TWO, MAYBE THREE PEOPLE WHO COULD HAVE PULLED THIS OFF.
BRAINIAC IS DEAD.
LUTHOR ISN'T A VILLAIN ANY--
BUT THEN THE BULLETS START.
THE GUNFIRE SOUNDS STRANGELY MUTED TO HIM IN HIS POD.
SLOW AND WATERY. PUM. PUM. PUM. LIKE DRUMS.

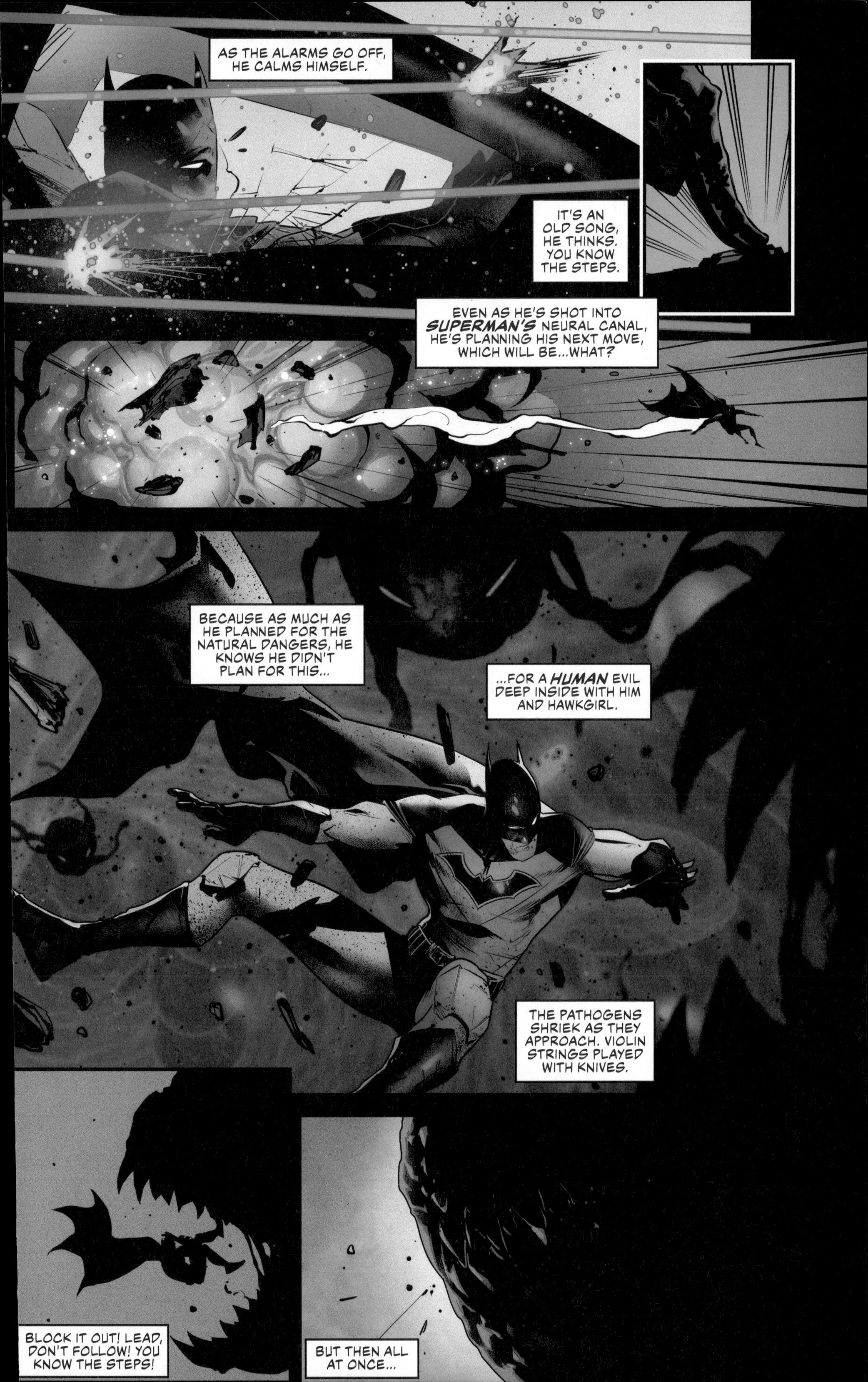
AS THE ALARMS GO OFF, HE CALMS HIMSELF.
IT'S AN OLD SONG, HE THINKS. YOU KNOW THE STEPS.
EVEN AS HE'S SHOT INTO SUPERMAN'S NEURAL CANAL, HE'S PLANNING HIS NEXT MOVE, WHICH WILL BE...WHAT?
BECAUSE AS MUCH AS HE PLANNED FOR THE NATURAL DANGERS, HE KNOWS HE DIDN'T PLAN FOR THIS...
...FOR A HUMAN EVIL DEEP INSIDE WITH HIM AND HAWKGIRL.
THE PATHOGENS SHRIEK AS THEY APPROACH. VIOLIN STRINGS PLAYED WITH KNIVES.
BLOCK IT OUT! LEAD, DON'T FOLLOW! YOU KNOW THE STEPS!
BUT THEN ALL AT ONCE...

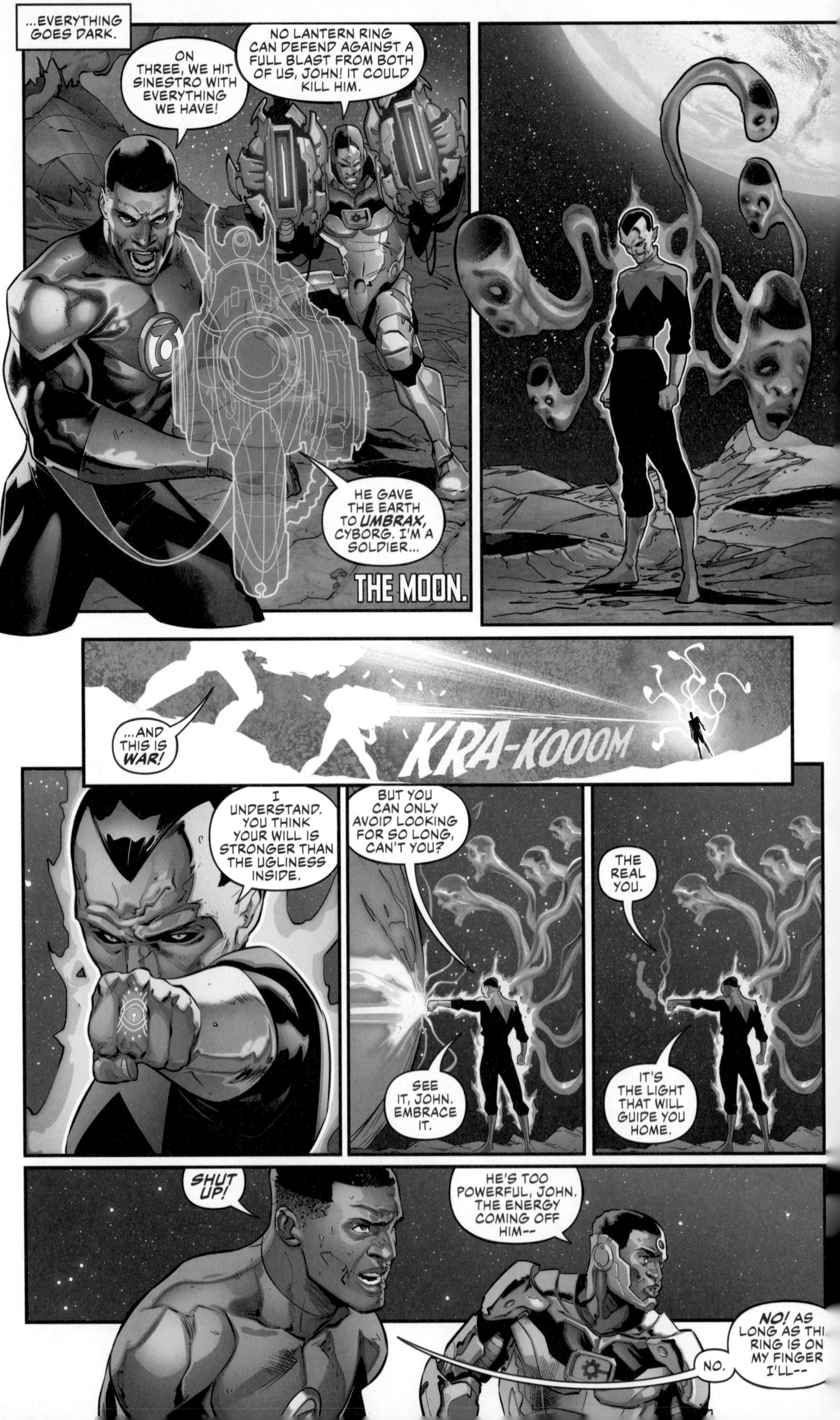
...EVERYTHING GOES DARK.
ON THREE, WE HIT SINESTRO WITH EVERYTHING WE HAVE!
NO LANTERN RING CAN DEFEND AGAINST A FULL BLAST FROM BOTH OF US, JOHN! IT COULD KILL HIM.
HE GAVE THE EARTH TO UMBRAX, CYBORG. I'M A SOLDIER...
THE MOON.
...AND THIS IS WAR!
KRA-KOOOM
I UNDERSTAND. YOUR THINK YOUR WILL IS STRONGER THAN THE UGLINESS INSIDE.
BUT YOU CAN ONLY AVOID LOOKING FOR SO LONG, CAN'T YOU?
SEE IT, JOHN. EMBRACE IT.
THE REAL YOU.
IT'S THE LIGHT THAT WILL GUIDE YOU HOME.
SHUT UP!
HE'S TOO POWERFUL, JOHN. THE ENERGY COMING OFF HIM--
NO.
NO! AS LONG AS THI RING IS ON MY FINGER I'LL--

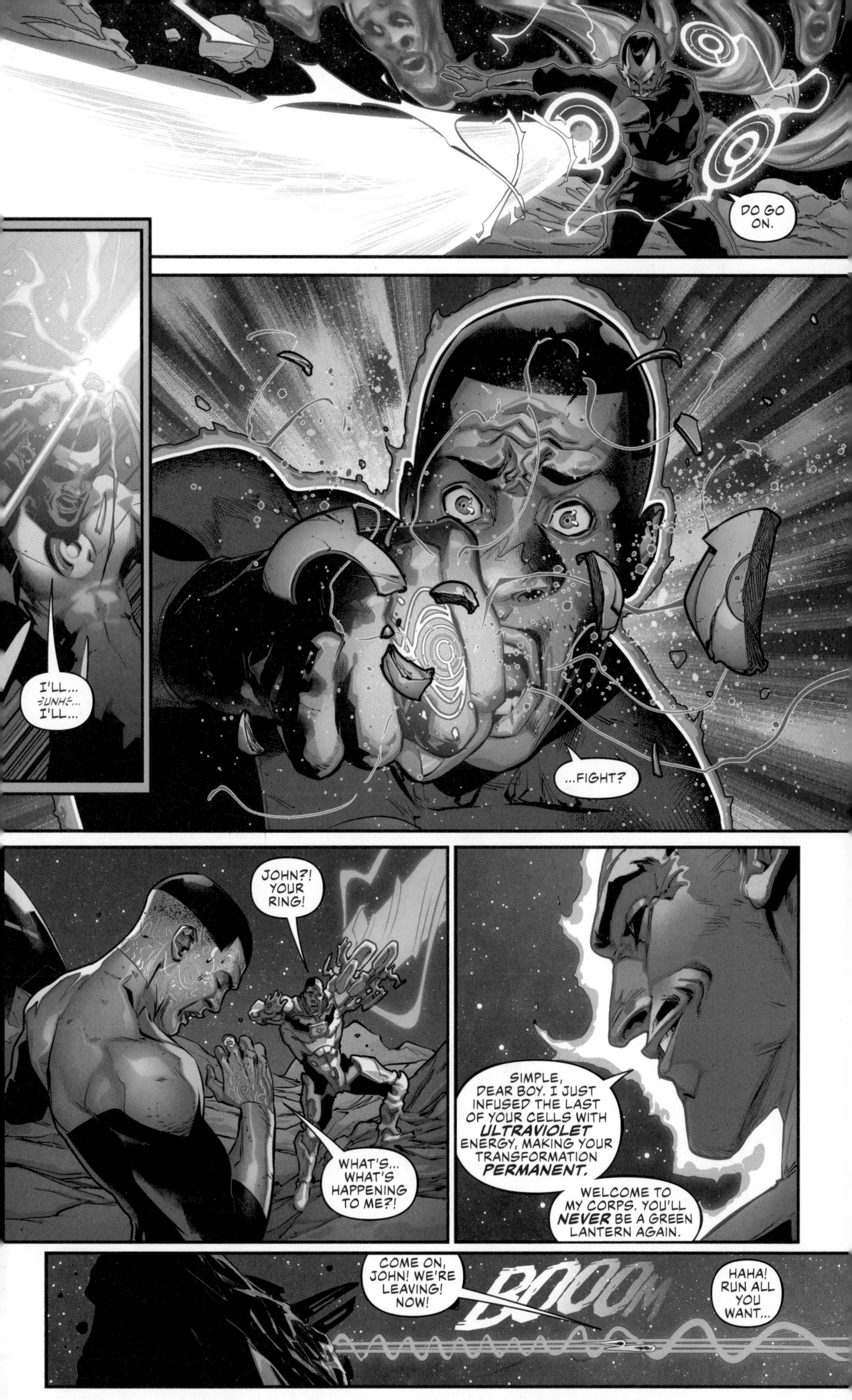

DO GO ON.
I'LL... UNH... I'LL...
...FIGHT?
JOHN?! YOUR RING!
WHAT'S... WHAT'S HAPPENING TO ME?!
SIMPLE, DEAR BOY. I JUST INFUSED THE LAST OF YOUR CELLS WITH ULTRAVIOLET ENERGY, MAKING YOUR TRANSFORMATION PERMANENT.
WELCOME TO MY CORPS. YOU'LL NEVER BE A GREEN LANTERN AGAIN.
COME ON, JOHN! WE'RE LEAVING! NOW!
BOOOM
HAHA! RUN ALL YOU WANT...

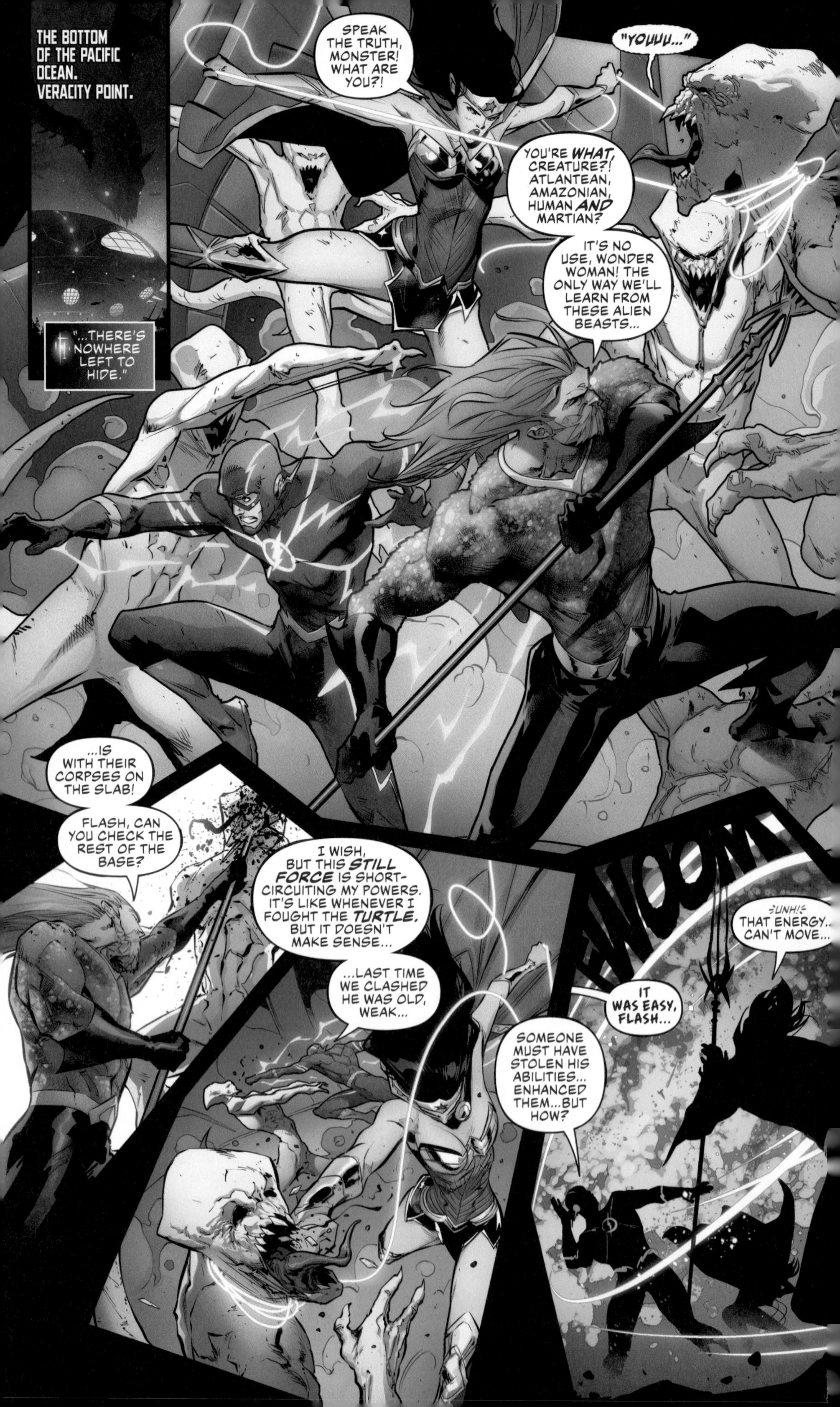

THE BOTTOM OF THE PACIFIC OCEAN. VERACITY POINT.
"...THERE'S NOWHERE LEFT TO HIDE."
SPEAK THE TRUTH, MONSTER! WHAT ARE YOU?!
"YOUUU..."
YOU'RE WHAT, CREATURE?! ATLANTEAN, AMAZONIAN, HUMAN AND MARTIAN?
IT'S NO USE, WONDER WOMAN! THE ONLY WAY WE'LL LEARN FROM THESE ALIEN BEASTS...
...IS WITH THEIR CORPSES ON THE SLAB!
FLASH, CAN YOU CHECK THE REST OF THE BASE?
I WISH, BUT THIS STILL FORCE IS SHORT-CIRCUITING MY POWERS. IT'S LIKE WHENEVER I FOUGHT THE TURTLE. BUT IT DOESN'T MAKE SENSE...
...LAST TIME WE CLASHED HE WAS OLD, WEAK...
SOMEONE MUST HAVE STOLEN HIS ABILITIES... ENHANCED THEM...BUT HOW?
IT WAS EASY, FLASH...
WHOOM
UNH! THAT ENERGY.. CAN'T MOVE...

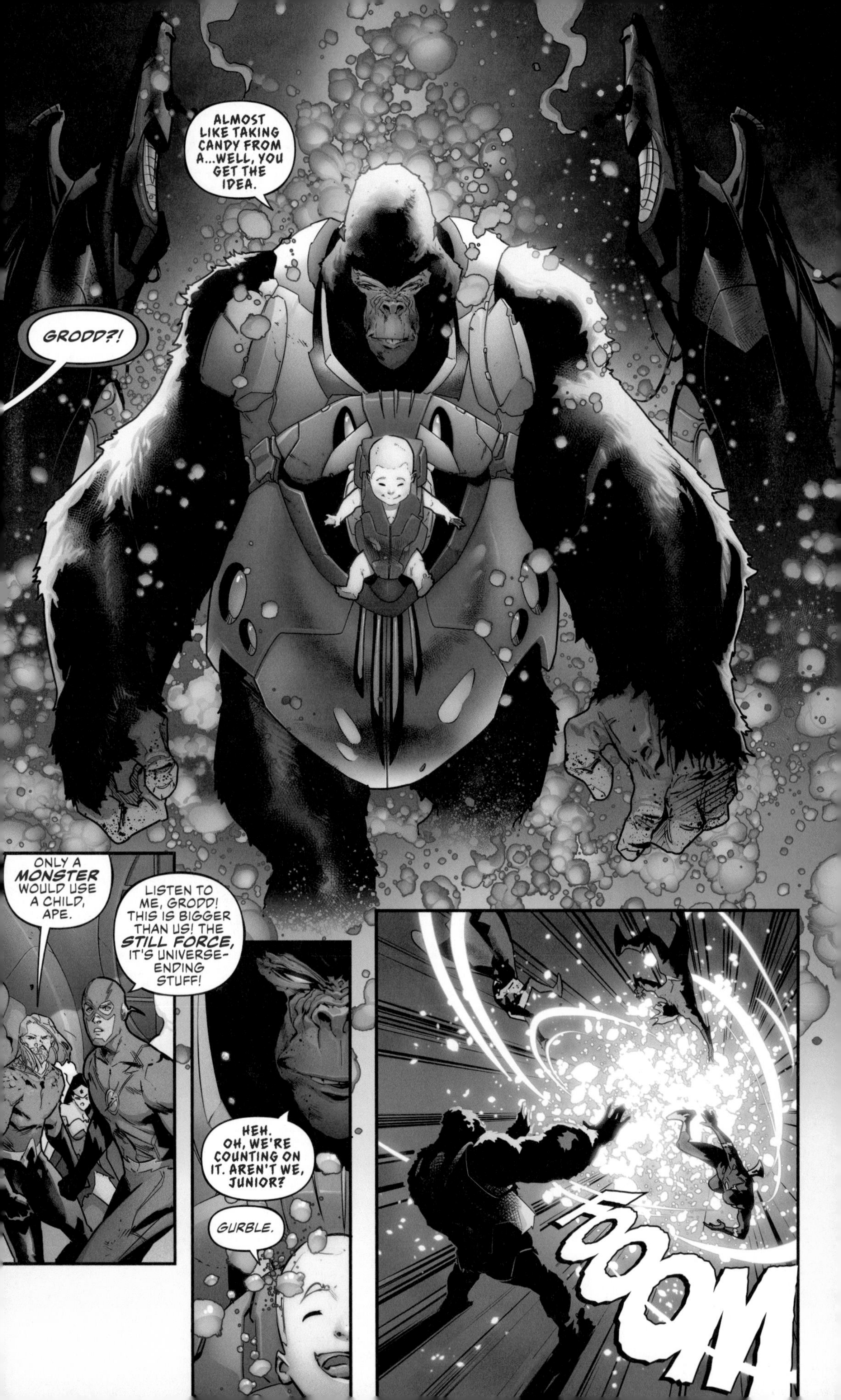
ALMOST LIKE TAKING CANDY FROM A...WELL, YOU GET THE IDEA.
GRODD?!
ONLY A MONSTER WOULD USE A CHILD, APE.
LISTEN TO ME, GRODD! THIS IS BIGGER THAN US! THE STILL FORCE, IT'S UNIVERSE-ENDING STUFF!
HEH. OH, WE'RE COUNTING ON IT. AREN'T WE, JUNIOR?
GURBLE.
WHOOOM

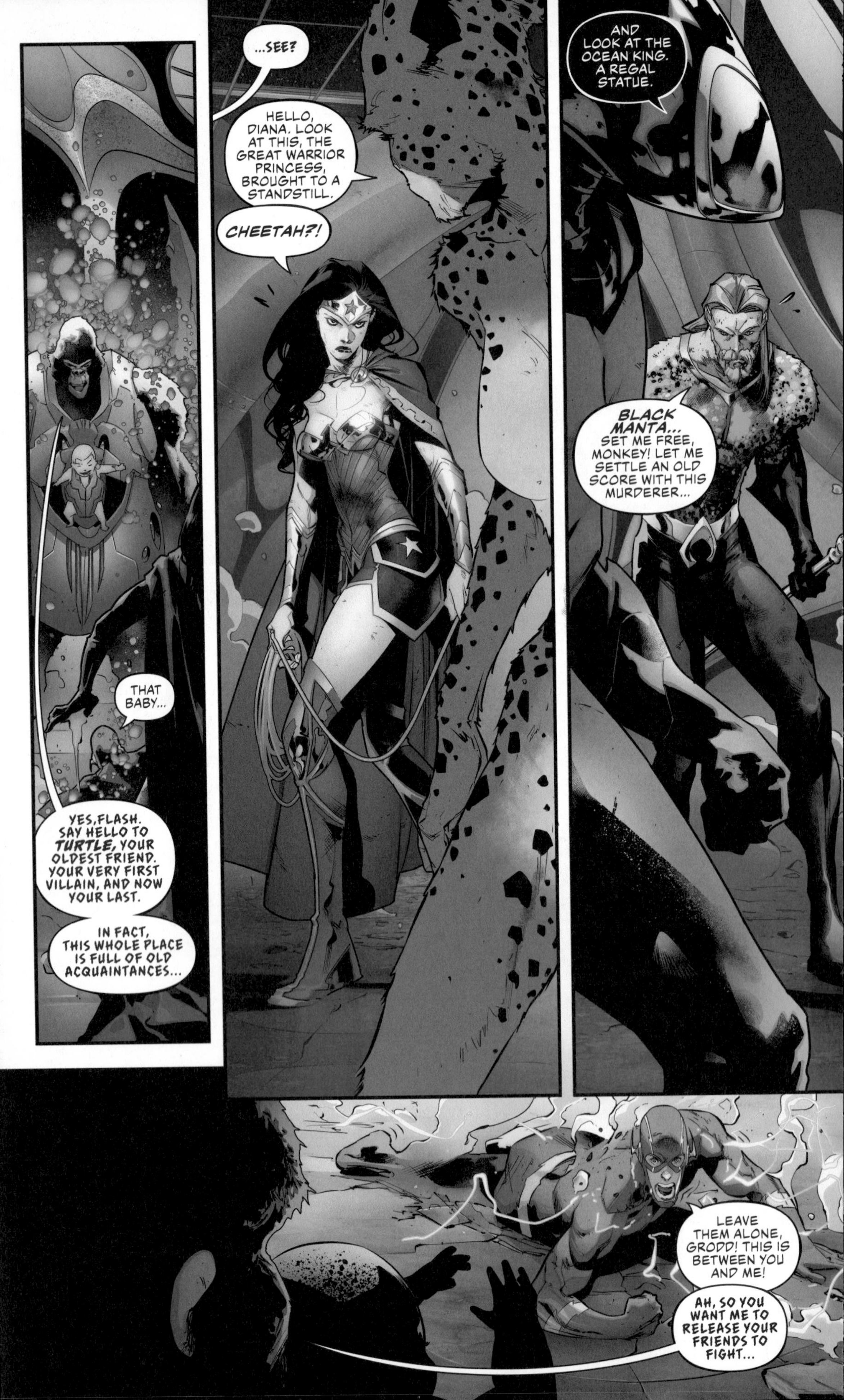

THAT BABY...
YES, FLASH. SAY HELLO TO TURTLE, YOUR OLDEST FRIEND. YOUR VERY FIRST VILLAIN, AND NOW YOUR LAST.
IN FACT, THIS WHOLE PLACE IS FULL OF OLD ACQUAINTANCES...
...SEE?
HELLO, DIANA. LOOK AT THIS, THE GREAT WARRIOR PRINCESS, BROUGHT TO A STANDSTILL.
CHEETAH?!
AND LOOK AT THE OCEAN KING. A REGAL STATUE.
BLACK MANTA... SET ME FREE, MONKEY! LET ME SETTLE AN OLD SCORE WITH THIS MURDERER...
LEAVE THEM ALONE, GRODD! THIS IS BETWEEN YOU AND ME!
AH, SO YOU WANT ME TO RELEASE YOUR FRIENDS TO FIGHT...

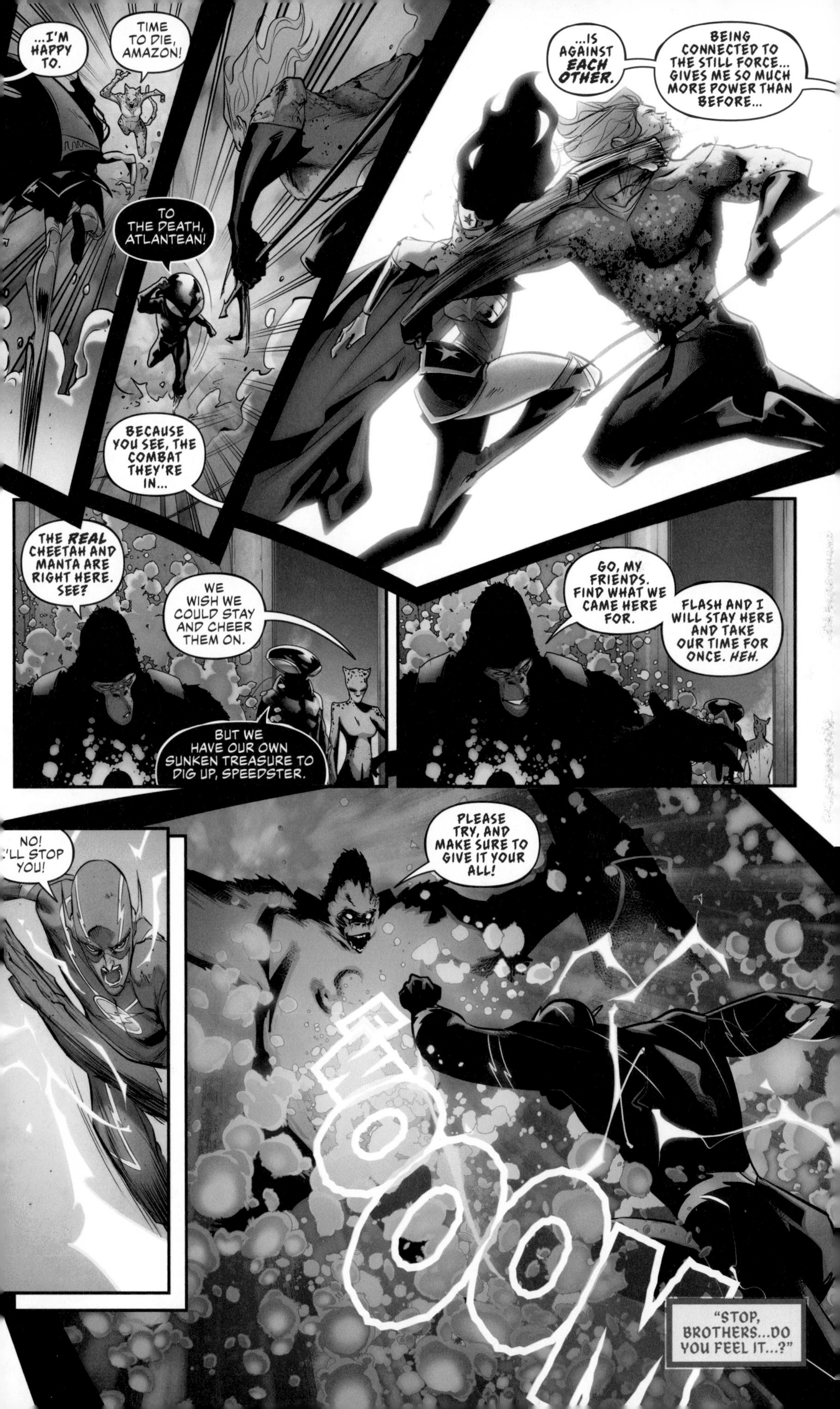
...I'M HAPPY TO.
TIME TO DIE, AMAZON!
TO THE DEATH, ATLANTEAN!
BECAUSE YOU SEE, THE COMBAT THEY'RE IN...
...IS AGAINST EACH OTHER.
BEING CONNECTED TO THE STILL FORCE... GIVES ME SO MUCH MORE POWER THAN BEFORE...
THE REAL CHEETAH AND MANTA ARE RIGHT HERE. SEE?
WE WISH WE COULD STAY AND CHEER THEM ON.
BUT WE HAVE OUR OWN SUNKEN TREASURE TO DIG UP, SPEEDSTER.
GO, MY FRIENDS. FIND WHAT WE CAME HERE FOR.
FLASH AND I WILL STAY HERE AND TAKE OUR TIME FOR ONCE. HEH.
NO! 'LL STOP YOU!
PLEASE TRY, AND MAKE SURE TO GIVE IT YOUR ALL!
"STOP, BROTHERS...DO YOU FEEL IT...?"

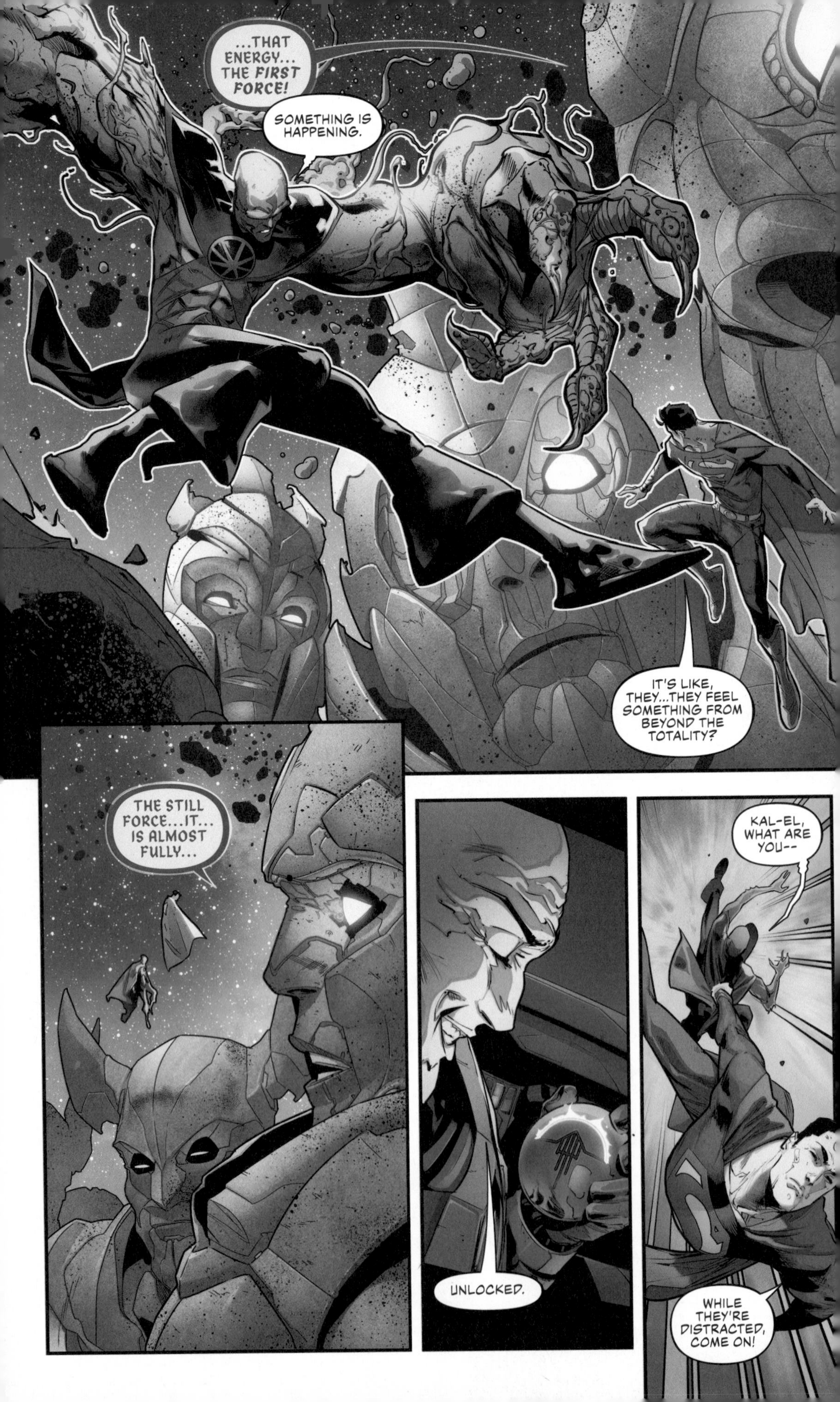
...THAT ENERGY... THE *FIRST FORCE!*
SOMETHING IS HAPPENING.
IT'S LIKE, THEY...THEY FEEL SOMETHING FROM BEYOND THE TOTALITY?
THE STILL FORCE...IT... IS ALMOST FULLY...
UNLOCKED.
KAL-EL, WHAT ARE YOU--
WHILE THEY'RE DISTRACTED, COME ON!

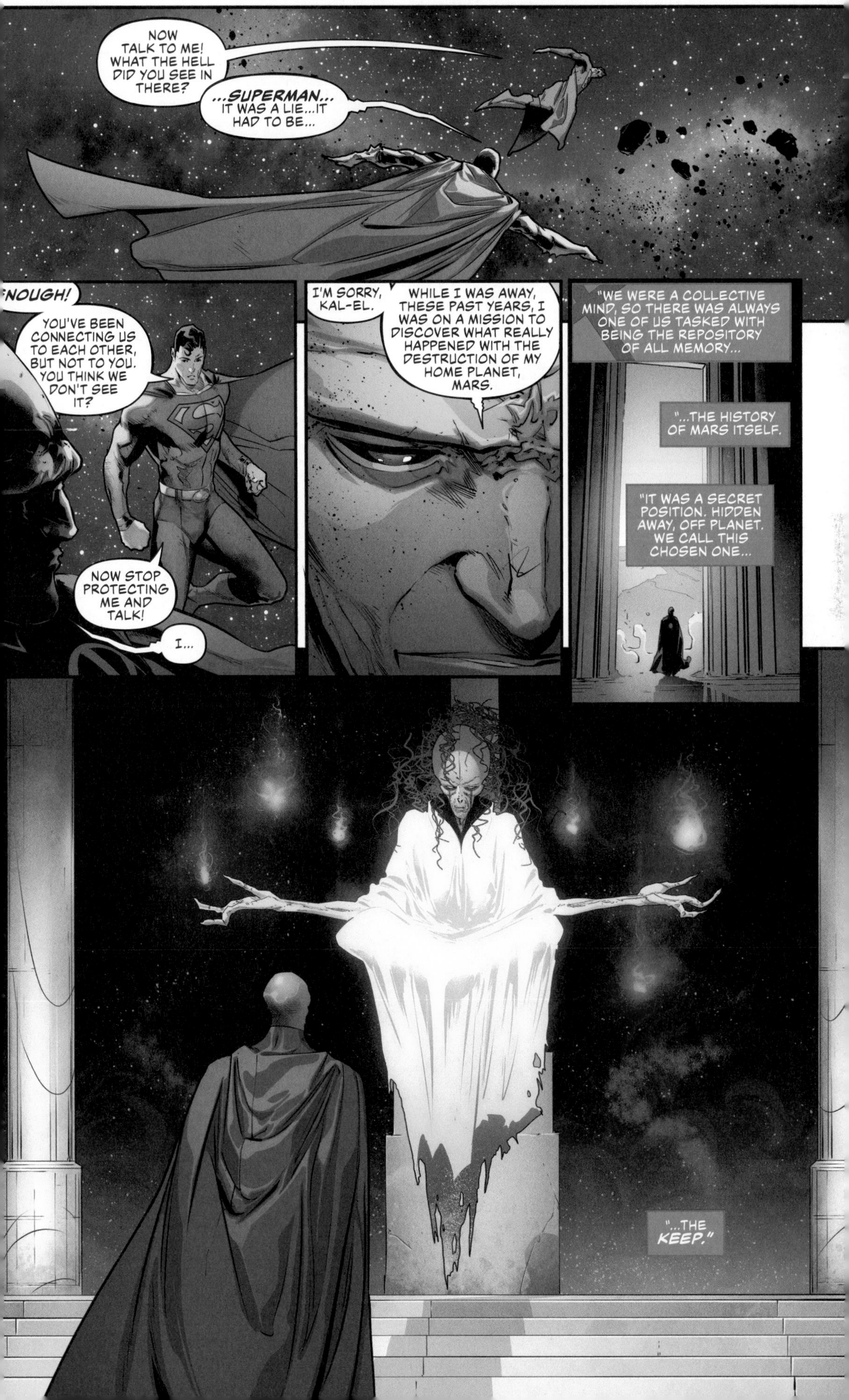

NOW TALK TO ME! WHAT THE HELL DID YOU SEE IN THERE?
...SUPERMAN... IT WAS A LIE...IT HAD TO BE...
ENOUGH!
YOU'VE BEEN CONNECTING US TO EACH OTHER, BUT NOT TO YOU. YOU THINK WE DON'T SEE IT?
NOW STOP PROTECTING ME AND TALK!
I...
I'M SORRY, KAL-EL.
WHILE I WAS AWAY, THESE PAST YEARS, I WAS ON A MISSION TO DISCOVER WHAT REALLY HAPPENED WITH THE DESTRUCTION OF MY HOME PLANET, MARS.
"WE WERE A COLLECTIVE MIND, SO THERE WAS ALWAYS ONE OF US TASKED WITH BEING THE REPOSITORY OF ALL MEMORY...
"...THE HISTORY OF MARS ITSELF.
"IT WAS A SECRET POSITION. HIDDEN AWAY, OFF PLANET. WE CALL THIS CHOSEN ONE...
"...THE KEEP."

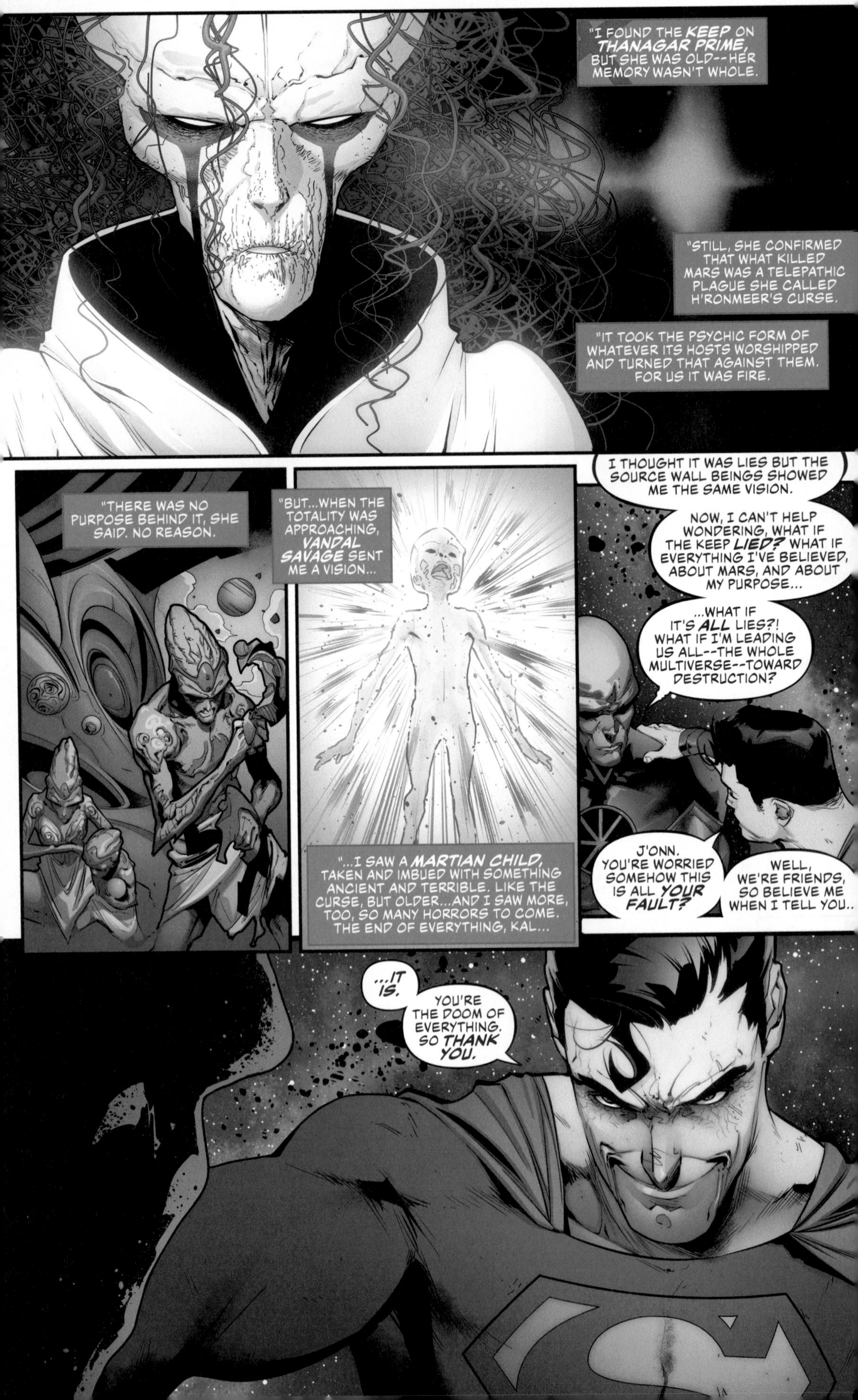
"I FOUND THE KEEP ON THANAGAR PRIME, BUT SHE WAS OLD--HER MEMORY WASN'T WHOLE.
"STILL, SHE CONFIRMED THAT WHAT KILLED MARS WAS A TELEPATHIC PLAGUE SHE CALLED H'RONMEER'S CURSE.
"IT TOOK THE PSYCHIC FORM OF WHATEVER ITS HOSTS WORSHIPPED AND TURNED THAT AGAINST THEM. FOR US IT WAS FIRE.
"THERE WAS NO PURPOSE BEHIND IT, SHE SAID. NO REASON.
"BUT...WHEN THE TOTALITY WAS APPROACHING, VANDAL SAVAGE SENT ME A VISION...
"...I SAW A MARTIAN CHILD, TAKEN AND IMBUED WITH SOMETHING ANCIENT AND TERRIBLE. LIKE THE CURSE, BUT OLDER...AND I SAW MORE, TOO, SO MANY HORRORS TO COME. THE END OF EVERYTHING, KAL...
I THOUGHT IT WAS LIES BUT THE SOURCE WALL BEINGS SHOWED ME THE SAME VISION.
NOW, I CAN'T HELP WONDERING, WHAT IF THE KEEP LIED? WHAT IF EVERYTHING I'VE BELIEVED, ABOUT MARS, AND ABOUT MY PURPOSE...
...WHAT IF IT'S ALL LIES?! WHAT IF I'M LEADING US ALL--THE WHOLE MULTIVERSE--TOWARD DESTRUCTION?
J'ONN. YOU'RE WORRIED SOMEHOW THIS IS ALL YOUR FAULT?
WELL, WE'RE FRIENDS, SO BELIEVE ME WHEN I TELL YOU...
...IT IS.
YOU'RE THE DOOM OF EVERYTHING. SO THANK YOU.

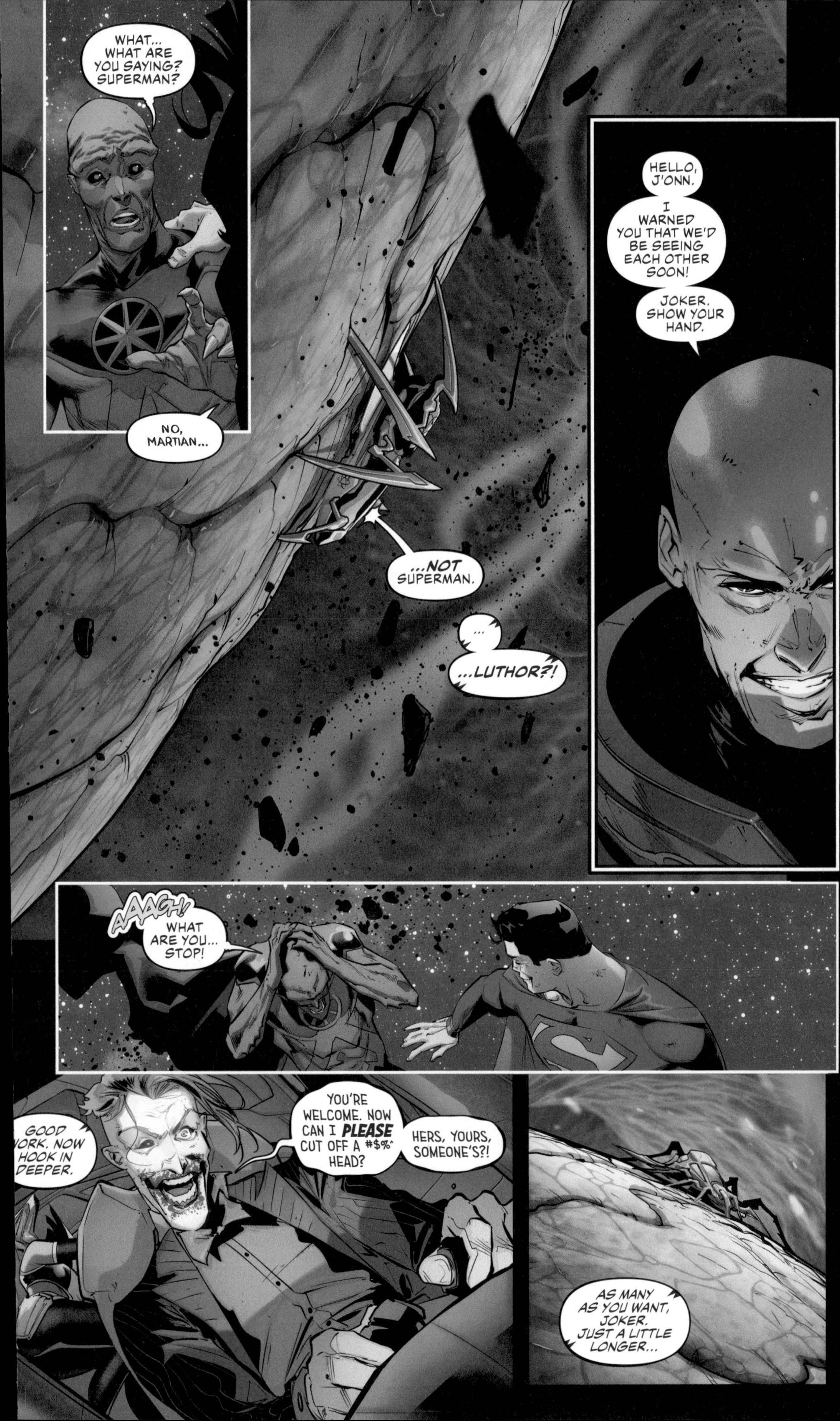
WHAT... WHAT ARE YOU SAYING? SUPERMAN?
NO, MARTIAN...
...NOT SUPERMAN.
...
...LUTHOR?!
HELLO, J'ONN.
I WARNED YOU THAT WE'D BE SEEING EACH OTHER SOON!
JOKER. SHOW YOUR HAND.
AAAGH!
WHAT ARE YOU... STOP!
GOOD WORK. NOW HOOK IN DEEPER.
YOU'RE WELCOME. NOW CAN I PLEASE CUT OFF A #$%^ HEAD?
HERS, YOURS, SOMEONE'S?!
AS MANY AS YOU WANT, JOKER. JUST A LITTLE LONGER...

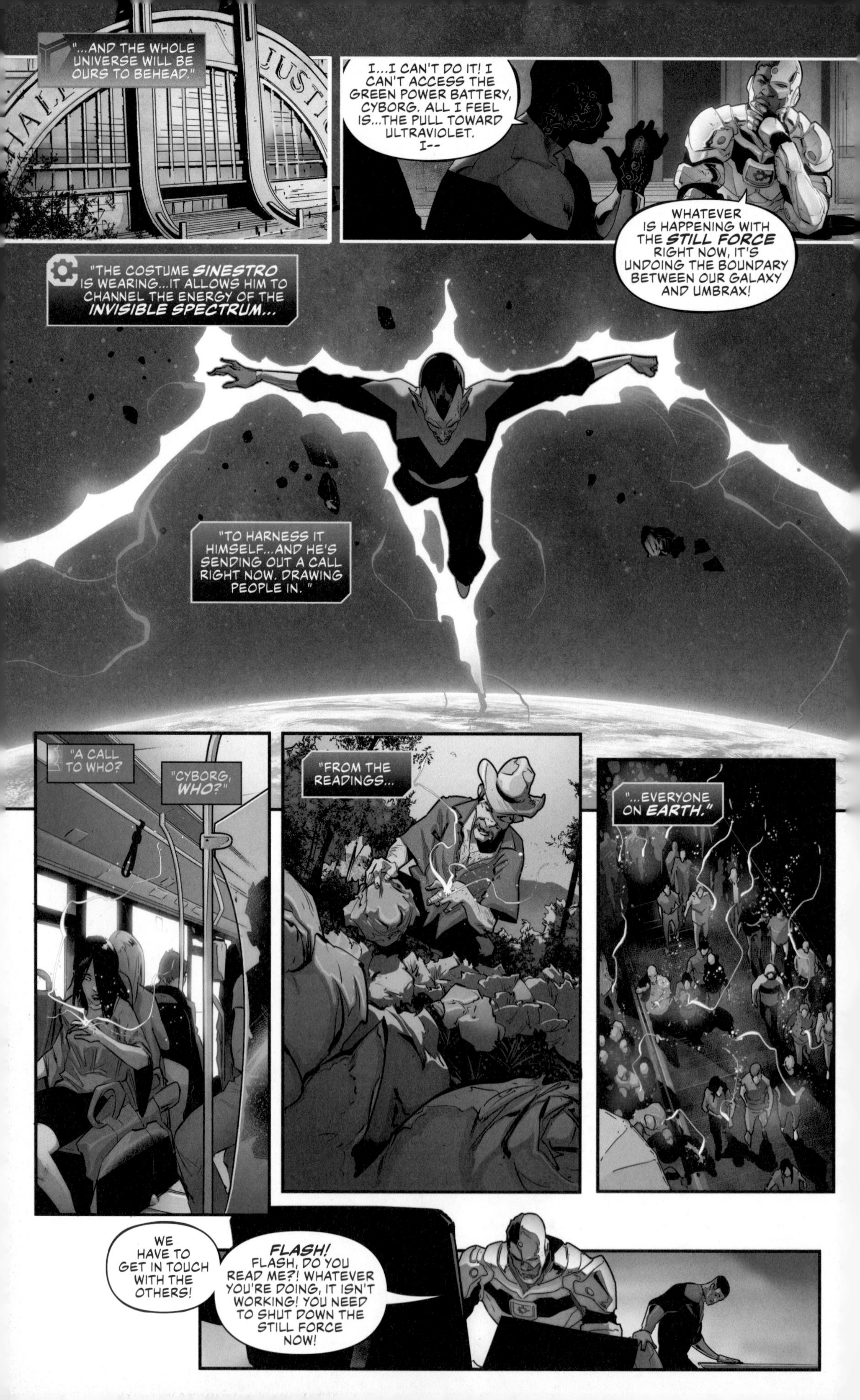
"...AND THE WHOLE UNIVERSE WILL BE OURS TO BEHEAD."
JUSTICE
I...I CAN'T DO IT! I CAN'T ACCESS THE GREEN POWER BATTERY, CYBORG. ALL I FEEL IS...THE PULL TOWARD ULTRAVIOLET. I--
WHATEVER IS HAPPENING WITH THE STILL FORCE RIGHT NOW, IT'S UNDOING THE BOUNDARY BETWEEN OUR GALAXY AND UMBRAX!
"THE COSTUME SINESTRO IS WEARING...IT ALLOWS HIM TO CHANNEL THE ENERGY OF THE INVISIBLE SPECTRUM...
"TO HARNESS IT HIMSELF...AND HE'S SENDING OUT A CALL RIGHT NOW. DRAWING PEOPLE IN."
"A CALL TO WHO?
"CYBORG, WHO?"
"FROM THE READINGS...
"...EVERYONE ON EARTH."
WE HAVE TO GET IN TOUCH WITH THE OTHERS!
FLASH! FLASH, DO YOU READ ME?! WHATEVER YOU'RE DOING, IT ISN'T WORKING! YOU NEED TO SHUT DOWN THE STILL FORCE NOW!

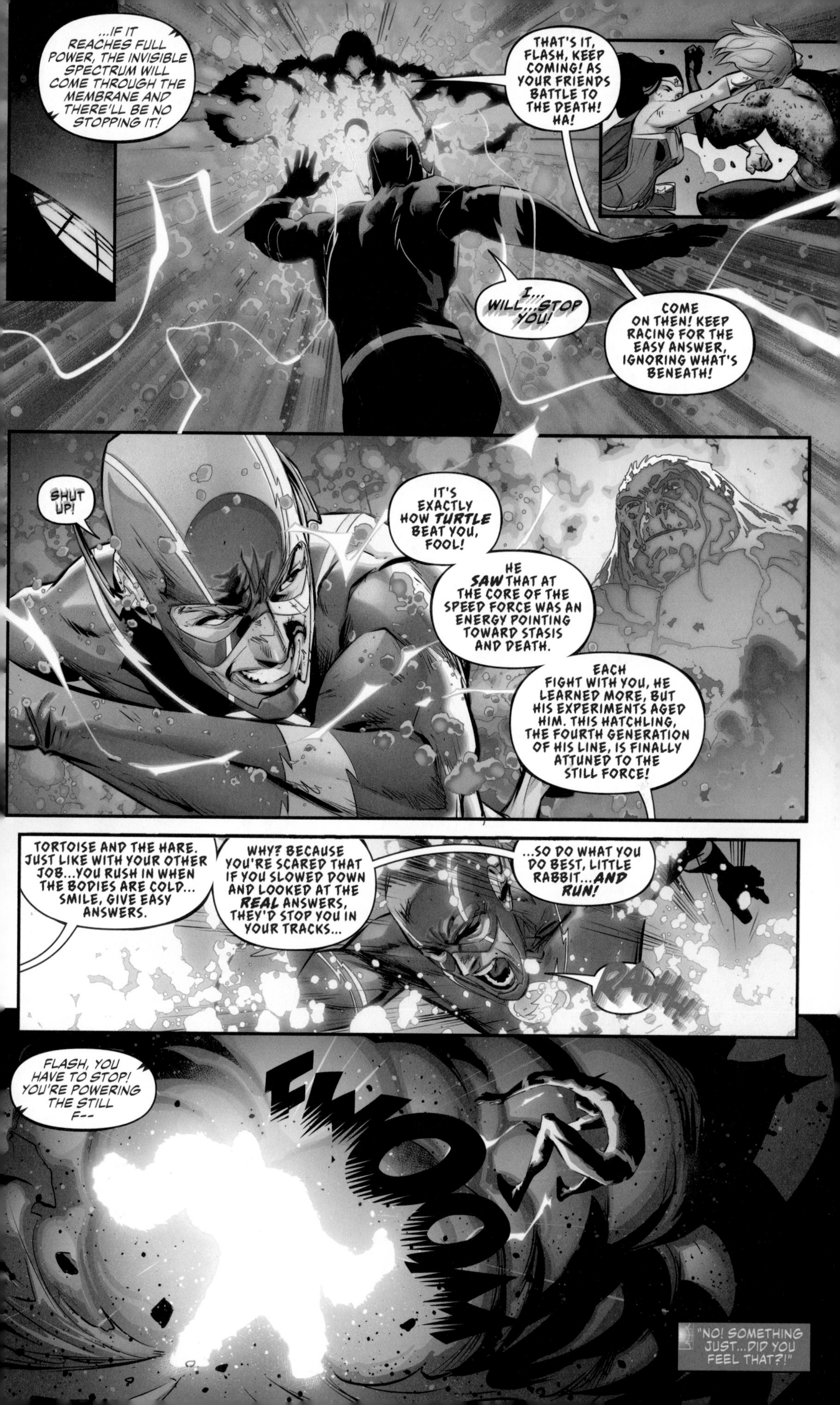
...IF IT REACHES FULL POWER, THE INVISIBLE SPECTRUM WILL COME THROUGH THE MEMBRANE AND THERE'LL BE NO STOPPING IT!
THAT'S IT, FLASH, KEEP COMING! AS YOUR FRIENDS BATTLE TO THE DEATH! HA!
I... WILL... STOP YOU!
COME ON THEN! KEEP RACING FOR THE EASY ANSWER, IGNORING WHAT'S BENEATH!
SHUT UP!
IT'S EXACTLY HOW TURTLE BEAT YOU, FOOL!
HE SAW THAT AT THE CORE OF THE SPEED FORCE WAS AN ENERGY POINTING TOWARD STASIS AND DEATH.
EACH FIGHT WITH YOU, HE LEARNED MORE, BUT HIS EXPERIMENTS AGED HIM. THIS HATCHLING, THE FOURTH GENERATION OF HIS LINE, IS FINALLY ATTUNED TO THE STILL FORCE!
TORTOISE AND THE HARE. JUST LIKE WITH YOUR OTHER JOB...YOU RUSH IN WHEN THE BODIES ARE COLD... SMILE, GIVE EASY ANSWERS.
WHY? BECAUSE YOU'RE SCARED THAT IF YOU SLOWED DOWN AND LOOKED AT THE REAL ANSWERS, THEY'D STOP YOU IN YOUR TRACKS...
...SO DO WHAT YOU DO BEST, LITTLE RABBIT...AND RUN!
RAHH!
FLASH, YOU HAVE TO STOP! YOU'RE POWERING THE STILL F--
FWOOM
"NO! SOMETHING JUST...DID YOU FEEL THAT?!"

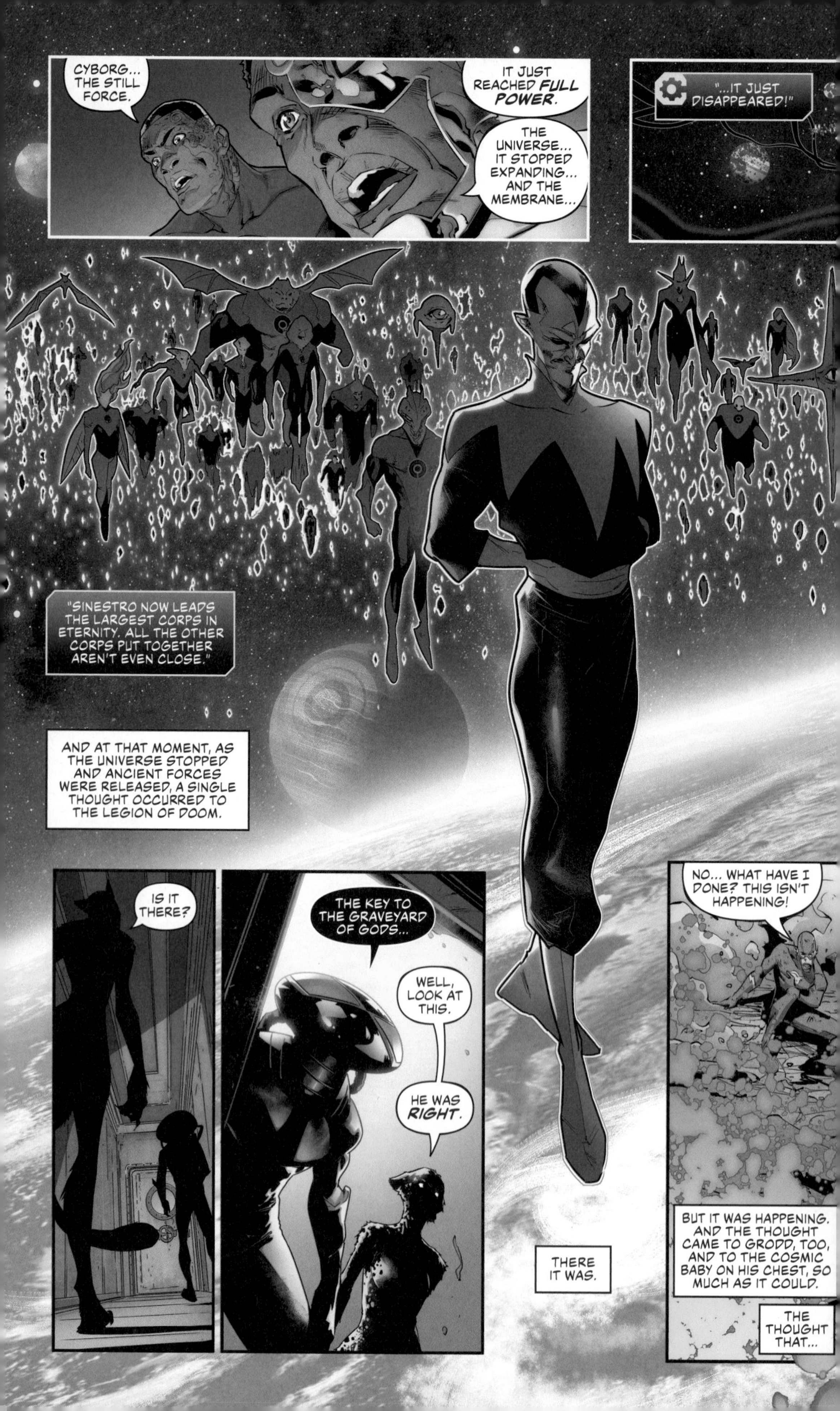
CYBORG... THE STILL FORCE.
IT JUST REACHED FULL POWER.
THE UNIVERSE... IT STOPPED EXPANDING... AND THE MEMBRANE...
"...IT JUST DISAPPEARED!"
"SINESTRO NOW LEADS THE LARGEST CORPS IN ETERNITY. ALL THE OTHER CORPS PUT TOGETHER AREN'T EVEN CLOSE."
AND AT THAT MOMENT, AS THE UNIVERSE STOPPED AND ANCIENT FORCES WERE RELEASED, A SINGLE THOUGHT OCCURRED TO THE LEGION OF DOOM.
IS IT THERE?
THE KEY TO THE GRAVEYARD OF GODS...
WELL, LOOK AT THIS.
HE WAS RIGHT.
THERE IT WAS.
NO... WHAT HAVE I DONE? THIS ISN'T HAPPENING!
BUT IT WAS HAPPENING. AND THE THOUGHT CAME TO GRODD, TOO, AND TO THE COSMIC BABY ON HIS CHEST, SO MUCH AS IT COULD.
THE THOUGHT THAT...

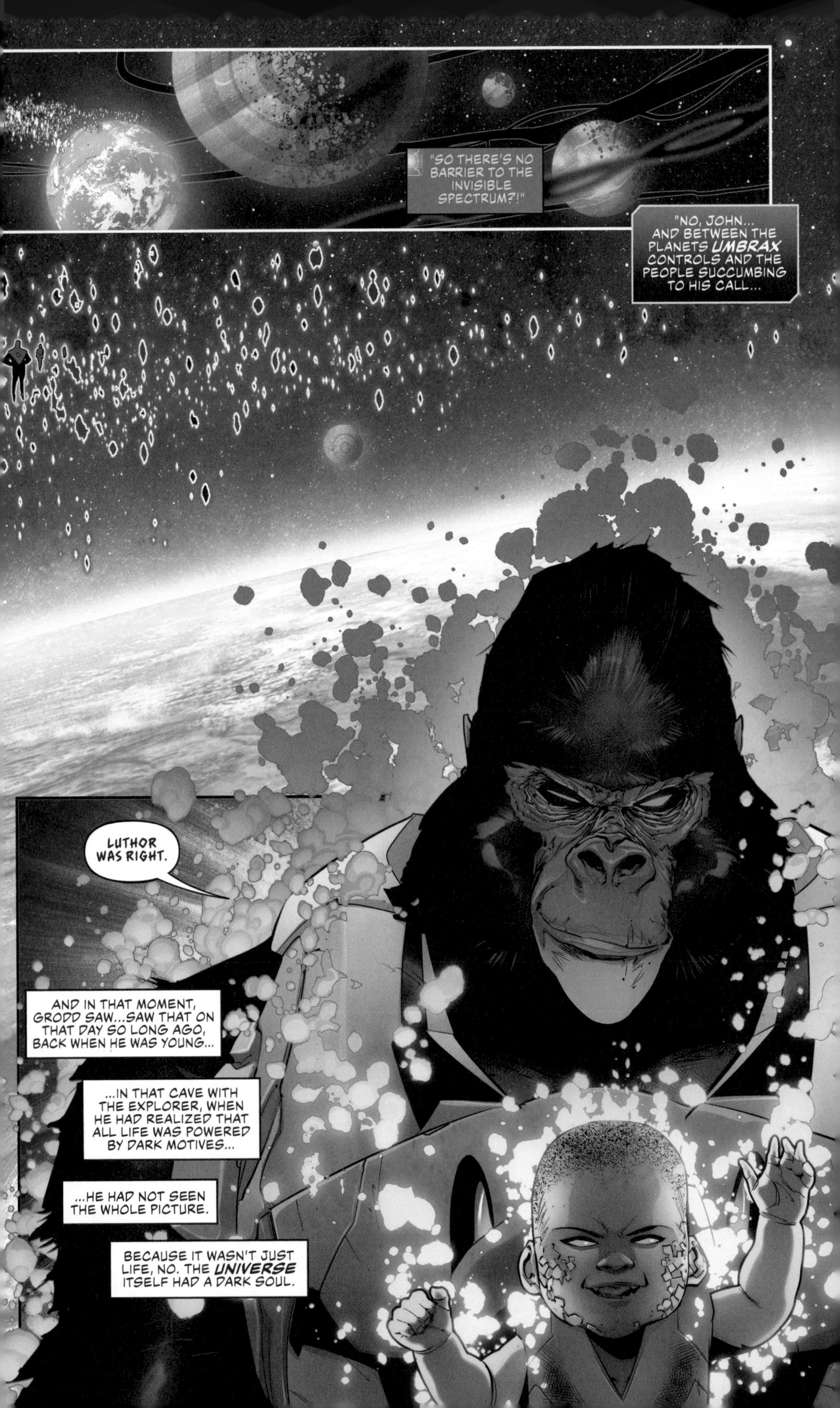

"SO THERE'S NO BARRIER TO THE INVISIBLE SPECTRUM?!"
"NO, JOHN... AND BETWEEN THE PLANETS UMBRAX CONTROLS AND THE PEOPLE SUCCUMBING TO HIS CALL...
LUTHOR WAS RIGHT.
AND IN THAT MOMENT, GRODD SAW...SAW THAT ON THAT DAY SO LONG AGO, BACK WHEN HE WAS YOUNG...
...IN THAT CAVE WITH THE EXPLORER, WHEN HE HAD REALIZED THAT ALL LIFE WAS POWERED BY DARK MOTIVES...
...HE HAD NOT SEEN THE WHOLE PICTURE.
BECAUSE IT WASN'T JUST LIFE, NO. THE UNIVERSE ITSELF HAD A DARK SOUL.

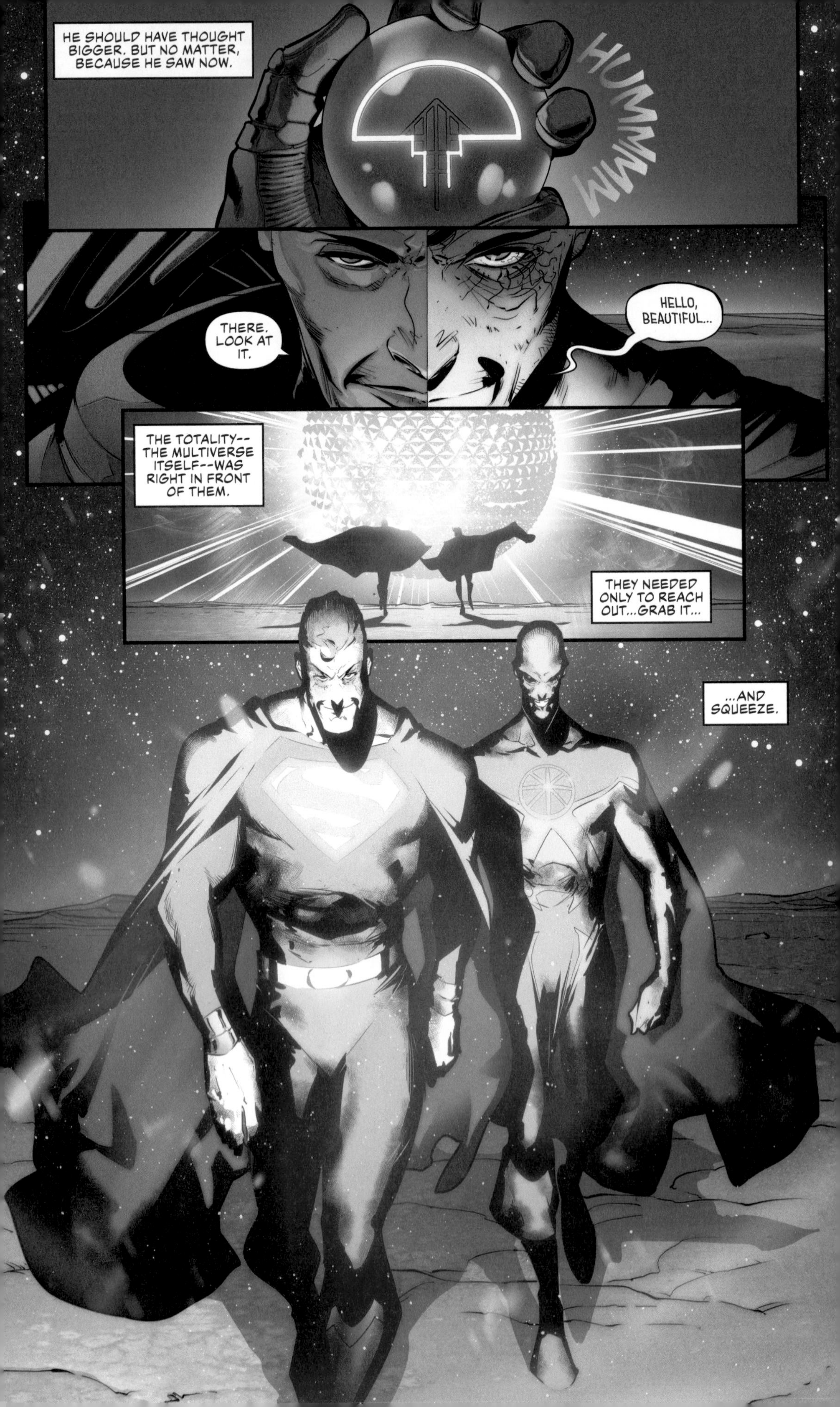
HE SHOULD HAVE THOUGHT BIGGER. BUT NO MATTER, BECAUSE HE SAW NOW.
HUMMMMMM
THERE. LOOK AT IT.
HELLO, BEAUTIFUL...
THE TOTALITY-- THE MULTIVERSE ITSELF--WAS RIGHT IN FRONT OF THEM.
THEY NEEDED ONLY TO REACH OUT...GRAB IT...
...AND SQUEEZE.

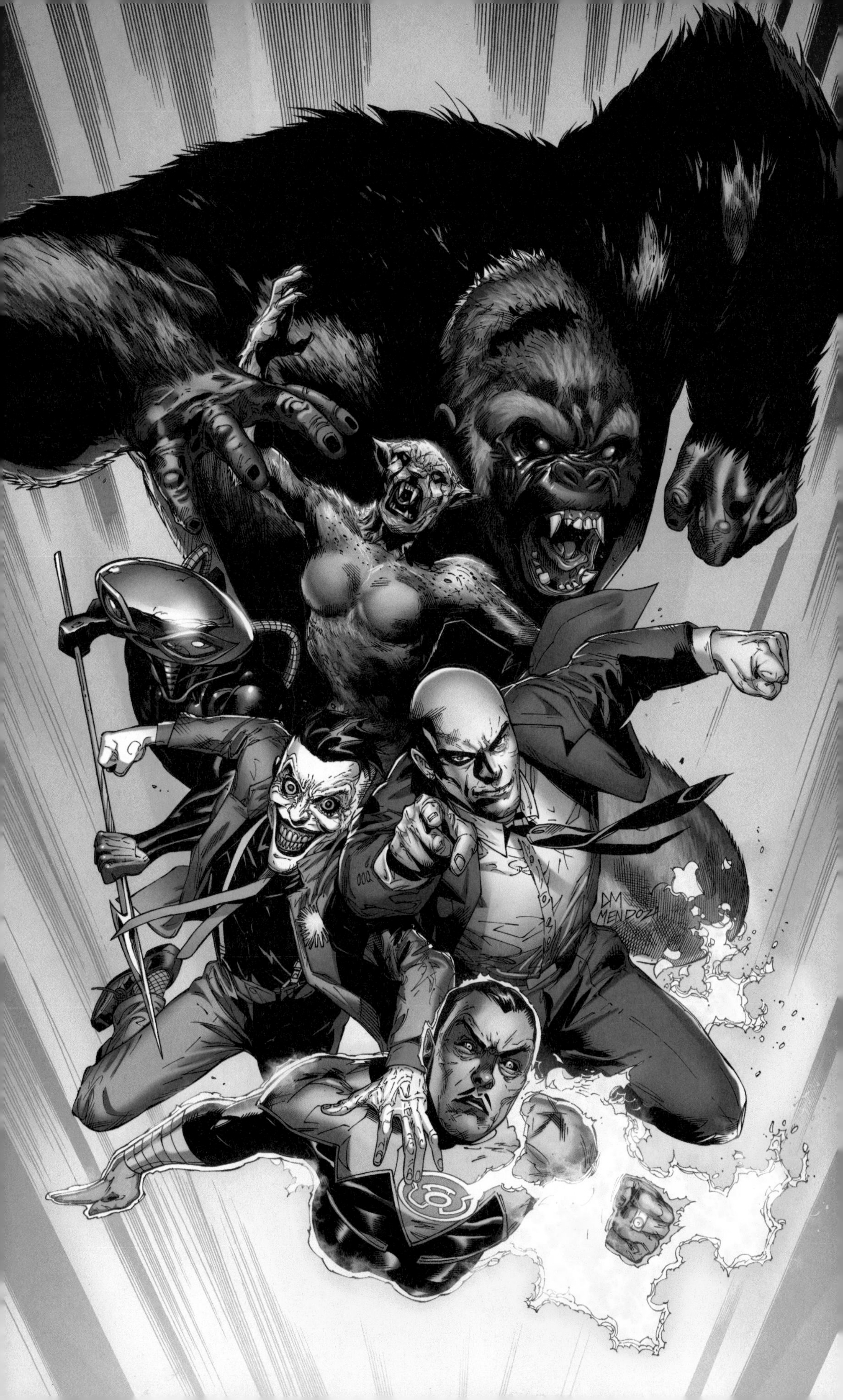

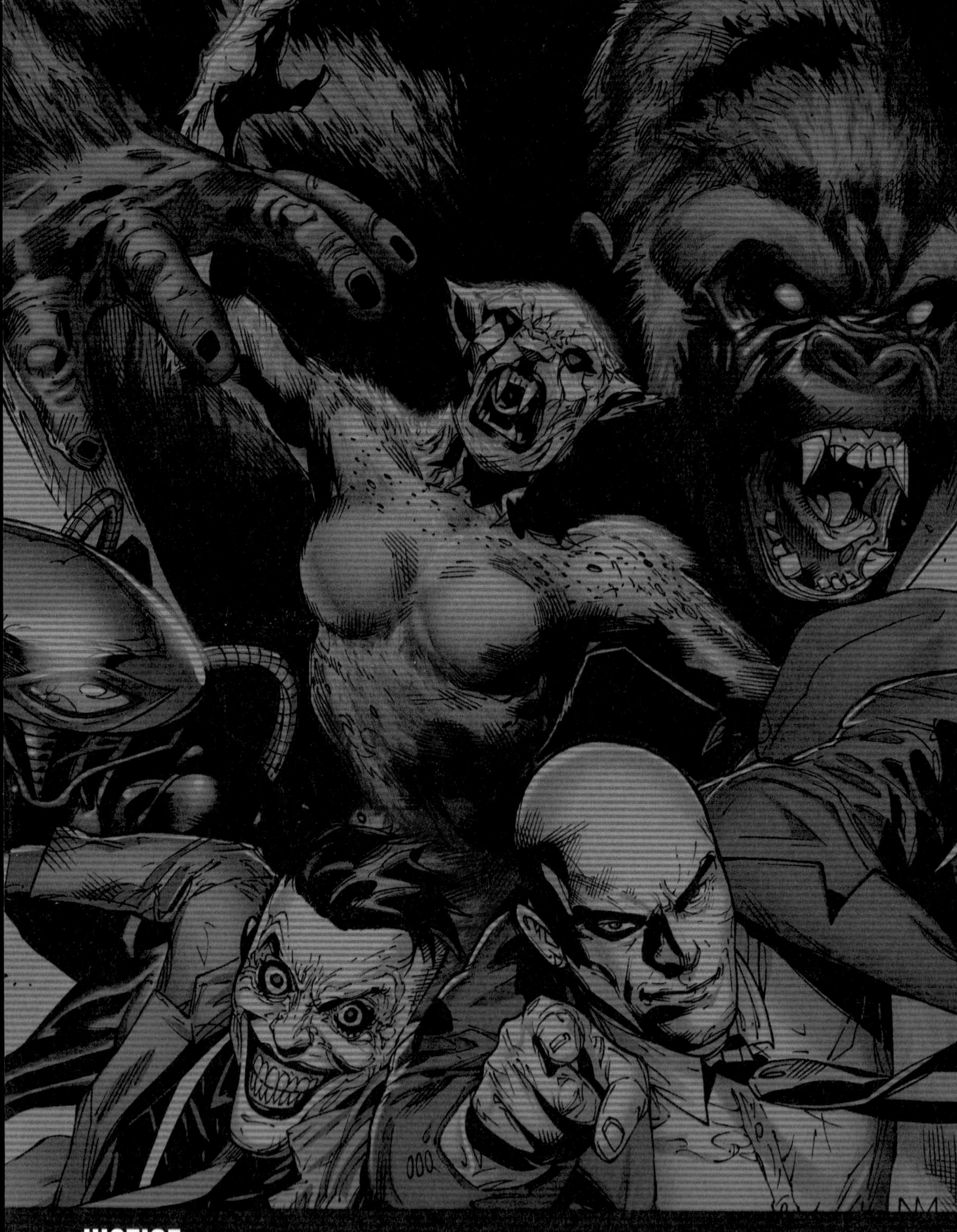

JUSTICE LEAGUE
#5

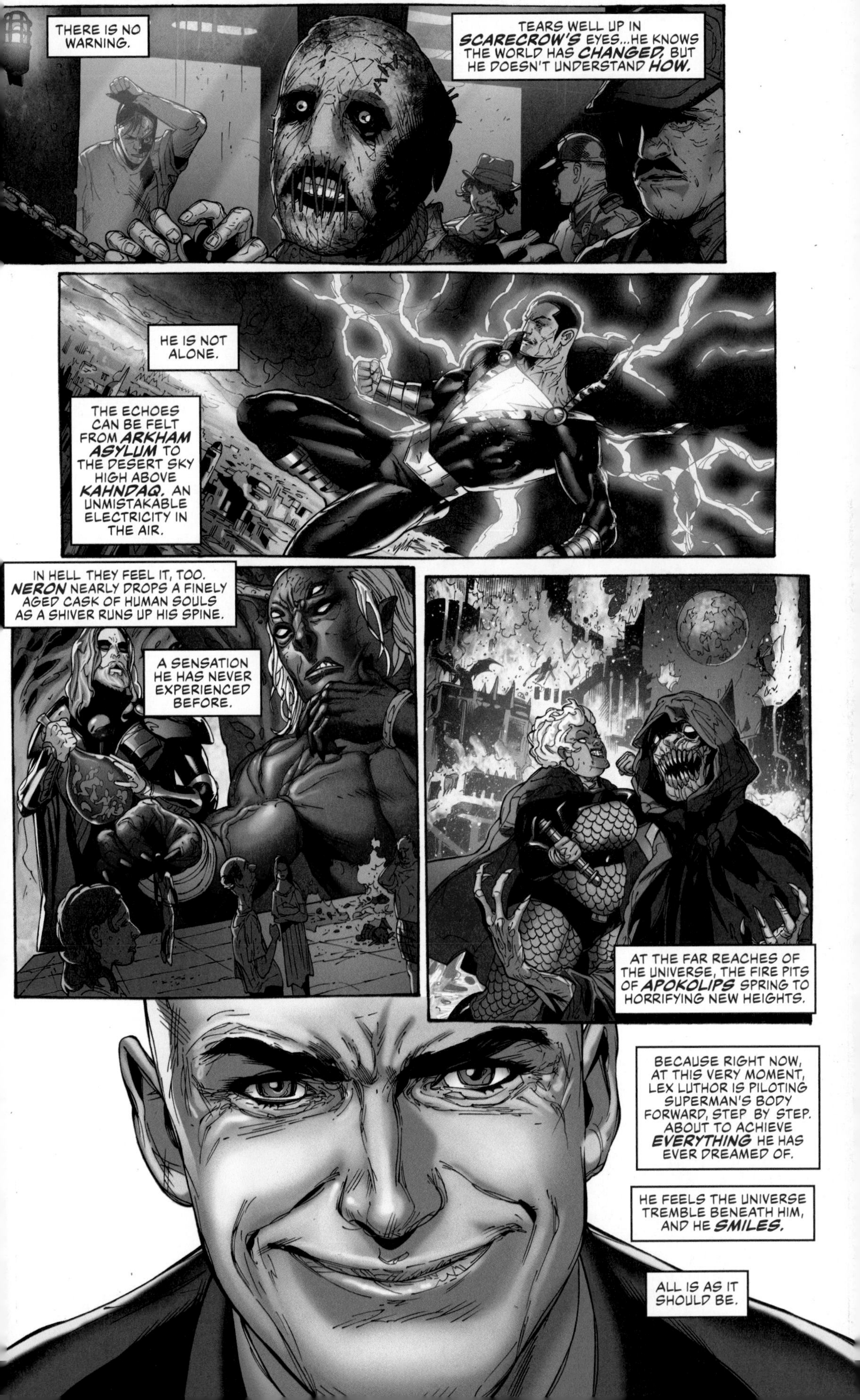
THERE IS NO WARNING.
TEARS WELL UP IN SCARECROW'S EYES...HE KNOWS THE WORLD HAS CHANGED, BUT HE DOESN'T UNDERSTAND HOW.
HE IS NOT ALONE.
THE ECHOES CAN BE FELT FROM ARKHAM ASYLUM TO THE DESERT SKY HIGH ABOVE KAHNDAQ. AN UNMISTAKABLE ELECTRICITY IN THE AIR.
IN HELL THEY FEEL IT, TOO. NERON NEARLY DROPS A FINELY AGED CASK OF HUMAN SOULS AS A SHIVER RUNS UP HIS SPINE.
A SENSATION HE HAS NEVER EXPERIENCED BEFORE.
AT THE FAR REACHES OF THE UNIVERSE, THE FIRE PITS OF APOKOLIPS SPRING TO HORRIFYING NEW HEIGHTS.
BECAUSE RIGHT NOW, AT THIS VERY MOMENT, LEX LUTHOR IS PILOTING SUPERMAN'S BODY FORWARD, STEP BY STEP. ABOUT TO ACHIEVE EVERYTHING HE HAS EVER DREAMED OF.
HE FEELS THE UNIVERSE TREMBLE BENEATH HIM, AND HE SMILES.
ALL IS AS IT SHOULD BE.

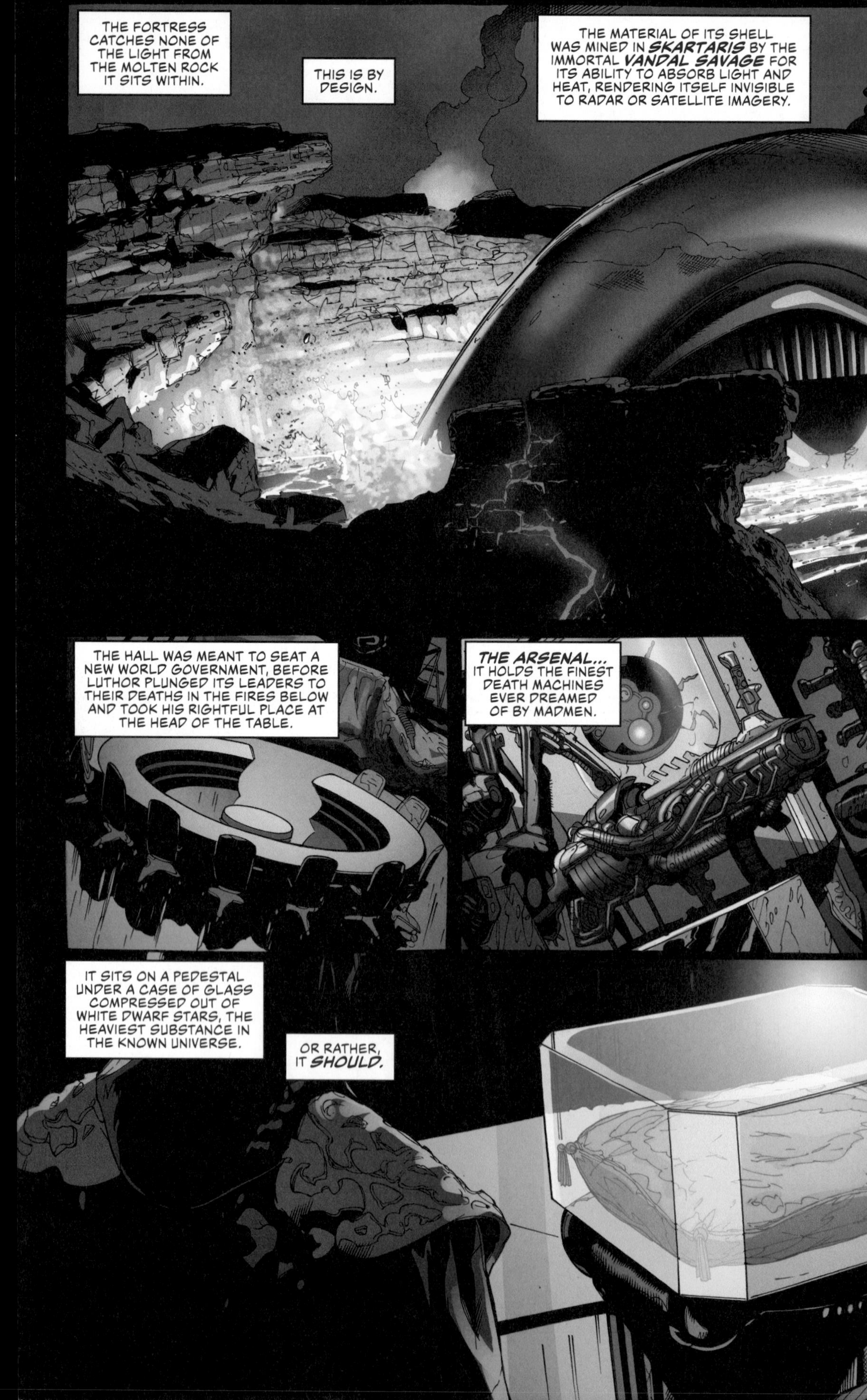
THE FORTRESS CATCHES NONE OF THE LIGHT FROM THE MOLTEN ROCK IT SITS WITHIN.
THIS IS BY DESIGN.
THE MATERIAL OF ITS SHELL WAS MINED IN SKARTARIS BY THE IMMORTAL VANDAL SAVAGE FOR ITS ABILITY TO ABSORB LIGHT AND HEAT, RENDERING ITSELF INVISIBLE TO RADAR OR SATELLITE IMAGERY.
THE HALL WAS MEANT TO SEAT A NEW WORLD GOVERNMENT, BEFORE LUTHOR PLUNGED ITS LEADERS TO THEIR DEATHS IN THE FIRES BELOW AND TOOK HIS RIGHTFUL PLACE AT THE HEAD OF THE TABLE.
THE ARSENAL... IT HOLDS THE FINEST DEATH MACHINES EVER DREAMED OF BY MADMEN.
IT SITS ON A PEDESTAL UNDER A CASE OF GLASS COMPRESSED OUT OF WHITE DWARF STARS, THE HEAVIEST SUBSTANCE IN THE KNOWN UNIVERSE.
OR RATHER, IT SHOULD.

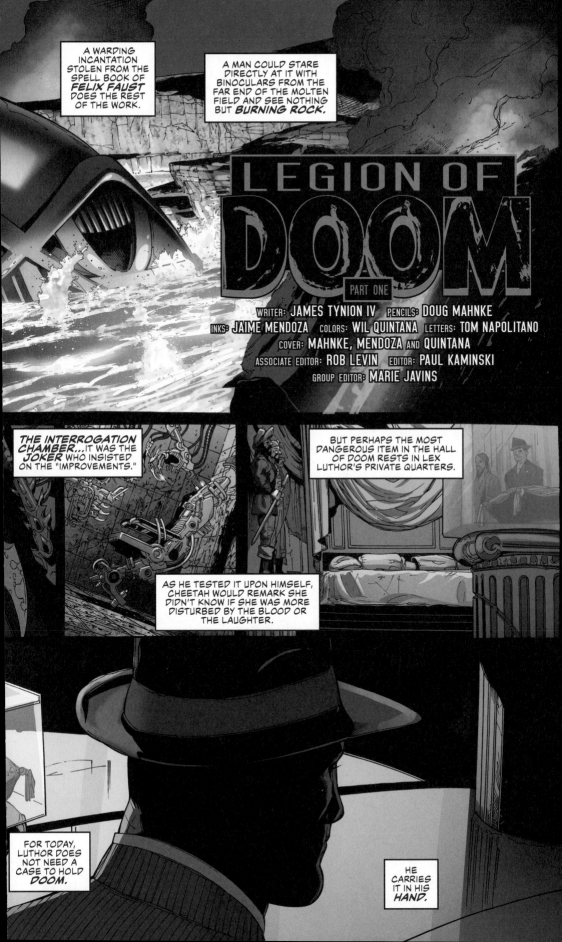

A WARDING INCANTATION STOLEN FROM THE SPELL BOOK OF *FELIX FAUST* DOES THE REST OF THE WORK.

A MAN COULD STARE DIRECTLY AT IT WITH BINOCULARS FROM THE FAR END OF THE MOLTEN FIELD AND SEE NOTHING BUT *BURNING ROCK.*

LEGION OF DOOM
PART ONE

WRITER: JAMES TYNION IV   PENCILS: DOUG MAHNKE

INKS: JAIME MENDOZA   COLORS: WIL QUINTANA   LETTERS: TOM NAPOLITANO

COVER: MAHNKE, MENDOZA AND QUINTANA

ASSOCIATE EDITOR: ROB LEVIN   EDITOR: PAUL KAMINSKI

GROUP EDITOR: MARIE JAVINS

THE INTERROGATION CHAMBER...IT WAS THE *JOKER* WHO INSISTED ON THE "IMPROVEMENTS."

BUT PERHAPS THE MOST DANGEROUS ITEM IN THE HALL OF DOOM RESTS IN LEX LUTHOR'S PRIVATE QUARTERS.

AS HE TESTED IT UPON HIMSELF, CHEETAH WOULD REMARK SHE DIDN'T KNOW IF SHE WAS MORE DISTURBED BY THE BLOOD OR THE LAUGHTER.

FOR TODAY, LUTHOR DOES NOT NEED A CASE TO HOLD *DOOM.*

HE CARRIES IT IN HIS *HAND.*

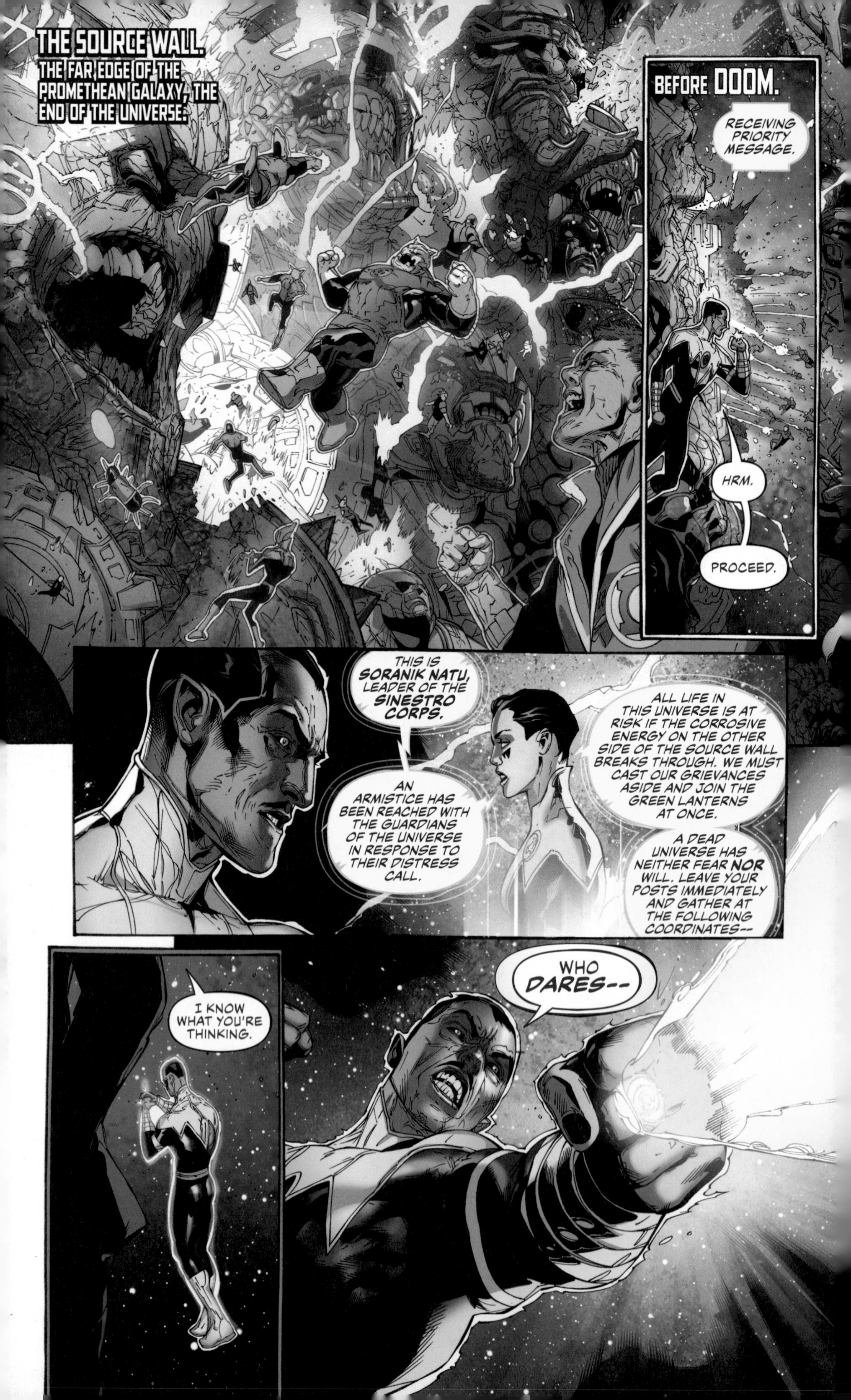
THE SOURCE WALL.
THE FAR EDGE OF THE PROMETHEAN GALAXY, THE END OF THE UNIVERSE.
BEFORE DOOM.
RECEIVING PRIORITY MESSAGE.
HRM.
PROCEED.
THIS IS SORANIK NATU, LEADER OF THE SINESTRO CORPS.
AN ARMISTICE HAS BEEN REACHED WITH THE GUARDIANS OF THE UNIVERSE IN RESPONSE TO THEIR DISTRESS CALL.
ALL LIFE IN THIS UNIVERSE IS AT RISK IF THE CORROSIVE ENERGY ON THE OTHER SIDE OF THE SOURCE WALL BREAKS THROUGH. WE MUST CAST OUR GRIEVANCES ASIDE AND JOIN THE GREEN LANTERNS AT ONCE.
A DEAD UNIVERSE HAS NEITHER FEAR NOR WILL. LEAVE YOUR POSTS IMMEDIATELY AND GATHER AT THE FOLLOWING COORDINATES--
I KNOW WHAT YOU'RE THINKING.
WHO DARES--

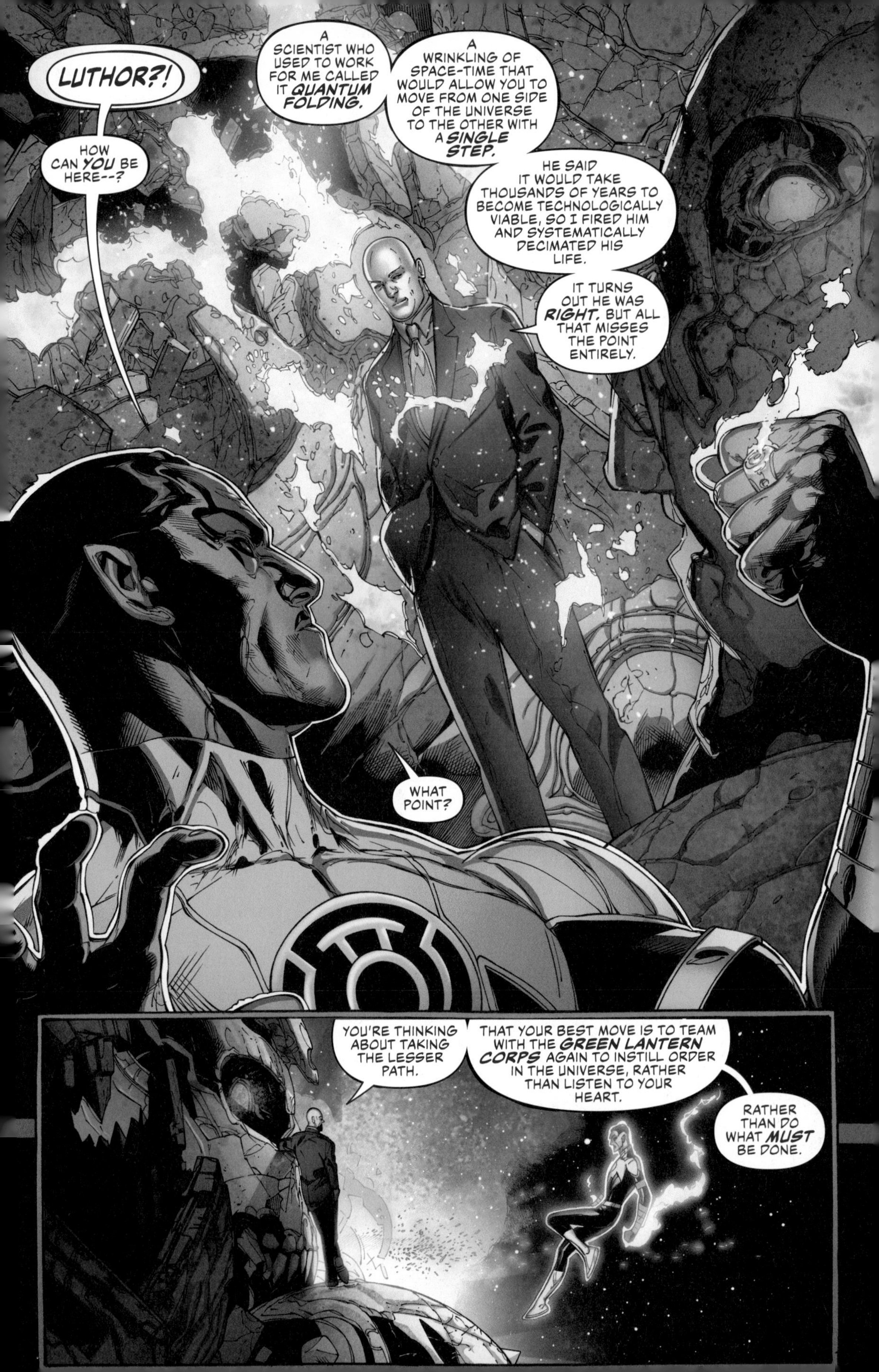
LUTHOR?!
HOW CAN YOU BE HERE--?
A SCIENTIST WHO USED TO WORK FOR ME CALLED IT QUANTUM FOLDING.
A WRINKLING OF SPACE-TIME THAT WOULD ALLOW YOU TO MOVE FROM ONE SIDE OF THE UNIVERSE TO THE OTHER WITH A SINGLE STEP.
HE SAID IT WOULD TAKE THOUSANDS OF YEARS TO BECOME TECHNOLOGICALLY VIABLE, SO I FIRED HIM AND SYSTEMATICALLY DECIMATED HIS LIFE.
IT TURNS OUT HE WAS RIGHT. BUT ALL THAT MISSES THE POINT ENTIRELY.
WHAT POINT?
YOU'RE THINKING ABOUT TAKING THE LESSER PATH.
THAT YOUR BEST MOVE IS TO TEAM WITH THE GREEN LANTERN CORPS AGAIN TO INSTILL ORDER IN THE UNIVERSE, RATHER THAN LISTEN TO YOUR HEART.
RATHER THAN DO WHAT MUST BE DONE.

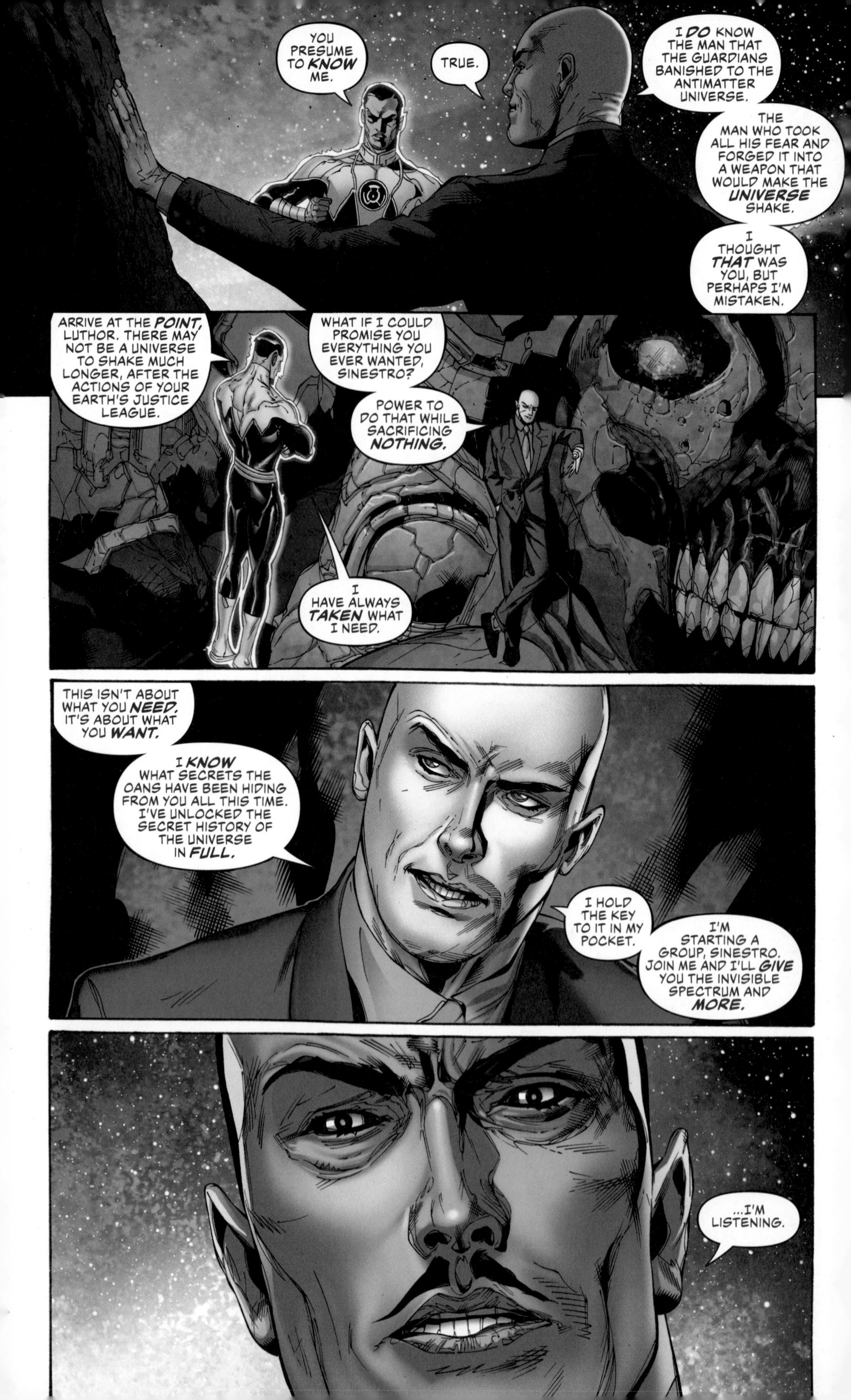
YOU PRESUME TO KNOW ME.
TRUE.
I DO KNOW THE MAN THAT THE GUARDIANS BANISHED TO THE ANTIMATTER UNIVERSE.
THE MAN WHO TOOK ALL HIS FEAR AND FORGED IT INTO A WEAPON THAT WOULD MAKE THE UNIVERSE SHAKE.
I THOUGHT THAT WAS YOU, BUT PERHAPS I'M MISTAKEN.
ARRIVE AT THE POINT, LUTHOR. THERE MAY NOT BE A UNIVERSE TO SHAKE MUCH LONGER, AFTER THE ACTIONS OF YOUR EARTH'S JUSTICE LEAGUE.
WHAT IF I COULD PROMISE YOU EVERYTHING YOU EVER WANTED, SINESTRO?
POWER TO DO THAT WHILE SACRIFICING NOTHING.
I HAVE ALWAYS TAKEN WHAT I NEED.
THIS ISN'T ABOUT WHAT YOU NEED. IT'S ABOUT WHAT YOU WANT.
I KNOW WHAT SECRETS THE OANS HAVE BEEN HIDING FROM YOU ALL THIS TIME. I'VE UNLOCKED THE SECRET HISTORY OF THE UNIVERSE IN FULL.
I HOLD THE KEY TO IT IN MY POCKET.
I'M STARTING A GROUP, SINESTRO. JOIN ME AND I'LL GIVE YOU THE INVISIBLE SPECTRUM AND MORE.
...I'M LISTENING.

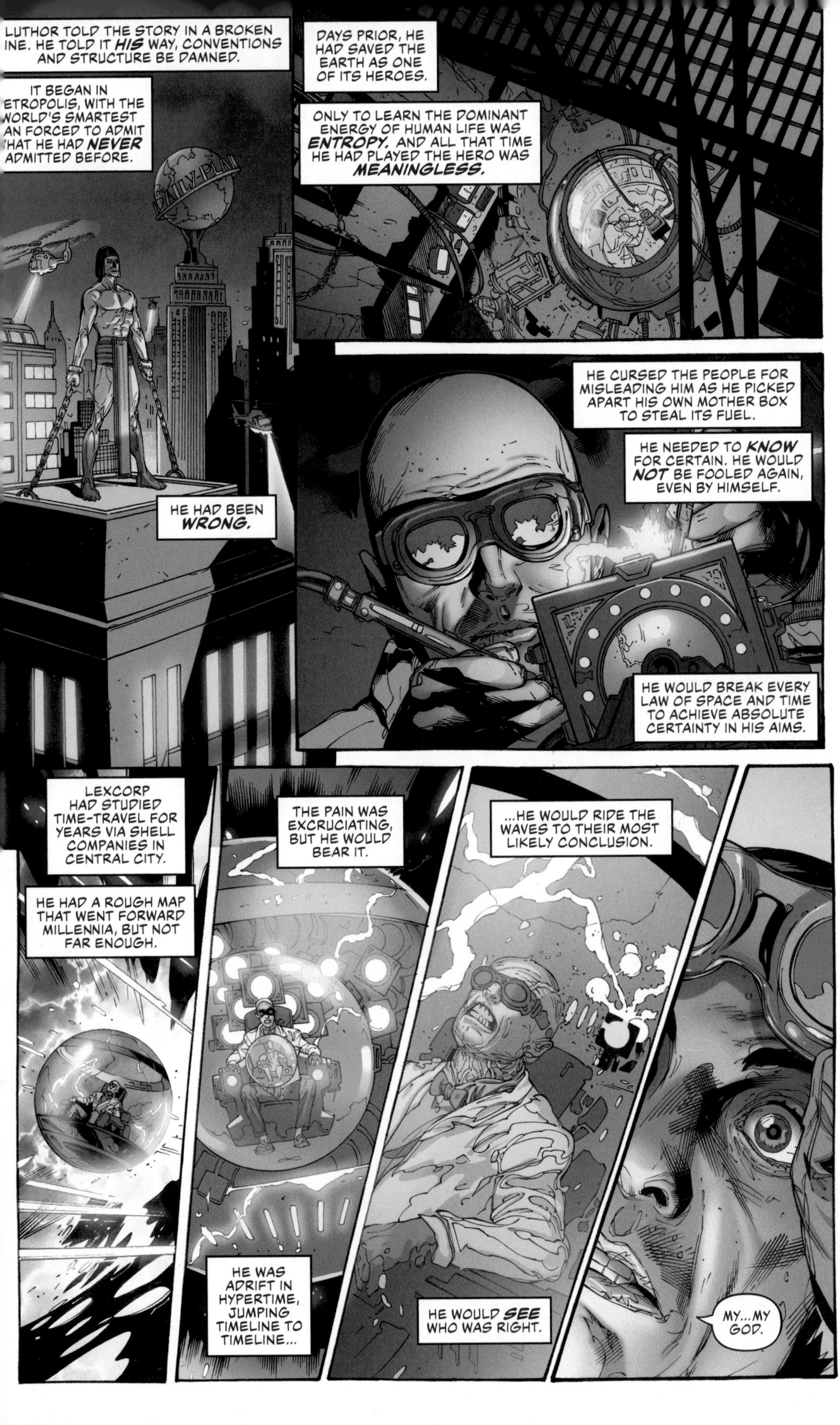
LUTHOR TOLD THE STORY IN A BROKEN INE. HE TOLD IT HIS WAY, CONVENTIONS AND STRUCTURE BE DAMNED.
IT BEGAN IN ETROPOLIS, WITH THE WORLD'S SMARTEST AN FORCED TO ADMIT THAT HE HAD NEVER ADMITTED BEFORE.
DAILY PLANET
HE HAD BEEN WRONG.
DAYS PRIOR, HE HAD SAVED THE EARTH AS ONE OF ITS HEROES.
ONLY TO LEARN THE DOMINANT ENERGY OF HUMAN LIFE WAS ENTROPY, AND ALL THAT TIME HE HAD PLAYED THE HERO WAS MEANINGLESS.
HE CURSED THE PEOPLE FOR MISLEADING HIM AS HE PICKED APART HIS OWN MOTHER BOX TO STEAL ITS FUEL.
HE NEEDED TO KNOW FOR CERTAIN. HE WOULD NOT BE FOOLED AGAIN, EVEN BY HIMSELF.
HE WOULD BREAK EVERY LAW OF SPACE AND TIME TO ACHIEVE ABSOLUTE CERTAINTY IN HIS AIMS.
LEXCORP HAD STUDIED TIME-TRAVEL FOR YEARS VIA SHELL COMPANIES IN CENTRAL CITY.
HE HAD A ROUGH MAP THAT WENT FORWARD MILLENNIA, BUT NOT FAR ENOUGH.
THE PAIN WAS EXCRUCIATING, BUT HE WOULD BEAR IT.
HE WAS ADRIFT IN HYPERTIME, JUMPING TIMELINE TO TIMELINE...
...HE WOULD RIDE THE WAVES TO THEIR MOST LIKELY CONCLUSION.
HE WOULD SEE WHO WAS RIGHT.
MY...MY GOD.

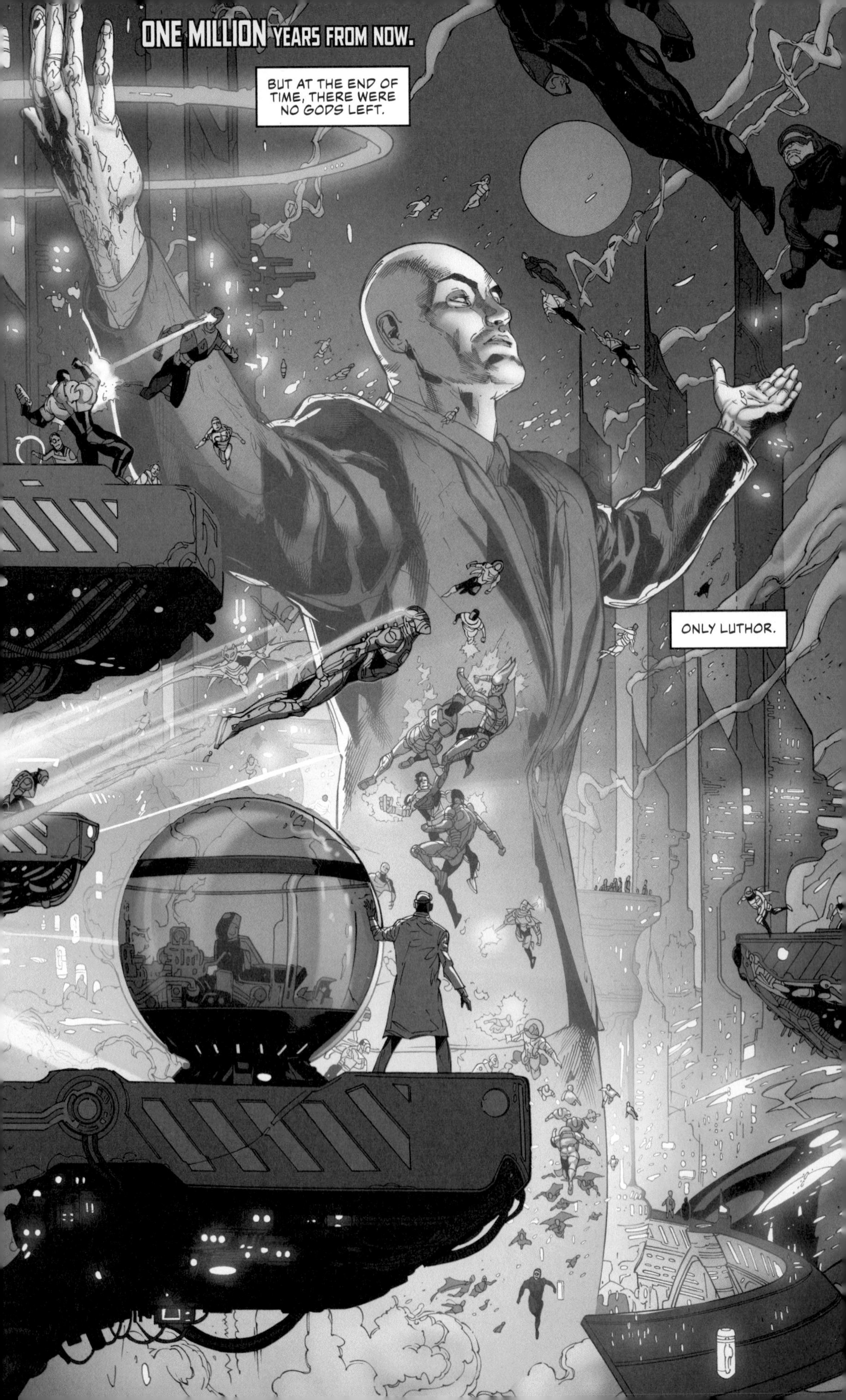
ONE MILLION YEARS FROM NOW.
BUT AT THE END OF TIME, THERE WERE NO GODS LEFT.
ONLY LUTHOR.

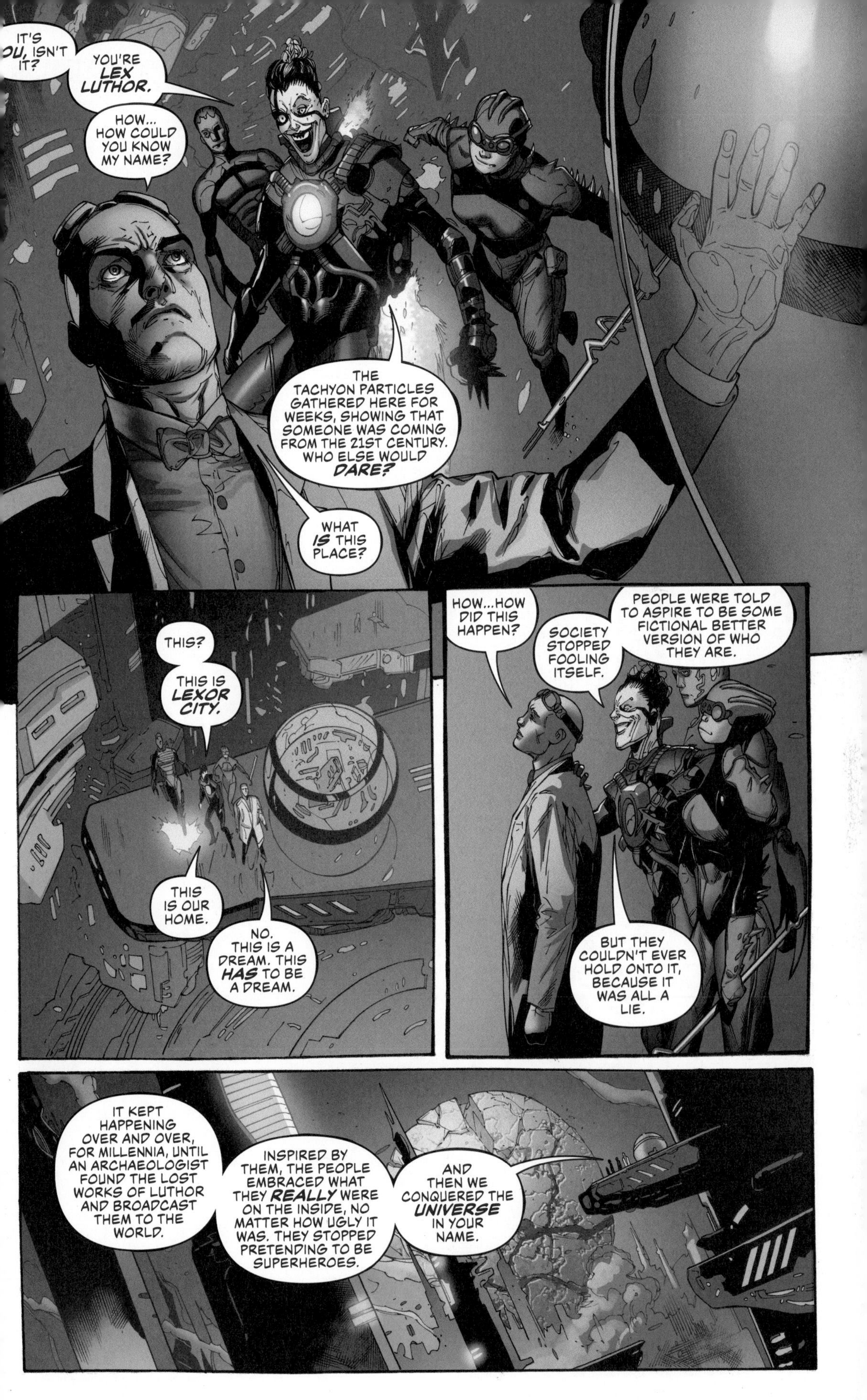
IT'S OU, ISN'T IT?
YOU'RE LEX LUTHOR.
HOW... HOW COULD YOU KNOW MY NAME?
THE TACHYON PARTICLES GATHERED HERE FOR WEEKS, SHOWING THAT SOMEONE WAS COMING FROM THE 21ST CENTURY. WHO ELSE WOULD DARE?
WHAT IS THIS PLACE?
THIS?
THIS IS LEXOR CITY.
THIS IS OUR HOME.
NO. THIS IS A DREAM. THIS HAS TO BE A DREAM.
HOW...HOW DID THIS HAPPEN?
SOCIETY STOPPED FOOLING ITSELF.
PEOPLE WERE TOLD TO ASPIRE TO BE SOME FICTIONAL BETTER VERSION OF WHO THEY ARE.
BUT THEY COULDN'T EVER HOLD ONTO IT, BECAUSE IT WAS ALL A LIE.
IT KEPT HAPPENING OVER AND OVER, FOR MILLENNIA, UNTIL AN ARCHAEOLOGIST FOUND THE LOST WORKS OF LUTHOR AND BROADCAST THEM TO THE WORLD.
INSPIRED BY THEM, THE PEOPLE EMBRACED WHAT THEY REALLY WERE ON THE INSIDE, NO MATTER HOW UGLY IT WAS. THEY STOPPED PRETENDING TO BE SUPERHEROES.
AND THEN WE CONQUERED THE UNIVERSE IN YOUR NAME.

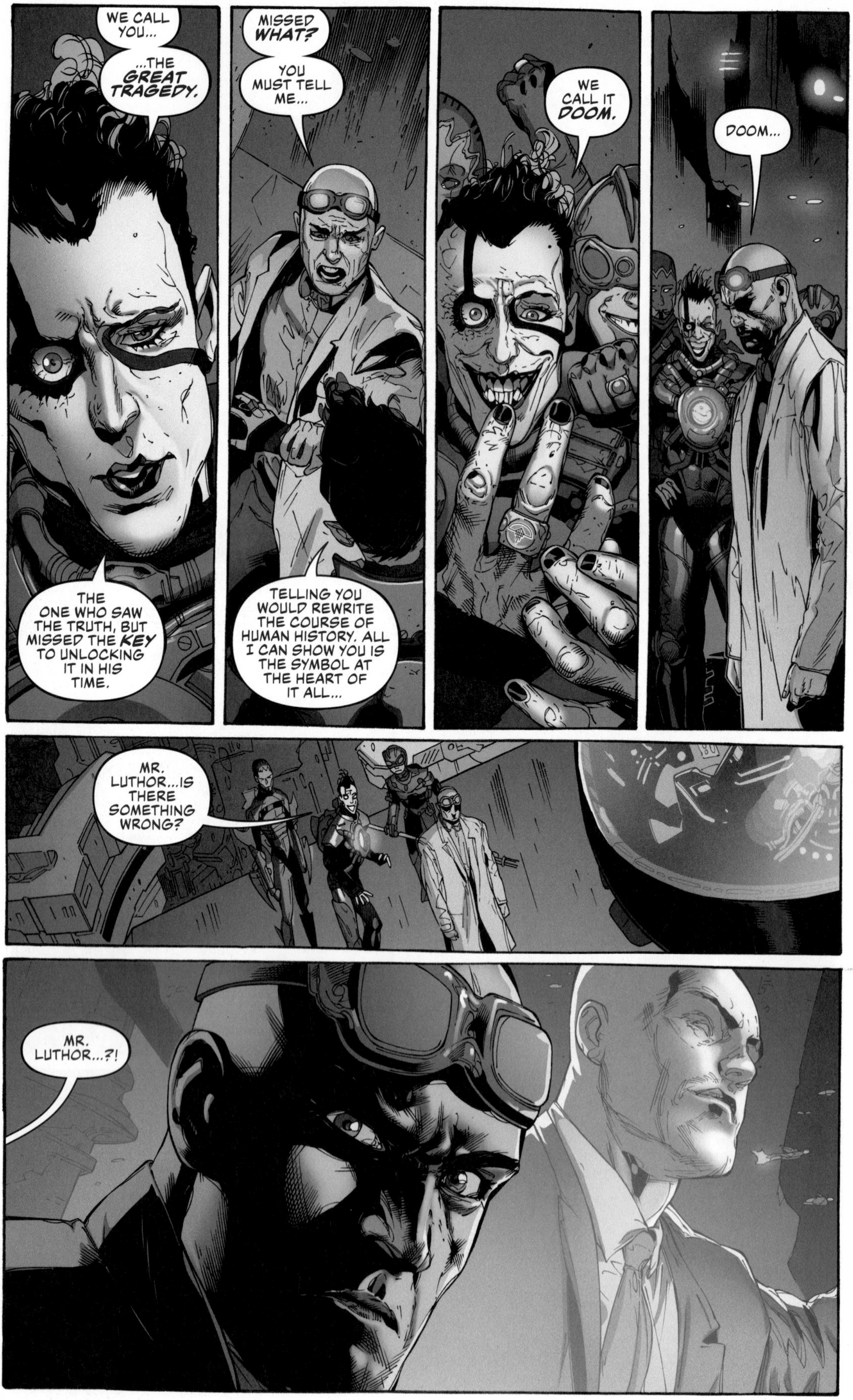
WE CALL YOU...
...THE GREAT TRAGEDY.
THE ONE WHO SAW THE TRUTH, BUT MISSED THE KEY TO UNLOCKING IT IN HIS TIME.
MISSED WHAT?
YOU MUST TELL ME...
TELLING YOU WOULD REWRITE THE COURSE OF HUMAN HISTORY. ALL I CAN SHOW YOU IS THE SYMBOL AT THE HEART OF IT ALL...
WE CALL IT DOOM.
DOOM...
MR. LUTHOR...IS THERE SOMETHING WRONG?
MR. LUTHOR...?!

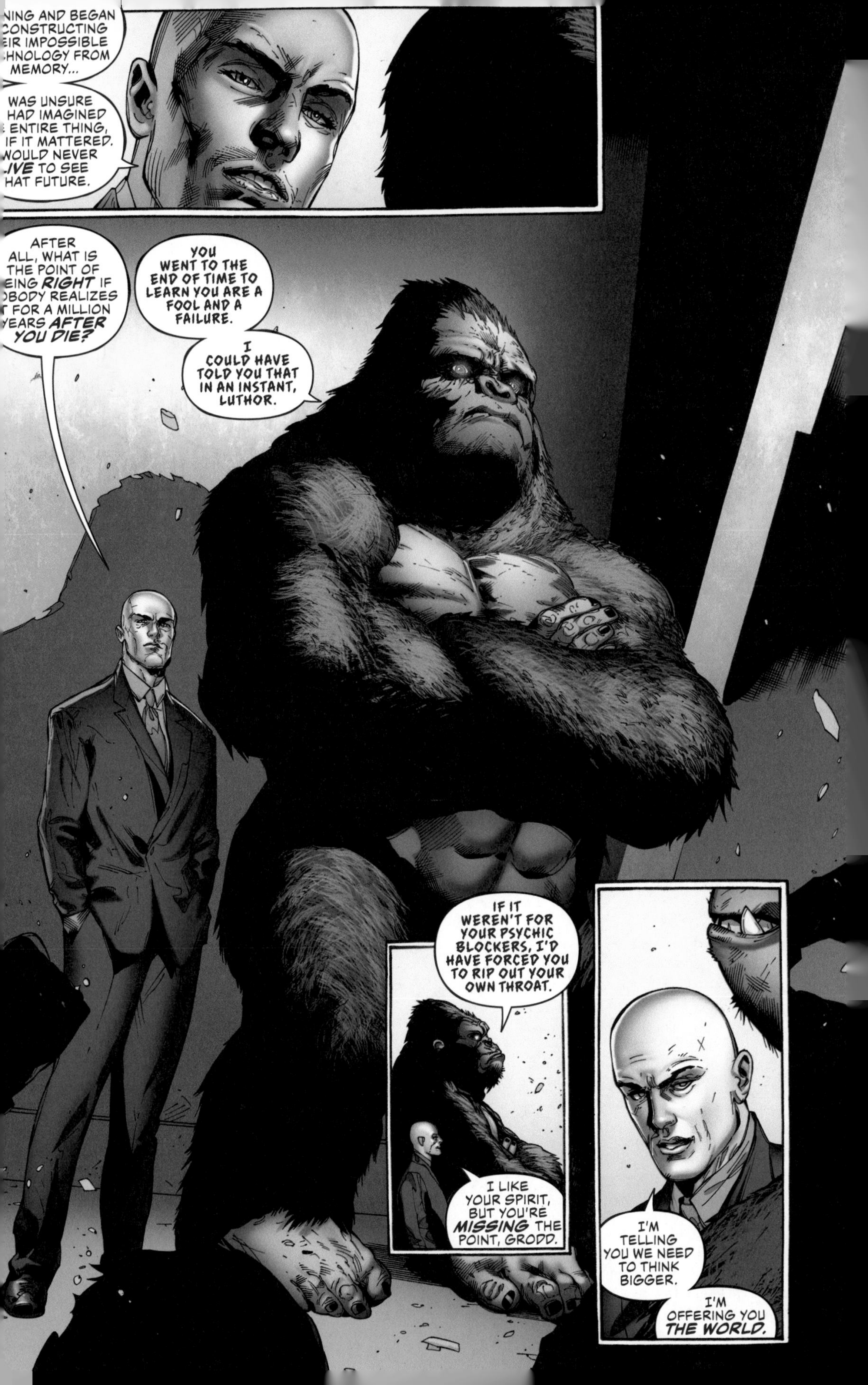

NING AND BEGAN CONSTRUCTING EIR IMPOSSIBLE CHNOLOGY FROM MEMORY...
WAS UNSURE HAD IMAGINED E ENTIRE THING, IF IT MATTERED. WOULD NEVER LIVE TO SEE HAT FUTURE.
AFTER ALL, WHAT IS THE POINT OF EING RIGHT IF OBODY REALIZES T FOR A MILLION YEARS AFTER YOU DIE?
YOU WENT TO THE END OF TIME TO LEARN YOU ARE A FOOL AND A FAILURE.
I COULD HAVE TOLD YOU THAT IN AN INSTANT, LUTHOR.
IF IT WEREN'T FOR YOUR PSYCHIC BLOCKERS, I'D HAVE FORCED YOU TO RIP OUT YOUR OWN THROAT.
I LIKE YOUR SPIRIT, BUT YOU'RE MISSING THE POINT, GRODD.
I'M TELLING YOU WE NEED TO THINK BIGGER.
I'M OFFERING YOU THE WORLD.

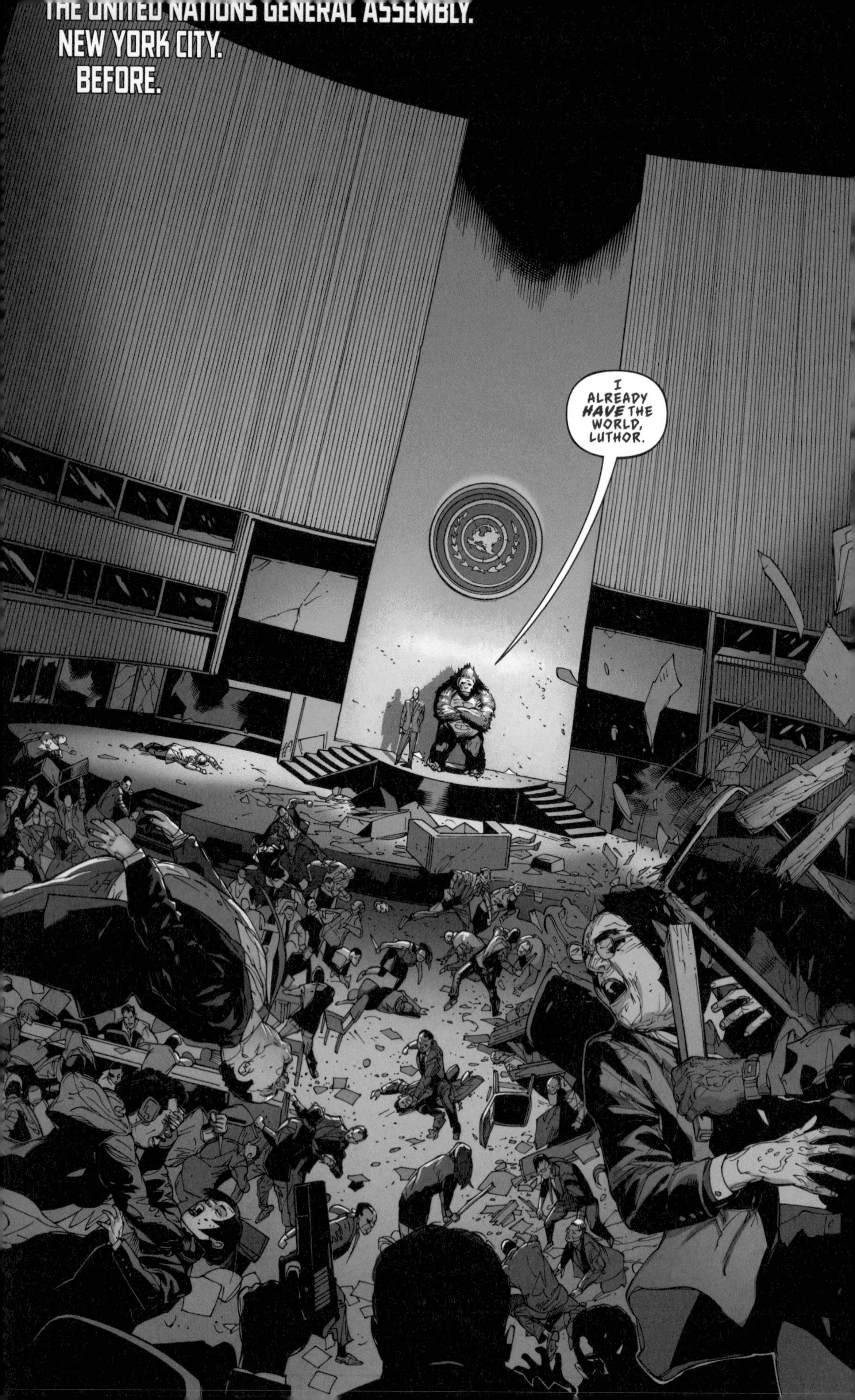
THE UNITED NATIONS GENERAL ASSEMBLY.
NEW YORK CITY.
BEFORE.
I ALREADY HAVE THE WORLD, LUTHOR.

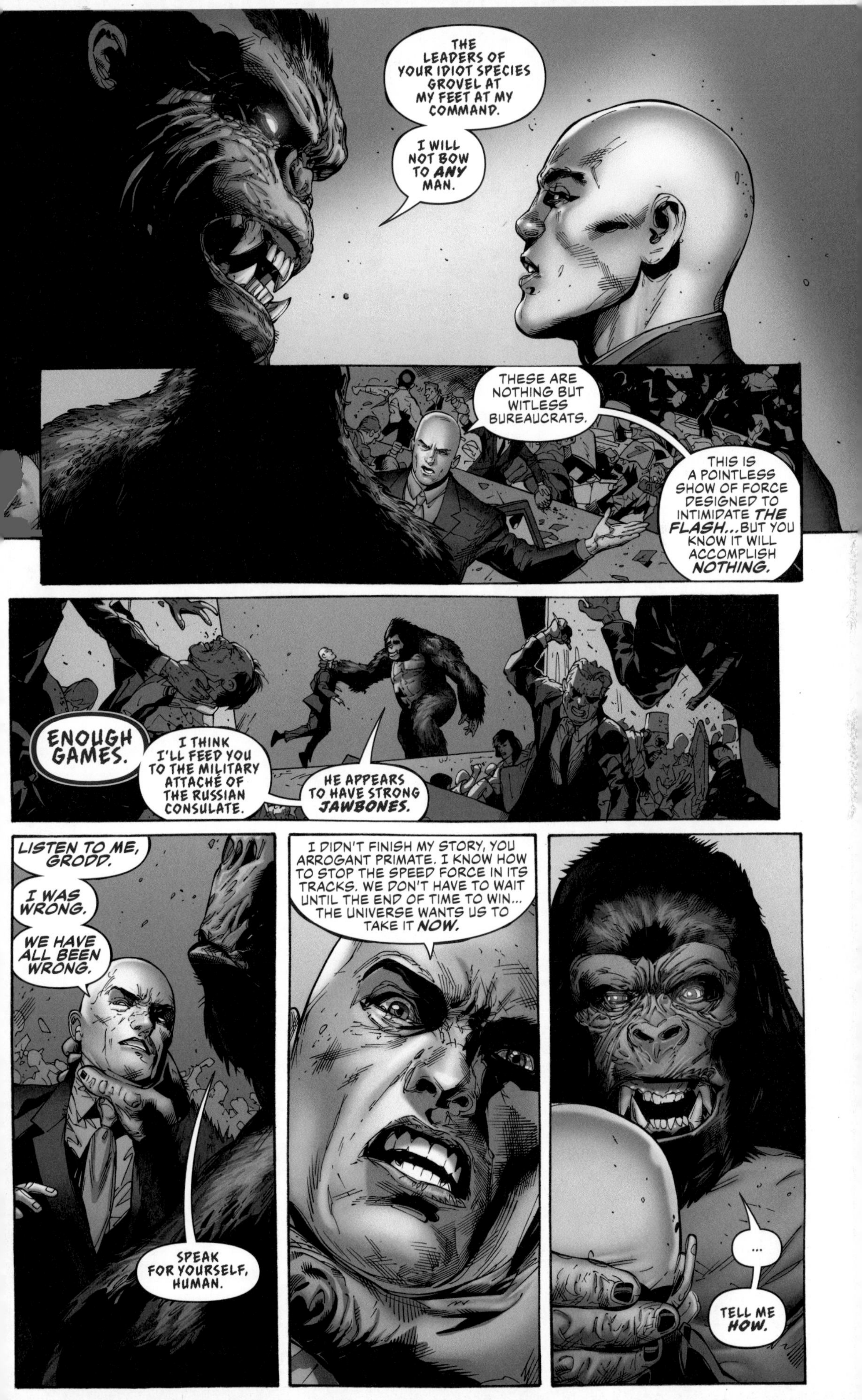
THE LEADERS OF YOUR IDIOT SPECIES GROVEL AT MY FEET AT MY COMMAND.
I WILL NOT BOW TO ANY MAN.
THESE ARE NOTHING BUT WITLESS BUREAUCRATS.
THIS IS A POINTLESS SHOW OF FORCE DESIGNED TO INTIMIDATE THE FLASH... BUT YOU KNOW IT WILL ACCOMPLISH NOTHING.
ENOUGH GAMES.
I THINK I'LL FEED YOU TO THE MILITARY ATTACHÉ OF THE RUSSIAN CONSULATE.
HE APPEARS TO HAVE STRONG JAWBONES.
LISTEN TO ME, GRODD.
I WAS WRONG.
WE HAVE ALL BEEN WRONG.
SPEAK FOR YOURSELF, HUMAN.
I DIDN'T FINISH MY STORY, YOU ARROGANT PRIMATE. I KNOW HOW TO STOP THE SPEED FORCE IN ITS TRACKS. WE DON'T HAVE TO WAIT UNTIL THE END OF TIME TO WIN... THE UNIVERSE WANTS US TO TAKE IT NOW.
...
TELL ME HOW.

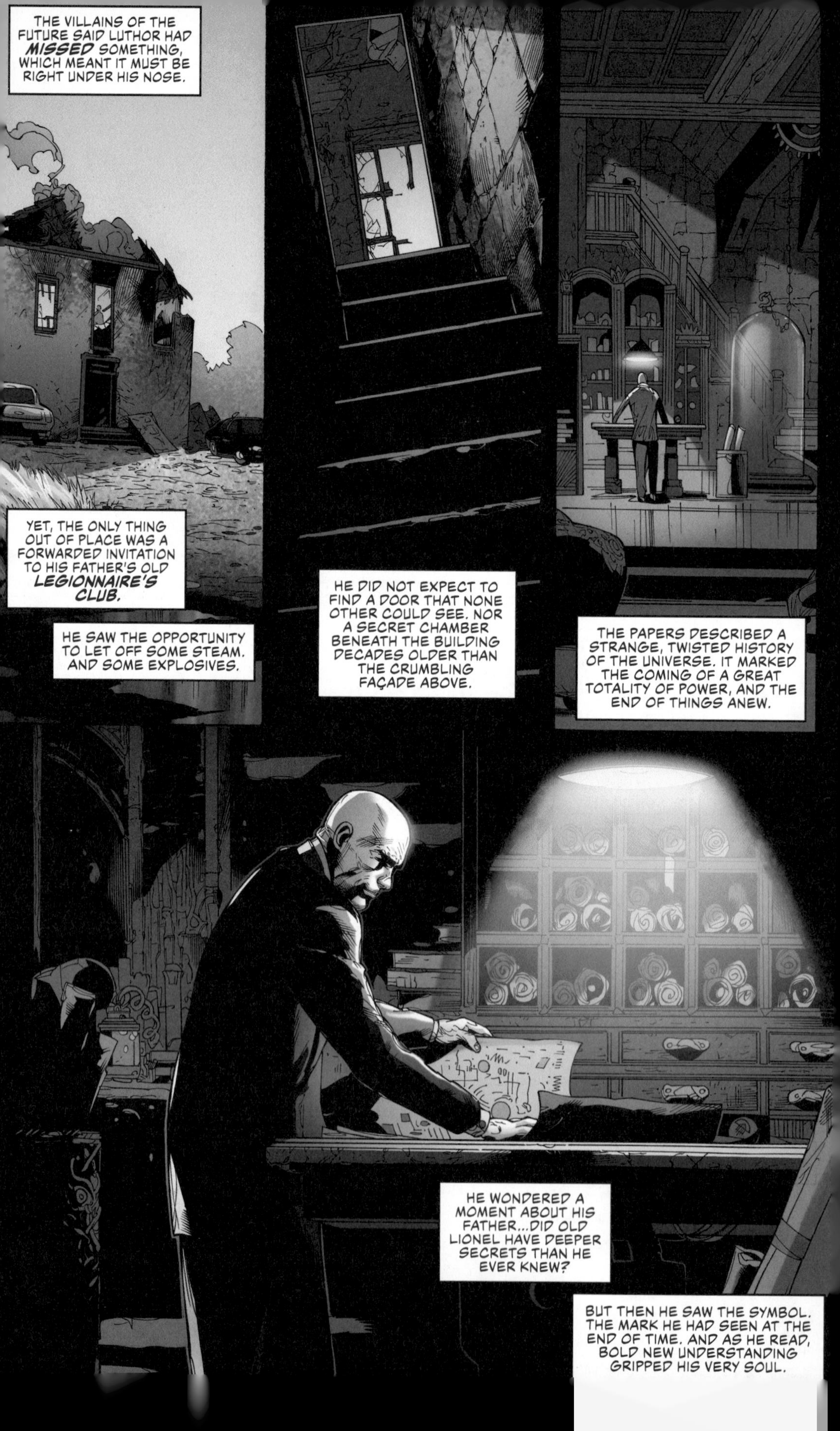
THE VILLAINS OF THE FUTURE SAID LUTHOR HAD MISSED SOMETHING, WHICH MEANT IT MUST BE RIGHT UNDER HIS NOSE.
YET, THE ONLY THING OUT OF PLACE WAS A FORWARDED INVITATION TO HIS FATHER'S OLD LEGIONNAIRE'S CLUB.
HE SAW THE OPPORTUNITY TO LET OFF SOME STEAM. AND SOME EXPLOSIVES.
HE DID NOT EXPECT TO FIND A DOOR THAT NONE OTHER COULD SEE. NOR A SECRET CHAMBER BENEATH THE BUILDING DECADES OLDER THAN THE CRUMBLING FAÇADE ABOVE.
THE PAPERS DESCRIBED A STRANGE, TWISTED HISTORY OF THE UNIVERSE. IT MARKED THE COMING OF A GREAT TOTALITY OF POWER, AND THE END OF THINGS ANEW.
HE WONDERED A MOMENT ABOUT HIS FATHER...DID OLD LIONEL HAVE DEEPER SECRETS THAN HE EVER KNEW?
BUT THEN HE SAW THE SYMBOL. THE MARK HE HAD SEEN AT THE END OF TIME. AND AS HE READ, BOLD NEW UNDERSTANDING GRIPPED HIS VERY SOUL.

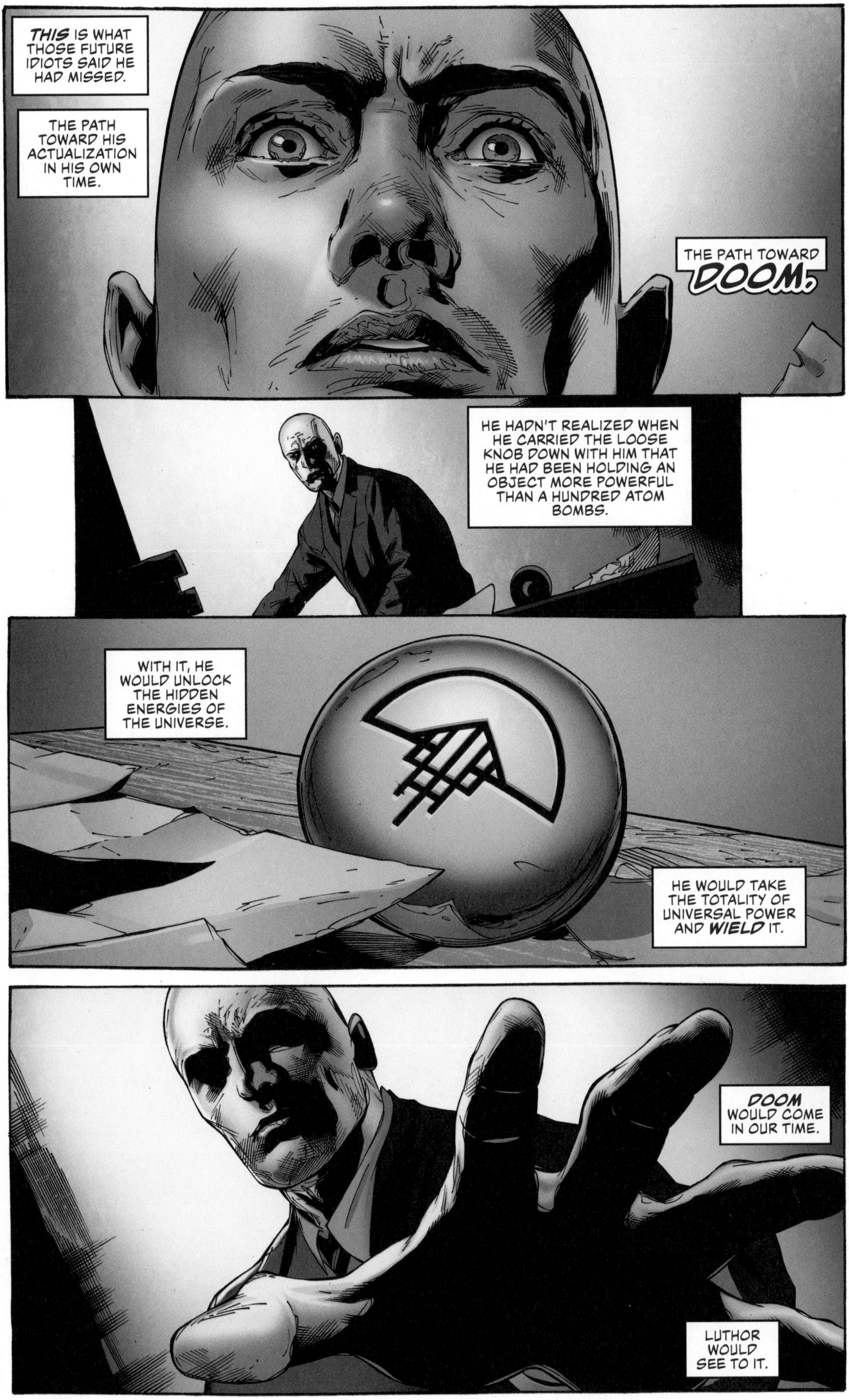
THIS IS WHAT THOSE FUTURE IDIOTS SAID HE HAD MISSED.
THE PATH TOWARD HIS ACTUALIZATION IN HIS OWN TIME.
THE PATH TOWARD DOOM.
HE HADN'T REALIZED WHEN HE CARRIED THE LOOSE KNOB DOWN WITH HIM THAT HE HAD BEEN HOLDING AN OBJECT MORE POWERFUL THAN A HUNDRED ATOM BOMBS.
WITH IT, HE WOULD UNLOCK THE HIDDEN ENERGIES OF THE UNIVERSE.
HE WOULD TAKE THE TOTALITY OF UNIVERSAL POWER AND WIELD IT.
DOOM WOULD COME IN OUR TIME.
LUTHOR WOULD SEE TO IT.

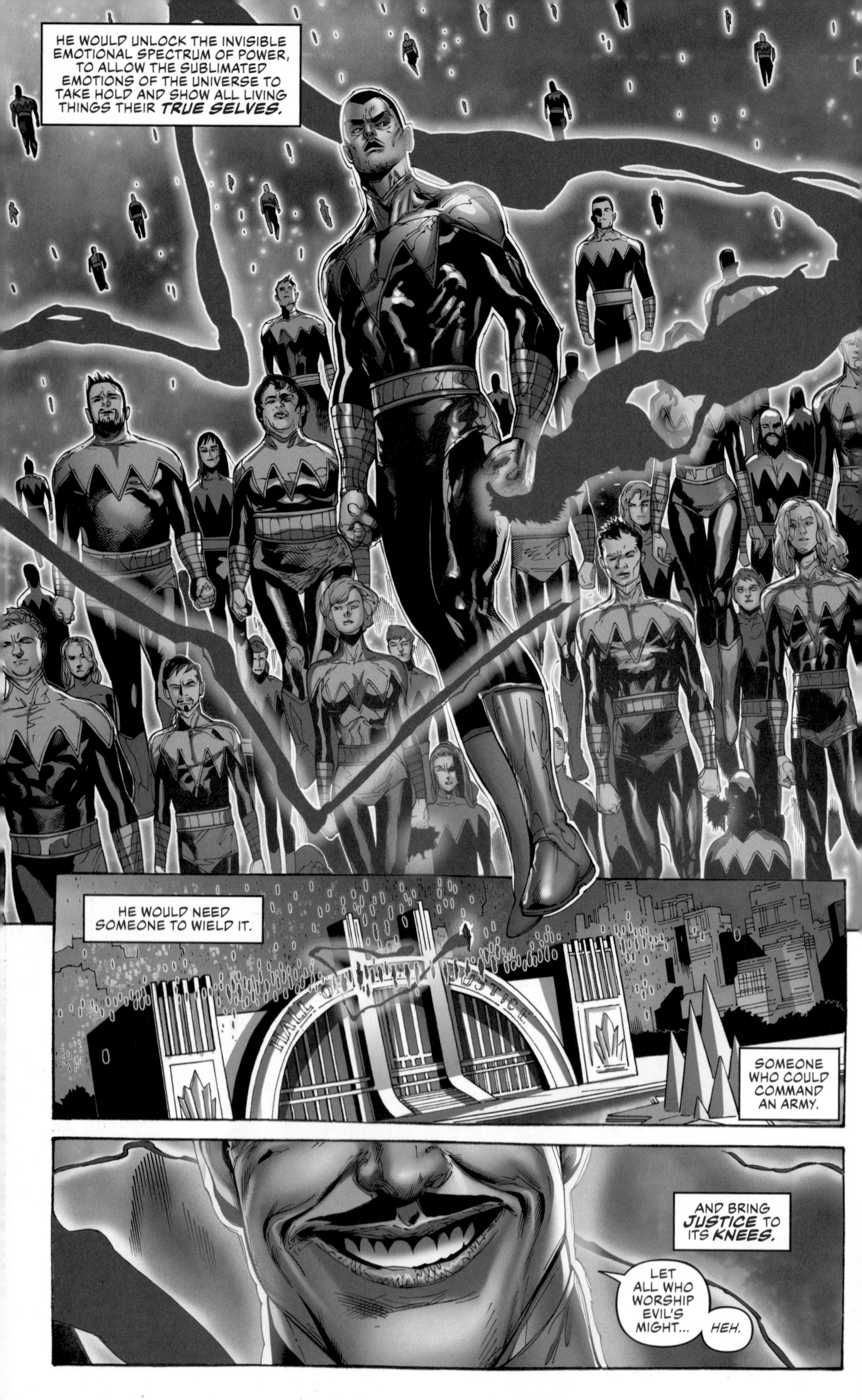
HE WOULD UNLOCK THE INVISIBLE EMOTIONAL SPECTRUM OF POWER, TO ALLOW THE SUBLIMATED EMOTIONS OF THE UNIVERSE TO TAKE HOLD AND SHOW ALL LIVING THINGS THEIR TRUE SELVES.
HE WOULD NEED SOMEONE TO WIELD IT.
HALL OF JUSTICE
SOMEONE WHO COULD COMMAND AN ARMY.
AND BRING JUSTICE TO ITS KNEES.
LET ALL WHO WORSHIP EVIL'S MIGHT...
HEH.

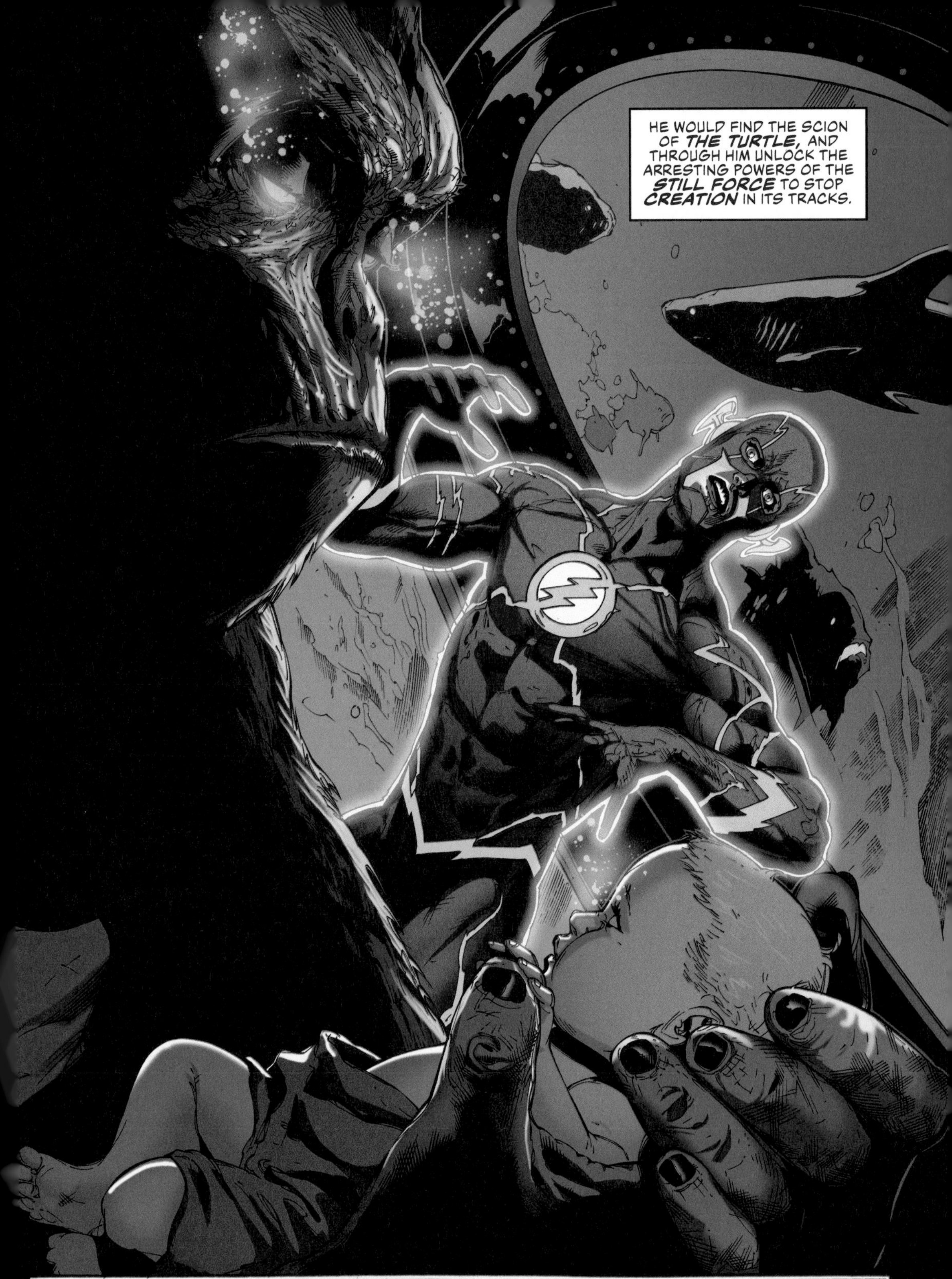
HE WOULD FIND THE SCION OF THE TURTLE, AND THROUGH HIM UNLOCK THE ARRESTING POWERS OF THE STILL FORCE TO STOP CREATION IN ITS TRACKS.

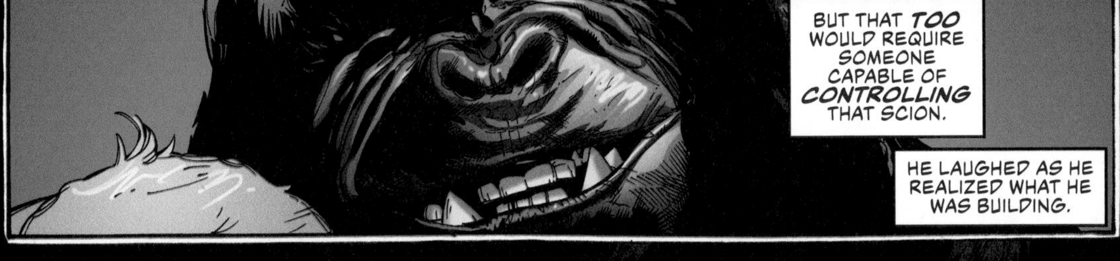
BUT THAT TOO WOULD REQUIRE SOMEONE CAPABLE OF CONTROLLING THAT SCION.
HE LAUGHED AS HE REALIZED WHAT HE WAS BUILDING.

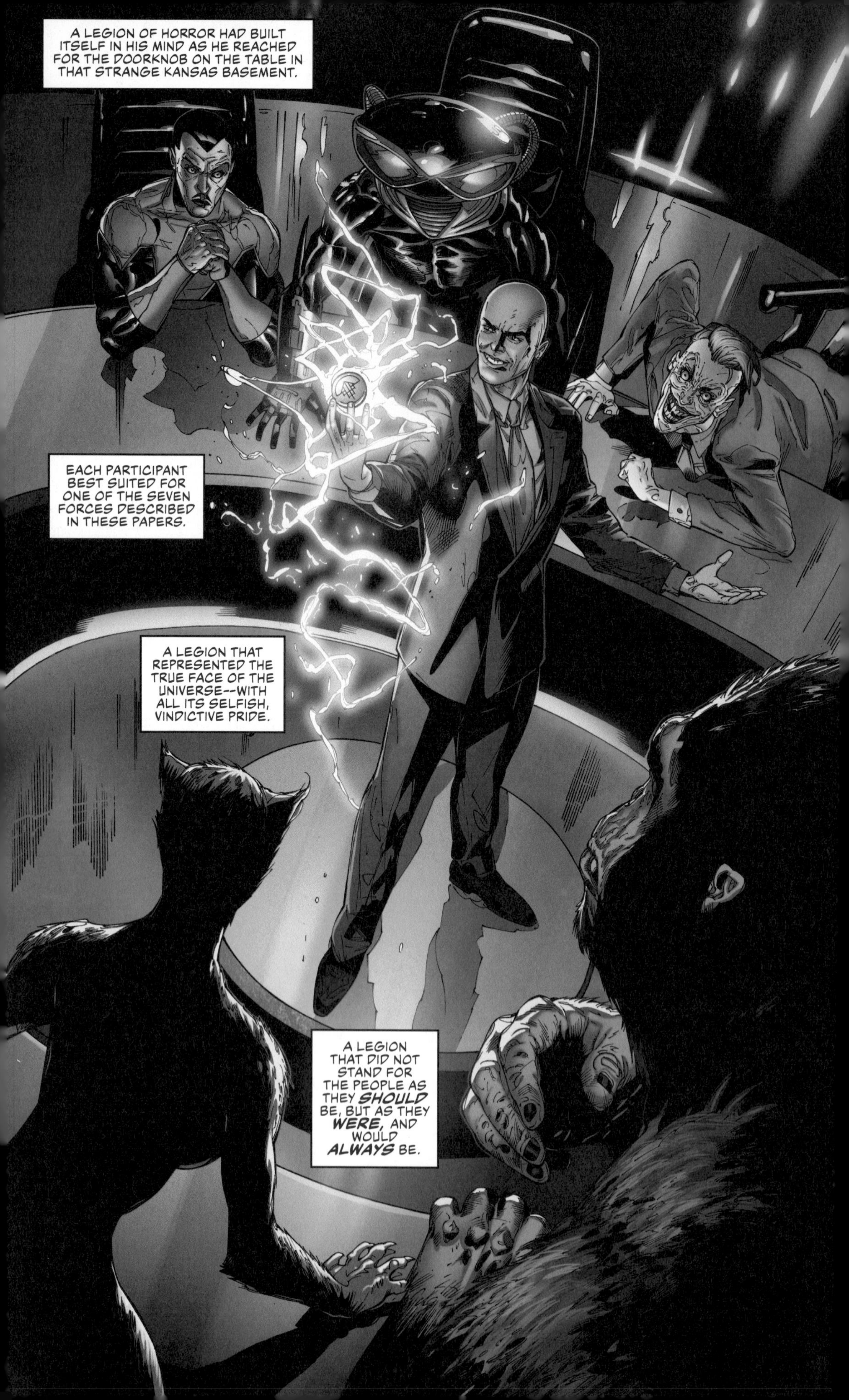
A LEGION OF HORROR HAD BUILT ITSELF IN HIS MIND AS HE REACHED FOR THE DOORKNOB ON THE TABLE IN THAT STRANGE KANSAS BASEMENT.
EACH PARTICIPANT BEST SUITED FOR ONE OF THE SEVEN FORCES DESCRIBED IN THESE PAPERS.
A LEGION THAT REPRESENTED THE TRUE FACE OF THE UNIVERSE--WITH ALL ITS SELFISH, VINDICTIVE PRIDE.
A LEGION THAT DID NOT STAND FOR THE PEOPLE AS THEY *SHOULD* BE, BUT AS THEY *WERE,* AND WOULD *ALWAYS* BE.

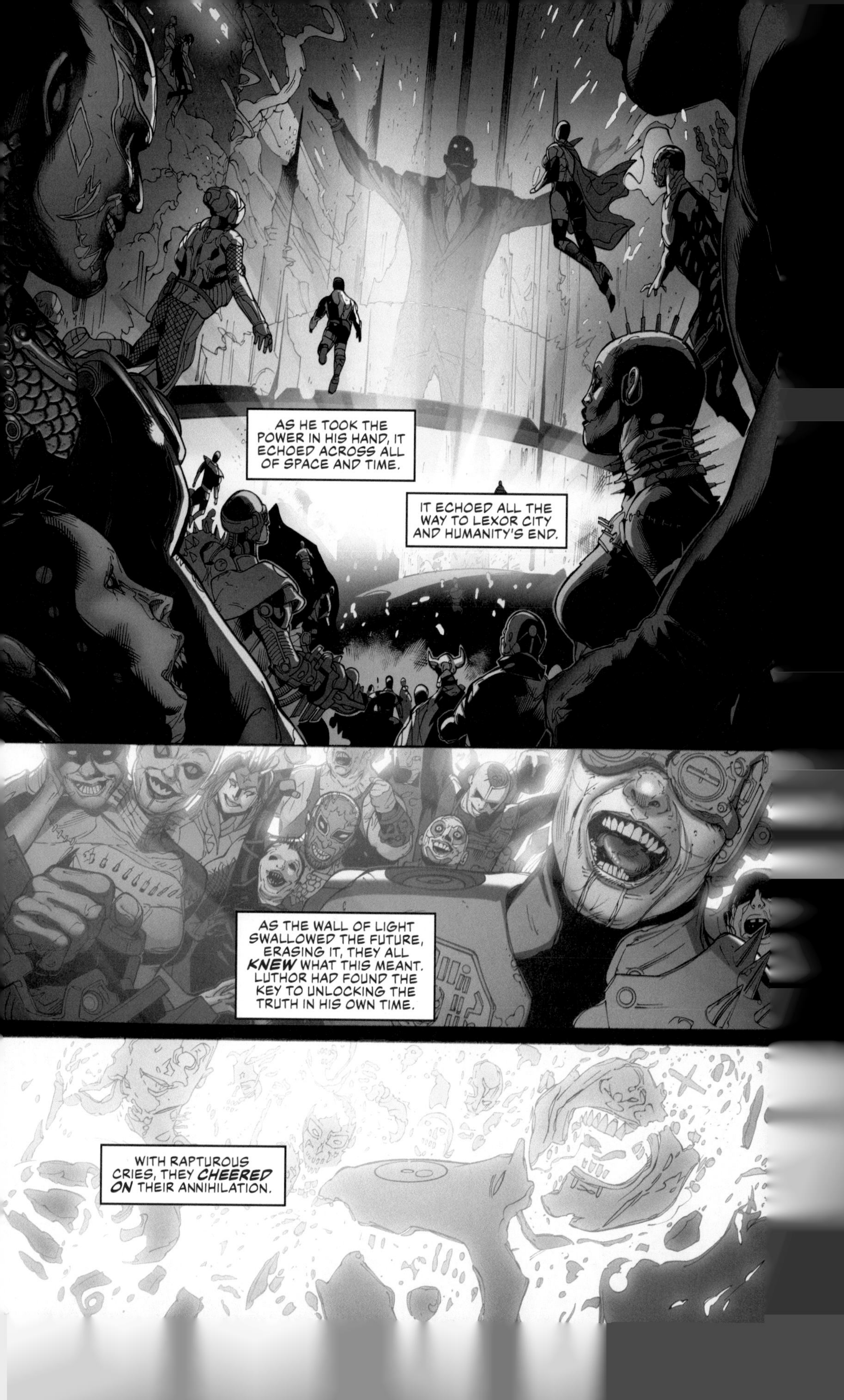
AS HE TOOK THE POWER IN HIS HAND, IT ECHOED ACROSS ALL OF SPACE AND TIME.
IT ECHOED ALL THE WAY TO LEXOR CITY AND HUMANITY'S END.
AS THE WALL OF LIGHT SWALLOWED THE FUTURE, ERASING IT, THEY ALL KNEW WHAT THIS MEANT. LUTHOR HAD FOUND THE KEY TO UNLOCKING THE TRUTH IN HIS OWN TIME.
WITH RAPTUROUS CRIES, THEY CHEERED ON THEIR ANNIHILATION.

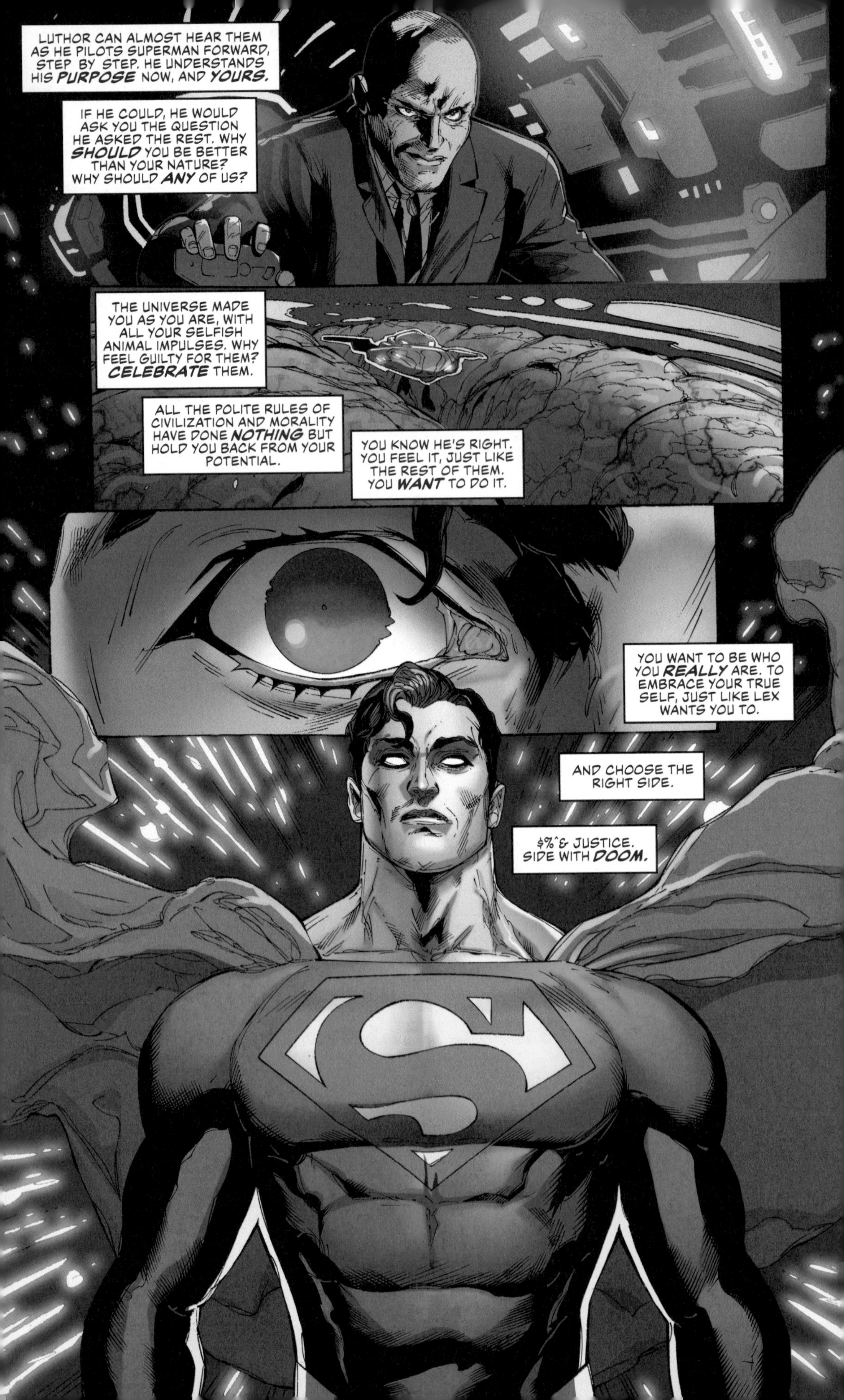
LUTHOR CAN ALMOST HEAR THEM AS HE PILOTS SUPERMAN FORWARD, STEP BY STEP. HE UNDERSTANDS HIS PURPOSE NOW, AND YOURS.
IF HE COULD, HE WOULD ASK YOU THE QUESTION HE ASKED THE REST. WHY SHOULD YOU BE BETTER THAN YOUR NATURE? WHY SHOULD ANY OF US?
THE UNIVERSE MADE YOU AS YOU ARE, WITH ALL YOUR SELFISH ANIMAL IMPULSES. WHY FEEL GUILTY FOR THEM? CELEBRATE THEM.
ALL THE POLITE RULES OF CIVILIZATION AND MORALITY HAVE DONE NOTHING BUT HOLD YOU BACK FROM YOUR POTENTIAL.
YOU KNOW HE'S RIGHT. YOU FEEL IT, JUST LIKE THE REST OF THEM. YOU WANT TO DO IT.
YOU WANT TO BE WHO YOU REALLY ARE. TO EMBRACE YOUR TRUE SELF, JUST LIKE LEX WANTS YOU TO.
AND CHOOSE THE RIGHT SIDE.
$%^& JUSTICE. SIDE WITH DOOM.

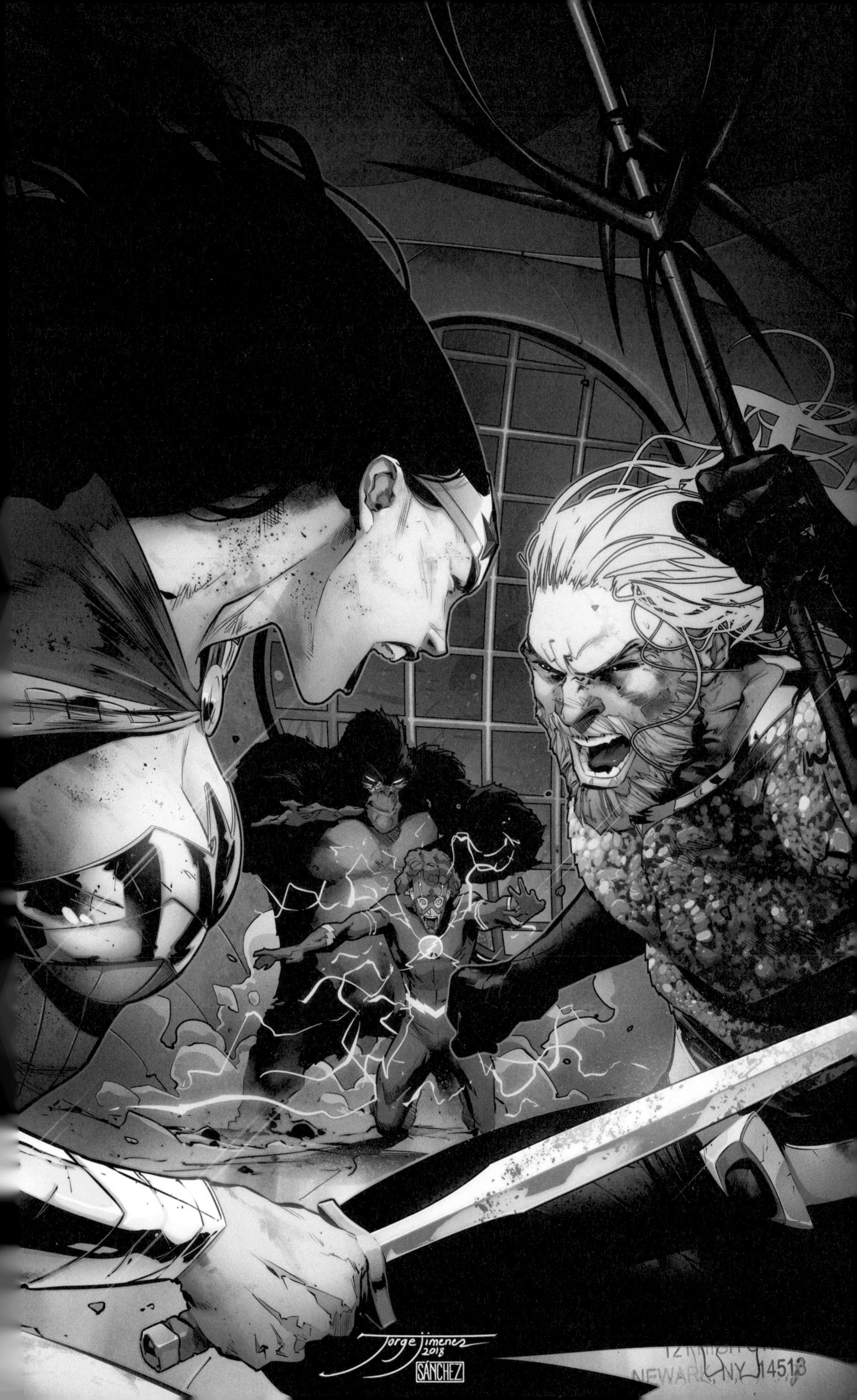
Jorge Jimenez 2018
SÁNCHEZ

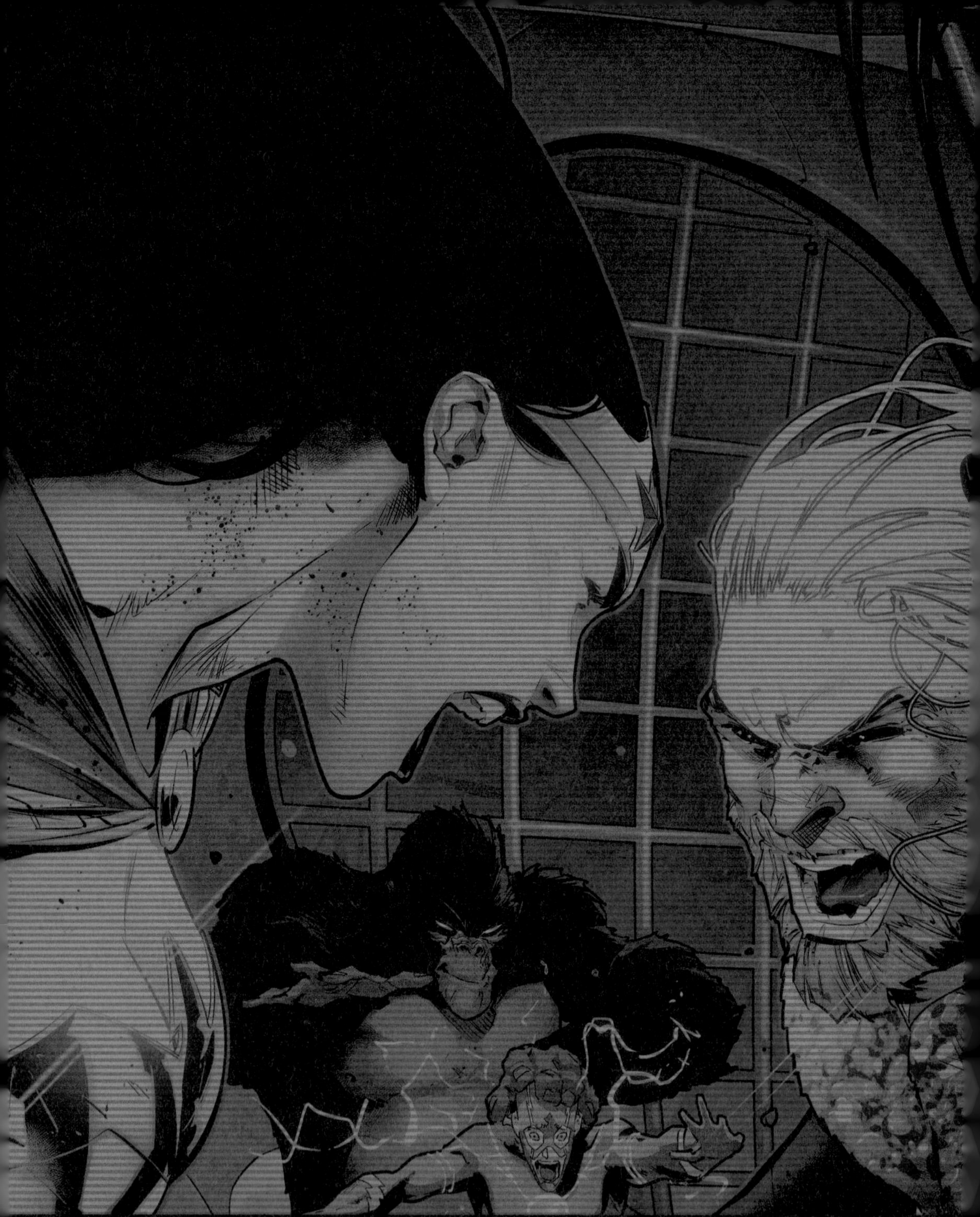

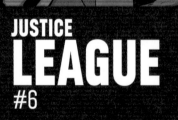

JUSTICE LEAGUE
#6

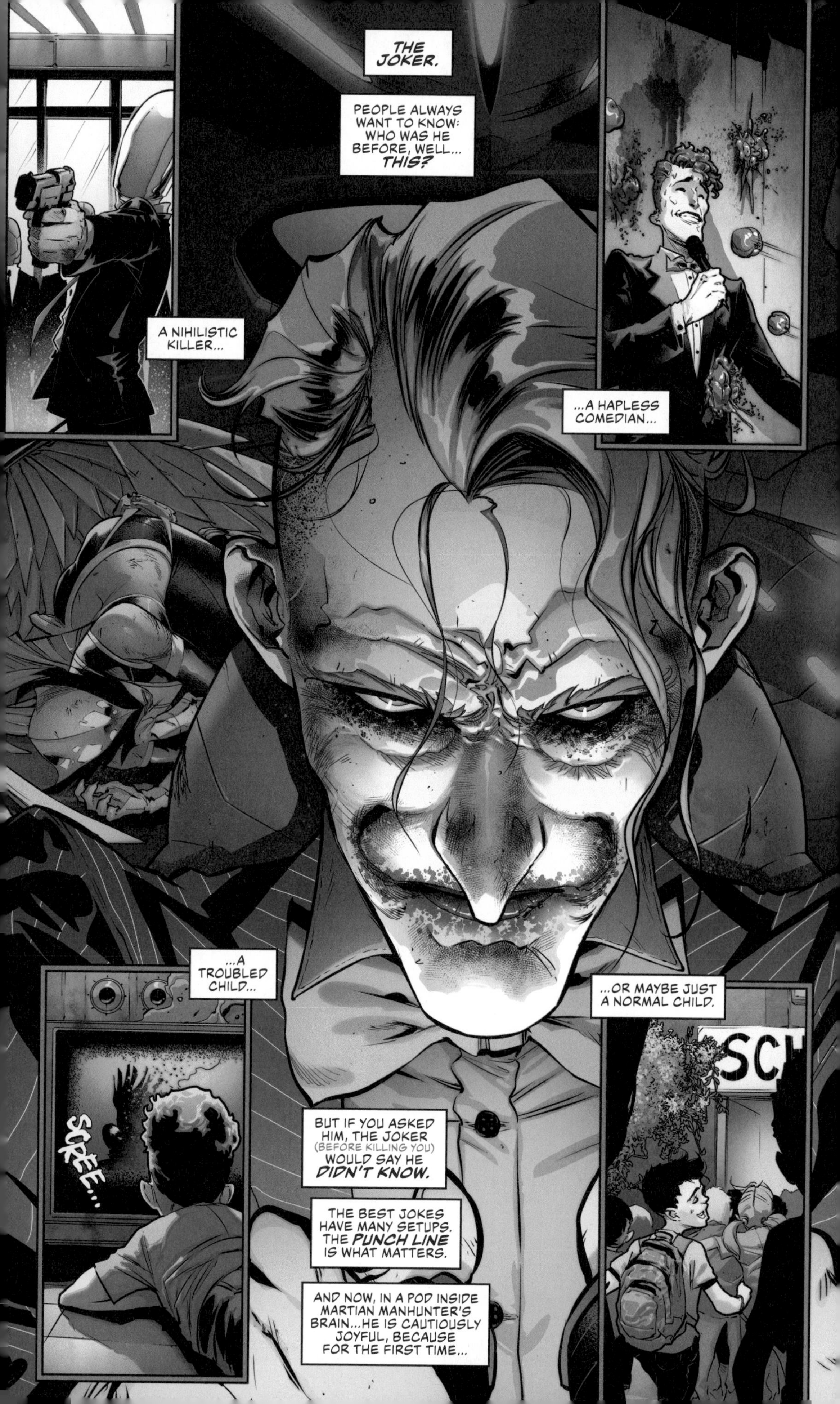
THE JOKER.
PEOPLE ALWAYS WANT TO KNOW: WHO WAS HE BEFORE, WELL... THIS?
A NIHILISTIC KILLER...
...A HAPLESS COMEDIAN...
...A TROUBLED CHILD...
SCREE...
...OR MAYBE JUST A NORMAL CHILD.
SCH
BUT IF YOU ASKED HIM, THE JOKER (BEFORE KILLING YOU) WOULD SAY HE DIDN'T KNOW.
THE BEST JOKES HAVE MANY SETUPS. THE PUNCH LINE IS WHAT MATTERS.
AND NOW, IN A POD INSIDE MARTIAN MANHUNTER'S BRAIN...HE IS CAUTIOUSLY JOYFUL, BECAUSE FOR THE FIRST TIME...

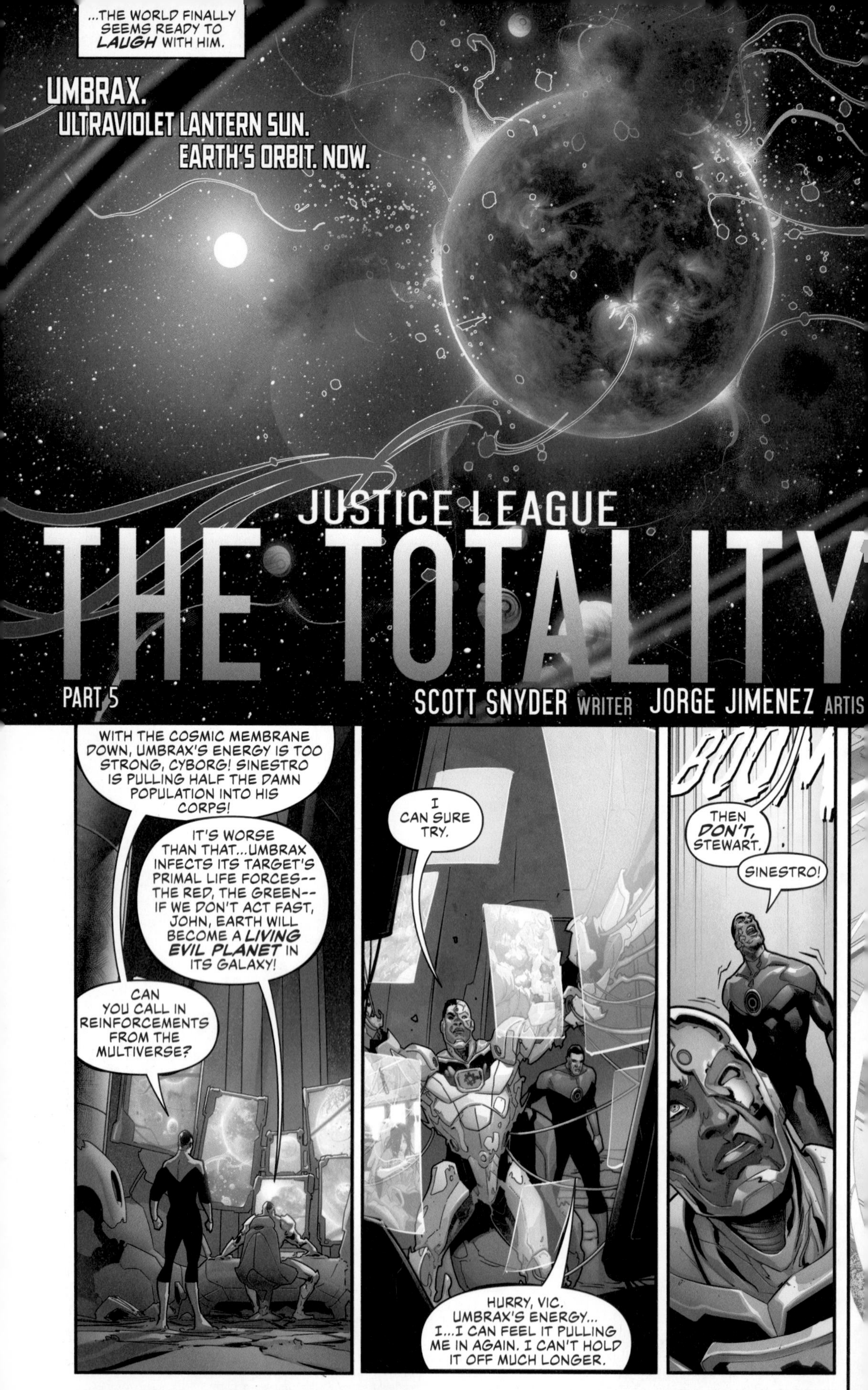

...THE WORLD FINALLY SEEMS READY TO LAUGH WITH HIM.
UMBRAX.
ULTRAVIOLET LANTERN SUN.
EARTH'S ORBIT. NOW.
JUSTICE LEAGUE
THE TOTALITY
PART 5
SCOTT SNYDER WRITER JORGE JIMENEZ ARTIS
WITH THE COSMIC MEMBRANE DOWN, UMBRAX'S ENERGY IS TOO STRONG, CYBORG! SINESTRO IS PULLING HALF THE DAMN POPULATION INTO HIS CORPS!
IT'S WORSE THAN THAT...UMBRAX INFECTS ITS TARGET'S PRIMAL LIFE FORCES--THE RED, THE GREEN--IF WE DON'T ACT FAST, JOHN, EARTH WILL BECOME A LIVING EVIL PLANET IN ITS GALAXY!
CAN YOU CALL IN REINFORCEMENTS FROM THE MULTIVERSE?
I CAN SURE TRY.
HURRY, VIC. UMBRAX'S ENERGY... I...I CAN FEEL IT PULLING ME IN AGAIN. I CAN'T HOLD IT OFF MUCH LONGER.
BOOM
THEN DON'T, STEWART.
SINESTRO!

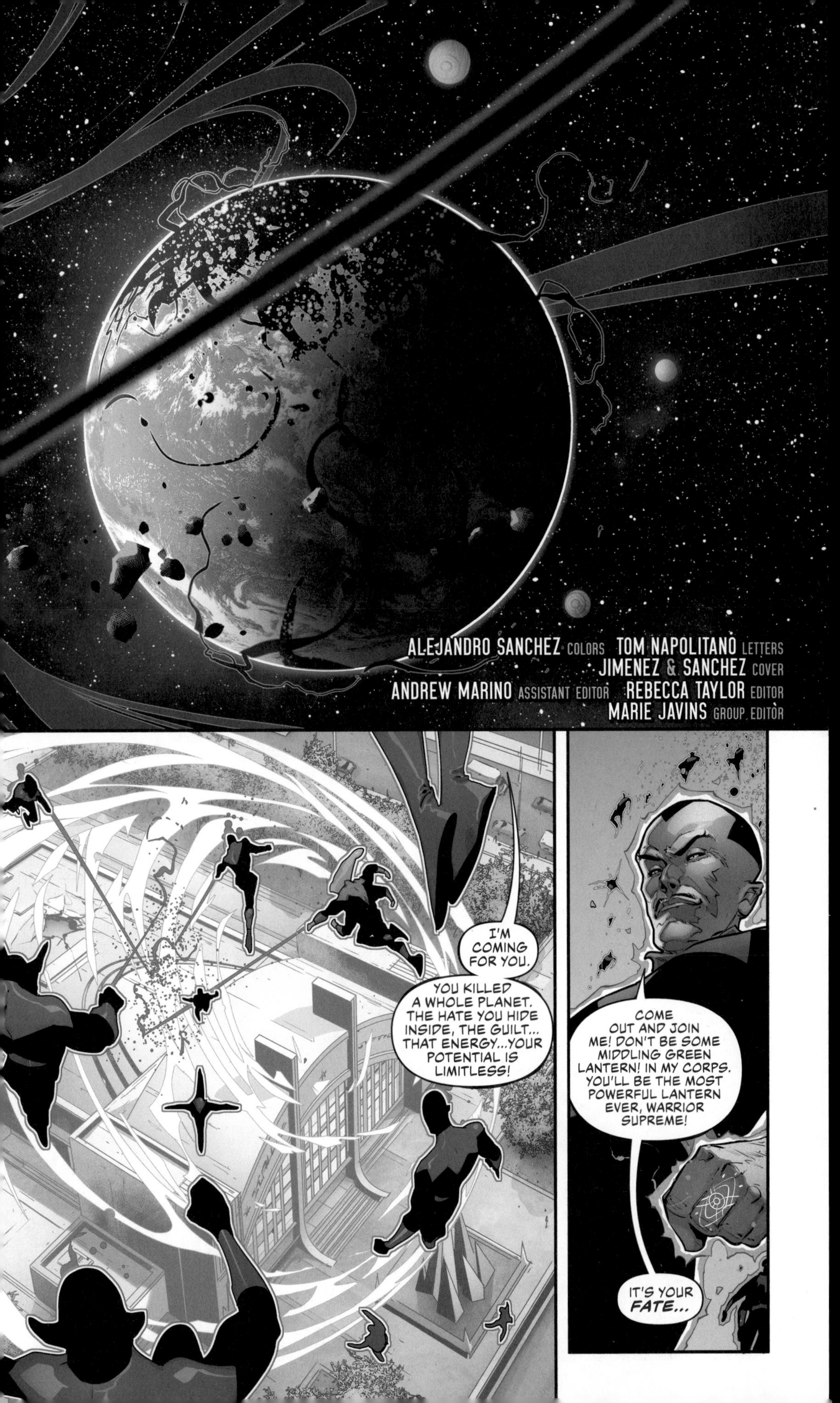
ALEJANDRO SANCHEZ COLORS TOM NAPOLITANO LETTERS
JIMENEZ & SANCHEZ COVER
ANDREW MARINO ASSISTANT EDITOR REBECCA TAYLOR EDITOR
MARIE JAVINS GROUP EDITOR
I'M COMING FOR YOU.
YOU KILLED A WHOLE PLANET. THE HATE YOU HIDE INSIDE, THE GUILT... THAT ENERGY...YOUR POTENTIAL IS LIMITLESS!
COME OUT AND JOIN ME! DON'T BE SOME MIDDLING GREEN LANTERN! IN MY CORPS, YOU'LL BE THE MOST POWERFUL LANTERN EVER, WARRIOR SUPREME!
IT'S YOUR FATE...

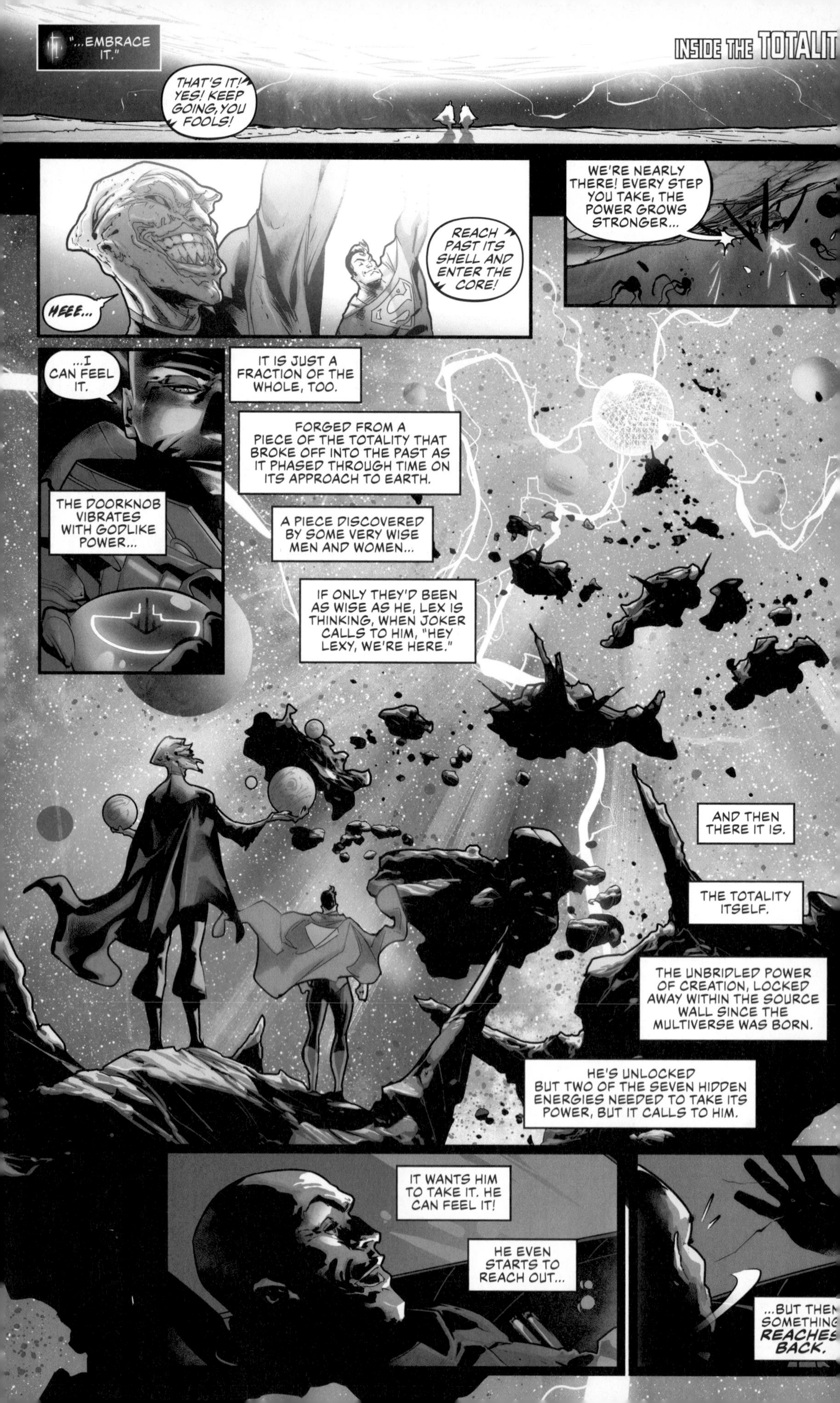
"...EMBRACE IT."
INSIDE THE TOTALIT
THAT'S IT! YES! KEEP GOING, YOU FOOLS!
HEEE...
REACH PAST ITS SHELL AND ENTER THE CORE!
WE'RE NEARLY THERE! EVERY STEP YOU TAKE, THE POWER GROWS STRONGER...
...I CAN FEEL IT.
THE DOORKNOB VIBRATES WITH GODLIKE POWER...
IT IS JUST A FRACTION OF THE WHOLE, TOO.
FORGED FROM A PIECE OF THE TOTALITY THAT BROKE OFF INTO THE PAST AS IT PHASED THROUGH TIME ON ITS APPROACH TO EARTH.
A PIECE DISCOVERED BY SOME VERY WISE MEN AND WOMEN...
IF ONLY THEY'D BEEN AS WISE AS HE, LEX IS THINKING, WHEN JOKER CALLS TO HIM, "HEY LEXY, WE'RE HERE."
AND THEN THERE IT IS.
THE TOTALITY ITSELF.
THE UNBRIDLED POWER OF CREATION, LOCKED AWAY WITHIN THE SOURCE WALL SINCE THE MULTIVERSE WAS BORN.
HE'S UNLOCKED BUT TWO OF THE SEVEN HIDDEN ENERGIES NEEDED TO TAKE ITS POWER, BUT IT CALLS TO HIM.
IT WANTS HIM TO TAKE IT. HE CAN FEEL IT!
HE EVEN STARTS TO REACH OUT...
...BUT THEN SOMETHING REACHES BACK.

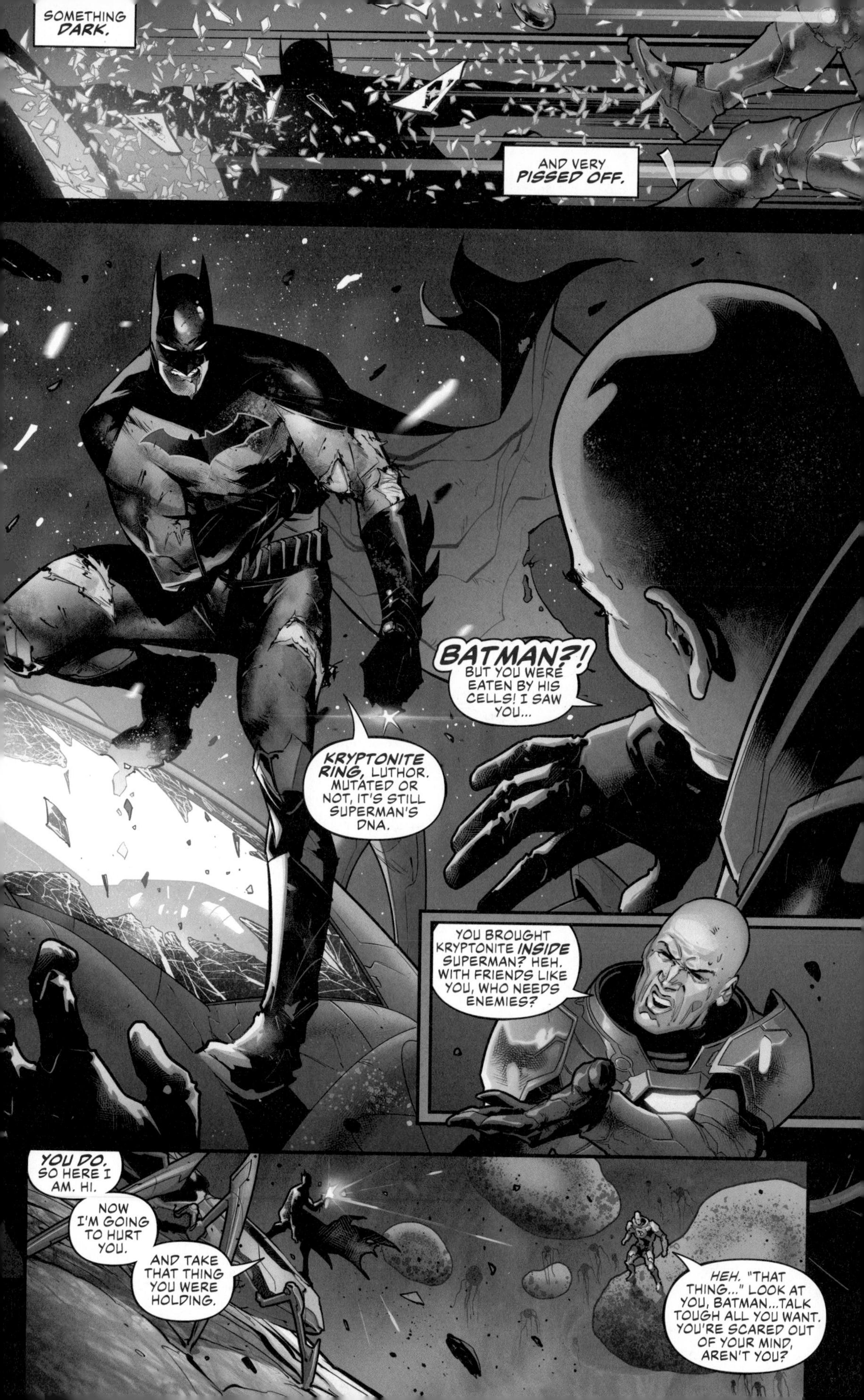
SOMETHING DARK.
AND VERY PISSED OFF.
BATMAN?! BUT YOU WERE EATEN BY HIS CELLS! I SAW YOU...
KRYPTONITE RING, LUTHOR. MUTATED OR NOT, IT'S STILL SUPERMAN'S DNA.
YOU BROUGHT KRYPTONITE INSIDE SUPERMAN? HEH. WITH FRIENDS LIKE YOU, WHO NEEDS ENEMIES?
YOU DO. SO HERE I AM. HI.
NOW I'M GOING TO HURT YOU.
AND TAKE THAT THING YOU WERE HOLDING.
HEH. "THAT THING..." LOOK AT YOU, BATMAN...TALK TOUGH ALL YOU WANT. YOU'RE SCARED OUT OF YOUR MIND, AREN'T YOU?

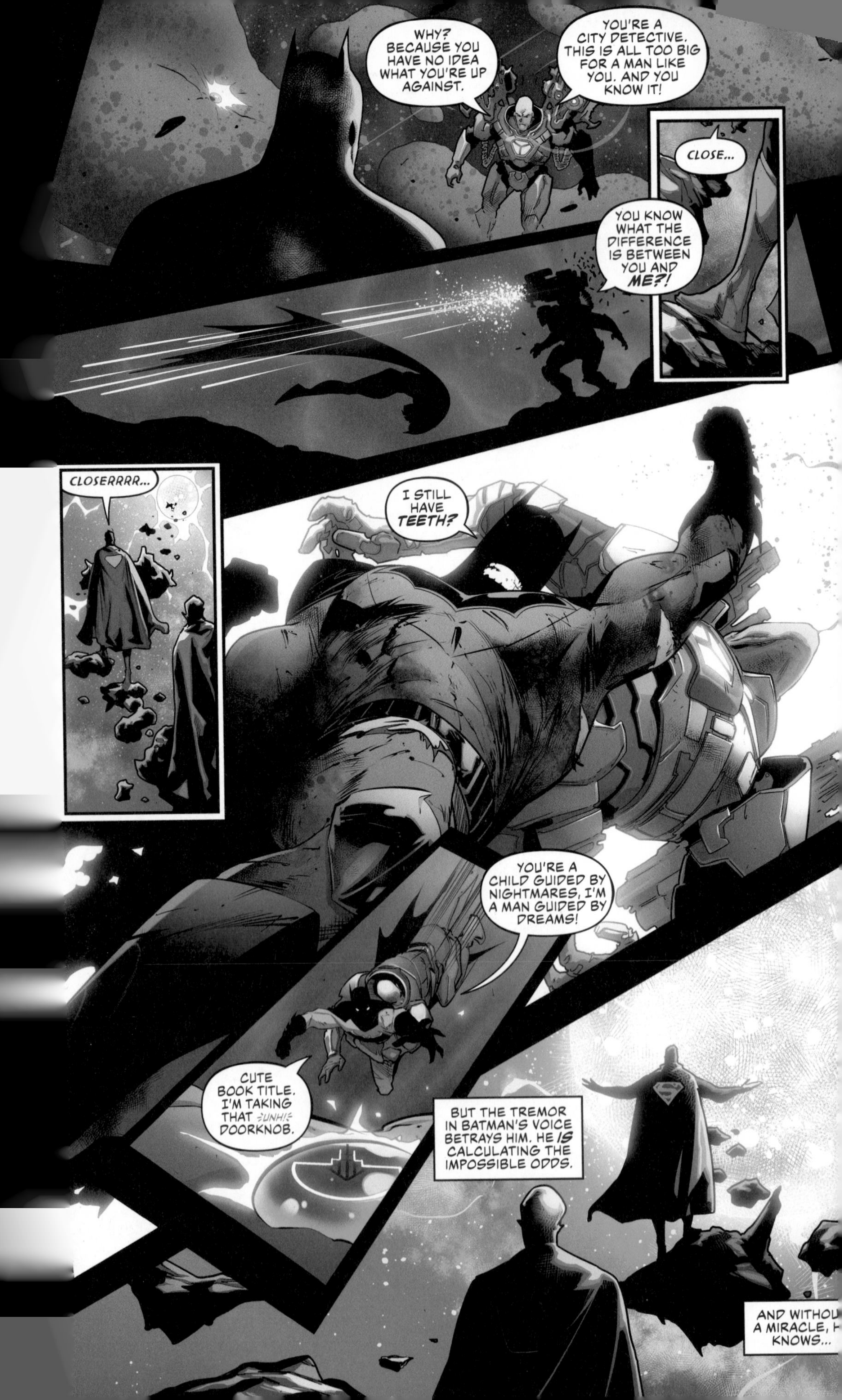

WHY? BECAUSE YOU HAVE NO IDEA WHAT YOU'RE UP AGAINST.
YOU'RE A CITY DETECTIVE. THIS IS ALL TOO BIG FOR A MAN LIKE YOU. AND YOU KNOW IT!
CLOSE...
YOU KNOW WHAT THE DIFFERENCE IS BETWEEN YOU AND ME?!
CLOSERRRR...
I STILL HAVE TEETH?
YOU'RE A CHILD GUIDED BY NIGHTMARES, I'M A MAN GUIDED BY DREAMS!
CUTE BOOK TITLE. I'M TAKING THAT UNH! DOORKNOB.
BUT THE TREMOR IN BATMAN'S VOICE BETRAYS HIM. HE IS CALCULATING THE IMPOSSIBLE ODDS.
AND WITHOU A MIRACLE, H KNOWS...

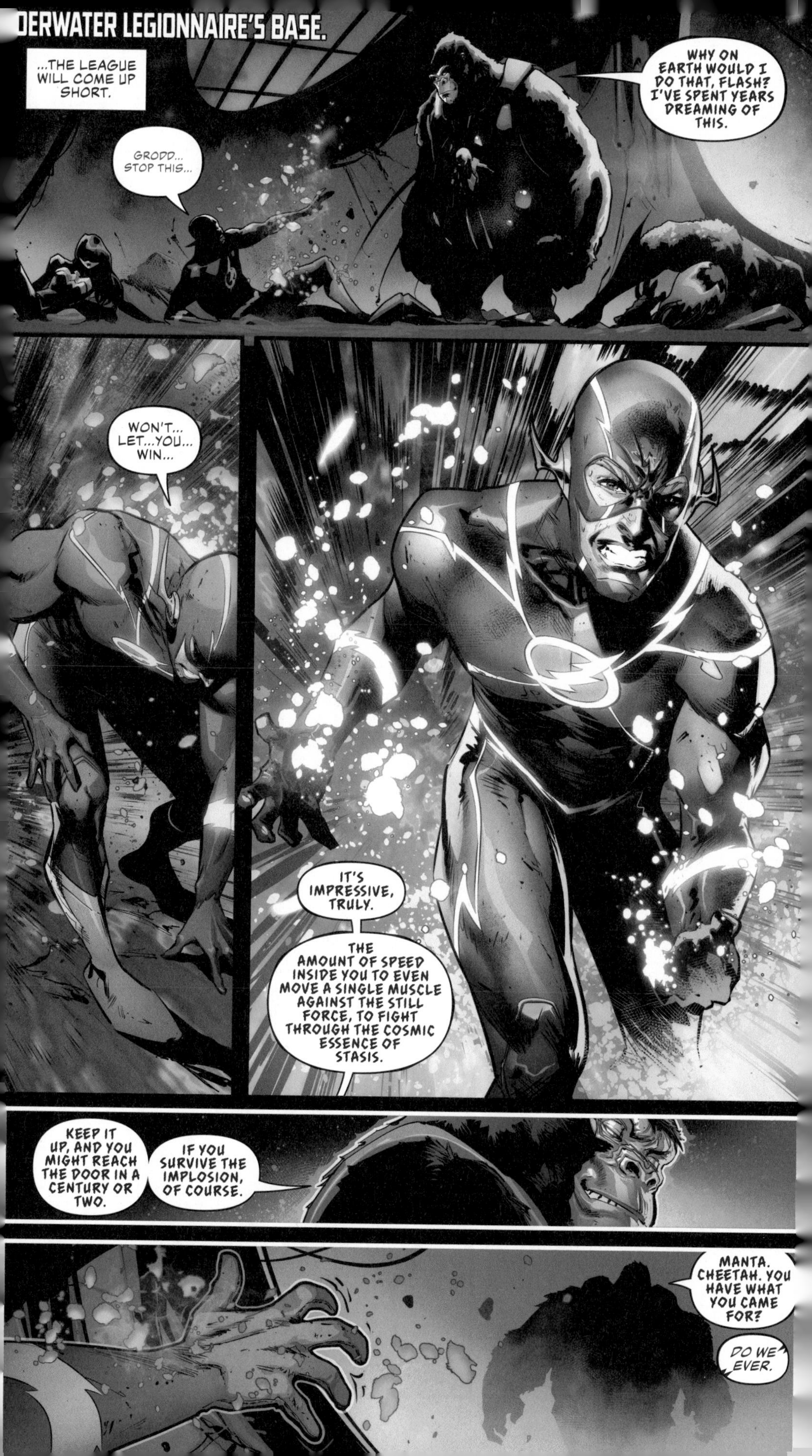
DERWATER LEGIONNAIRE'S BASE.
...THE LEAGUE WILL COME UP SHORT.
GRODD... STOP THIS...
WHY ON EARTH WOULD I DO THAT, FLASH? I'VE SPENT YEARS DREAMING OF THIS.
WON'T... LET...YOU... WIN...
IT'S IMPRESSIVE, TRULY.
THE AMOUNT OF SPEED INSIDE YOU TO EVEN MOVE A SINGLE MUSCLE AGAINST THE STILL FORCE, TO FIGHT THROUGH THE COSMIC ESSENCE OF STASIS.
KEEP IT UP, AND YOU MIGHT REACH THE DOOR IN A CENTURY OR TWO.
IF YOU SURVIVE THE IMPLOSION, OF COURSE.
MANTA. CHEETAH. YOU HAVE WHAT YOU CAME FOR?
DO WE EVER.

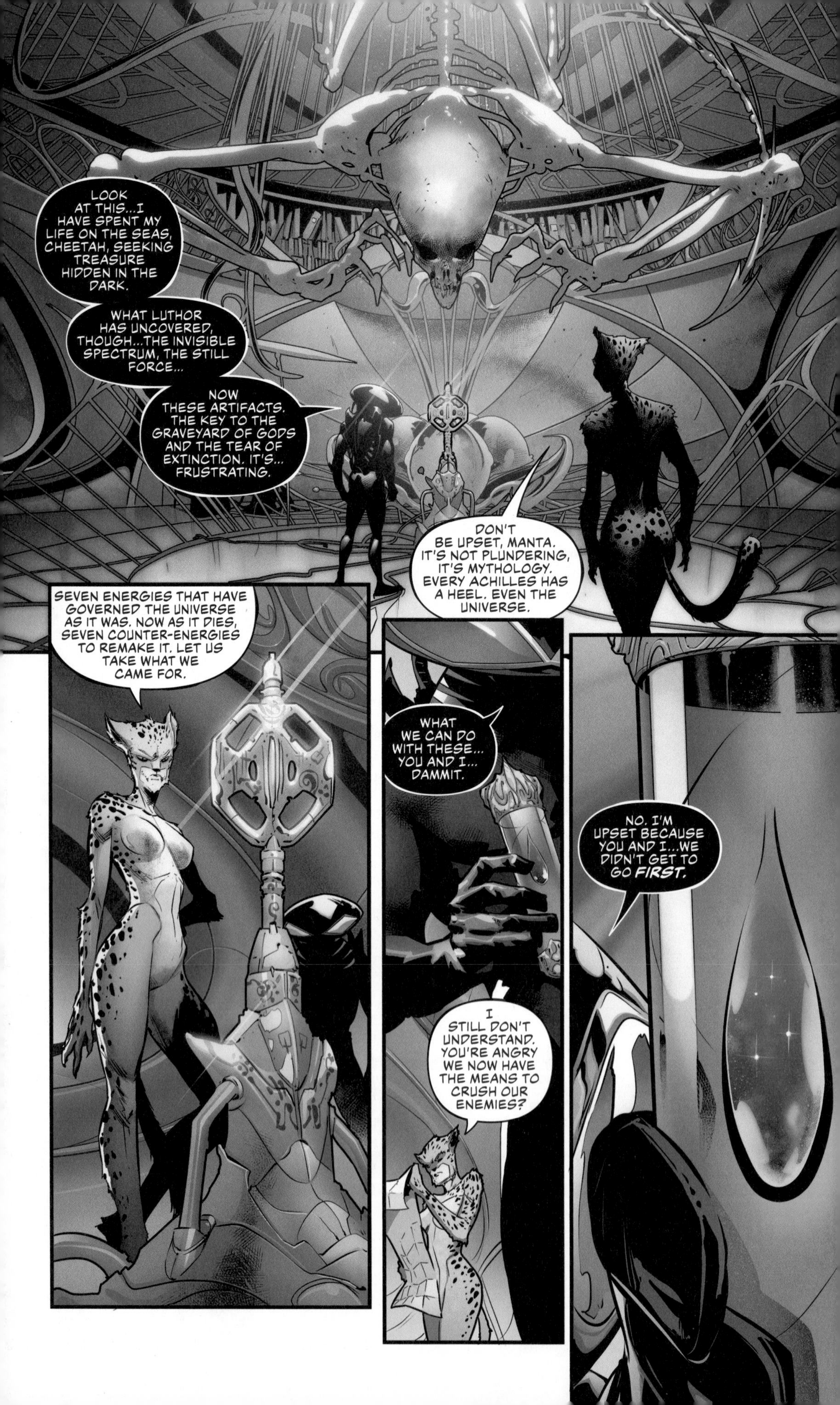

LOOK AT THIS...I HAVE SPENT MY LIFE ON THE SEAS, CHEETAH, SEEKING TREASURE HIDDEN IN THE DARK.
WHAT LUTHOR HAS UNCOVERED, THOUGH...THE INVISIBLE SPECTRUM, THE STILL FORCE...
NOW THESE ARTIFACTS. THE KEY TO THE GRAVEYARD OF GODS AND THE TEAR OF EXTINCTION. IT'S... FRUSTRATING.
DON'T BE UPSET, MANTA. IT'S NOT PLUNDERING, IT'S MYTHOLOGY. EVERY ACHILLES HAS A HEEL. EVEN THE UNIVERSE.
SEVEN ENERGIES THAT HAVE GOVERNED THE UNIVERSE AS IT WAS. NOW AS IT DIES, SEVEN COUNTER-ENERGIES TO REMAKE IT. LET US TAKE WHAT WE CAME FOR.
WHAT WE CAN DO WITH THESE... YOU AND I... DAMMIT.
I STILL DON'T UNDERSTAND. YOU'RE ANGRY WE NOW HAVE THE MEANS TO CRUSH OUR ENEMIES?
NO. I'M UPSET BECAUSE YOU AND I...WE DIDN'T GET TO GO FIRST.

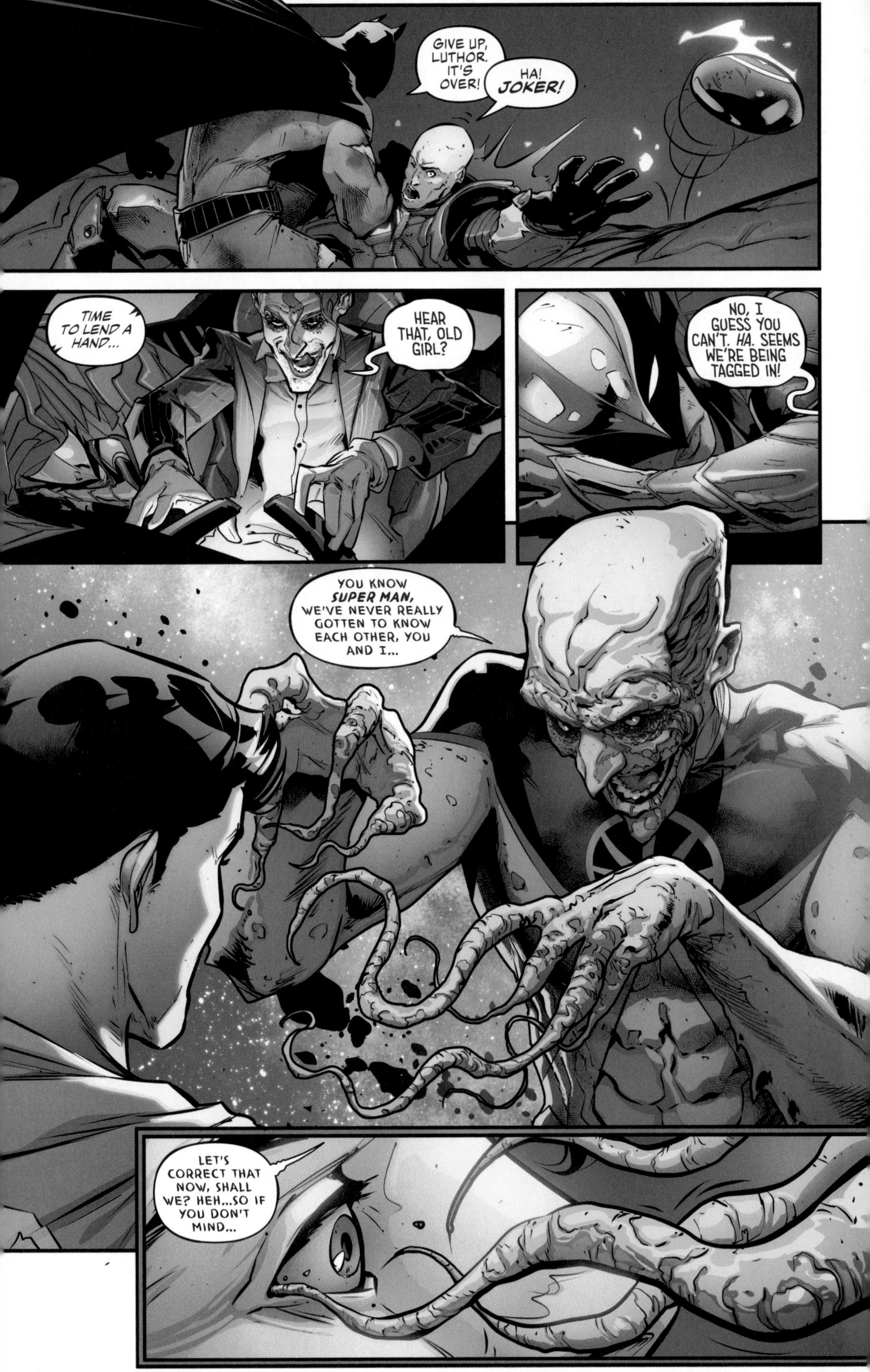
GIVE UP, LUTHOR. IT'S OVER!
HA! JOKER!
TIME TO LEND A HAND...
HEAR THAT, OLD GIRL?
NO, I GUESS YOU CAN'T. HA. SEEMS WE'RE BEING TAGGED IN!
YOU KNOW SUPER MAN, WE'VE NEVER REALLY GOTTEN TO KNOW EACH OTHER, YOU AND I...
LET'S CORRECT THAT NOW, SHALL WE? HEH...SO IF YOU DON'T MIND...

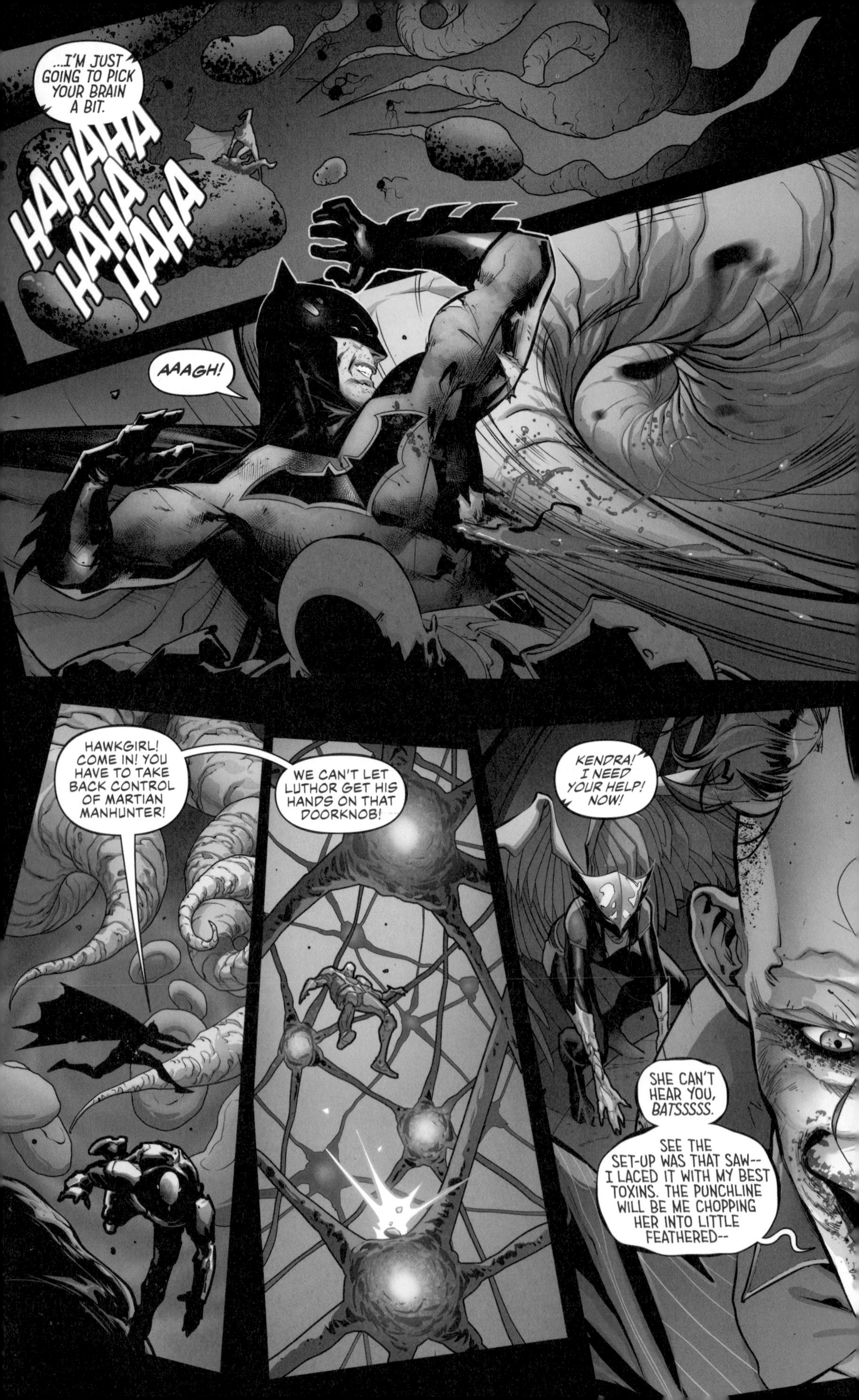
...I'M JUST GOING TO PICK YOUR BRAIN A BIT.
HAHAHA HAHA HAHA
AAAGH!
HAWKGIRL! COME IN! YOU HAVE TO TAKE BACK CONTROL OF MARTIAN MANHUNTER!
WE CAN'T LET LUTHOR GET HIS HANDS ON THAT DOORKNOB!
KENDRA! I NEED YOUR HELP! NOW!
SHE CAN'T HEAR YOU, BATSSSSS.
SEE THE SET-UP WAS THAT SAW-- I LACED IT WITH MY BEST TOXINS. THE PUNCHLINE WILL BE ME CHOPPING HER INTO LITTLE FEATHERED--

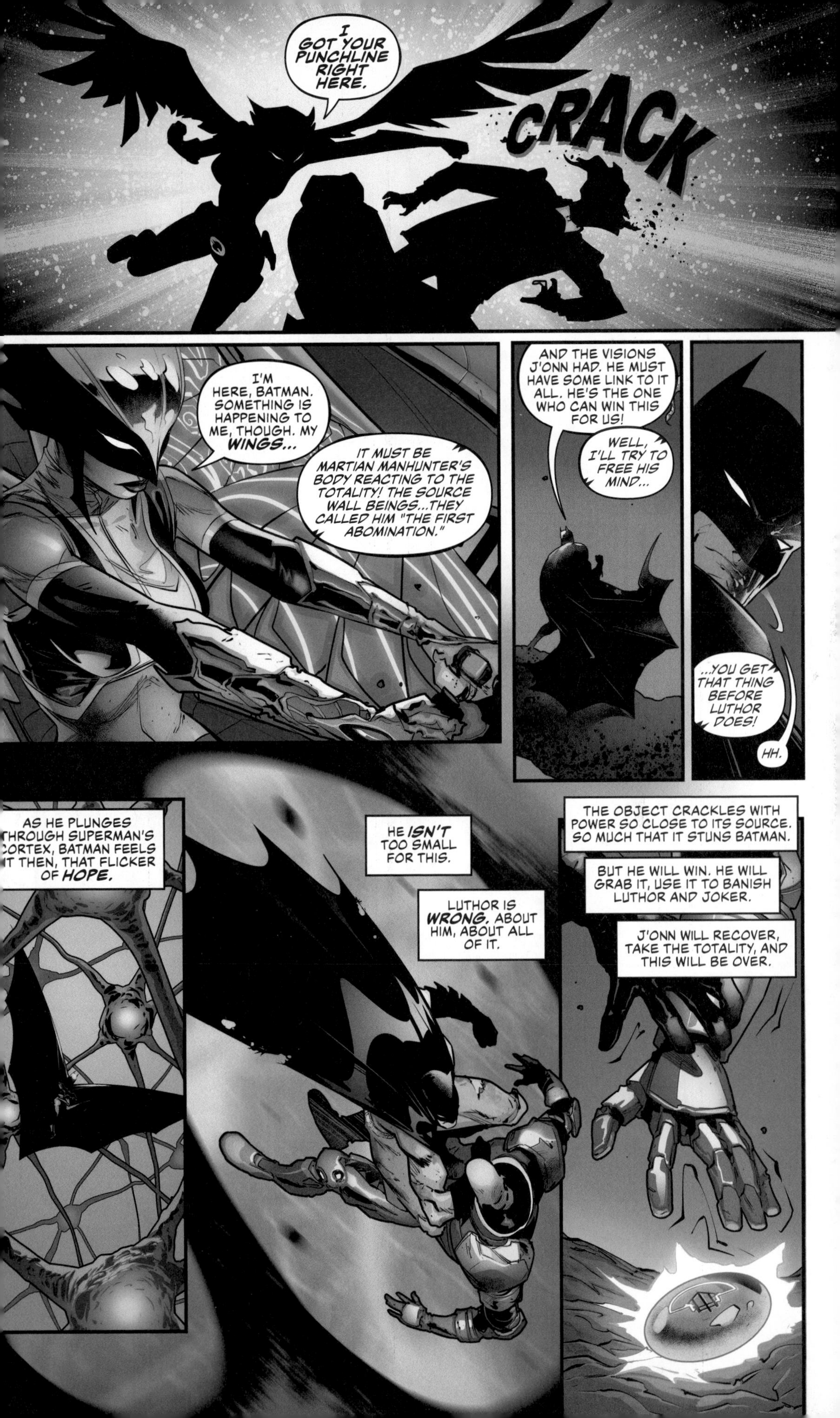
I GOT YOUR PUNCHLINE RIGHT HERE.
CRACK
I'M HERE, BATMAN. SOMETHING IS HAPPENING TO ME, THOUGH. MY WINGS...
IT MUST BE MARTIAN MANHUNTER'S BODY REACTING TO THE TOTALITY! THE SOURCE WALL BEINGS...THEY CALLED HIM "THE FIRST ABOMINATION."
AND THE VISIONS J'ONN HAD. HE MUST HAVE SOME LINK TO IT ALL. HE'S THE ONE WHO CAN WIN THIS FOR US!
WELL, I'LL TRY TO FREE HIS MIND...
...YOU GET THAT THING BEFORE LUTHOR DOES!
HH.
AS HE PLUNGES THROUGH SUPERMAN'S CORTEX, BATMAN FEELS IT THEN, THAT FLICKER OF HOPE.
HE ISN'T TOO SMALL FOR THIS.
LUTHOR IS WRONG. ABOUT HIM, ABOUT ALL OF IT.
THE OBJECT CRACKLES WITH POWER SO CLOSE TO ITS SOURCE. SO MUCH THAT IT STUNS BATMAN.
BUT HE WILL WIN. HE WILL GRAB IT, USE IT TO BANISH LUTHOR AND JOKER.
J'ONN WILL RECOVER, TAKE THE TOTALITY, AND THIS WILL BE OVER.

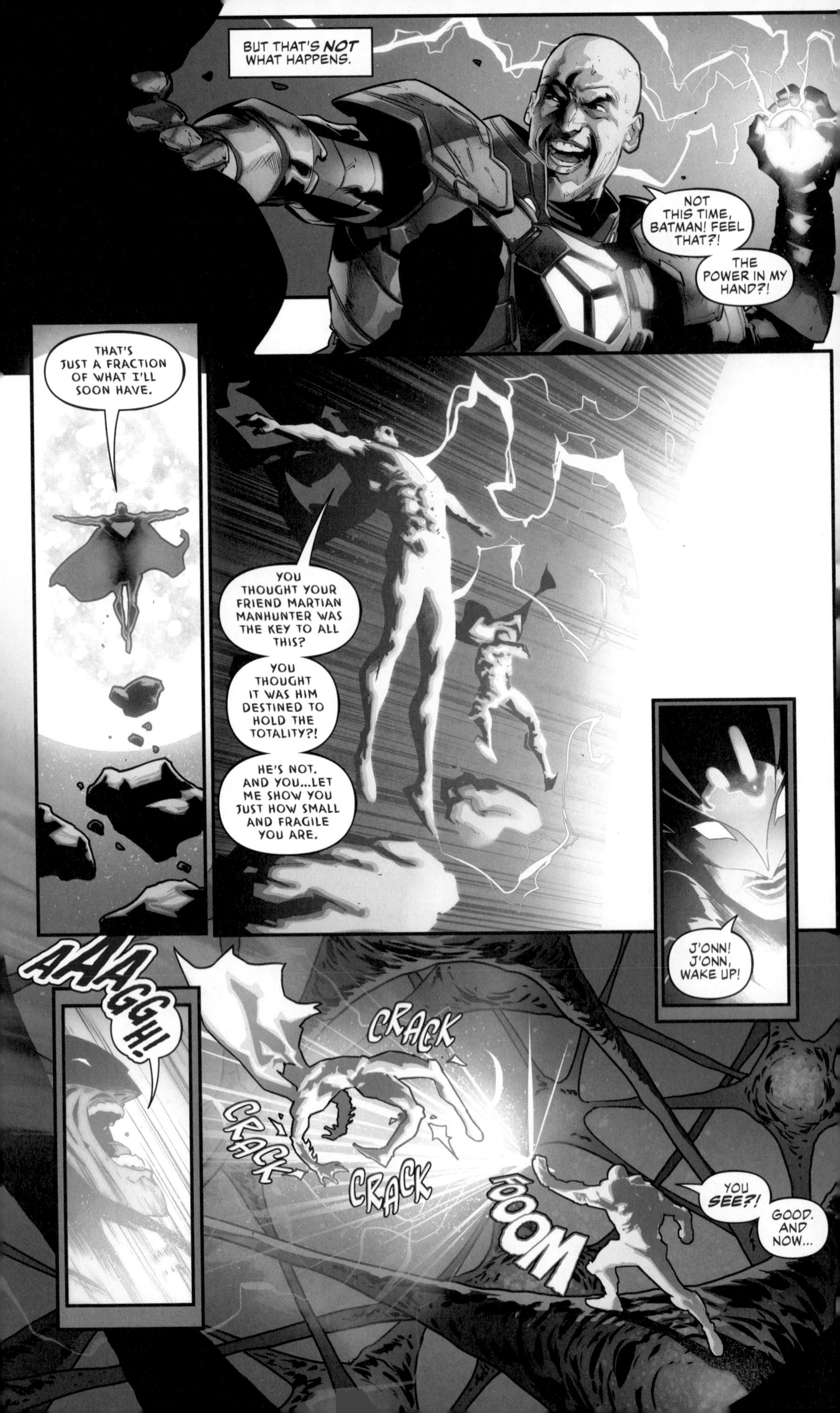
BUT THAT'S NOT WHAT HAPPENS.
NOT THIS TIME, BATMAN! FEEL THAT?!
THE POWER IN MY HAND?!
THAT'S JUST A FRACTION OF WHAT I'LL SOON HAVE.
YOU THOUGHT YOUR FRIEND MARTIAN MANHUNTER WAS THE KEY TO ALL THIS?
YOU THOUGHT IT WAS HIM DESTINED TO HOLD THE TOTALITY?!
HE'S NOT. AND YOU...LET ME SHOW YOU JUST HOW SMALL AND FRAGILE YOU ARE.
J'ONN! J'ONN, WAKE UP!
AAAGGH!
CRACK
CRACK
CRACK
FOOOOM
YOU SEE?!
GOOD. AND NOW...

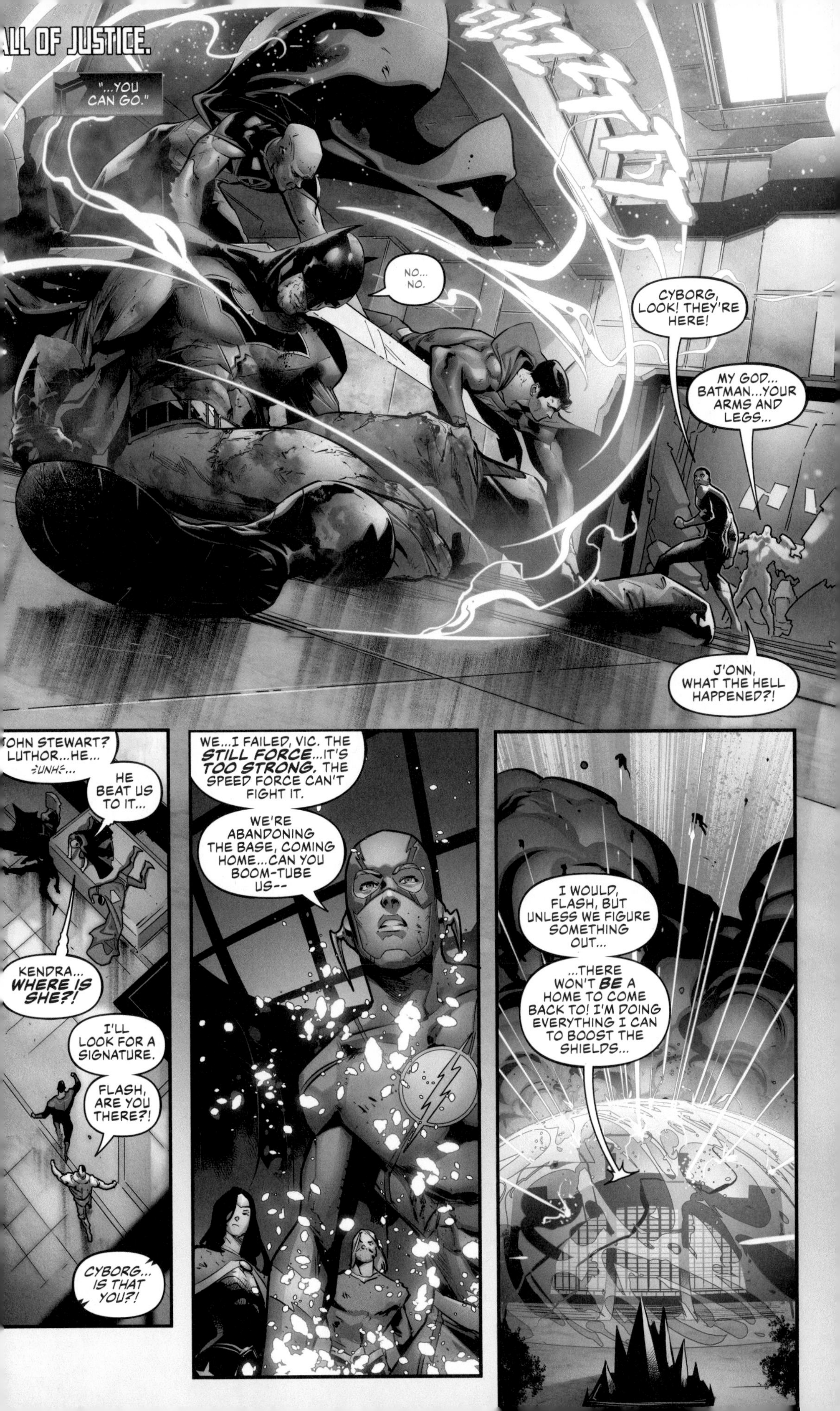
ALL OF JUSTICE.
"...YOU CAN GO."
ZZZZT
NO... NO.
CYBORG, LOOK! THEY'RE HERE!
MY GOD... BATMAN...YOUR ARMS AND LEGS...
J'ONN, WHAT THE HELL HAPPENED?!
JOHN STEWART? LUTHOR...HE... =UNH=...
HE BEAT US TO IT...
KENDRA... WHERE IS SHE?!
I'LL LOOK FOR A SIGNATURE.
FLASH, ARE YOU THERE?!
CYBORG... IS THAT YOU?!
WE...I FAILED, VIC. THE STILL FORCE...IT'S TOO STRONG. THE SPEED FORCE CAN'T FIGHT IT.
WE'RE ABANDONING THE BASE, COMING HOME...CAN YOU BOOM-TUBE US--
I WOULD, FLASH, BUT UNLESS WE FIGURE SOMETHING OUT...
...THERE WON'T BE A HOME TO COME BACK TO! I'M DOING EVERYTHING I CAN TO BOOST THE SHIELDS...

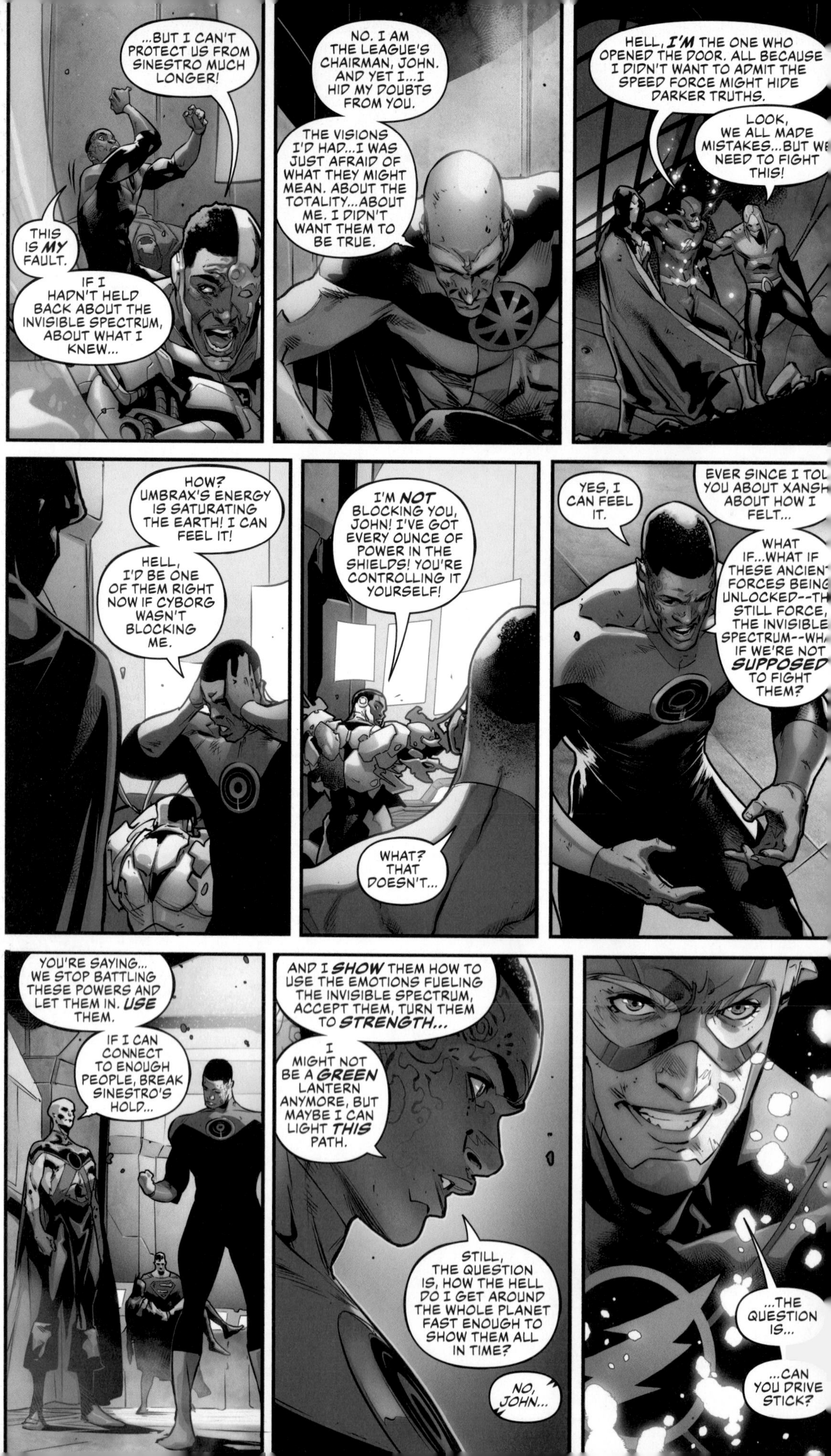
...BUT I CAN'T PROTECT US FROM SINESTRO MUCH LONGER!
THIS IS MY FAULT.
IF I HADN'T HELD BACK ABOUT THE INVISIBLE SPECTRUM, ABOUT WHAT I KNEW...
NO. I AM THE LEAGUE'S CHAIRMAN, JOHN. AND YET I...I HID MY DOUBTS FROM YOU.
THE VISIONS I'D HAD...I WAS JUST AFRAID OF WHAT THEY MIGHT MEAN. ABOUT THE TOTALITY...ABOUT ME. I DIDN'T WANT THEM TO BE TRUE.
HELL, I'M THE ONE WHO OPENED THE DOOR. ALL BECAUSE I DIDN'T WANT TO ADMIT THE SPEED FORCE MIGHT HIDE DARKER TRUTHS.
LOOK, WE ALL MADE MISTAKES...BUT WE NEED TO FIGHT THIS!
HOW? UMBRAX'S ENERGY IS SATURATING THE EARTH! I CAN FEEL IT!
HELL, I'D BE ONE OF THEM RIGHT NOW IF CYBORG WASN'T BLOCKING ME.
I'M NOT BLOCKING YOU, JOHN! I'VE GOT EVERY OUNCE OF POWER IN THE SHIELDS! YOU'RE CONTROLLING IT YOURSELF!
WHAT? THAT DOESN'T...
YES, I CAN FEEL IT.
EVER SINCE I TOL YOU ABOUT XANSH ABOUT HOW I FELT...
WHAT IF...WHAT IF THESE ANCIENT FORCES BEING UNLOCKED--TH STILL FORCE, THE INVISIBLE SPECTRUM--WHA IF WE'RE NOT SUPPOSED TO FIGHT THEM?
YOU'RE SAYING... WE STOP BATTLING THESE POWERS AND LET THEM IN. USE THEM.
IF I CAN CONNECT TO ENOUGH PEOPLE, BREAK SINESTRO'S HOLD...
AND I SHOW THEM HOW TO USE THE EMOTIONS FUELING THE INVISIBLE SPECTRUM, ACCEPT THEM, TURN THEM TO STRENGTH...
I MIGHT NOT BE A GREEN LANTERN ANYMORE, BUT MAYBE I CAN LIGHT THIS PATH.
STILL, THE QUESTION IS, HOW THE HELL DO I GET AROUND THE WHOLE PLANET FAST ENOUGH TO SHOW THEM ALL IN TIME?
NO, JOHN...
...THE QUESTION IS...
...CAN YOU DRIVE STICK?

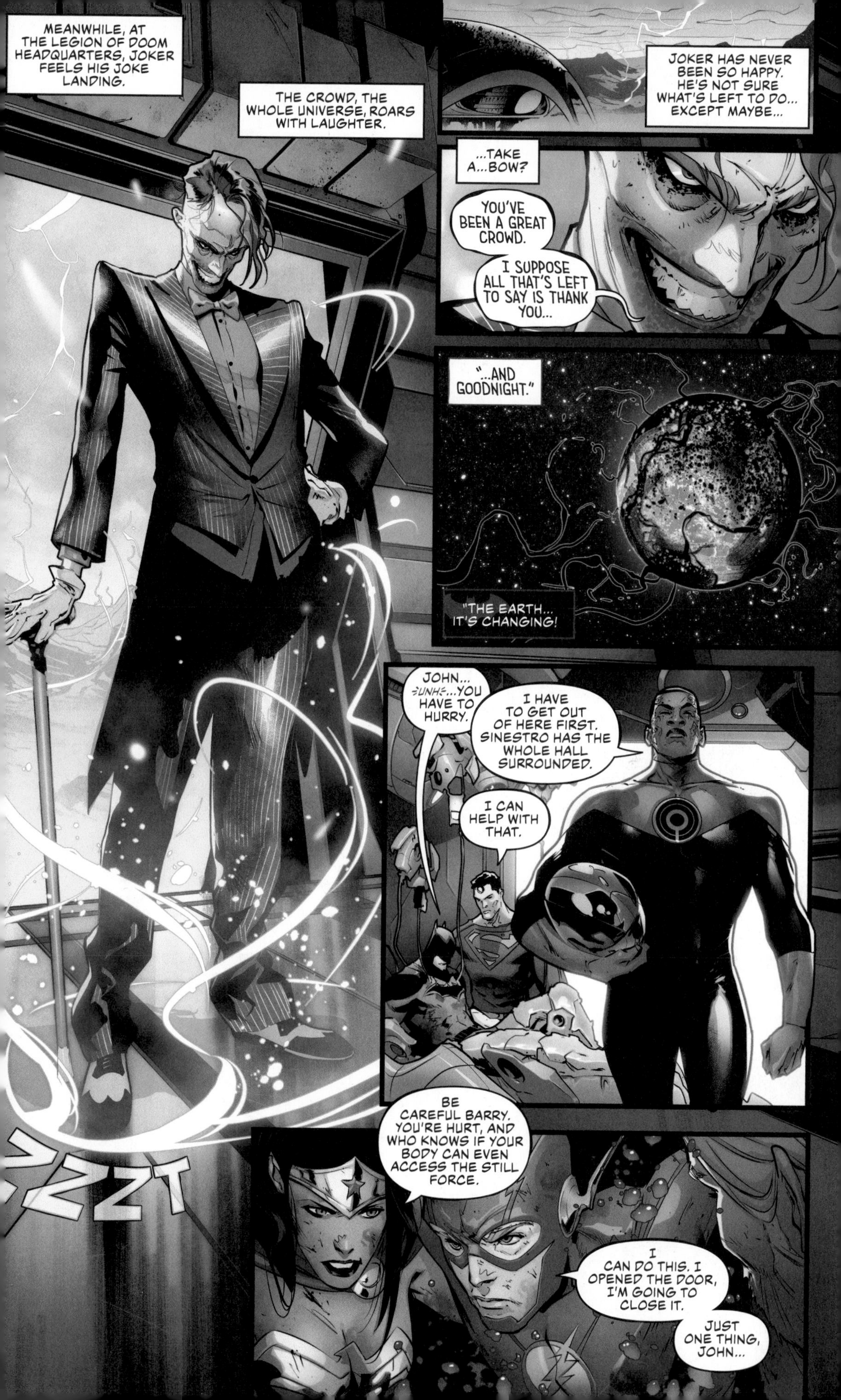
MEANWHILE, AT THE LEGION OF DOOM HEADQUARTERS, JOKER FEELS HIS JOKE LANDING.
THE CROWD, THE WHOLE UNIVERSE, ROARS WITH LAUGHTER.
JOKER HAS NEVER BEEN SO HAPPY. HE'S NOT SURE WHAT'S LEFT TO DO... EXCEPT MAYBE...
...TAKE A...BOW?
YOU'VE BEEN A GREAT CROWD.
I SUPPOSE ALL THAT'S LEFT TO SAY IS THANK YOU...
"...AND GOODNIGHT."
"THE EARTH... IT'S CHANGING!
JOHN... UNH...YOU HAVE TO HURRY.
I HAVE TO GET OUT OF HERE FIRST. SINESTRO HAS THE WHOLE HALL SURROUNDED.
I CAN HELP WITH THAT.
ZZZT
BE CAREFUL BARRY. YOU'RE HURT, AND WHO KNOWS IF YOUR BODY CAN EVEN ACCESS THE STILL FORCE.
I CAN DO THIS. I OPENED THE DOOR, I'M GOING TO CLOSE IT.
JUST ONE THING, JOHN...

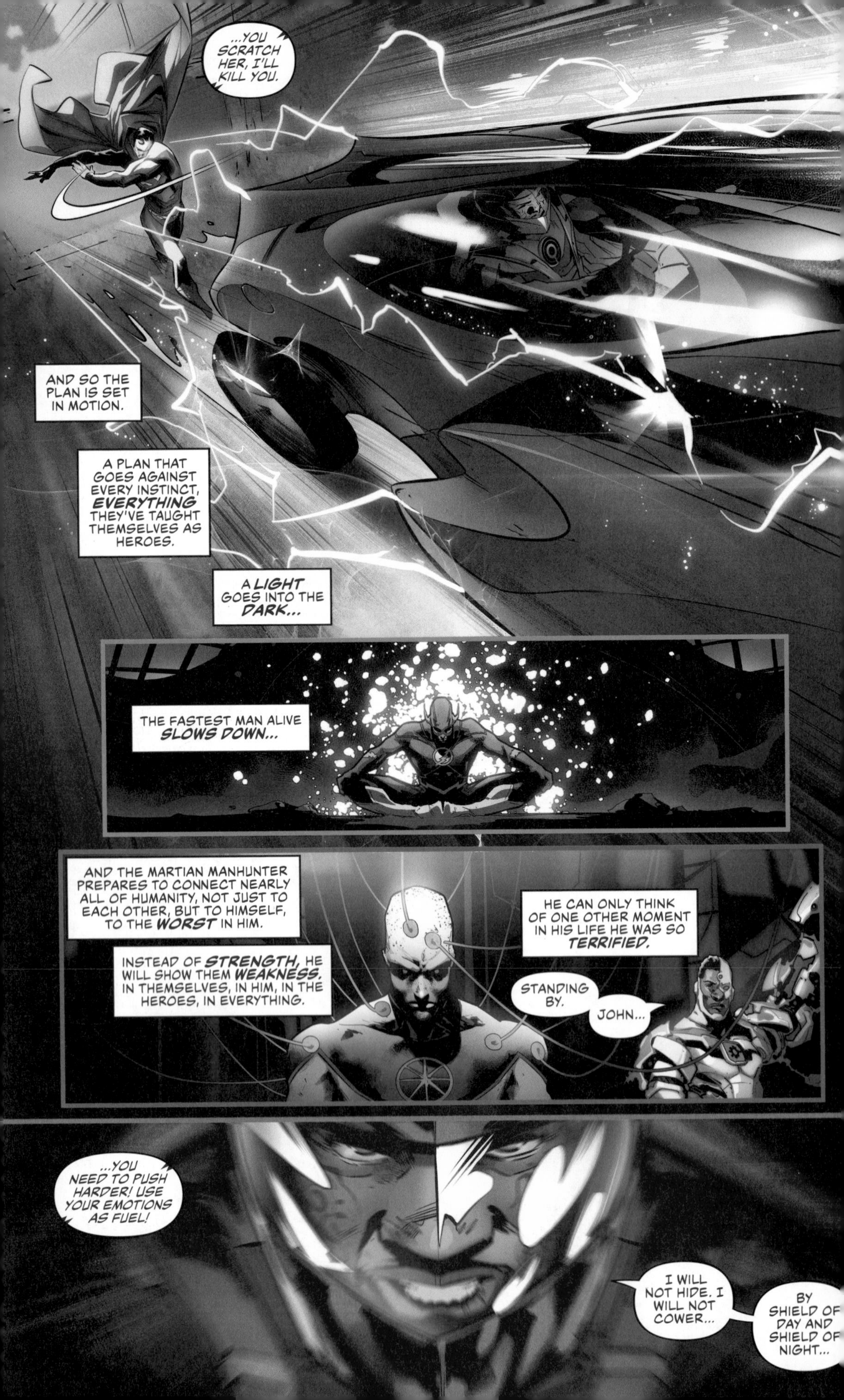

...YOU SCRATCH HER, I'LL KILL YOU.
AND SO THE PLAN IS SET IN MOTION.
A PLAN THAT GOES AGAINST EVERY INSTINCT, EVERYTHING THEY'VE TAUGHT THEMSELVES AS HEROES.
A LIGHT GOES INTO THE DARK...
THE FASTEST MAN ALIVE SLOWS DOWN...
AND THE MARTIAN MANHUNTER PREPARES TO CONNECT NEARLY ALL OF HUMANITY, NOT JUST TO EACH OTHER, BUT TO HIMSELF, TO THE WORST IN HIM.
INSTEAD OF STRENGTH, HE WILL SHOW THEM WEAKNESS. IN THEMSELVES, IN HIM, IN THE HEROES, IN EVERYTHING.
HE CAN ONLY THINK OF ONE OTHER MOMENT IN HIS LIFE HE WAS SO TERRIFIED.
STANDING BY.
JOHN...
...YOU NEED TO PUSH HARDER! USE YOUR EMOTIONS AS FUEL!
I WILL NOT HIDE. I WILL NOT COWER...
BY SHIELD OF DAY AND SHIELD OF NIGHT...

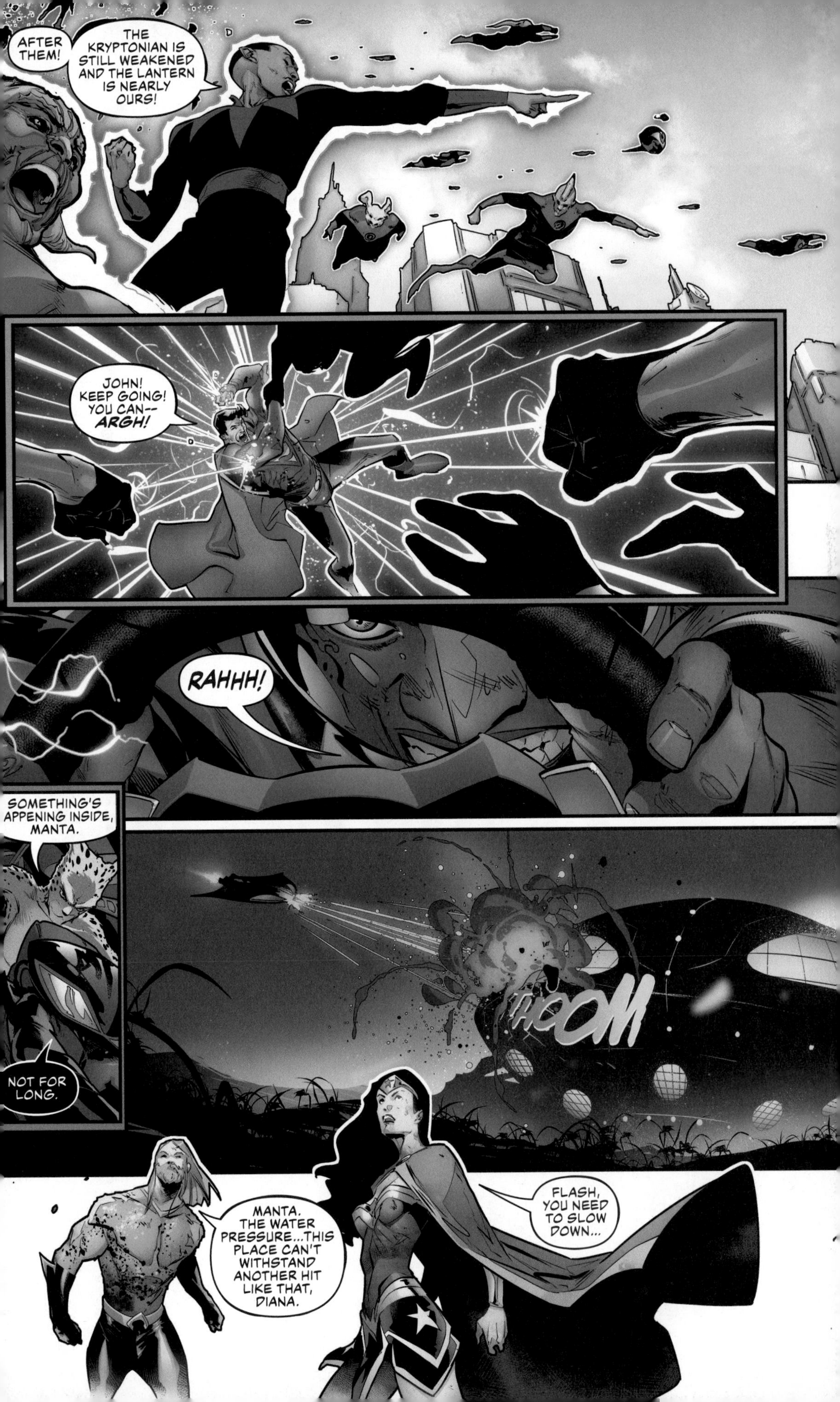
AFTER THEM!
THE KRYPTONIAN IS STILL WEAKENED AND THE LANTERN IS NEARLY OURS!
JOHN! KEEP GOING! YOU CAN-- ARGH!
RAHHH!
SOMETHING'S APPENING INSIDE, MANTA.
NOT FOR LONG.
THOOM
MANTA. THE WATER PRESSURE...THIS PLACE CAN'T WITHSTAND ANOTHER HIT LIKE THAT, DIANA.
FLASH, YOU NEED TO SLOW DOWN...

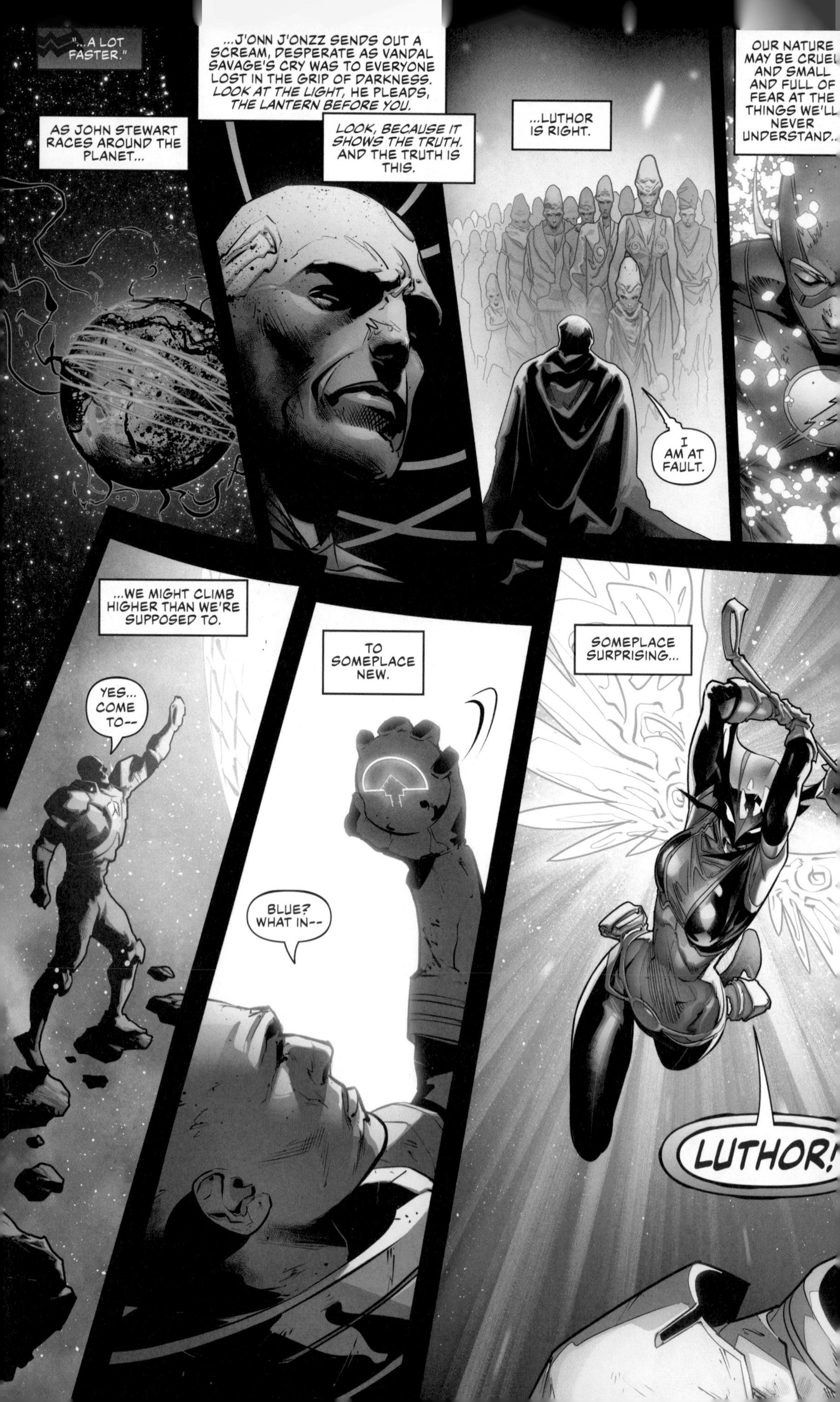
"...A LOT FASTER."
AS JOHN STEWART RACES AROUND THE PLANET...
...J'ONN J'ONZZ SENDS OUT A SCREAM, DESPERATE AS VANDAL SAVAGE'S CRY WAS TO EVERYONE LOST IN THE GRIP OF DARKNESS. LOOK AT THE LIGHT, HE PLEADS, THE LANTERN BEFORE YOU.
LOOK, BECAUSE IT SHOWS THE TRUTH. AND THE TRUTH IS THIS.
...LUTHOR IS RIGHT.
I AM AT FAULT.
OUR NATURE MAY BE CRUEL AND SMALL AND FULL OF FEAR AT THE THINGS WE'LL NEVER UNDERSTAND...
...WE MIGHT CLIMB HIGHER THAN WE'RE SUPPOSED TO.
YES... COME TO--
TO SOMEPLACE NEW.
BLUE? WHAT IN--
SOMEPLACE SURPRISING...
LUTHOR!

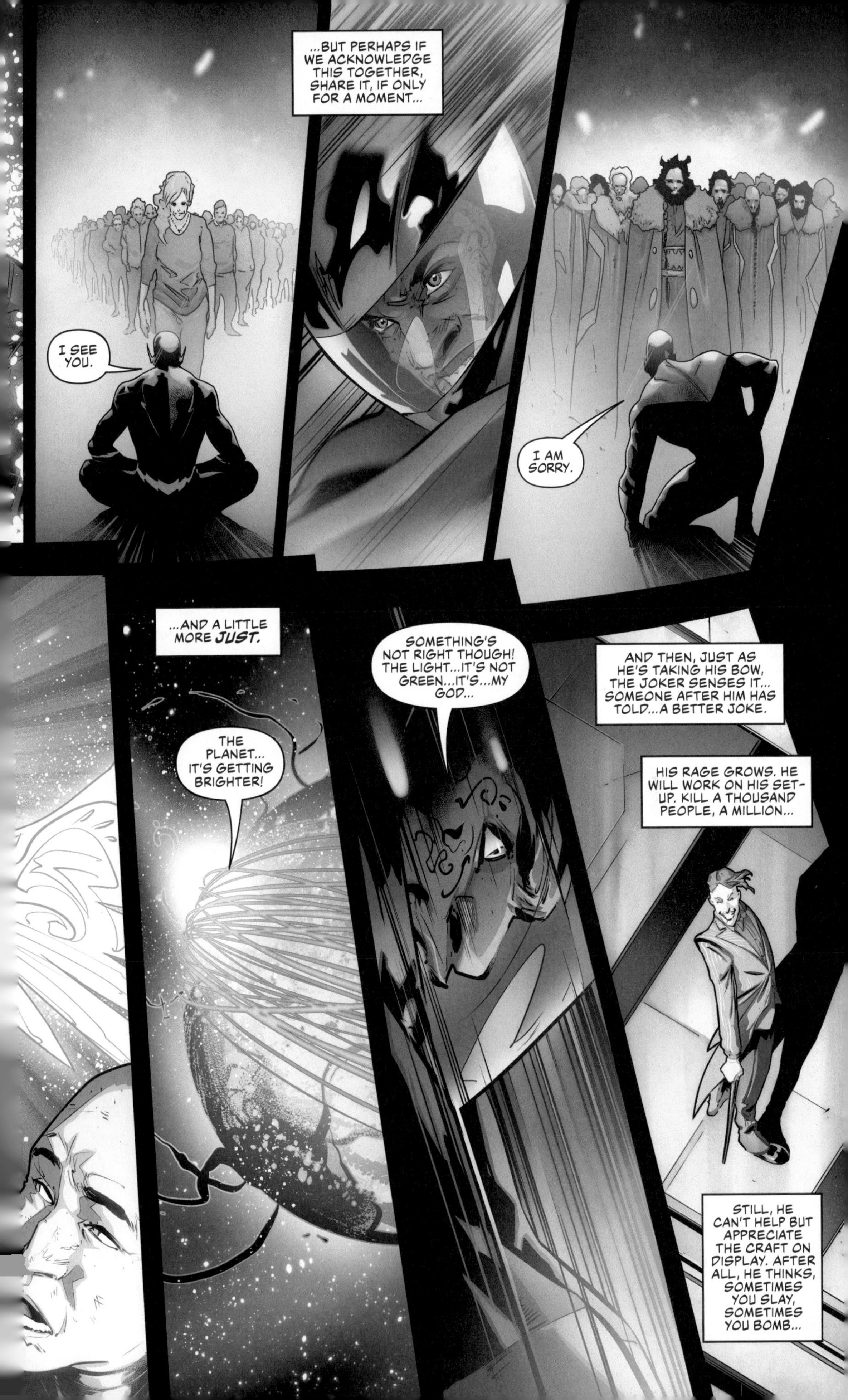
...BUT PERHAPS IF WE ACKNOWLEDGE THIS TOGETHER, SHARE IT, IF ONLY FOR A MOMENT...
I SEE YOU.
I AM SORRY.
...AND A LITTLE MORE JUST.
THE PLANET... IT'S GETTING BRIGHTER!
SOMETHING'S NOT RIGHT THOUGH! THE LIGHT...IT'S NOT GREEN...IT'S...MY GOD...
AND THEN, JUST AS HE'S TAKING HIS BOW, THE JOKER SENSES IT... SOMEONE AFTER HIM HAS TOLD...A BETTER JOKE.
HIS RAGE GROWS. HE WILL WORK ON HIS SET-UP. KILL A THOUSAND PEOPLE, A MILLION...
STILL, HE CAN'T HELP BUT APPRECIATE THE CRAFT ON DISPLAY. AFTER ALL, HE THINKS, SOMETIMES YOU SLAY, SOMETIMES YOU BOMB...

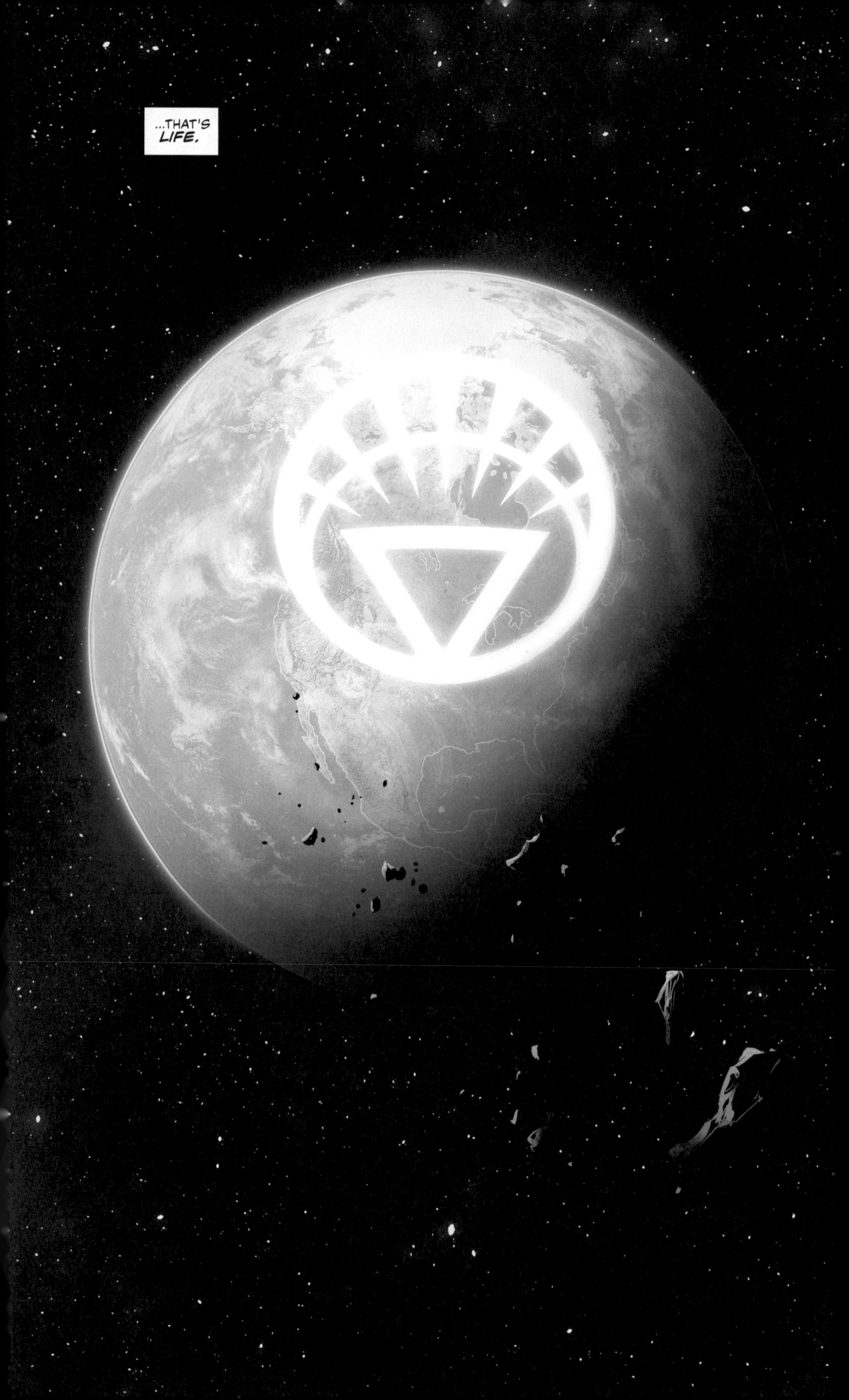
...THAT'S LIFE.

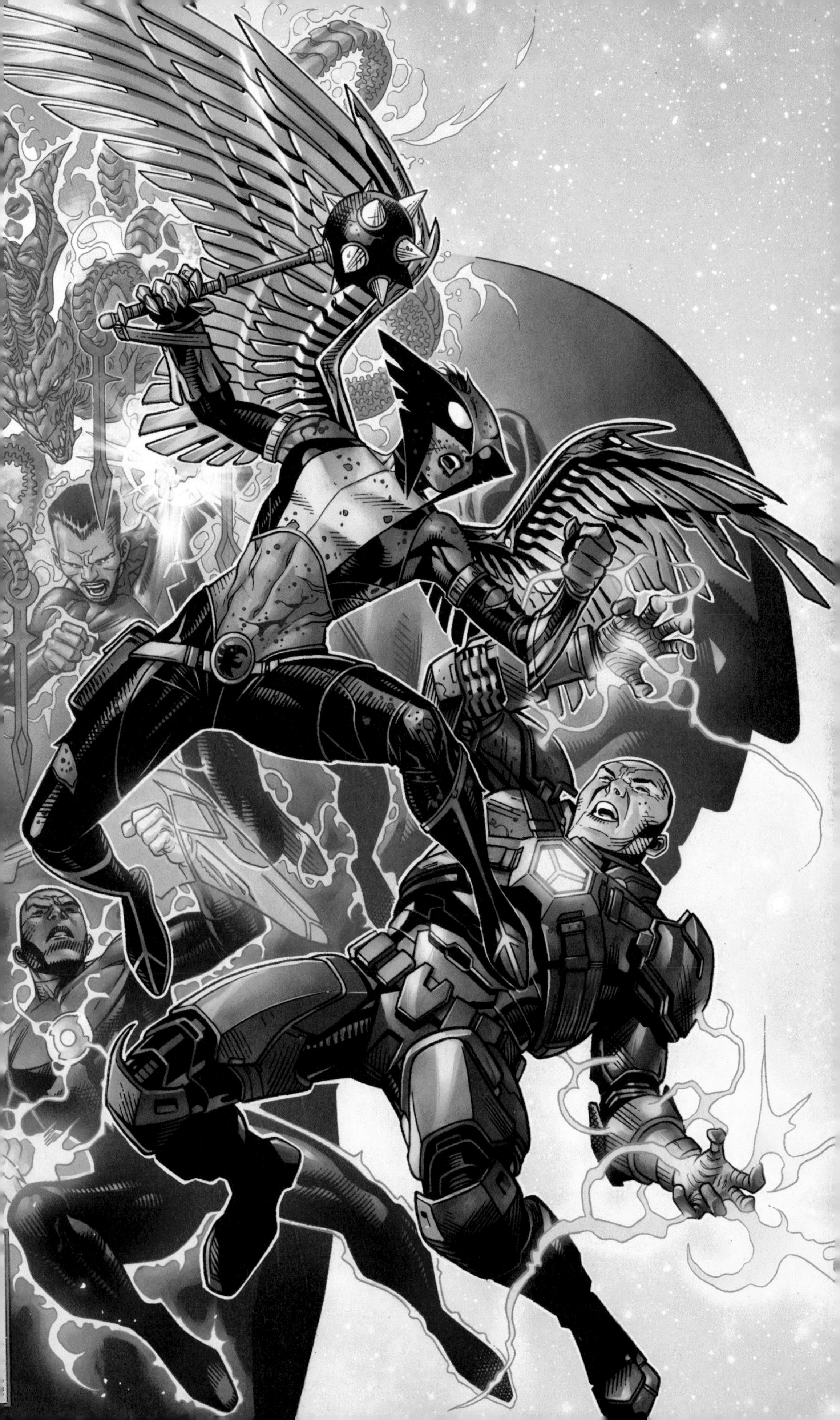

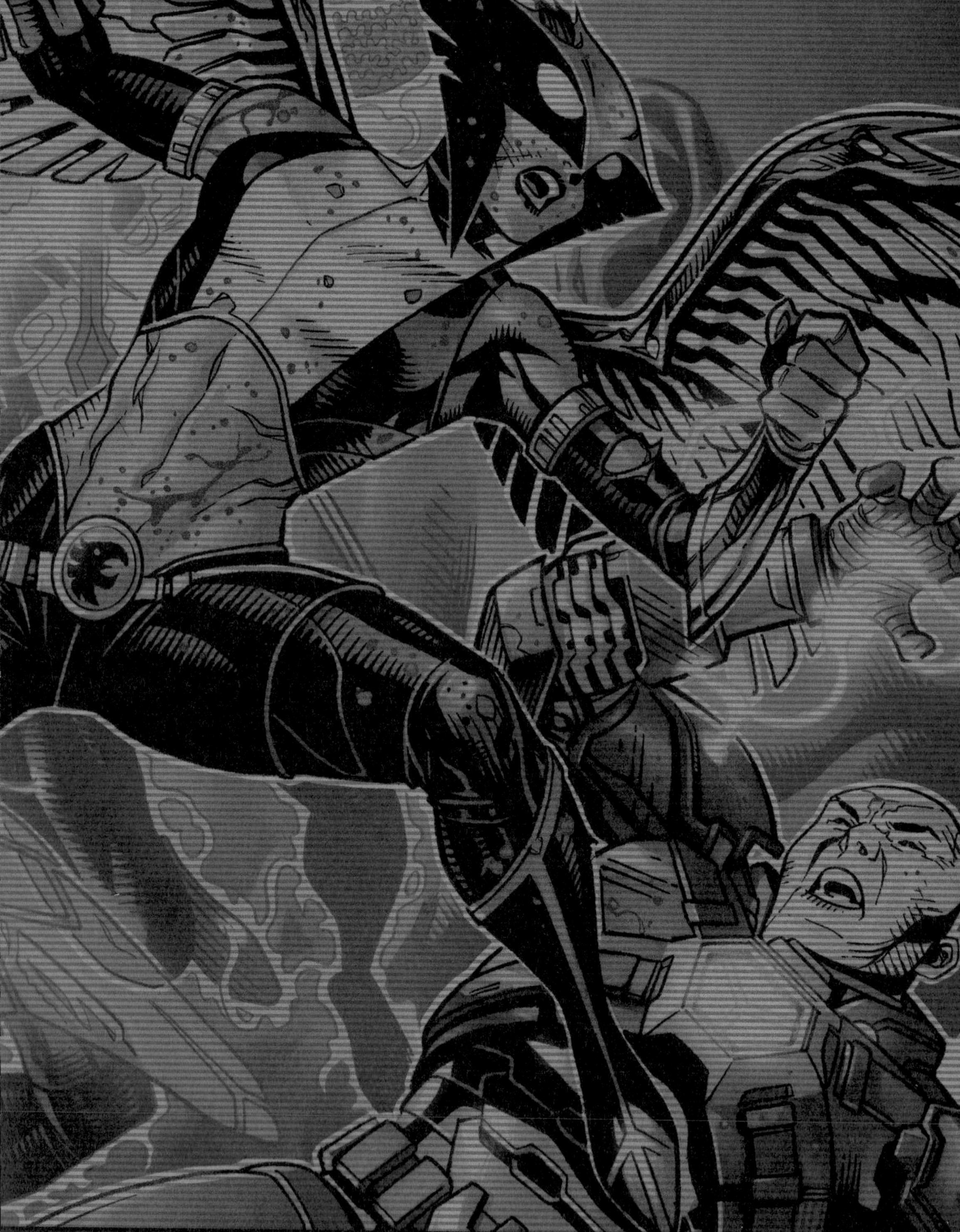

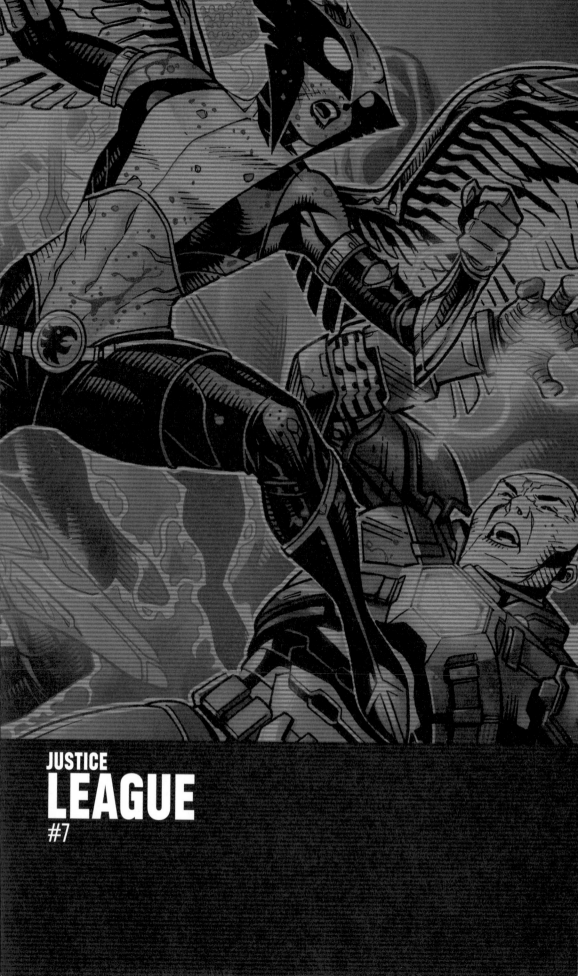

JUSTICE LEAGUE
#7

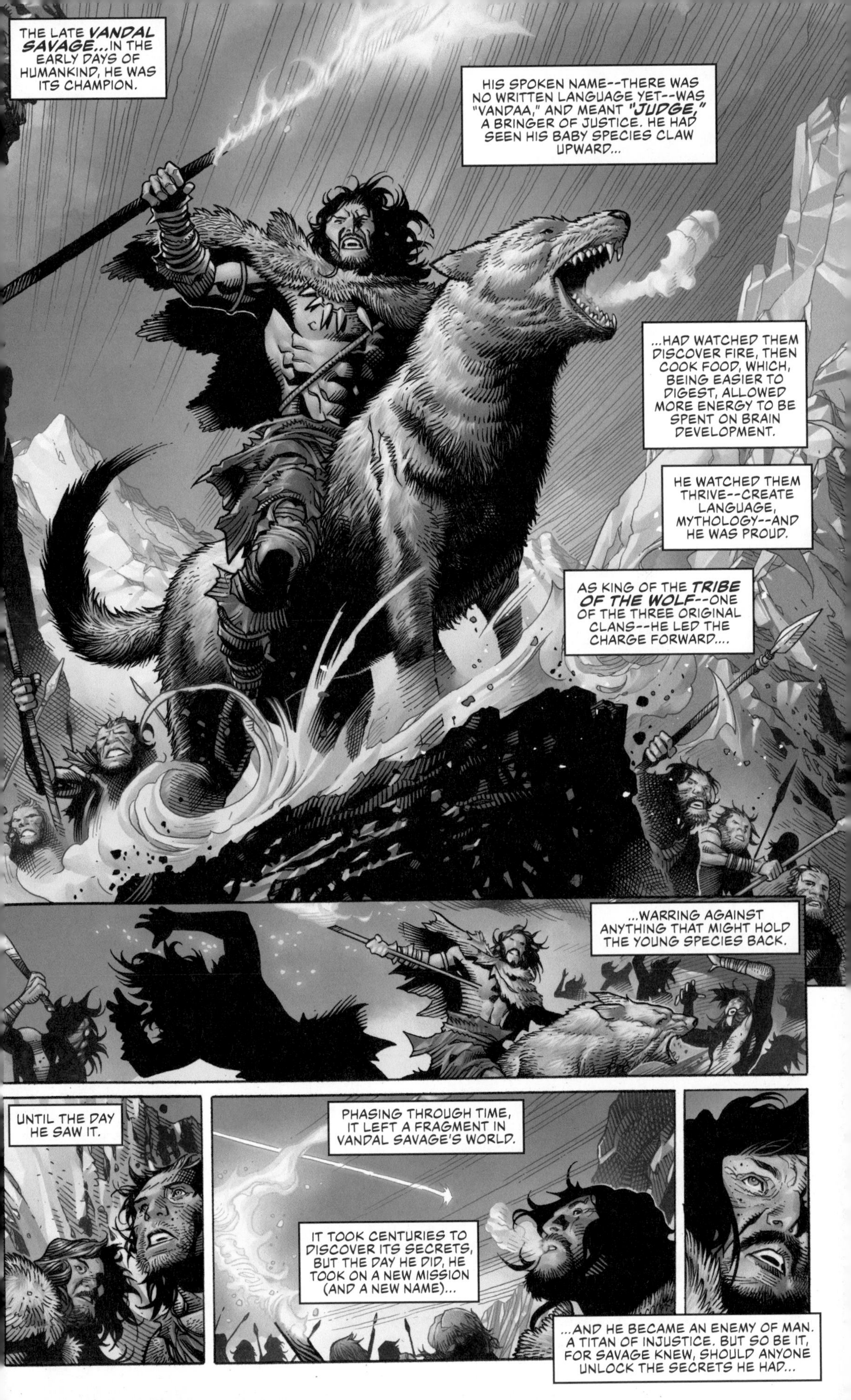
THE LATE VANDAL SAVAGE...IN THE EARLY DAYS OF HUMANKIND, HE WAS ITS CHAMPION.
HIS SPOKEN NAME--THERE WAS NO WRITTEN LANGUAGE YET--WAS "VANDAA," AND MEANT "JUDGE," A BRINGER OF JUSTICE. HE HAD SEEN HIS BABY SPECIES CLAW UPWARD...
...HAD WATCHED THEM DISCOVER FIRE, THEN COOK FOOD, WHICH, BEING EASIER TO DIGEST, ALLOWED MORE ENERGY TO BE SPENT ON BRAIN DEVELOPMENT.
HE WATCHED THEM THRIVE--CREATE LANGUAGE, MYTHOLOGY--AND HE WAS PROUD.
AS KING OF THE TRIBE OF THE WOLF--ONE OF THE THREE ORIGINAL CLANS--HE LED THE CHARGE FORWARD....
...WARRING AGAINST ANYTHING THAT MIGHT HOLD THE YOUNG SPECIES BACK.
UNTIL THE DAY HE SAW IT.
PHASING THROUGH TIME, IT LEFT A FRAGMENT IN VANDAL SAVAGE'S WORLD.
IT TOOK CENTURIES TO DISCOVER ITS SECRETS, BUT THE DAY HE DID, HE TOOK ON A NEW MISSION (AND A NEW NAME)...
...AND HE BECAME AN ENEMY OF MAN. A TITAN OF INJUSTICE. BUT SO BE IT, FOR SAVAGE KNEW, SHOULD ANYONE UNLOCK THE SECRETS HE HAD...

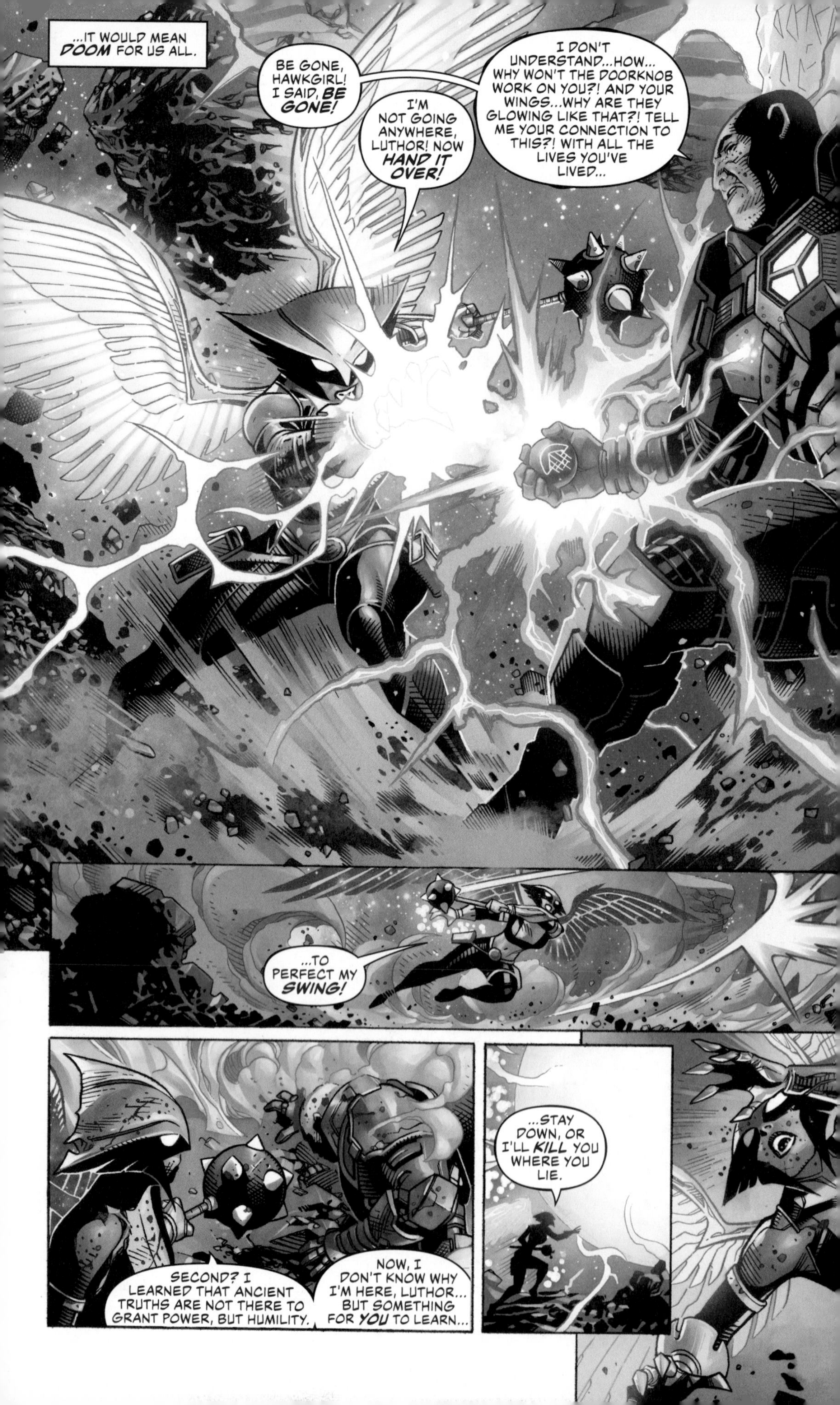
...IT WOULD MEAN DOOM FOR US ALL.
BE GONE, HAWKGIRL! I SAID, BE GONE!
I'M NOT GOING ANYWHERE, LUTHOR! NOW HAND IT OVER!
I DON'T UNDERSTAND...HOW... WHY WON'T THE DOORKNOB WORK ON YOU?! AND YOUR WINGS...WHY ARE THEY GLOWING LIKE THAT?! TELL ME YOUR CONNECTION TO THIS?! WITH ALL THE LIVES YOU'VE LIVED...
...TO PERFECT MY SWING!
SECOND? I LEARNED THAT ANCIENT TRUTHS ARE NOT THERE TO GRANT POWER, BUT HUMILITY.
NOW, I DON'T KNOW WHY I'M HERE, LUTHOR... BUT SOMETHING FOR YOU TO LEARN...
...STAY DOWN, OR I'LL KILL YOU WHERE YOU LIE.

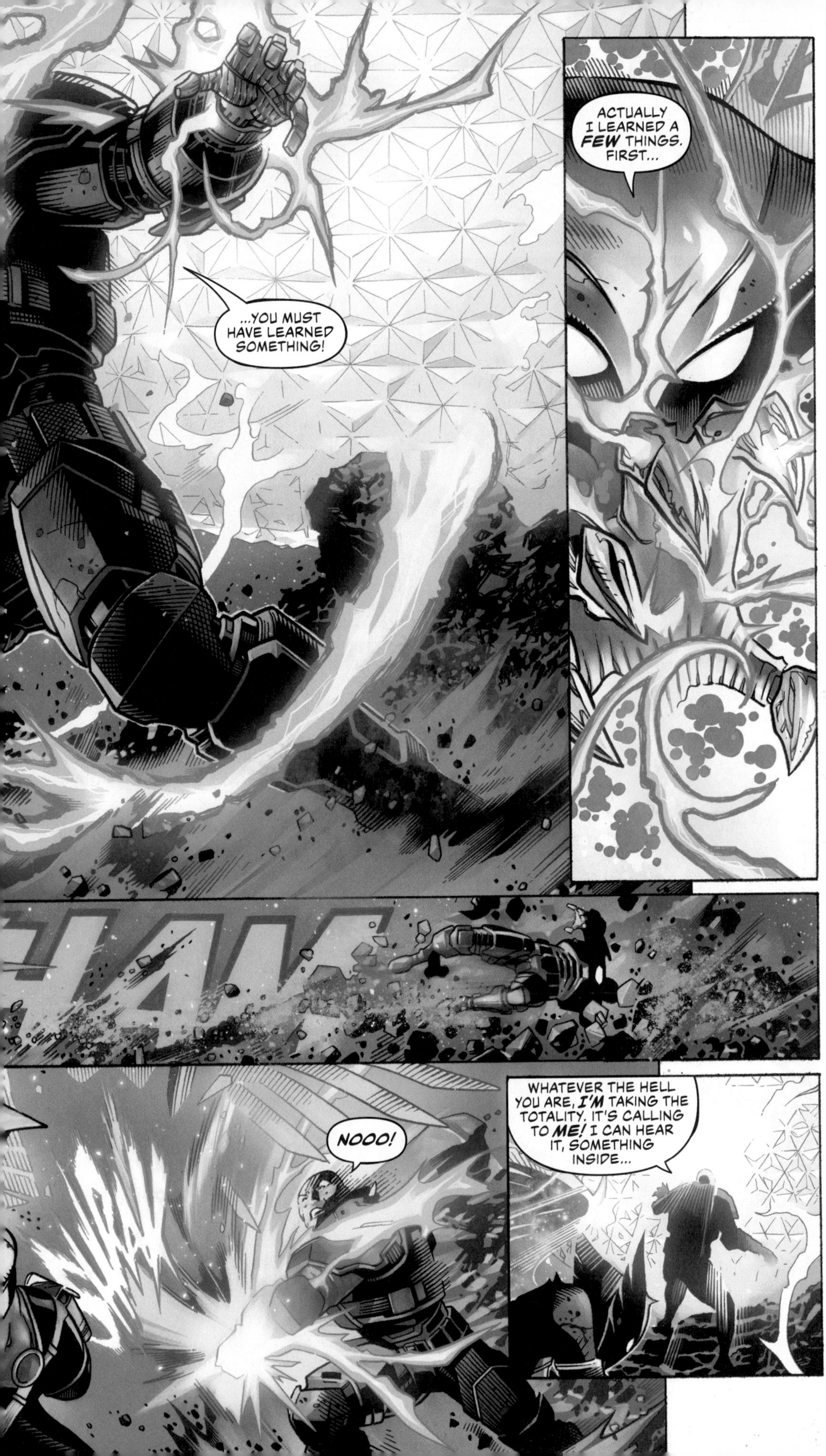
...YOU MUST HAVE LEARNED SOMETHING!
ACTUALLY I LEARNED A FEW THINGS. FIRST...
NOOO!
WHATEVER THE HELL YOU ARE, I'M TAKING THE TOTALITY. IT'S CALLING TO ME! I CAN HEAR IT, SOMETHING INSIDE...

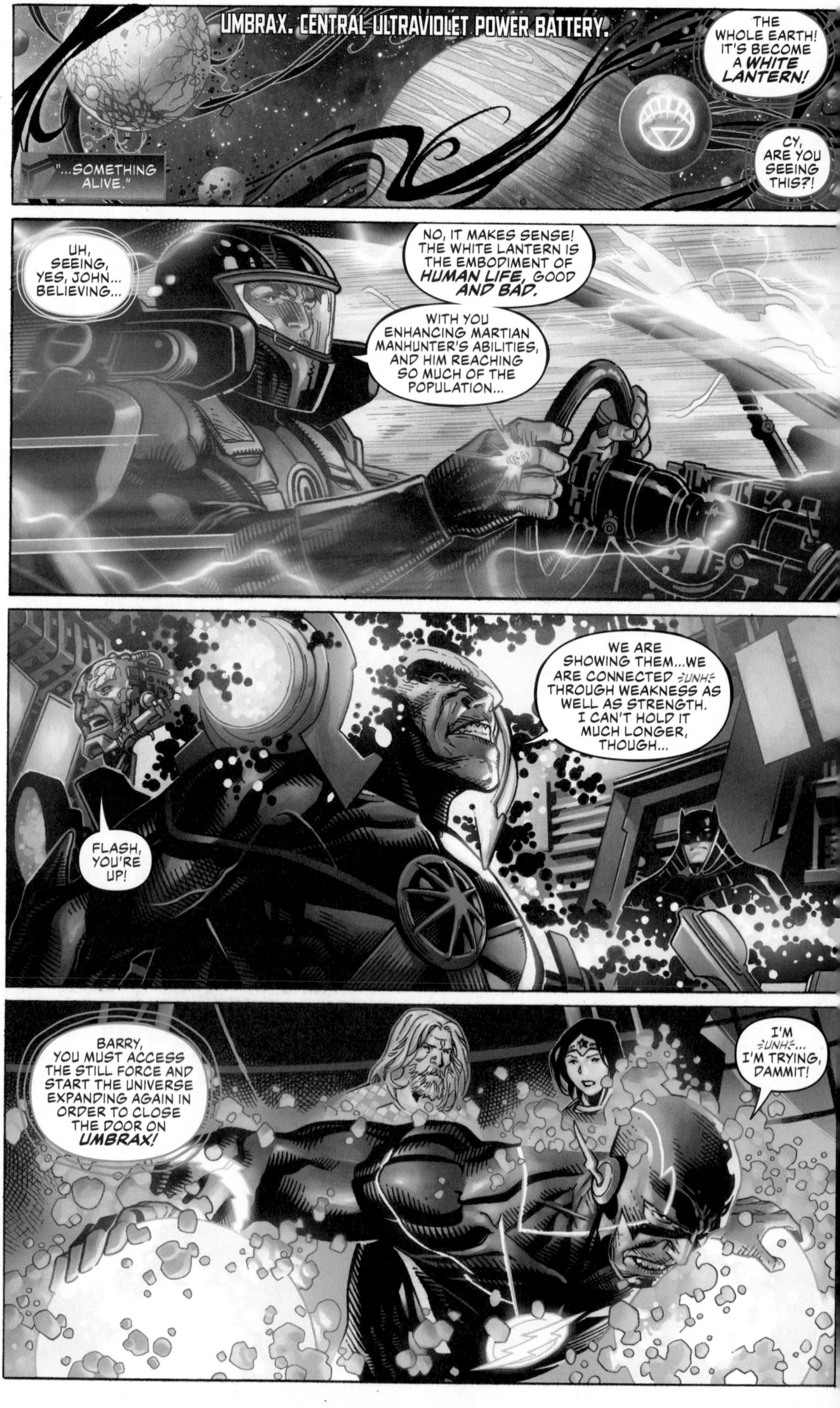
UMBRAX. CENTRAL ULTRAVIOLET POWER BATTERY.
"...SOMETHING ALIVE."
THE WHOLE EARTH! IT'S BECOME A *WHITE LANTERN!*
CY, ARE YOU SEEING THIS?!
UH, SEEING, YES, JOHN... BELIEVING...
NO, IT MAKES SENSE! THE WHITE LANTERN IS THE EMBODIMENT OF *HUMAN LIFE,* GOOD *AND BAD.*
WITH YOU ENHANCING MARTIAN MANHUNTER'S ABILITIES, AND HIM REACHING SO MUCH OF THE POPULATION...
WE ARE SHOWING THEM...WE ARE CONNECTED *UNH* THROUGH WEAKNESS AS WELL AS STRENGTH. I CAN'T HOLD IT MUCH LONGER, THOUGH...
FLASH, YOU'RE UP!
BARRY, YOU MUST ACCESS THE STILL FORCE AND START THE UNIVERSE EXPANDING AGAIN IN ORDER TO CLOSE THE DOOR ON *UMBRAX!*
I'M *UNH*... I'M TRYING, DAMMIT!

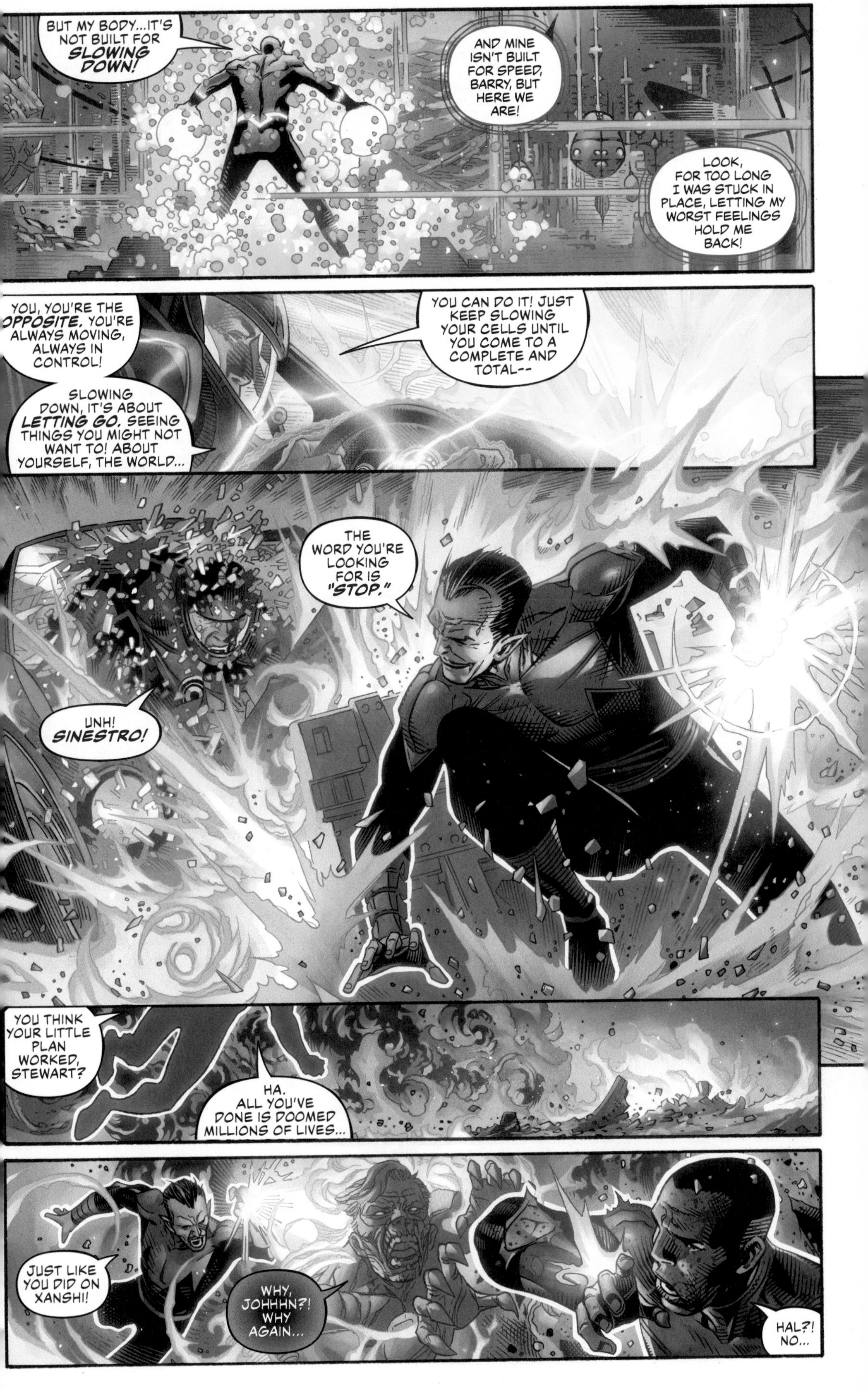
BUT MY BODY...IT'S NOT BUILT FOR SLOWING DOWN!
AND MINE ISN'T BUILT FOR SPEED, BARRY, BUT HERE WE ARE!
LOOK, FOR TOO LONG I WAS STUCK IN PLACE, LETTING MY WORST FEELINGS HOLD ME BACK!
YOU, YOU'RE THE OPPOSITE. YOU'RE ALWAYS MOVING, ALWAYS IN CONTROL!
SLOWING DOWN, IT'S ABOUT LETTING GO. SEEING THINGS YOU MIGHT NOT WANT TO! ABOUT YOURSELF, THE WORLD...
YOU CAN DO IT! JUST KEEP SLOWING YOUR CELLS UNTIL YOU COME TO A COMPLETE AND TOTAL--
THE WORD YOU'RE LOOKING FOR IS "STOP."
UNH! SINESTRO!
YOU THINK YOUR LITTLE PLAN WORKED, STEWART?
HA. ALL YOU'VE DONE IS DOOMED MILLIONS OF LIVES...
JUST LIKE YOU DID ON XANSHI!
WHY, JOHHHN?! WHY AGAIN...
HAL?! NO...

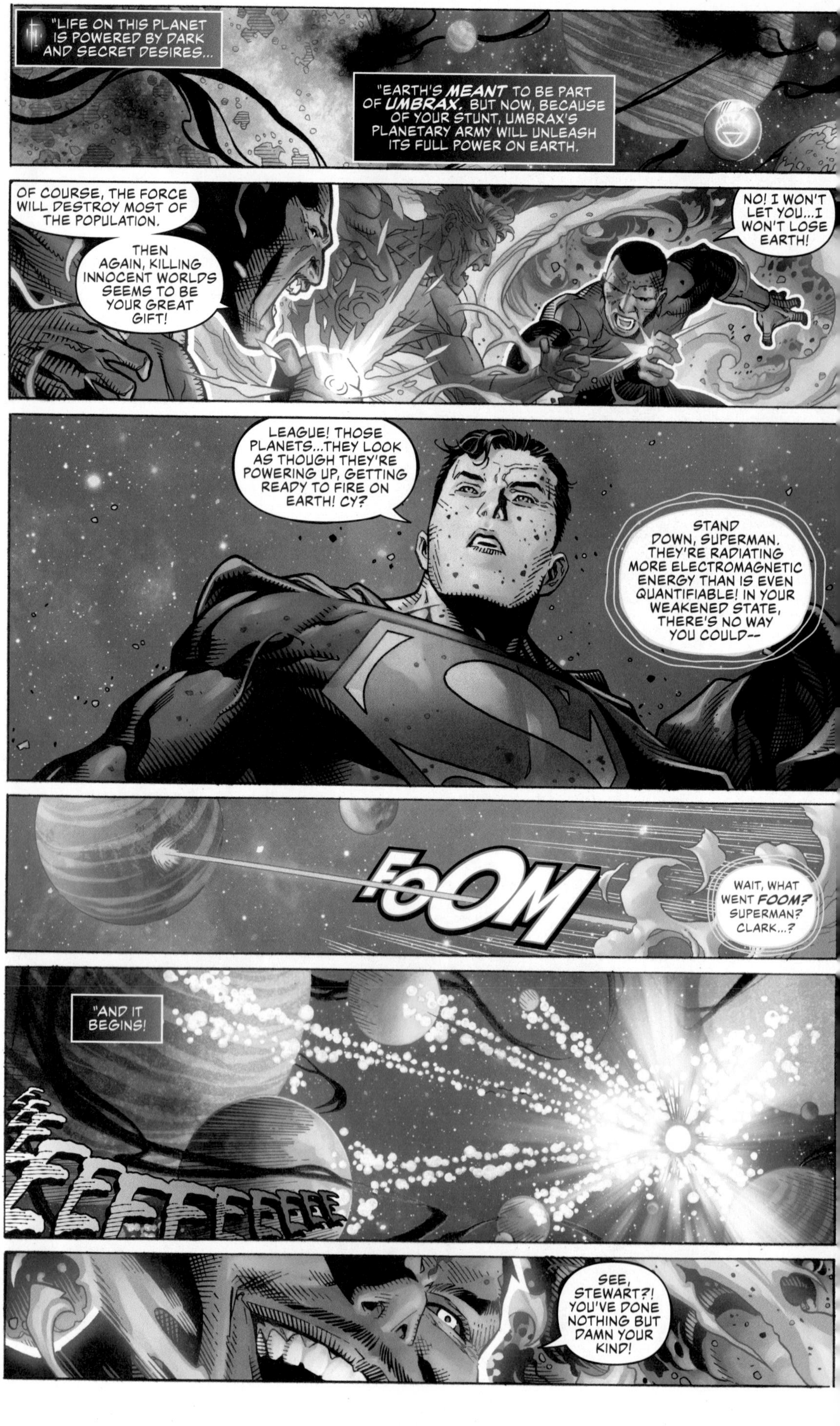
"LIFE ON THIS PLANET IS POWERED BY DARK AND SECRET DESIRES...
"EARTH'S **MEANT** TO BE PART OF **UMBRAX.** BUT NOW, BECAUSE OF YOUR STUNT, UMBRAX'S PLANETARY ARMY WILL UNLEASH ITS FULL POWER ON EARTH.
OF COURSE, THE FORCE WILL DESTROY MOST OF THE POPULATION.
THEN AGAIN, KILLING INNOCENT WORLDS SEEMS TO BE YOUR GREAT GIFT!
NO! I WON'T LET YOU...I WON'T LOSE EARTH!
LEAGUE! THOSE PLANETS...THEY LOOK AS THOUGH THEY'RE POWERING UP, GETTING READY TO FIRE ON EARTH! CY?
STAND DOWN, SUPERMAN. THEY'RE RADIATING MORE ELECTROMAGNETIC ENERGY THAN IS EVEN QUANTIFIABLE! IN YOUR WEAKENED STATE, THERE'S NO WAY YOU COULD--
FOOM
WAIT, WHAT WENT **FOOM?** SUPERMAN? CLARK...?
"AND IT BEGINS!
EEEEEEEEEE
SEE, STEWART?! YOU'VE DONE NOTHING BUT DAMN YOUR KIND!

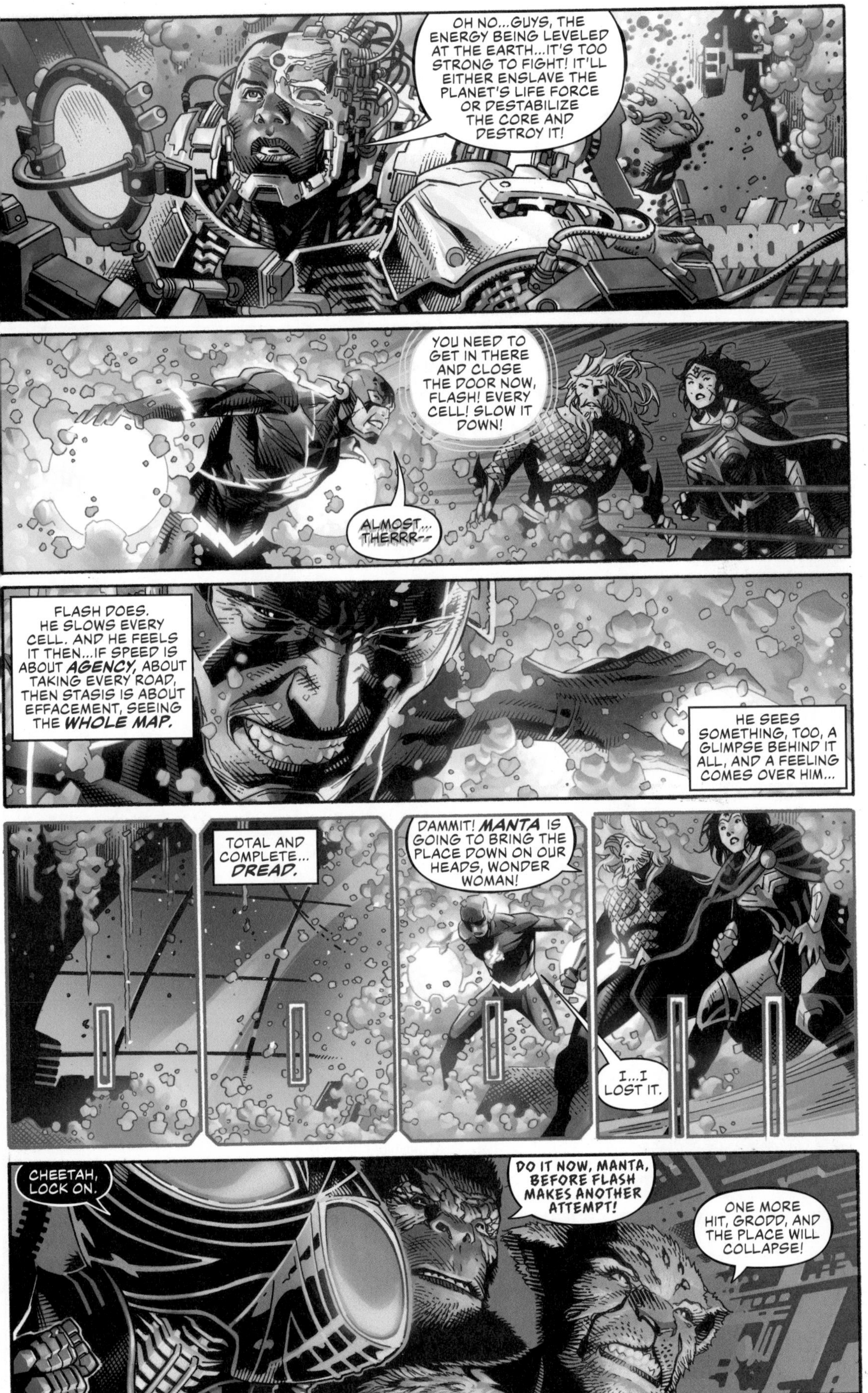
OH NO...GUYS, THE ENERGY BEING LEVELED AT THE EARTH...IT'S TOO STRONG TO FIGHT! IT'LL EITHER ENSLAVE THE PLANET'S LIFE FORCE OR DESTABILIZE THE CORE AND DESTROY IT!
YOU NEED TO GET IN THERE AND CLOSE THE DOOR NOW, FLASH! EVERY CELL! SLOW IT DOWN!
ALMOST... THERRR--
FLASH DOES. HE SLOWS EVERY CELL. AND HE FEELS IT THEN...IF SPEED IS ABOUT AGENCY, ABOUT TAKING EVERY ROAD, THEN STASIS IS ABOUT EFFACEMENT, SEEING THE WHOLE MAP.
HE SEES SOMETHING, TOO, A GLIMPSE BEHIND IT ALL, AND A FEELING COMES OVER HIM...
TOTAL AND COMPLETE... DREAD.
DAMMIT! MANTA IS GOING TO BRING THE PLACE DOWN ON OUR HEADS, WONDER WOMAN!
I...I LOST IT.
CHEETAH, LOCK ON.
DO IT NOW, MANTA, BEFORE FLASH MAKES ANOTHER ATTEMPT!
ONE MORE HIT, GRODD, AND THE PLACE WILL COLLAPSE!

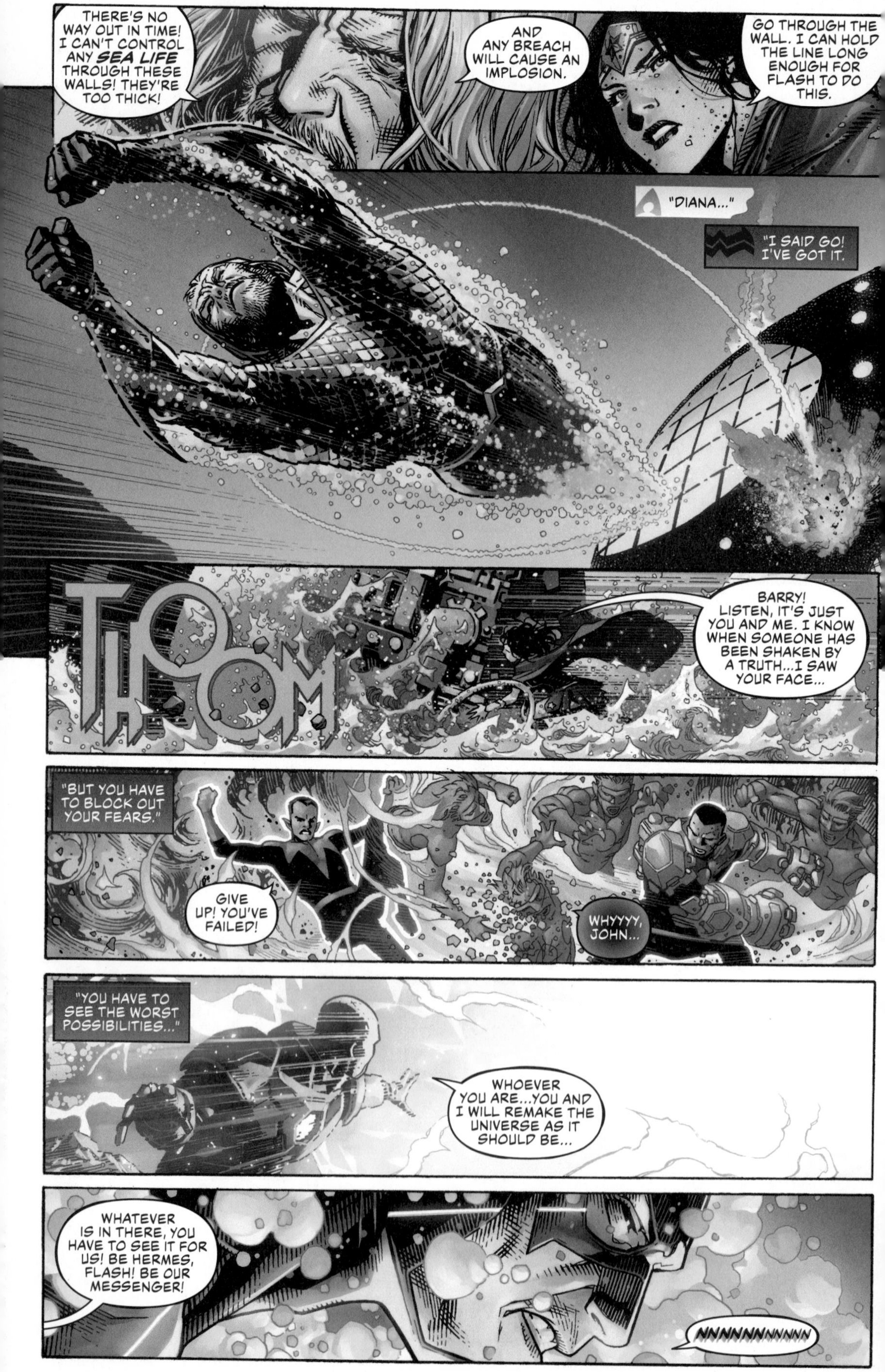

THERE'S NO WAY OUT IN TIME! I CAN'T CONTROL ANY SEA LIFE THROUGH THESE WALLS! THEY'RE TOO THICK!
AND ANY BREACH WILL CAUSE AN IMPLOSION.
GO THROUGH THE WALL. I CAN HOLD THE LINE LONG ENOUGH FOR FLASH TO DO THIS.
"DIANA..."
"I SAID GO! I'VE GOT IT.
THOOM
BARRY! LISTEN, IT'S JUST YOU AND ME. I KNOW WHEN SOMEONE HAS BEEN SHAKEN BY A TRUTH...I SAW YOUR FACE...
"BUT YOU HAVE TO BLOCK OUT YOUR FEARS."
GIVE UP! YOU'VE FAILED!
WHYYYY, JOHN...
"YOU HAVE TO SEE THE WORST POSSIBILITIES..."
WHOEVER YOU ARE...YOU AND I WILL REMAKE THE UNIVERSE AS IT SHOULD BE...
WHATEVER IS IN THERE, YOU HAVE TO SEE IT FOR US! BE HERMES, FLASH! BE OUR MESSENGER!
NNNNNNNNNNN

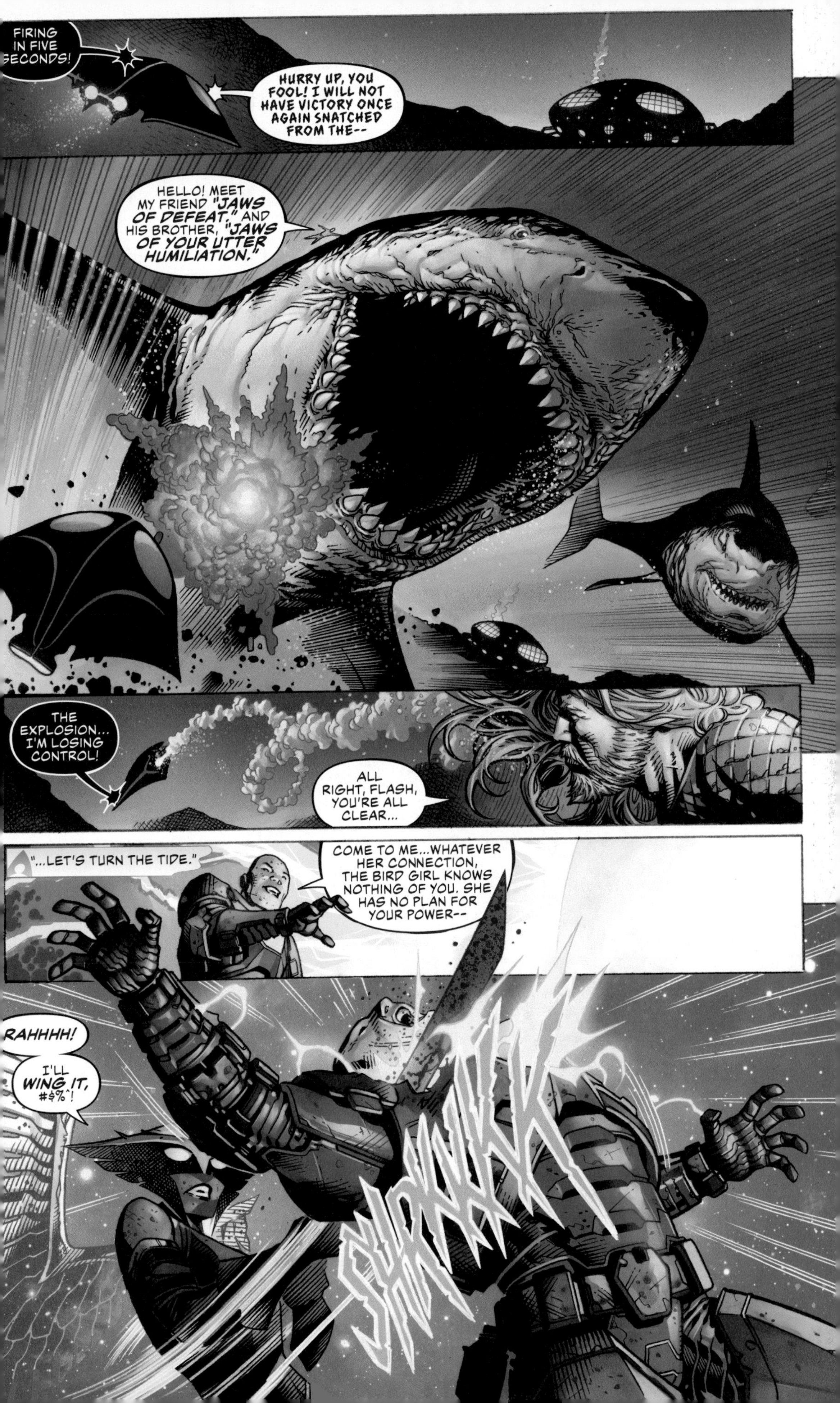
FIRING IN FIVE SECONDS!
HURRY UP, YOU FOOL! I WILL NOT HAVE VICTORY ONCE AGAIN SNATCHED FROM THE--
HELLO! MEET MY FRIEND "JAWS OF DEFEAT," AND HIS BROTHER, "JAWS OF YOUR UTTER HUMILIATION."
THE EXPLOSION... I'M LOSING CONTROL!
ALL RIGHT, FLASH, YOU'RE ALL CLEAR...
"...LET'S TURN THE TIDE."
COME TO ME...WHATEVER HER CONNECTION, THE BIRD GIRL KNOWS NOTHING OF YOU. SHE HAS NO PLAN FOR YOUR POWER--
RAHHHH!
I'LL WING IT, #$%^!
SHUNK

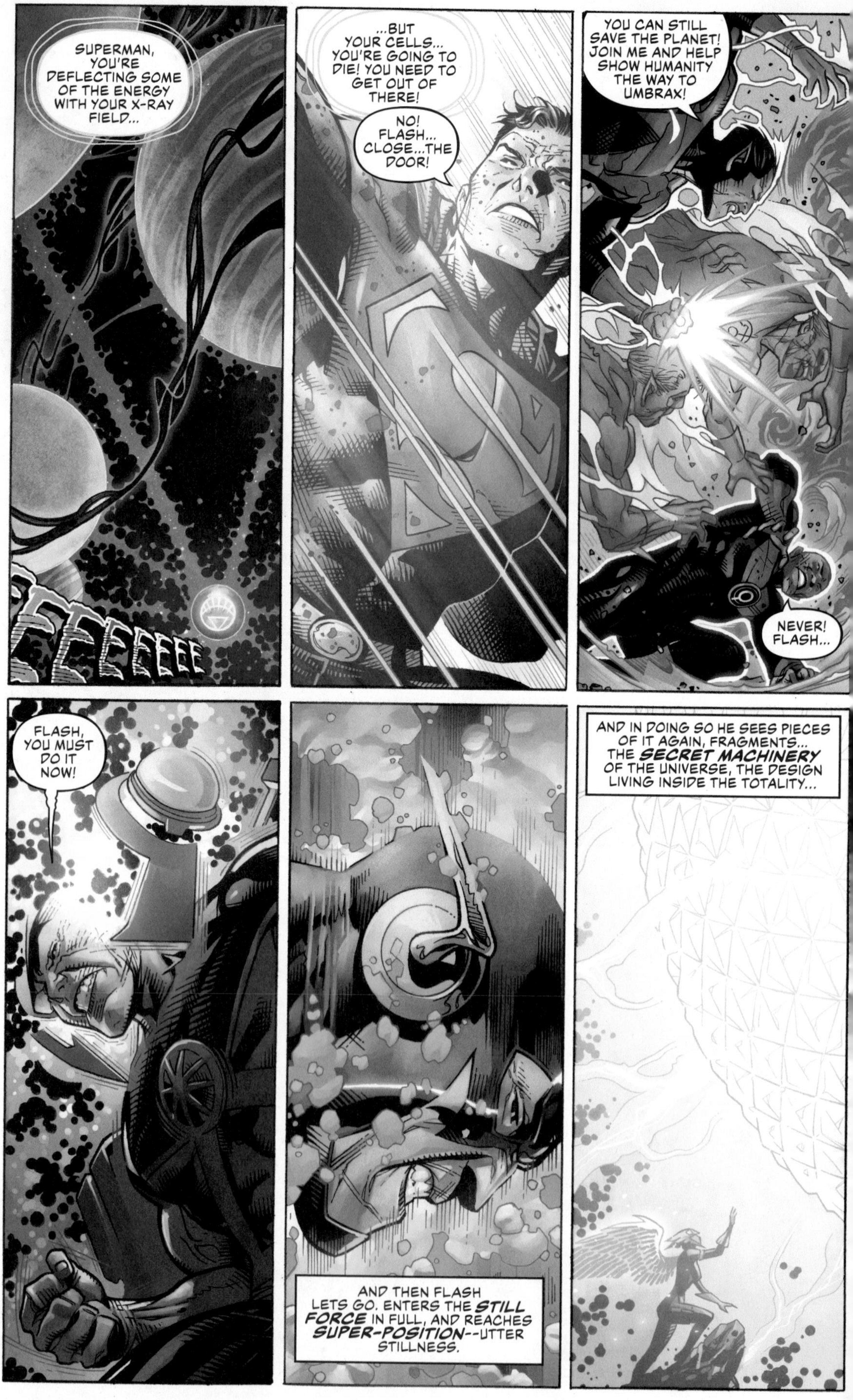
SUPERMAN, YOU'RE DEFLECTING SOME OF THE ENERGY WITH YOUR X-RAY FIELD...
EEEEEEE
...BUT YOUR CELLS... YOU'RE GOING TO DIE! YOU NEED TO GET OUT OF THERE!
NO! FLASH... CLOSE...THE DOOR!
YOU CAN STILL SAVE THE PLANET! JOIN ME AND HELP SHOW HUMANITY THE WAY TO UMBRAX!
NEVER! FLASH...
FLASH, YOU MUST DO IT NOW!
AND THEN FLASH LETS GO. ENTERS THE STILL FORCE IN FULL, AND REACHES SUPER-POSITION--UTTER STILLNESS.
AND IN DOING SO HE SEES PIECES OF IT AGAIN, FRAGMENTS... THE SECRET MACHINERY OF THE UNIVERSE, THE DESIGN LIVING INSIDE THE TOTALITY...

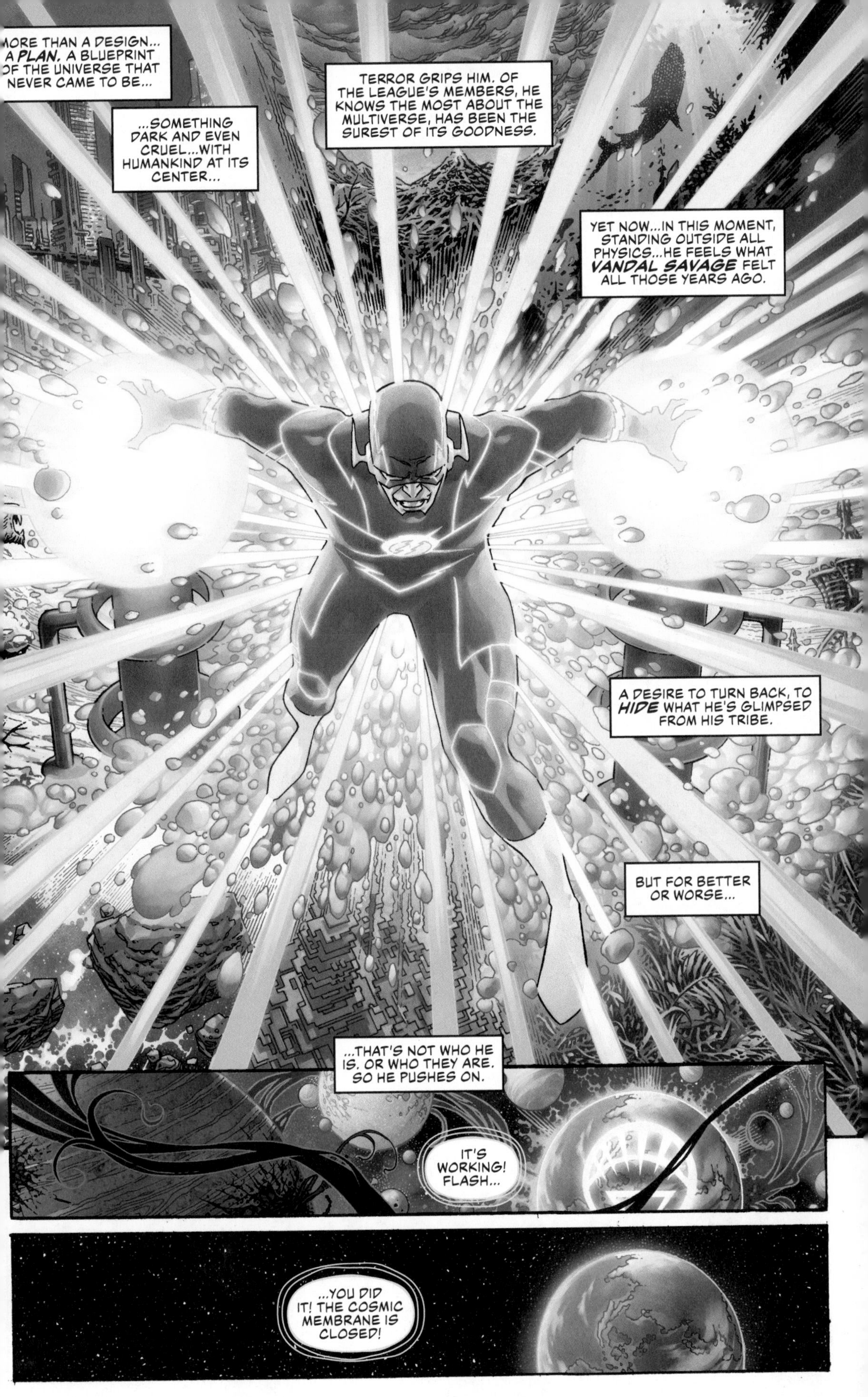
MORE THAN A DESIGN... A *PLAN*, A BLUEPRINT OF THE UNIVERSE THAT NEVER CAME TO BE...
...SOMETHING DARK AND EVEN CRUEL...WITH HUMANKIND AT ITS CENTER...
TERROR GRIPS HIM. OF THE LEAGUE'S MEMBERS, HE KNOWS THE MOST ABOUT THE MULTIVERSE, HAS BEEN THE SUREST OF ITS GOODNESS.
YET NOW...IN THIS MOMENT, STANDING OUTSIDE ALL PHYSICS...HE FEELS WHAT *VANDAL SAVAGE* FELT ALL THOSE YEARS AGO.
A DESIRE TO TURN BACK, TO *HIDE* WHAT HE'S GLIMPSED FROM HIS TRIBE.
BUT FOR BETTER OR WORSE...
...THAT'S NOT WHO HE IS. OR WHO THEY ARE. SO HE PUSHES ON.
IT'S WORKING! FLASH...
...YOU DID IT! THE COSMIC MEMBRANE IS CLOSED!

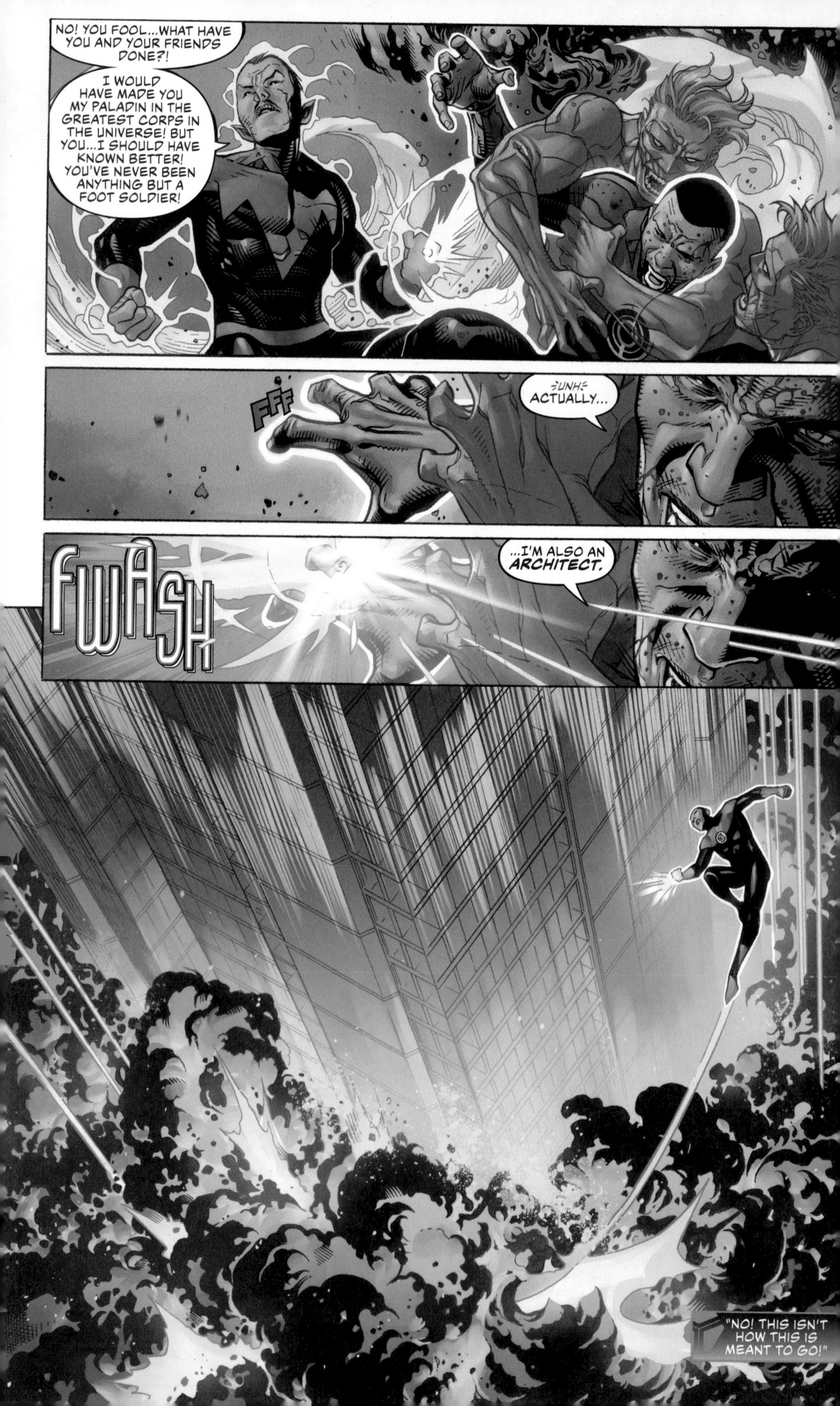
NO! YOU FOOL...WHAT HAVE YOU AND YOUR FRIENDS DONE?!
I WOULD HAVE MADE YOU MY PALADIN IN THE GREATEST CORPS IN THE UNIVERSE! BUT YOU...I SHOULD HAVE KNOWN BETTER! YOU'VE NEVER BEEN ANYTHING BUT A FOOT SOLDIER!
FFF
UNH ACTUALLY...
FWASH
...I'M ALSO AN ARCHITECT.
"NO! THIS ISN'T HOW THIS IS MEANT TO GO!"

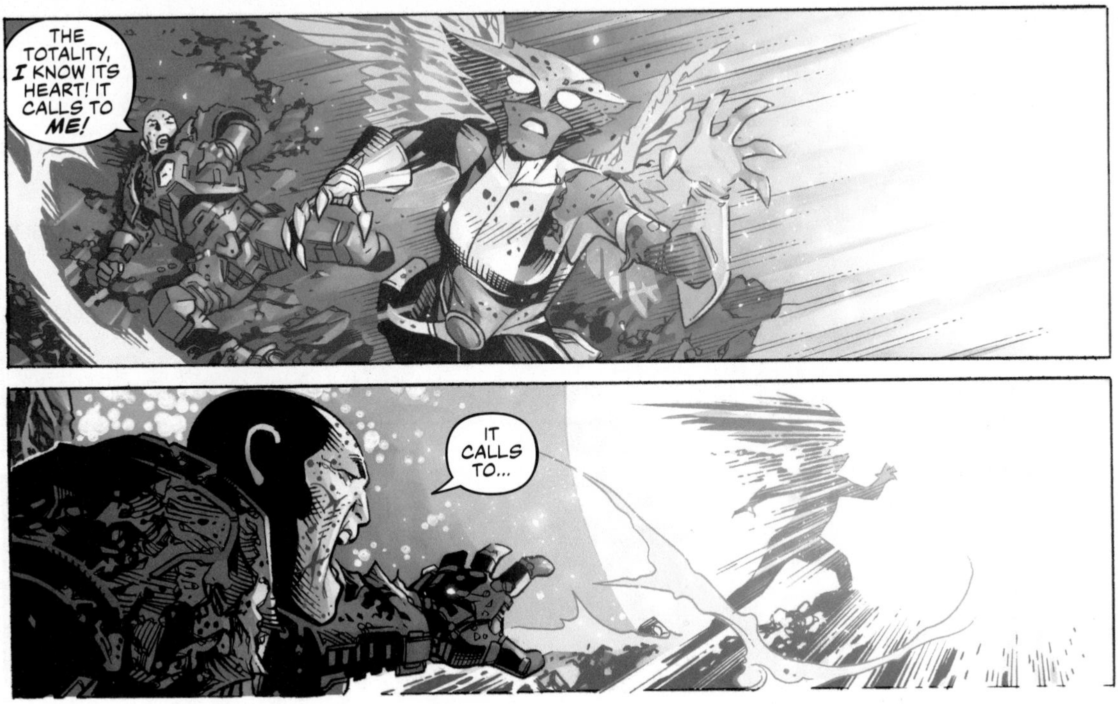
THE TOTALITY, *I* KNOW ITS HEART! IT CALLS TO *ME!*
IT CALLS TO...

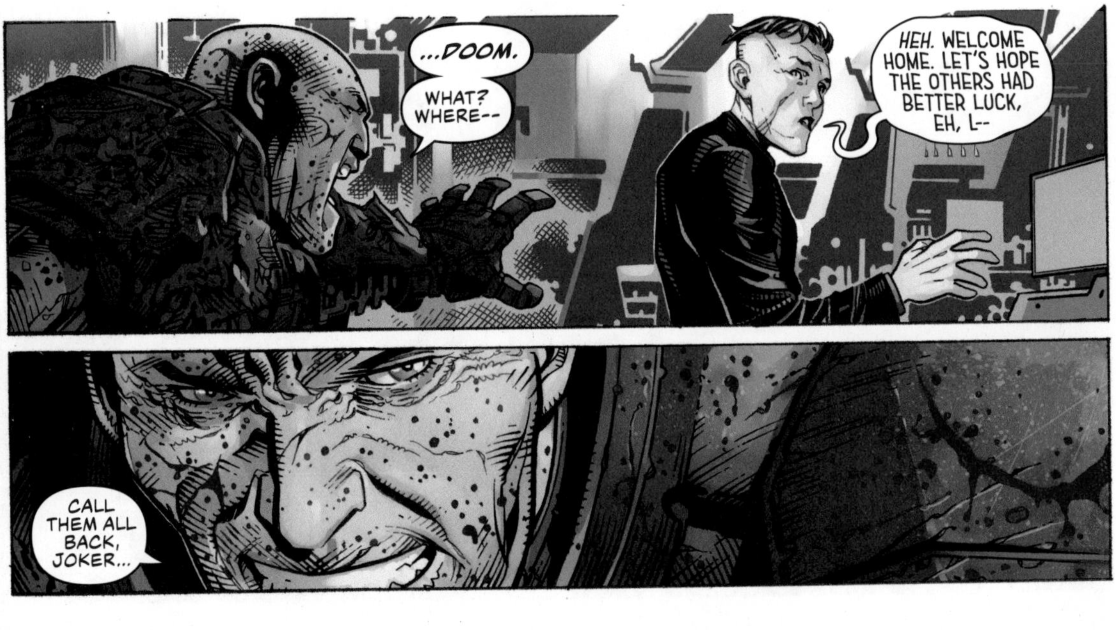
...*DOOM.*
WHAT? WHERE--
HEH. WELCOME HOME. LET'S HOPE THE OTHERS HAD BETTER LUCK, EH, L--
CALL THEM ALL BACK, JOKER...

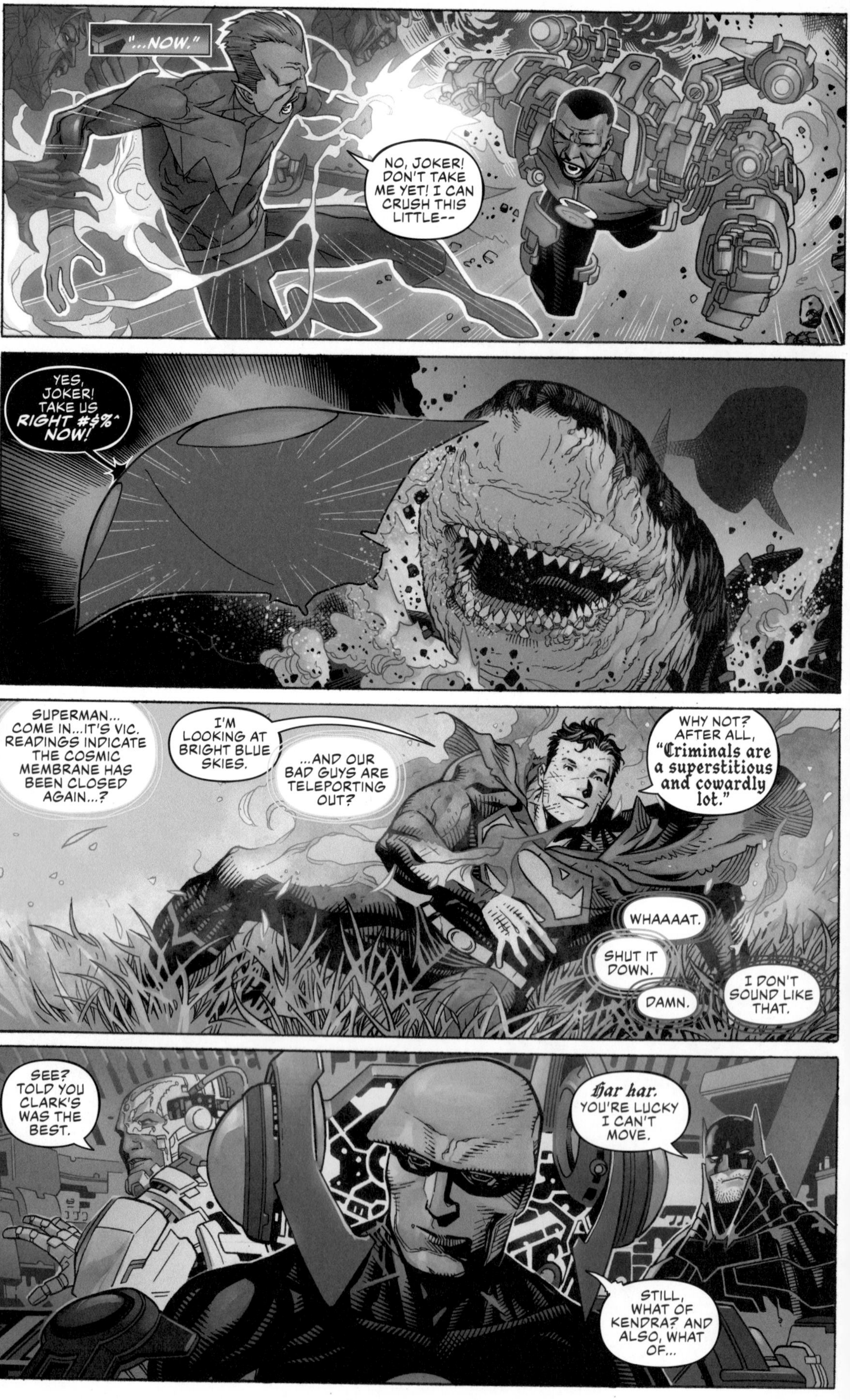
"...NOW."
NO, JOKER! DON'T TAKE ME YET! I CAN CRUSH THIS LITTLE--
YES, JOKER! TAKE US RIGHT #$%^ NOW!
SUPERMAN... COME IN...IT'S VIC. READINGS INDICATE THE COSMIC MEMBRANE HAS BEEN CLOSED AGAIN...?
I'M LOOKING AT BRIGHT BLUE SKIES.
...AND OUR BAD GUYS ARE TELEPORTING OUT?
WHY NOT? AFTER ALL, "Criminals are a superstitious and cowardly lot."
WHAAAAT.
SHUT IT DOWN.
DAMN.
I DON'T SOUND LIKE THAT.
SEE? TOLD YOU CLARK'S WAS THE BEST.
Har har. YOU'RE LUCKY I CAN'T MOVE.
STILL, WHAT OF KENDRA? AND ALSO, WHAT OF...

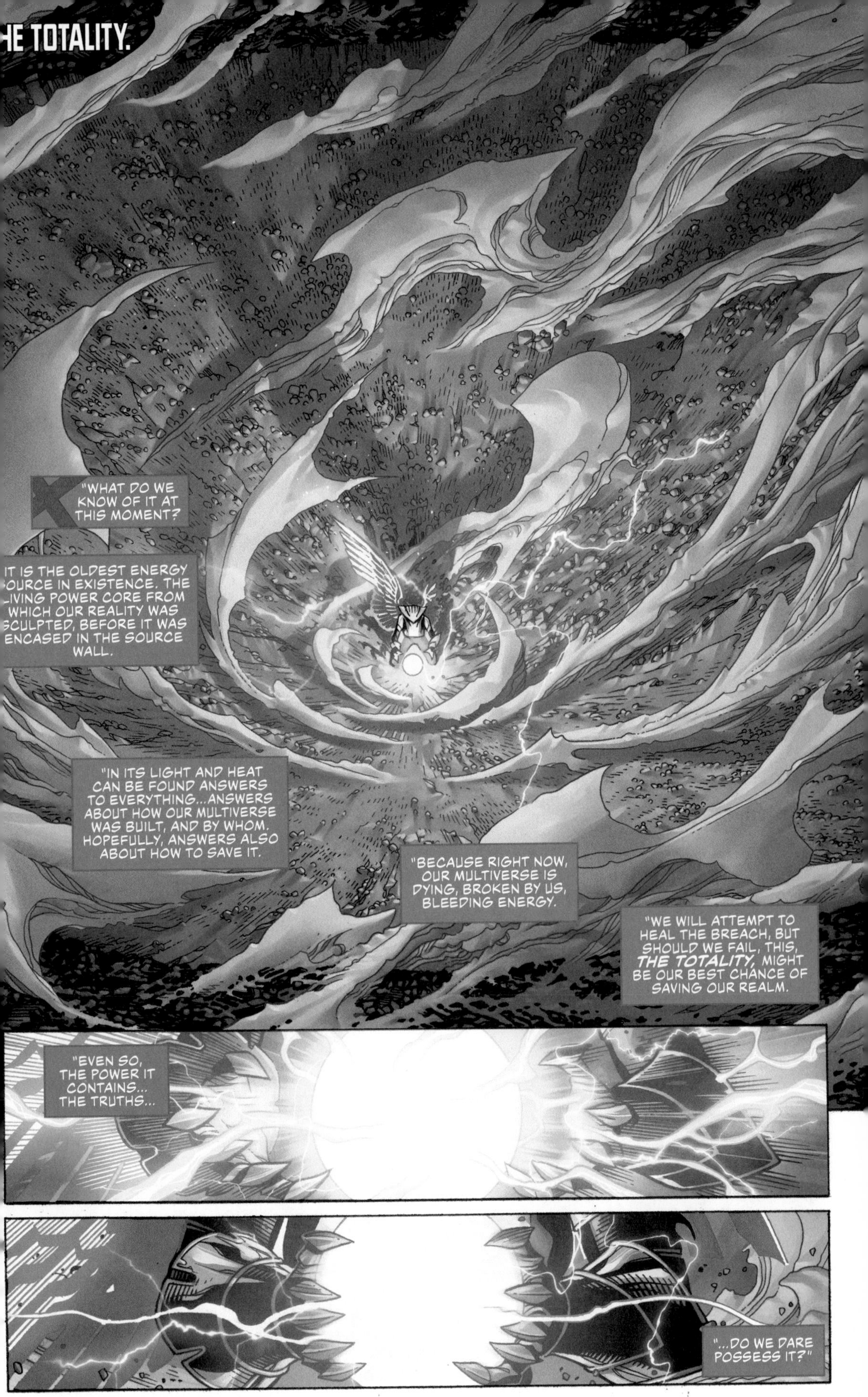
HE TOTALITY.
"WHAT DO WE KNOW OF IT AT THIS MOMENT?
IT IS THE OLDEST ENERGY SOURCE IN EXISTENCE. THE LIVING POWER CORE FROM WHICH OUR REALITY WAS SCULPTED, BEFORE IT WAS ENCASED IN THE SOURCE WALL.
"IN ITS LIGHT AND HEAT CAN BE FOUND ANSWERS TO EVERYTHING...ANSWERS ABOUT HOW OUR MULTIVERSE WAS BUILT, AND BY WHOM. HOPEFULLY, ANSWERS ALSO ABOUT HOW TO SAVE IT.
"BECAUSE RIGHT NOW, OUR MULTIVERSE IS DYING, BROKEN BY US, BLEEDING ENERGY.
"WE WILL ATTEMPT TO HEAL THE BREACH, BUT SHOULD WE FAIL, THIS, *THE TOTALITY,* MIGHT BE OUR BEST CHANCE OF SAVING OUR REALM.
"EVEN SO, THE POWER IT CONTAINS... THE TRUTHS...
"...DO WE DARE POSSESS IT?"

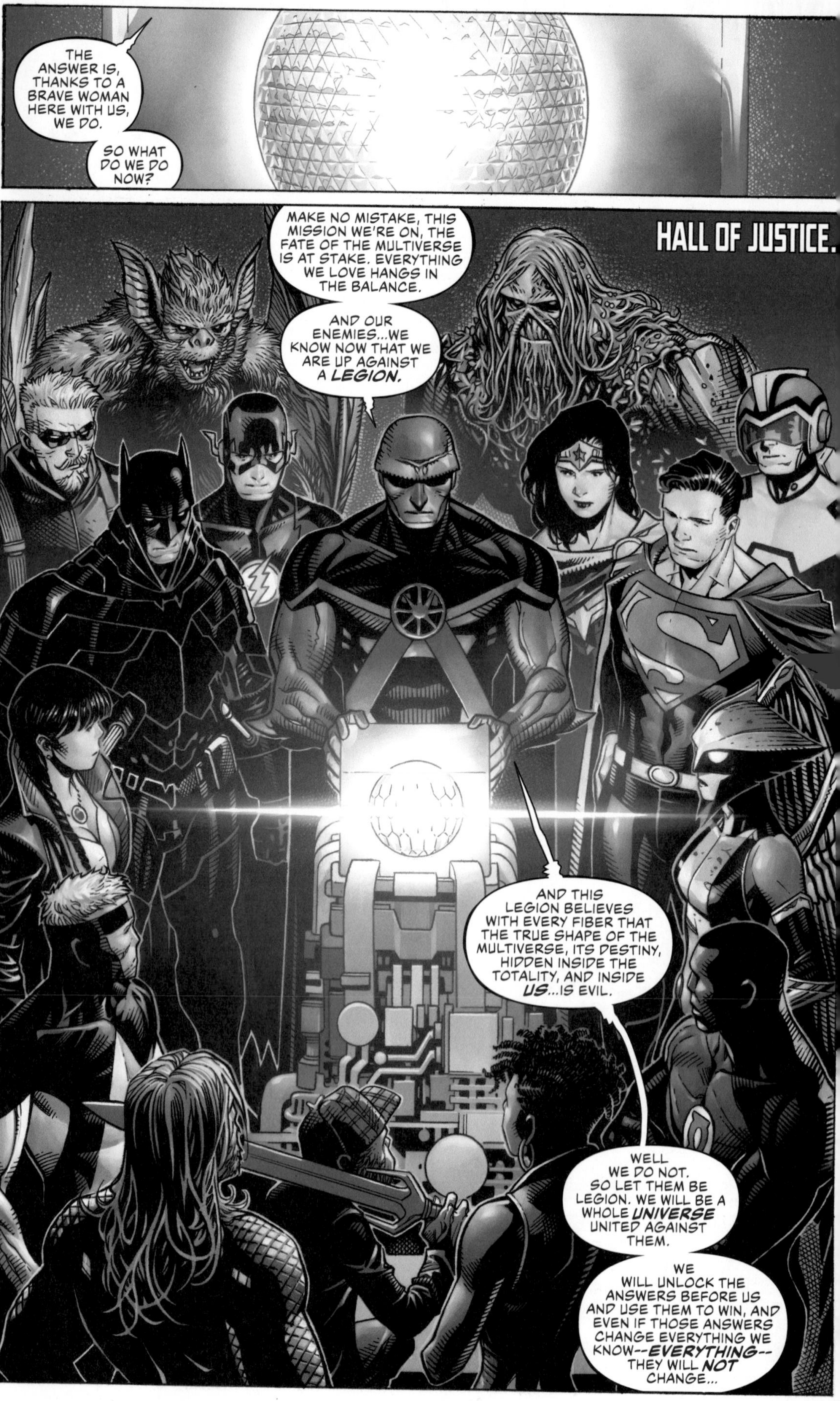

THE ANSWER IS, THANKS TO A BRAVE WOMAN HERE WITH US, WE DO.
SO WHAT DO WE DO NOW?
HALL OF JUSTICE.
MAKE NO MISTAKE, THIS MISSION WE'RE ON, THE FATE OF THE MULTIVERSE IS AT STAKE. EVERYTHING WE LOVE HANGS IN THE BALANCE.
AND OUR ENEMIES...WE KNOW NOW THAT WE ARE UP AGAINST A *LEGION.*
AND THIS LEGION BELIEVES WITH EVERY FIBER THAT THE TRUE SHAPE OF THE MULTIVERSE, ITS DESTINY, HIDDEN INSIDE THE TOTALITY, AND INSIDE *US*...IS EVIL.
WELL WE DO NOT. SO LET THEM BE LEGION. WE WILL BE A WHOLE *UNIVERSE* UNITED AGAINST THEM.
WE WILL UNLOCK THE ANSWERS BEFORE US AND USE THEM TO WIN, AND EVEN IF THOSE ANSWERS CHANGE EVERYTHING WE KNOW--*EVERYTHING*--THEY WILL *NOT* CHANGE...

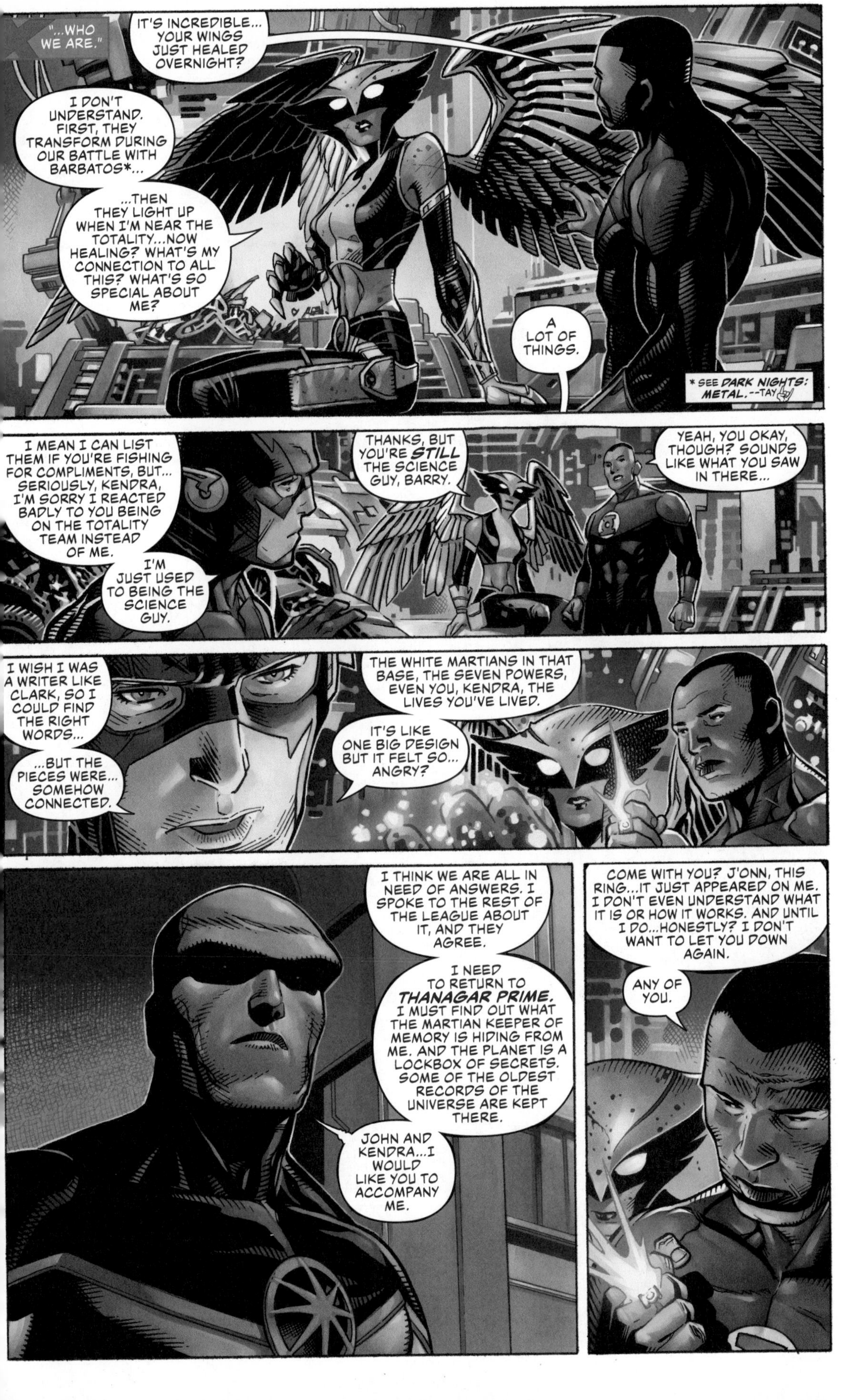
"...WHO WE ARE."
IT'S INCREDIBLE... YOUR WINGS JUST HEALED OVERNIGHT?
I DON'T UNDERSTAND. FIRST, THEY TRANSFORM DURING OUR BATTLE WITH BARBATOS*...
...THEN THEY LIGHT UP WHEN I'M NEAR THE TOTALITY...NOW HEALING? WHAT'S MY CONNECTION TO ALL THIS? WHAT'S SO SPECIAL ABOUT ME?
A LOT OF THINGS.
* SEE DARK NIGHTS: METAL. --TAY
I MEAN I CAN LIST THEM IF YOU'RE FISHING FOR COMPLIMENTS, BUT... SERIOUSLY, KENDRA, I'M SORRY I REACTED BADLY TO YOU BEING ON THE TOTALITY TEAM INSTEAD OF ME.
I'M JUST USED TO BEING THE SCIENCE GUY.
THANKS, BUT YOU'RE STILL THE SCIENCE GUY, BARRY.
YEAH, YOU OKAY, THOUGH? SOUNDS LIKE WHAT YOU SAW IN THERE...
I WISH I WAS A WRITER LIKE CLARK, SO I COULD FIND THE RIGHT WORDS...
...BUT THE PIECES WERE... SOMEHOW CONNECTED.
THE WHITE MARTIANS IN THAT BASE, THE SEVEN POWERS, EVEN YOU, KENDRA, THE LIVES YOU'VE LIVED.
IT'S LIKE ONE BIG DESIGN BUT IT FELT SO... ANGRY?
I THINK WE ARE ALL IN NEED OF ANSWERS. I SPOKE TO THE REST OF THE LEAGUE ABOUT IT, AND THEY AGREE.
I NEED TO RETURN TO THANAGAR PRIME. I MUST FIND OUT WHAT THE MARTIAN KEEPER OF MEMORY IS HIDING FROM ME. AND THE PLANET IS A LOCKBOX OF SECRETS. SOME OF THE OLDEST RECORDS OF THE UNIVERSE ARE KEPT THERE.
JOHN AND KENDRA...I WOULD LIKE YOU TO ACCOMPANY ME.
COME WITH YOU? J'ONN, THIS RING...IT JUST APPEARED ON ME. I DON'T EVEN UNDERSTAND WHAT IT IS OR HOW IT WORKS. AND UNTIL I DO...HONESTLY? I DON'T WANT TO LET YOU DOWN AGAIN.
ANY OF YOU.

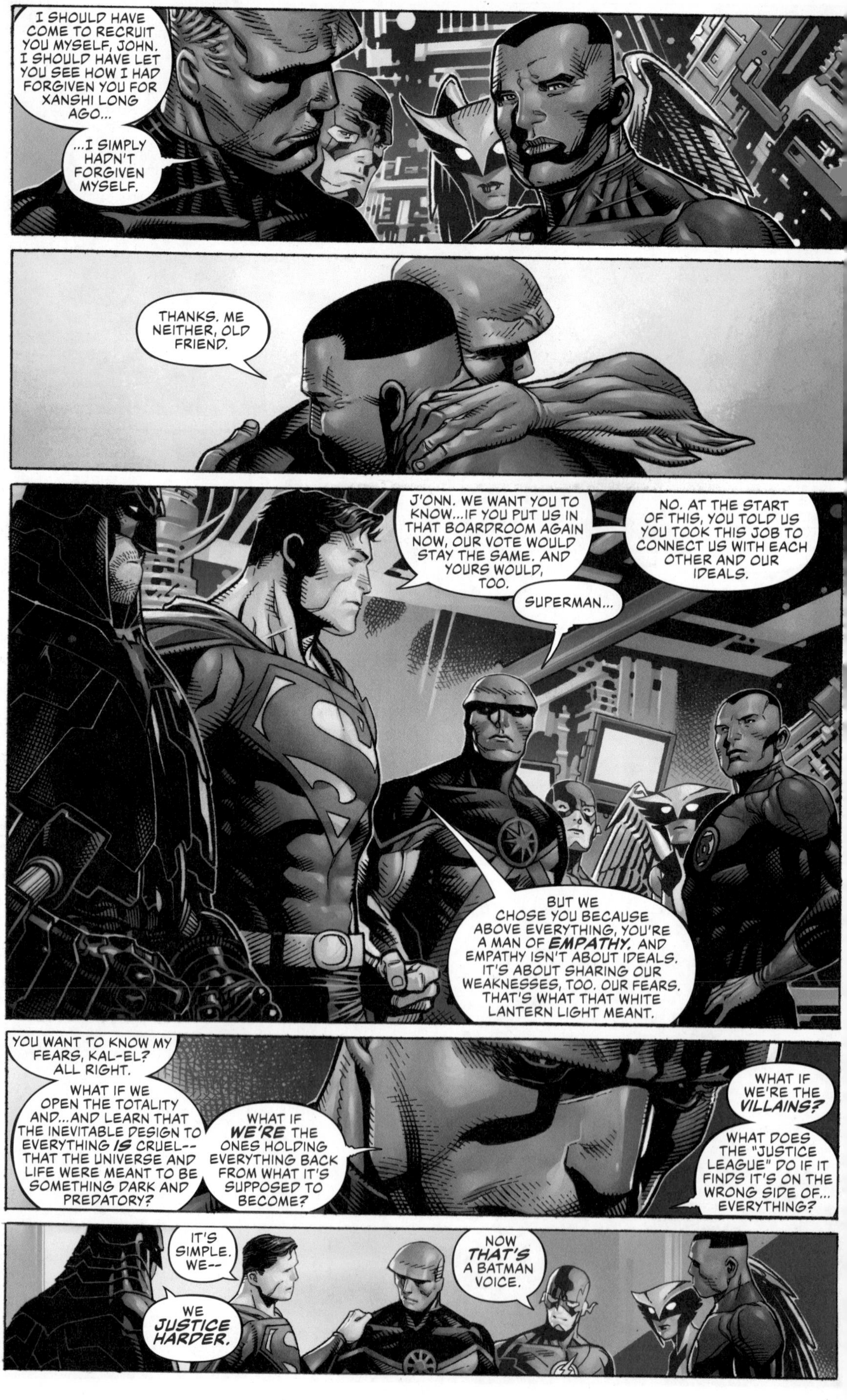
I SHOULD HAVE COME TO RECRUIT YOU MYSELF, JOHN. I SHOULD HAVE LET YOU SEE HOW I HAD FORGIVEN YOU FOR XANSHI LONG AGO...
...I SIMPLY HADN'T FORGIVEN MYSELF.
THANKS. ME NEITHER, OLD FRIEND.
J'ONN. WE WANT YOU TO KNOW...IF YOU PUT US IN THAT BOARDROOM AGAIN NOW, OUR VOTE WOULD STAY THE SAME. AND YOURS WOULD, TOO.
NO. AT THE START OF THIS, YOU TOLD US YOU TOOK THIS JOB TO CONNECT US WITH EACH OTHER AND OUR IDEALS.
SUPERMAN...
BUT WE CHOSE YOU BECAUSE ABOVE EVERYTHING, YOU'RE A MAN OF EMPATHY. AND EMPATHY ISN'T ABOUT IDEALS. IT'S ABOUT SHARING OUR WEAKNESSES, TOO. OUR FEARS. THAT'S WHAT THAT WHITE LANTERN LIGHT MEANT.
YOU WANT TO KNOW MY FEARS, KAL-EL? ALL RIGHT.
WHAT IF WE OPEN THE TOTALITY AND...AND LEARN THAT THE INEVITABLE DESIGN TO EVERYTHING IS CRUEL--THAT THE UNIVERSE AND LIFE WERE MEANT TO BE SOMETHING DARK AND PREDATORY?
WHAT IF WE'RE THE ONES HOLDING EVERYTHING BACK FROM WHAT IT'S SUPPOSED TO BECOME?
WHAT IF WE'RE THE VILLAINS?
WHAT DOES THE "JUSTICE LEAGUE" DO IF IT FINDS IT'S ON THE WRONG SIDE OF... EVERYTHING?
IT'S SIMPLE. WE--
WE JUSTICE HARDER.
NOW THAT'S A BATMAN VOICE.

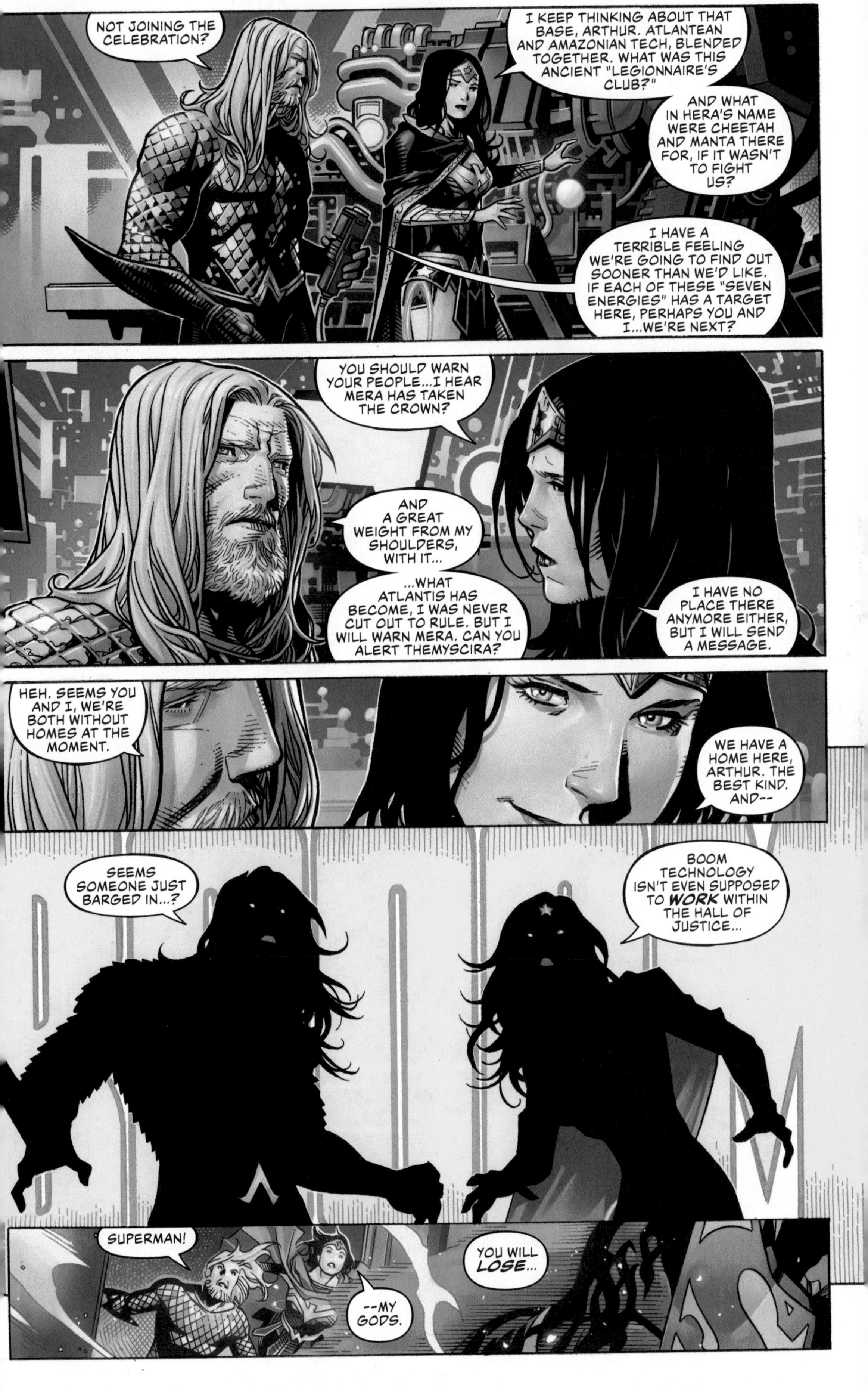
NOT JOINING THE CELEBRATION?
I KEEP THINKING ABOUT THAT BASE, ARTHUR. ATLANTEAN AND AMAZONIAN TECH, BLENDED TOGETHER. WHAT WAS THIS ANCIENT "LEGIONNAIRE'S CLUB?"
AND WHAT IN HERA'S NAME WERE CHEETAH AND MANTA THERE FOR, IF IT WASN'T TO FIGHT US?
I HAVE A TERRIBLE FEELING WE'RE GOING TO FIND OUT SOONER THAN WE'D LIKE. IF EACH OF THESE "SEVEN ENERGIES" HAS A TARGET HERE, PERHAPS YOU AND I...WE'RE NEXT?
YOU SHOULD WARN YOUR PEOPLE...I HEAR MERA HAS TAKEN THE CROWN?
AND A GREAT WEIGHT FROM MY SHOULDERS, WITH IT...
...WHAT ATLANTIS HAS BECOME, I WAS NEVER CUT OUT TO RULE. BUT I WILL WARN MERA. CAN YOU ALERT THEMYSCIRA?
I HAVE NO PLACE THERE ANYMORE EITHER, BUT I WILL SEND A MESSAGE.
HEH. SEEMS YOU AND I, WE'RE BOTH WITHOUT HOMES AT THE MOMENT.
WE HAVE A HOME HERE, ARTHUR. THE BEST KIND. AND--
SEEMS SOMEONE JUST BARGED IN...?
BOOM TECHNOLOGY ISN'T EVEN SUPPOSED TO WORK WITHIN THE HALL OF JUSTICE...
SUPERMAN!
--MY GODS.
YOU WILL LOSE...

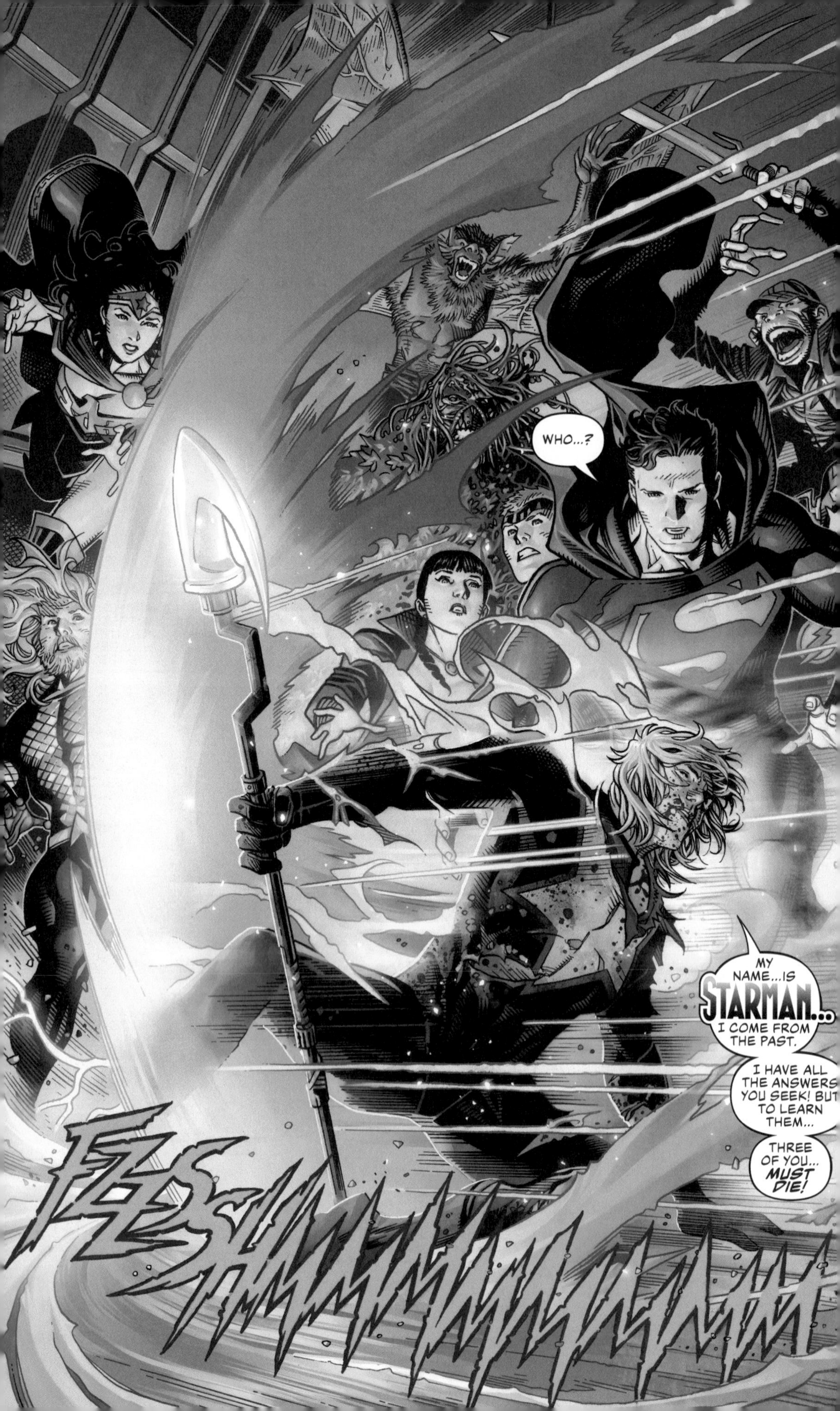
WHO...?
MY NAME...IS STARMAN... I COME FROM THE PAST.
I HAVE ALL THE ANSWERS YOU SEEK! BUT TO LEARN THEM...
THREE OF YOU... MUST DIE!
FZSHMMMMMMMMMM

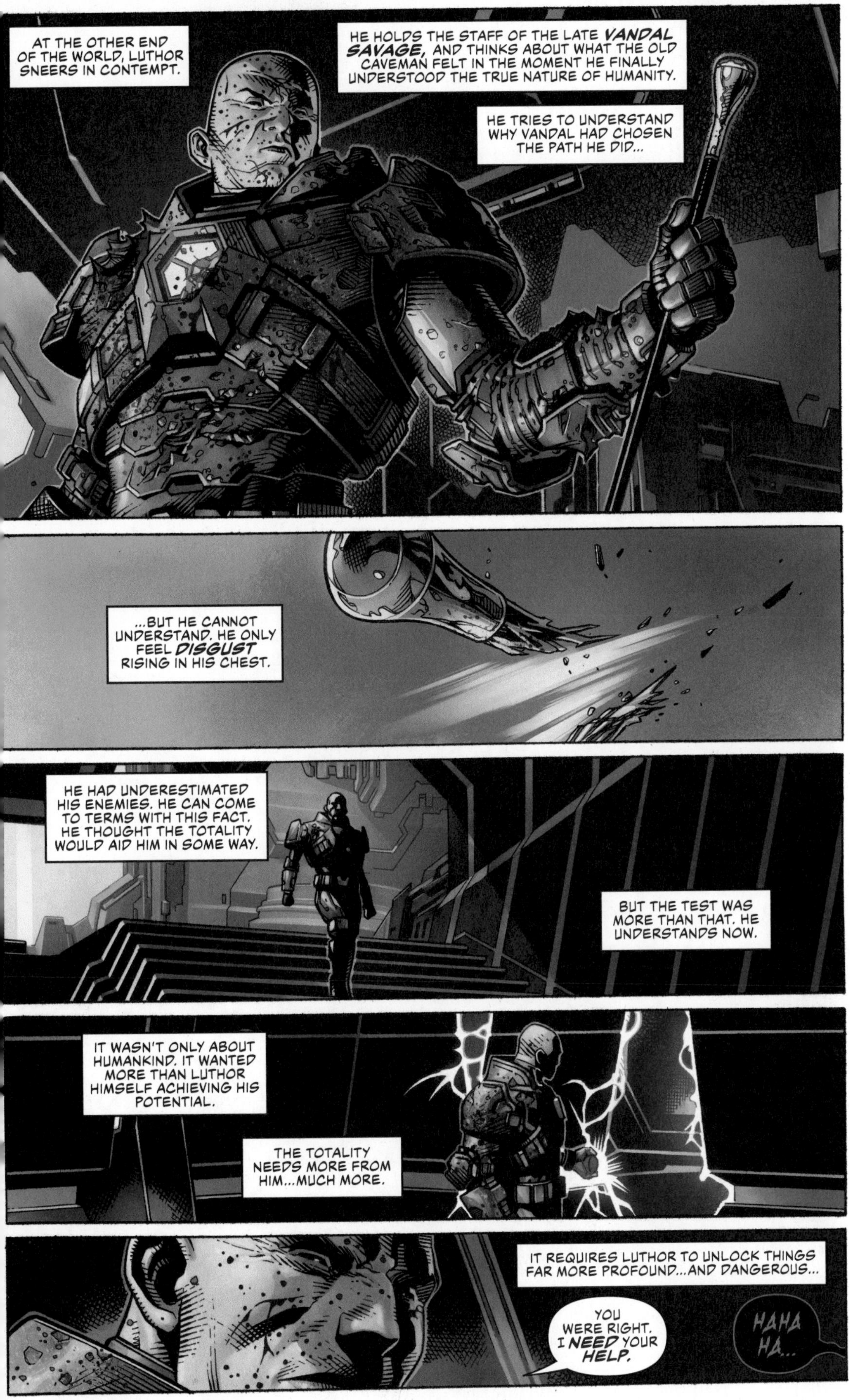

AT THE OTHER END OF THE WORLD, LUTHOR SNEERS IN CONTEMPT.
HE HOLDS THE STAFF OF THE LATE VANDAL SAVAGE, AND THINKS ABOUT WHAT THE OLD CAVEMAN FELT IN THE MOMENT HE FINALLY UNDERSTOOD THE TRUE NATURE OF HUMANITY.
HE TRIES TO UNDERSTAND WHY VANDAL HAD CHOSEN THE PATH HE DID...
...BUT HE CANNOT UNDERSTAND. HE ONLY FEEL DISGUST RISING IN HIS CHEST.
HE HAD UNDERESTIMATED HIS ENEMIES. HE CAN COME TO TERMS WITH THIS FACT. HE THOUGHT THE TOTALITY WOULD AID HIM IN SOME WAY.
BUT THE TEST WAS MORE THAN THAT. HE UNDERSTANDS NOW.
IT WASN'T ONLY ABOUT HUMANKIND. IT WANTED MORE THAN LUTHOR HIMSELF ACHIEVING HIS POTENTIAL.
THE TOTALITY NEEDS MORE FROM HIM...MUCH MORE.
IT REQUIRES LUTHOR TO UNLOCK THINGS FAR MORE PROFOUND...AND DANGEROUS...
YOU WERE RIGHT. I NEED YOUR HELP.
HAHA HA...

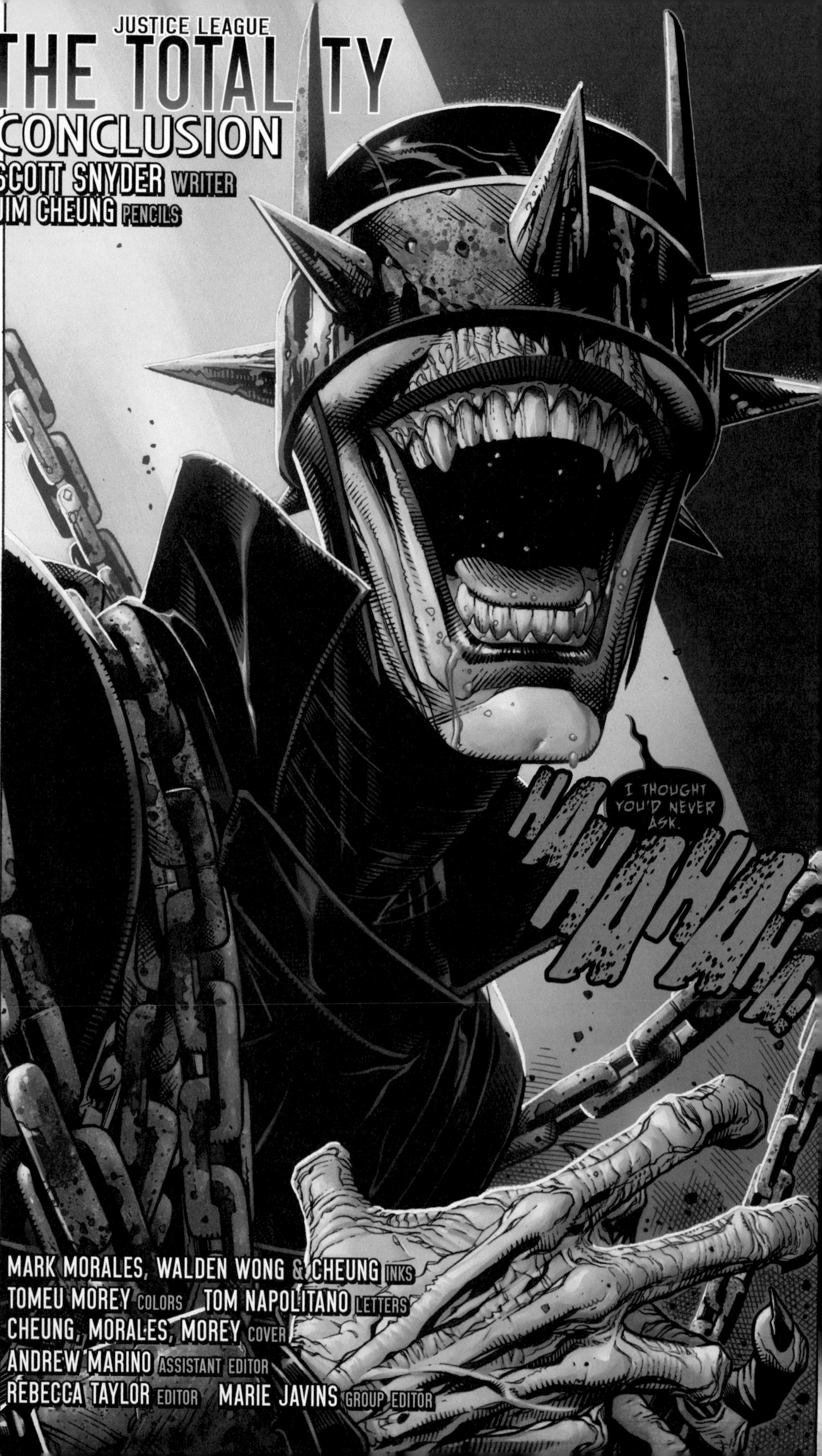
JUSTICE LEAGUE
THE TOTALITY
CONCLUSION
SCOTT SNYDER WRITER
JIM CHEUNG PENCILS
I THOUGHT YOU'D NEVER ASK.
MARK MORALES, WALDEN WONG & CHEUNG INKS
TOMEU MOREY COLORS TOM NAPOLITANO LETTERS
CHEUNG, MORALES, MOREY COVER
ANDREW MARINO ASSISTANT EDITOR
REBECCA TAYLOR EDITOR MARIE JAVINS GROUP EDITOR

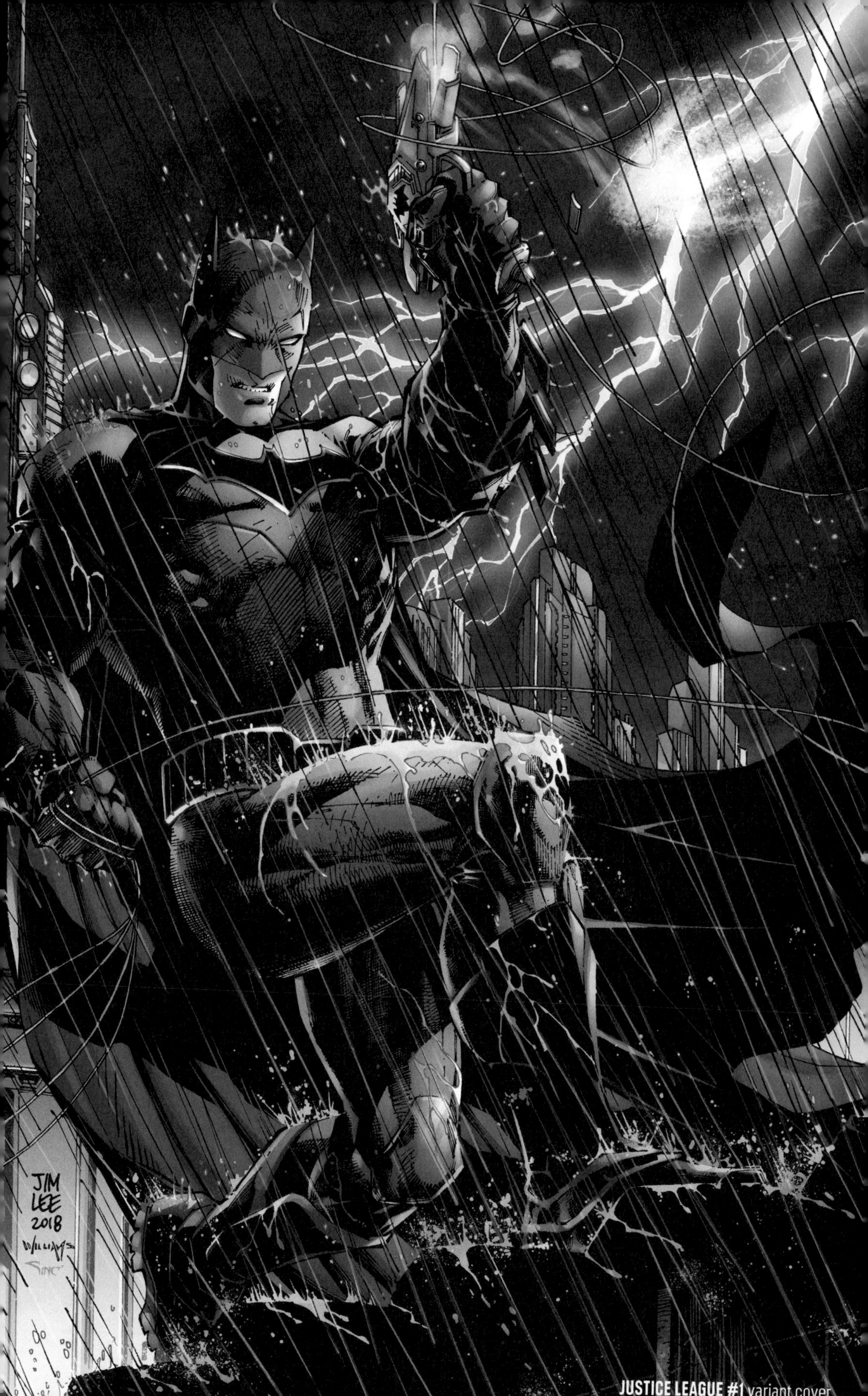

JUSTICE LEAGUE #1 variant cover
by JIM LEE, SCOTT WILLIAMS and ALEX SINCLAIR

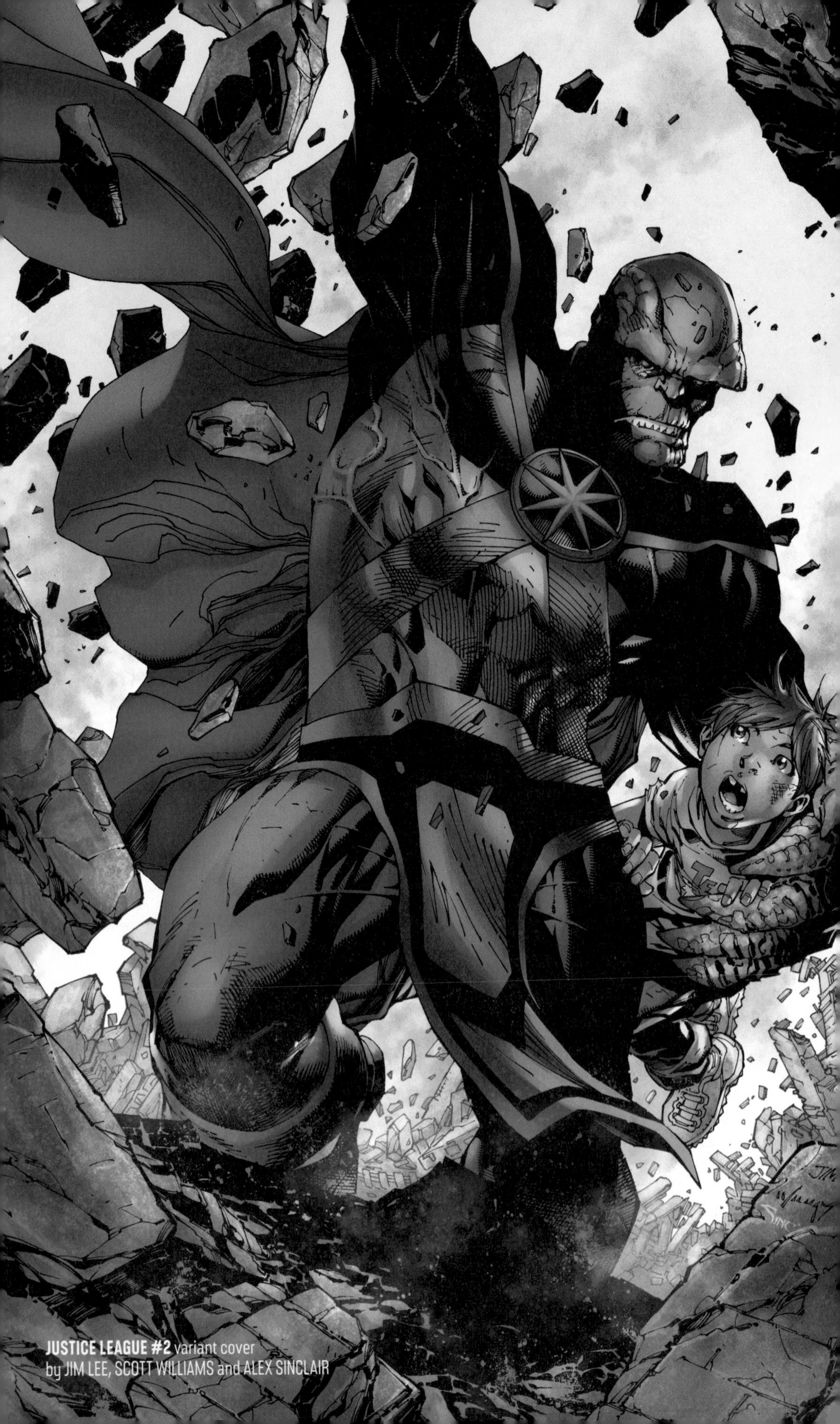

JUSTICE LEAGUE #2 variant cover
by JIM LEE, SCOTT WILLIAMS and ALEX SINCLAIR

JUSTICE LEAGUE #3 variant cover
by JIM LEE, SANDRA HOPE and TOMEU MOREY

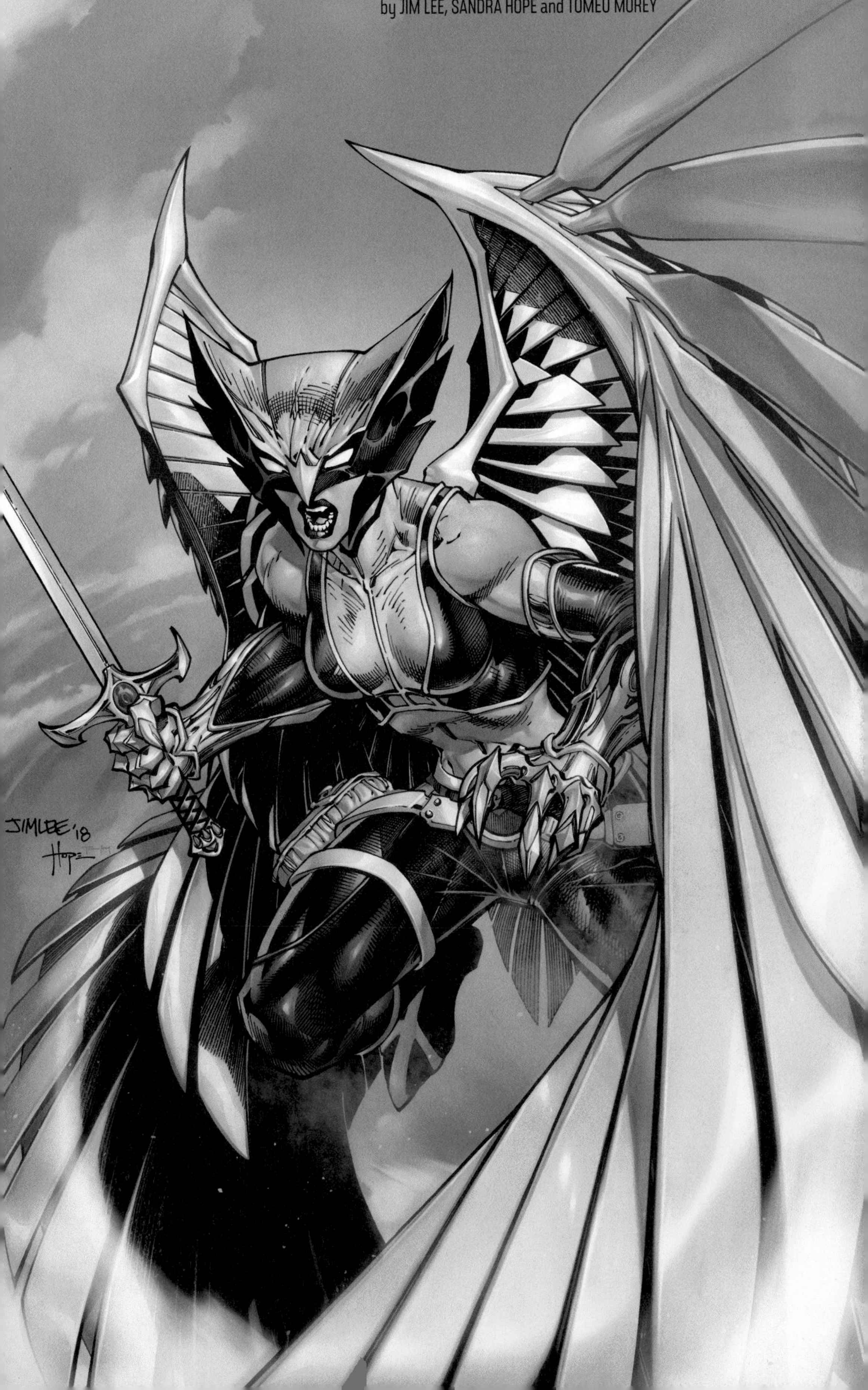
JIMLEE '18
HOPE

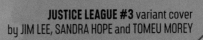

JUSTICE LEAGUE #4 variant cover
by JIM LEE, SANDRA HOPE and LAURA MARTIN

JUSTICE LEAGUE #5 variant cover
by JIM LEE, SCOTT WILLIAMS and ALEX SINCLAIR

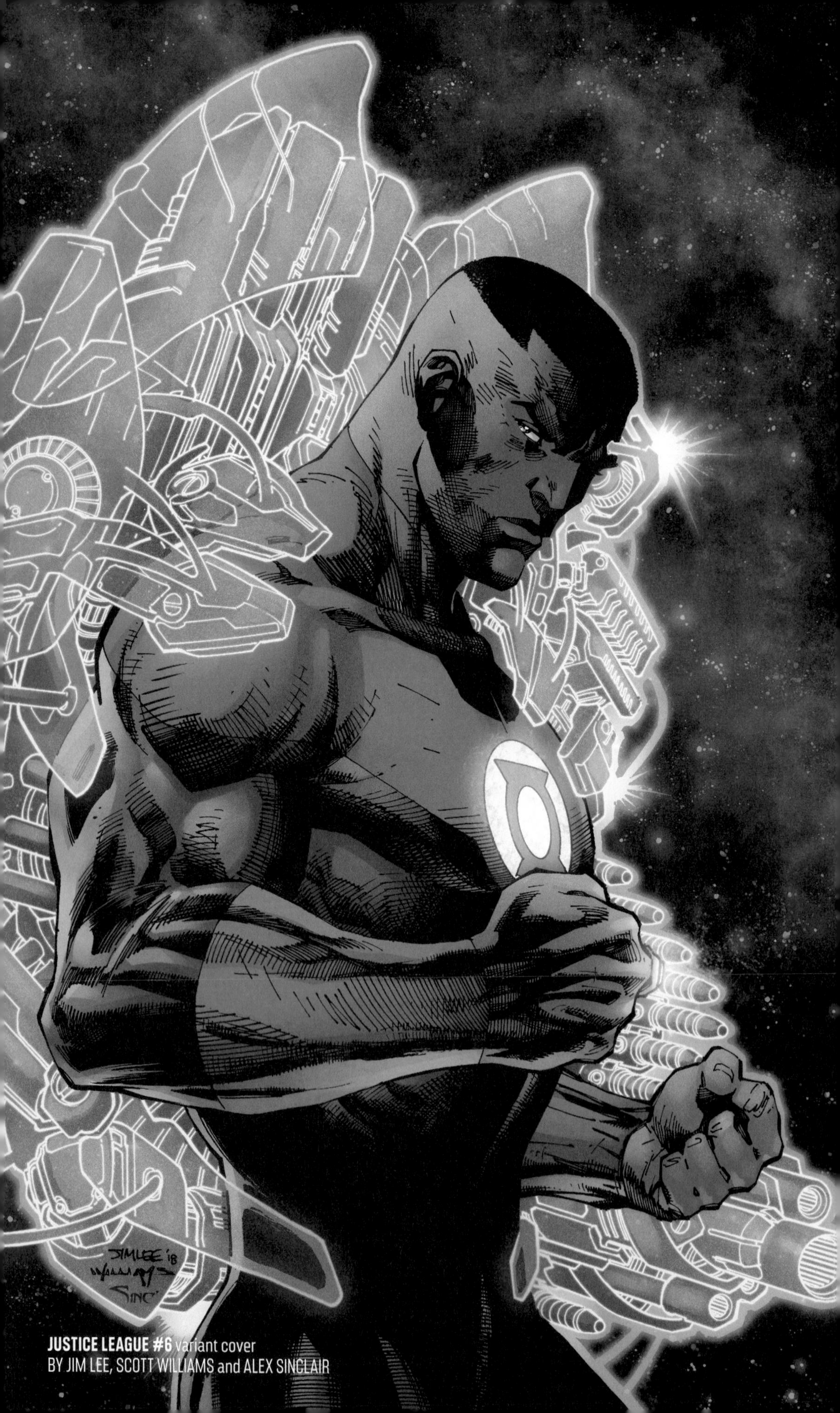

JUSTICE LEAGUE #6 variant cover
BY JIM LEE, SCOTT WILLIAMS and ALEX SINCLAIR

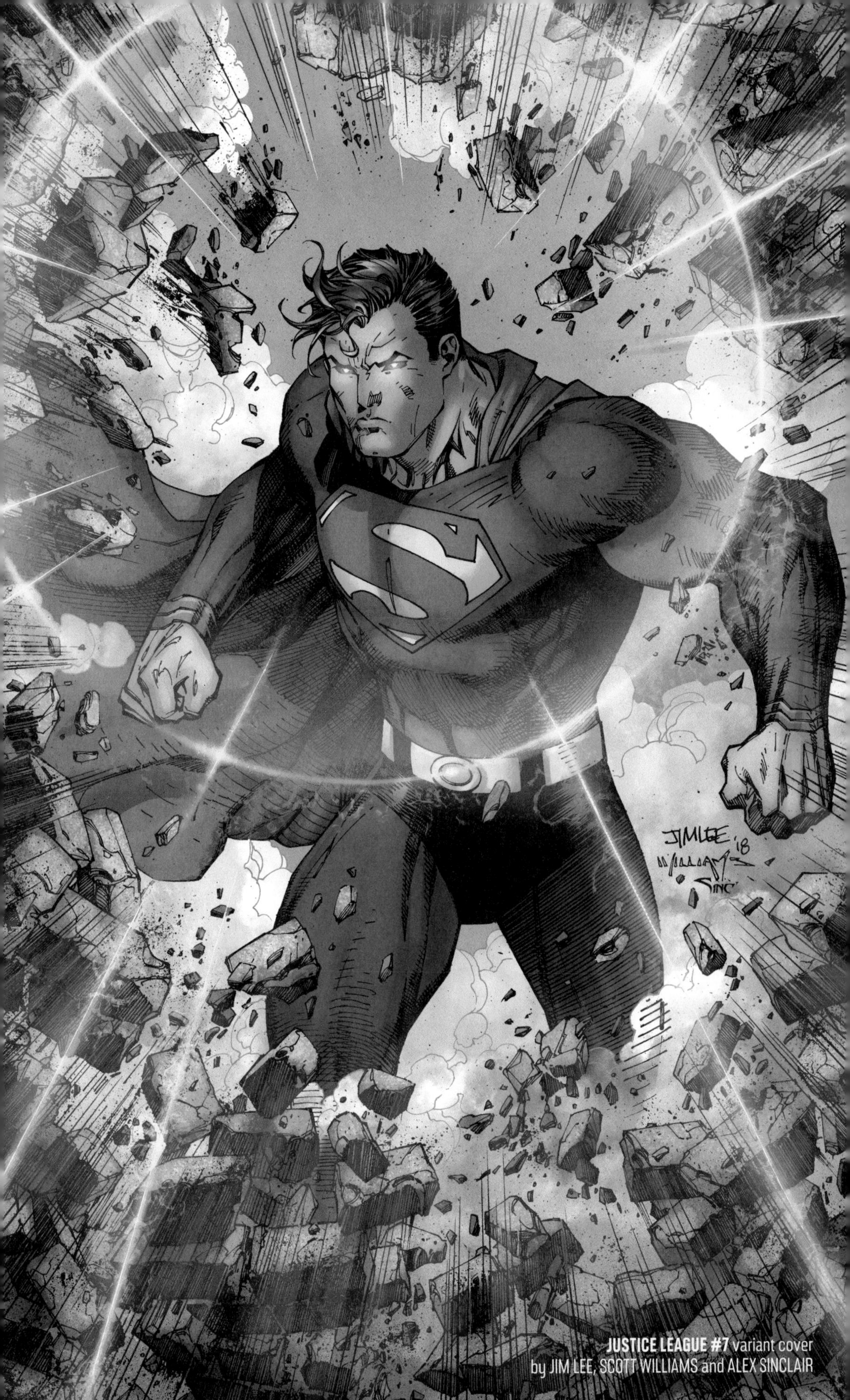

JUSTICE LEAGUE #7 variant cover
by JIM LEE, SCOTT WILLIAMS and ALEX SINCLAIR

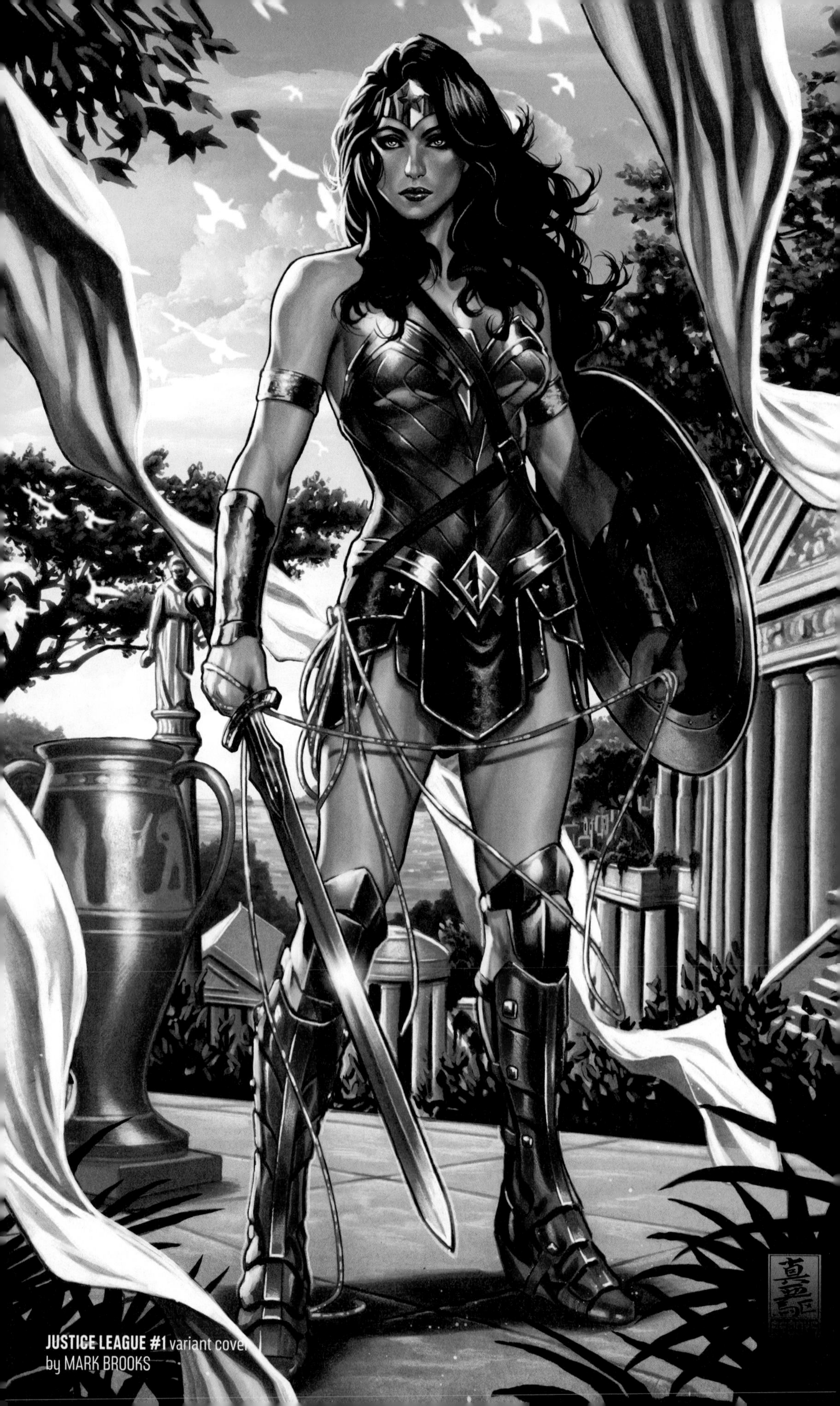

JUSTICE LEAGUE #1 variant cover
by MARK BROOKS

JUSTICE LEAGUE #1 variant cover
by CLAYTON CRAIN

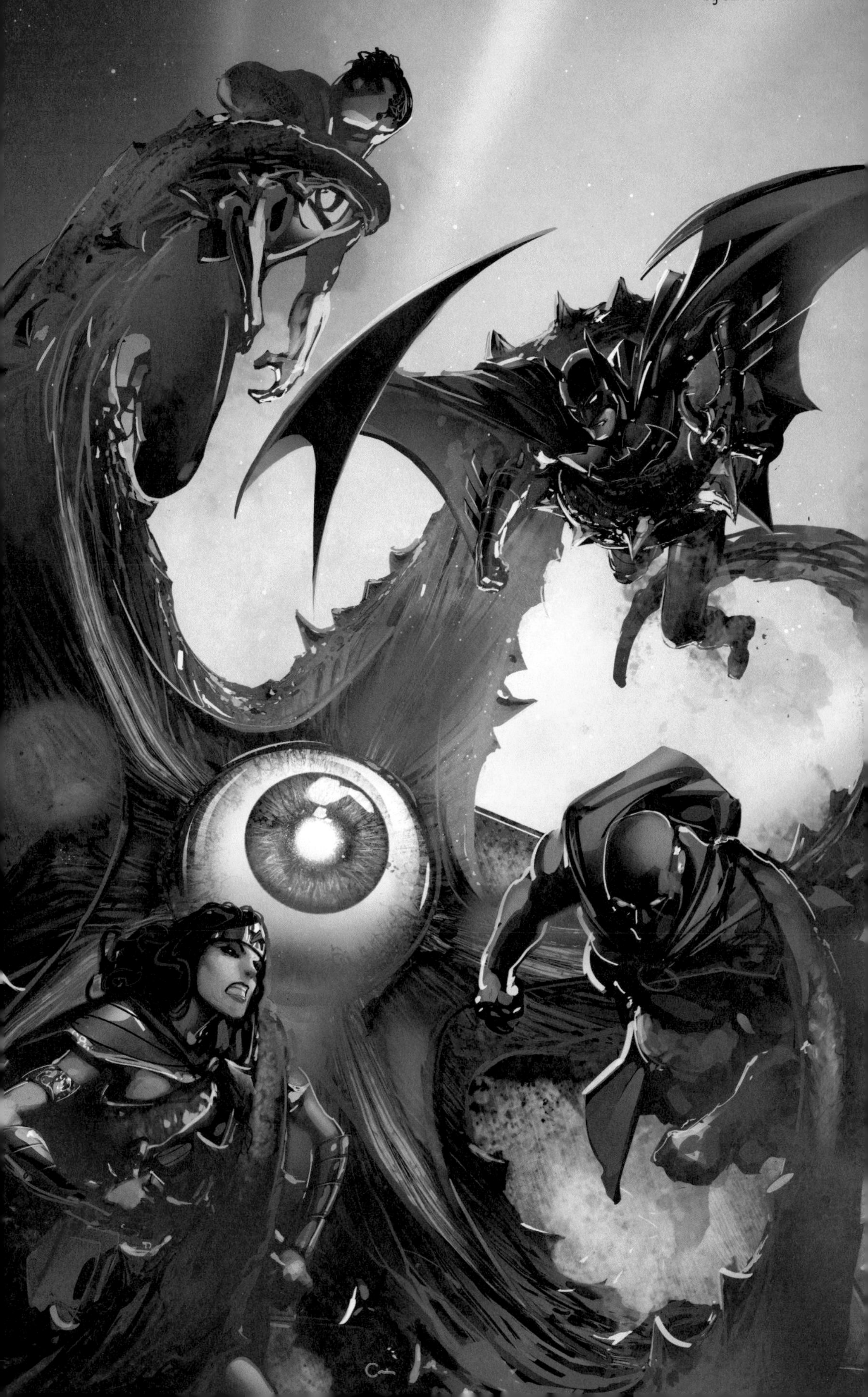

JUSTICE LEAGUE #1 variant cover
by JOCK

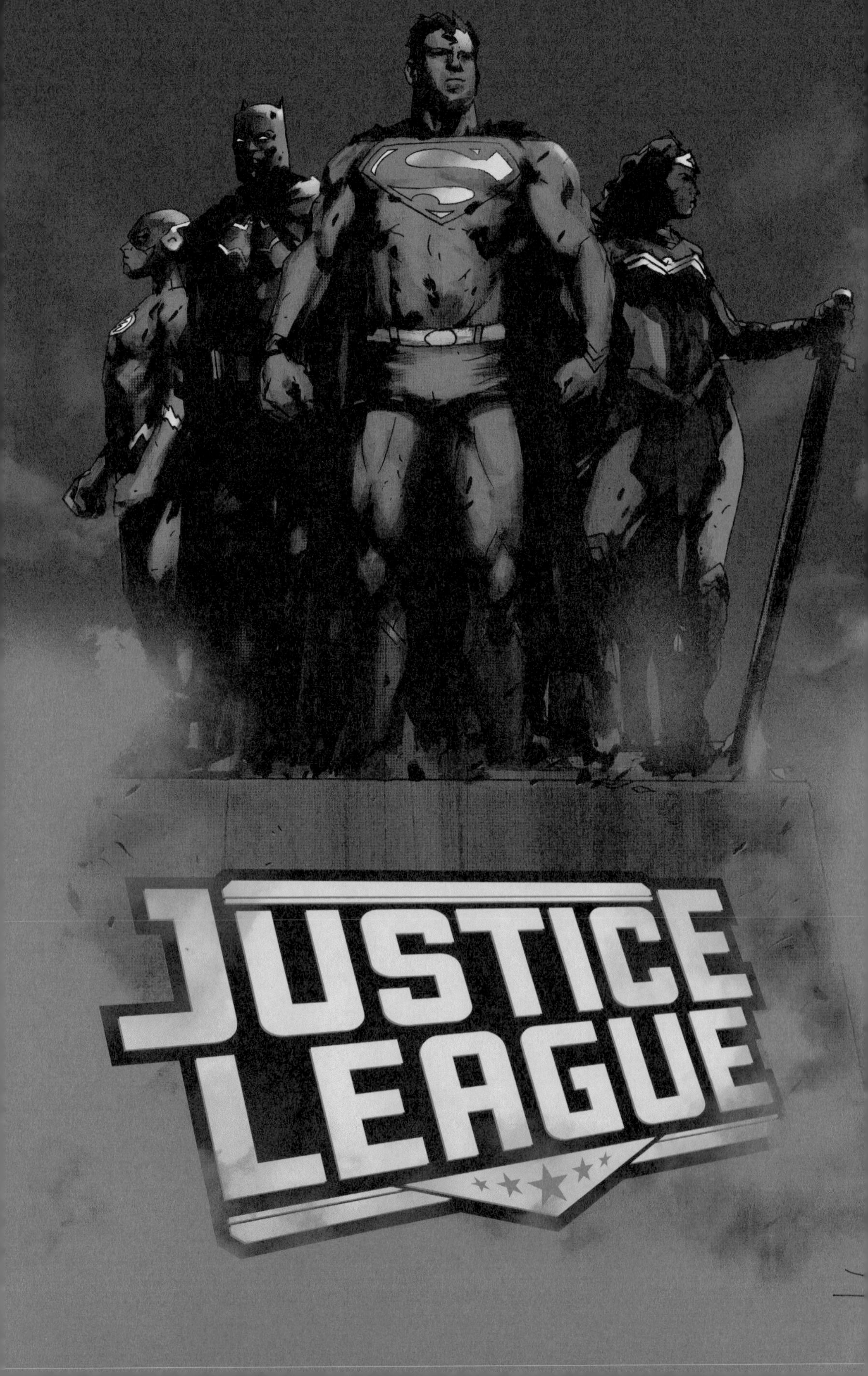
JUSTICE
LEAGUE

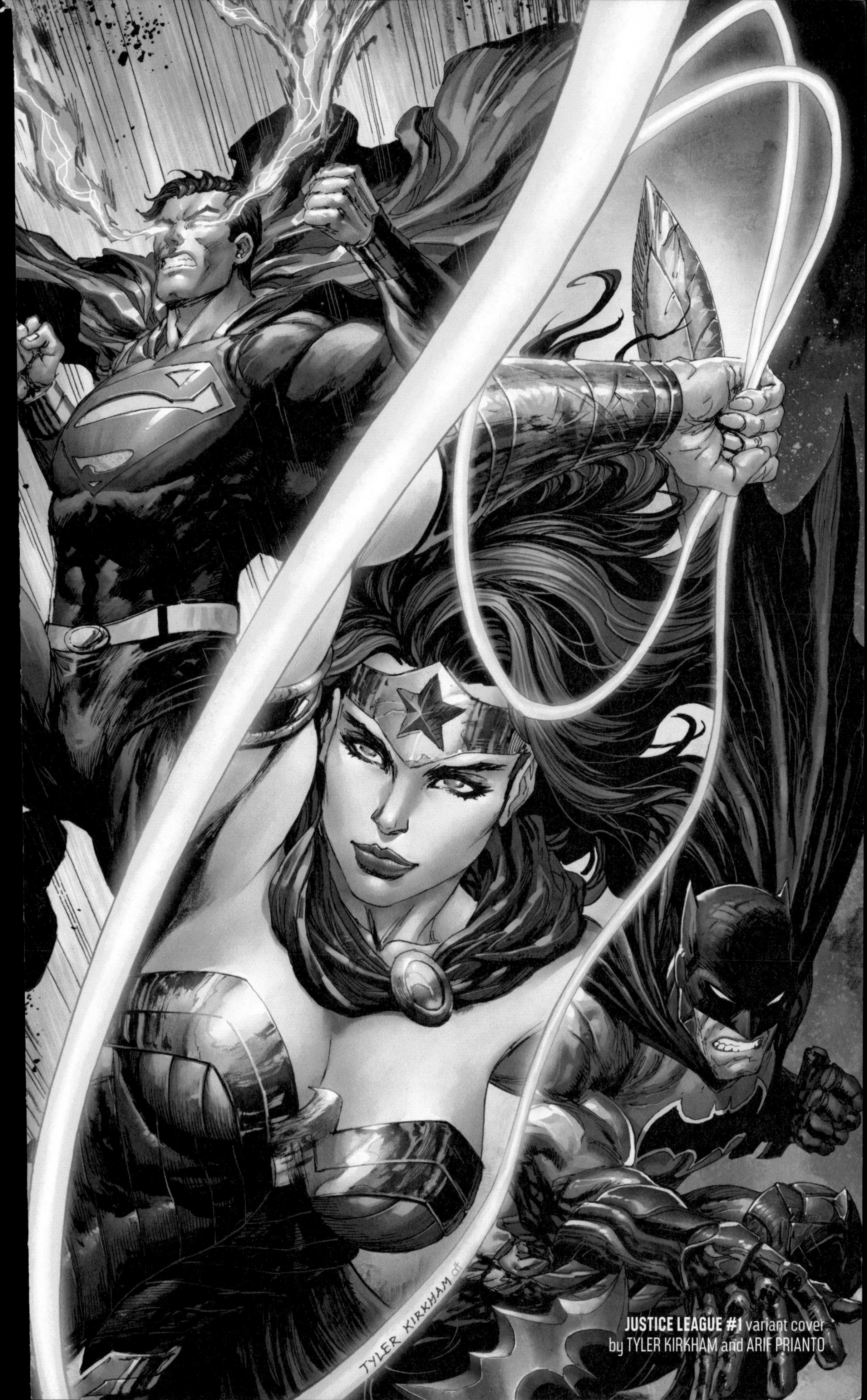
TYLER KIRKHAM

JUSTICE LEAGUE #1 variant cover
by TYLER KIRKHAM and ARIF PRIANTO

JUSTICE LEAGUE #1 variant cover
by WARREN LOUW

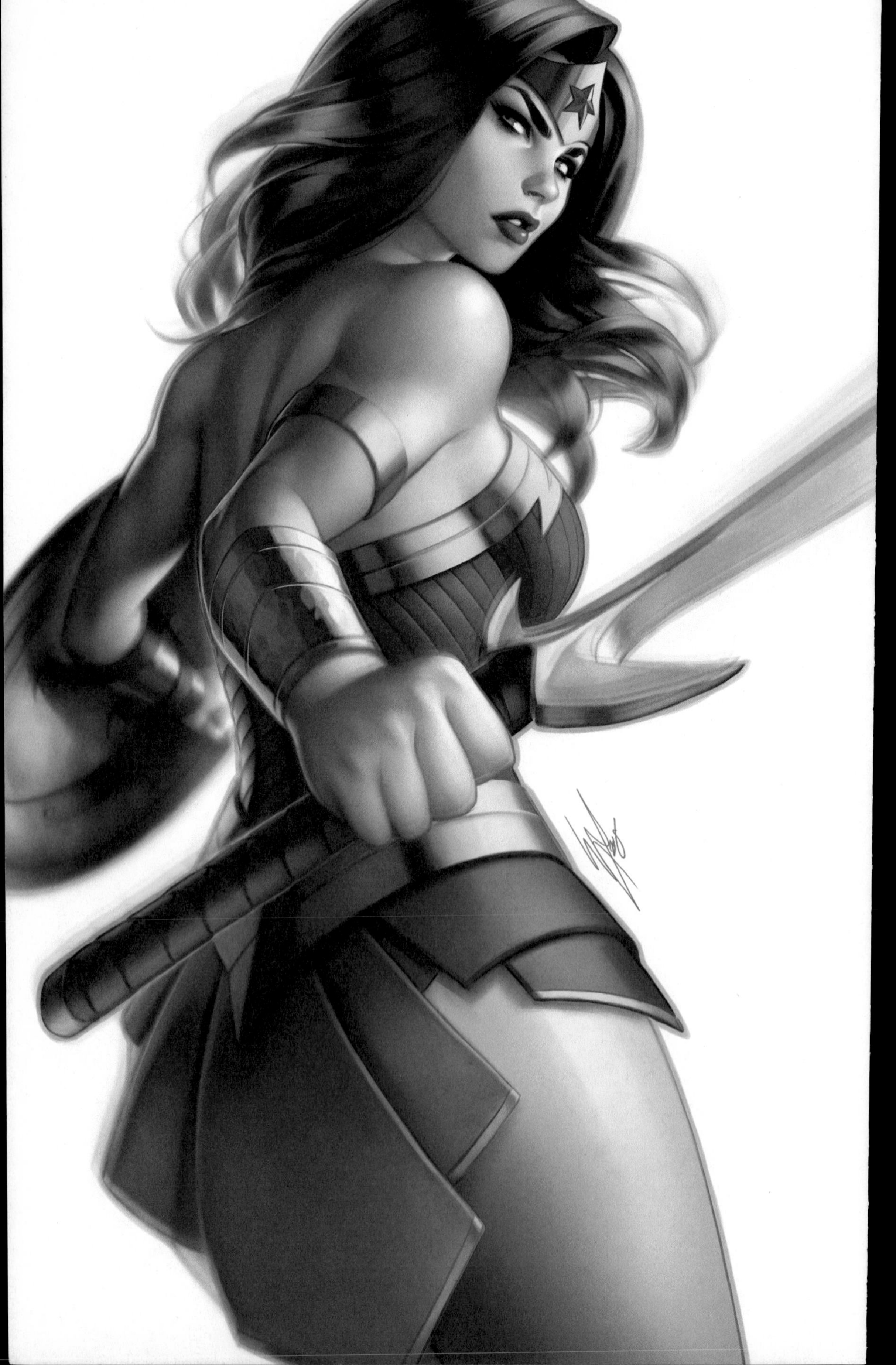

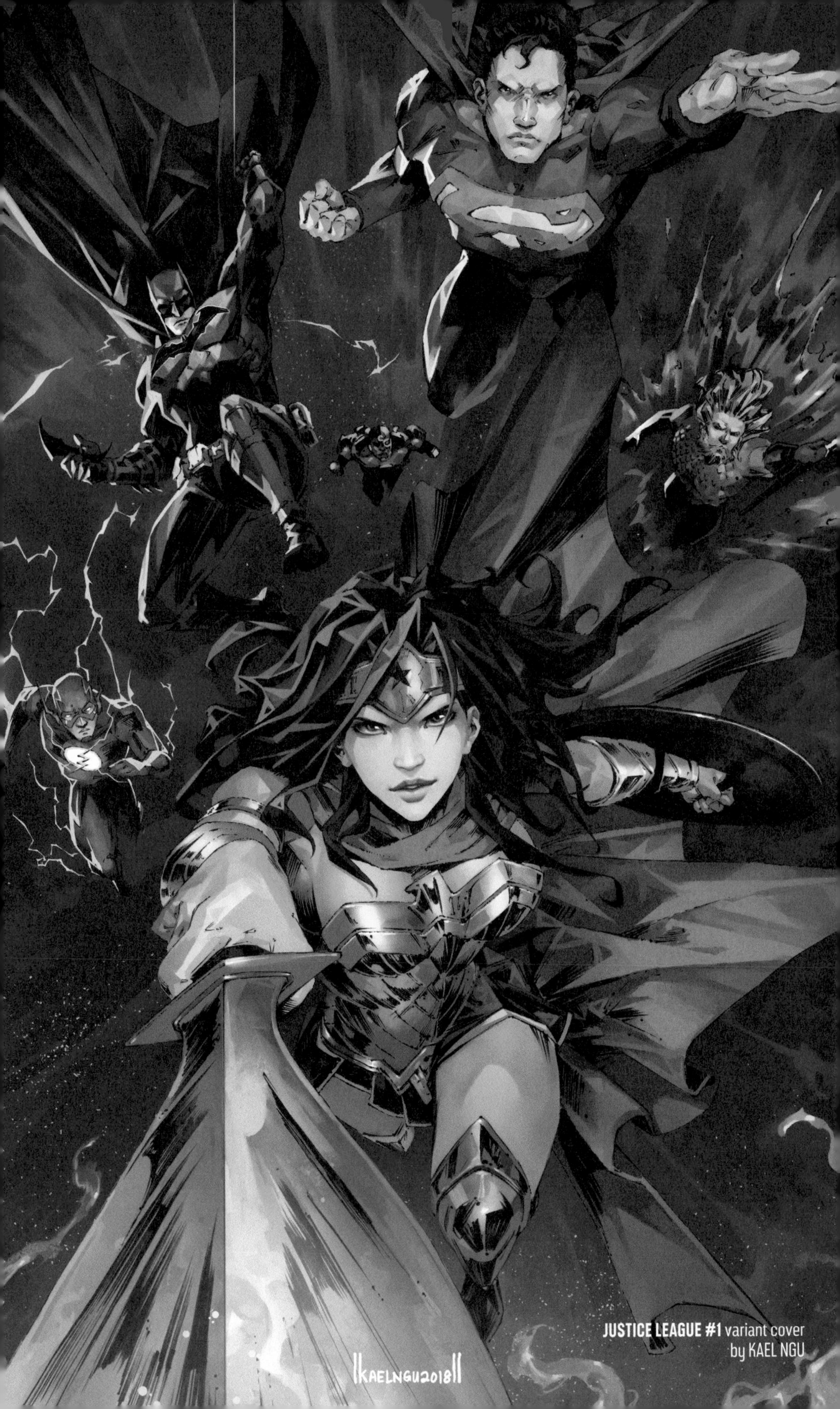
KAELNGU2018

JUSTICE LEAGUE #1 variant cover
by KAEL NGU

JUSTICE LEAGUE #1 variant cover
by BEN OLIVER

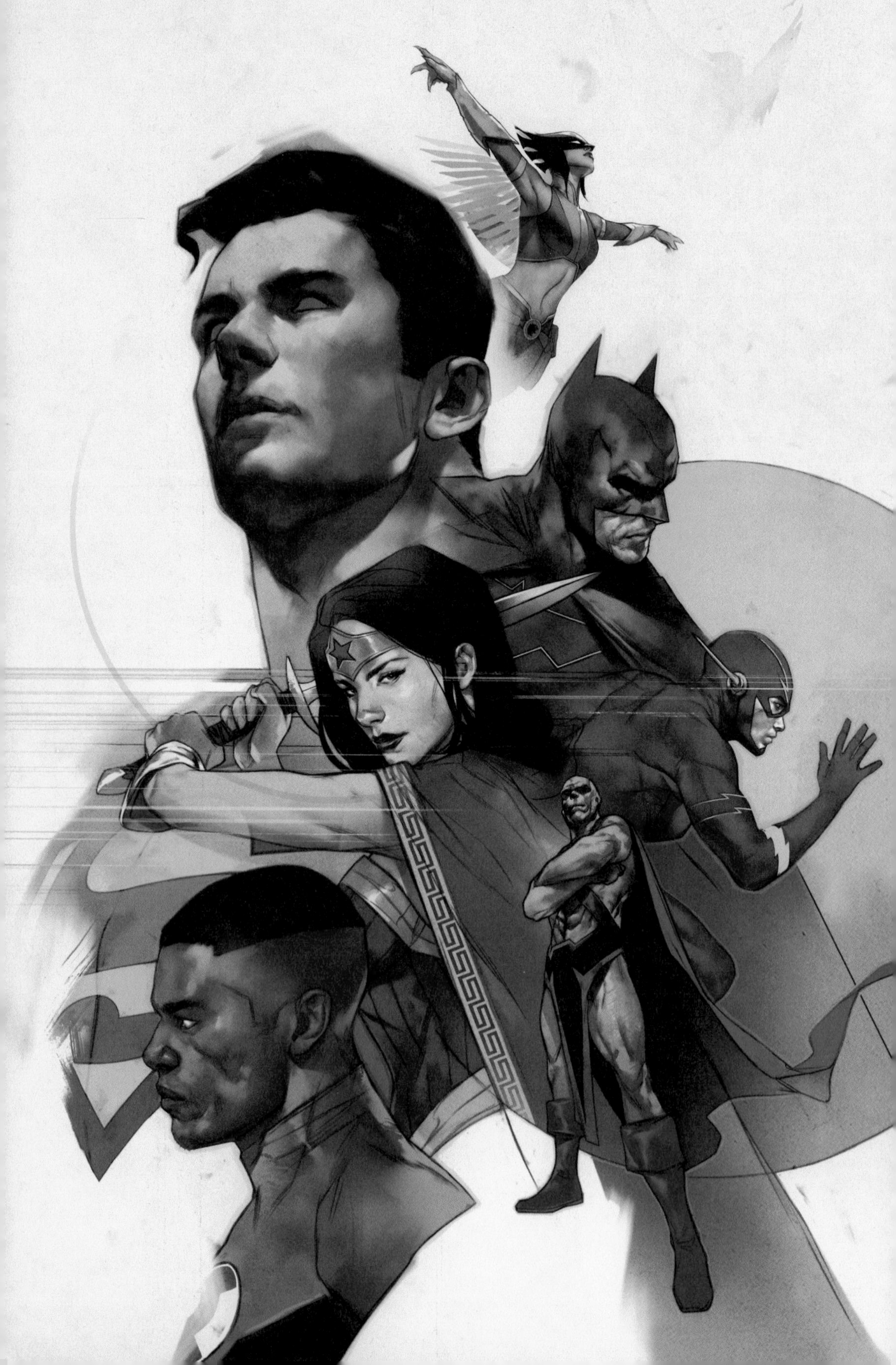